Abhinaya Darpanam

An Illustrated Translation

July, 2025

Thank you for being an inspiration for dancers around the globe.

Gratefully

[illegible]

Abhinaya Darpanam

An Illustrated Translation

Anita Vallabh Ph.D.

B.R. Rhythms
Delhi-110052

Published by:
B.R. Rhythms
B-22, 1st Floor, Left Portion, Phase-1, Ashok Vihar, Near PNB
Delhi-110 052
E-Mail : *brpc73@gmail.com*

2024 : 4th EDITION

COVER DESIGN AND DRAWINGS: SIGNET DESIGNS

ILLUSTRATIONS: Venkatesh & A. Selvaraj

ISBN 9788188827343

Printed at Chetan Offset, Delhi.

Cataloging in Publication Data--DK
Courtesy: D.K. Agencies (P) Ltd. <docinfo@dkagencies.com>

Nandikeśvara, author.
Abhinaya darpanam : an illustrated translation / Anita Vallabh (Ph.D.). -- 4th edition.
pages cm
English and Sanskrit (Sanskrit in Devanagari and Latin).
Includes bibliographical references.
ISBN 9788188827343

1. Gesture in dance--India--Early works to 1800. 2. Theater--India--Early works to 1800. 3. Dance--India--Early works to 1800. I. Vallabh, Anita, editor, translator. II. Nandikeśvara. Abhinayadarpaṇa. III. Nandikeśvara. Abhinayadarpaṇa. English. IV. Title.

LCC GV1693.N36 2024 | DDC 793.31954 23

नर्तक आत्मा

'Nartaka Atma'

(Siva Sutra 9)

'Such a one who has realized his essential spiritual nature is a self that is only an actor (on the world stage)'.

This book is dedicated to all learners and dancers whose performances reflected significant shifts in the dance field and provided much of the inspiration for me to write.

CONTENTS

		Verses	Page No.
	Foreword		xxiii
	Acknowledgement		xxvii
	An Expression of Faith		xxix
	About the Book		xxxvii
	Note on Translation		xliv
	Transliteration		xlvi
1.	**Avatārika**		
	Namaskriyā	(1)	1
	Nandikeśvara Devendra Samvādam	(2-9)	2
2.	**Nāṭyotpattiḥ**	(10-14)	6
	Nāṭya Praśaṃsā	(15-18)	8
	Naṭanabhedāḥ	(19)	10
	Naṭana Prayoga Kālaḥ	(20-25)	11
	Sabhāpatilakṣaṇam	(26-27)	14
	Mantrilakṣaṇam	(28-29)	15
	Sabhālakṣaṇam	(30-33)	16
	Sabhāracanā	(34-36)	18
	Pātralakṣaṇam	(37-40)	20
	Varjanīyapātrāṇī	(41)	21
	Pātrasya Prāṇāḥ	(42-43)	22
	Pātra bahi Prāṇah	(44-45)	23
	Kiṅkinīlakṣaṇam	(46-47)	24

		Verses	Page No.
	Naṭa / Nartaka Lakṣaṇam	(48-49)	25
	Pūrvaraṅgam	(50-52)	26
	Prārthanādikam	(53-54)	27
	Raṅgādhidevatāstutiḥ	(55)	28
	Puṣpāñjaliḥ	(56-57)	29
	Nāṭyakramaḥ	(58-60)	30
	Abhinayaḥ	(61-64)	31
	Āṅgikābhinayasādhanāni	(65-70)	35
3.	**Śirobhedāḥ (9)**		40
	1. Sama	(72-73)	41
	2. Udvāhita	(74)	42
	3. Adhomukha	(75-76)	43
	4. Ālolita	(77)	44
	5. Dhuta	(78-80)	45
	6. Kampita	(81-82)	47
	7. Parāvṛṛta	(83)	48
	8. Utkṣipta	(84-85)	49
	9. Parivāhita	(86)	50
4.	**Dṛṣṭi Bhedāḥ (8)**		52
	1. Sama	(89)	53
	2. Ālokita	(90-91)	54
	3. Sācī	(92-93)	55
	4. Pralokita	(94)	56
	5. Nimīlita	(95-96)	57

		Verses	Page No.
	6. Ullokita	(97)	58
	7. Anuvṛtta	(98)	59
	8. Avalokita	(99-100)	60
5.	**Bhrū Bhedāḥ (6)**	(101)	62
	1. Sahaja	(102)	62
	2. Patita	(103)	63
	3. Utkṣipta	(104)	64
	4. Catura	(105)	65
	5. Recita	(106)	66
	6. Kuñcita	(107)	66
6.	**Grīvā Bhedāḥ (4)**	(108)	67
	1. Sundarī	(109-110)	68
	2. Tiraścīnā	(111)	69
	3. Parivartitā	(112-113)	70
	4. Prakampitā	(114-115)	71
7.	**Hasta Prāṇām (12)**	(116-117)	72
	1. Praśaraṇam	(118)	73
	2. Kuñcitam	(118)	73
	3. Recitam	(119)	74
	4. Puṃkhitam	(119)	74
	5. Apaveṣṭitaṃ	(120)	75
	6. Preritaṃ	(121)	75
	7. Udveṣṭitaṃ	(122)	76
	8. Vyāvṛttam	(123)	76

	Verses	Page No.
9. Parivṛttaṃ	(123)	77
10. Saṃketaṃ	(124)	77
11. Cihnaṃ	(125-128)	78
12. Padārthatīka	(129)	79
Hasta Bhedāḥ	(130)	80
8. Asaṃyuta Hastāḥ (28)	(131-134)	81
1. Patāka	(135-142)	82
2. Tripatāka	(143-144)	84
3. Ardhapatāka	(145-146)	85
4. Kartarīmukha	(147-149)	86
5. Mayūra	(150-152)	87
6. Ardhacandra	(153-155)	88
7. Arāla	(156)	89
8. Śukatuṇḍa	(157-158)	90
9. Muśṭi	(159-160)	91
10. Śikhara	(161-163)	92
11. Kapittha	(164-166)	93
12. Kaṭakāmukha	(167-169)	94
13. Sūcī Hasta	(170-173)	96
14. Candrakalā	(174-175)	97
15. Padmakośa	(176-179)	98
16. Sarpaśīrṣa	(180-181)	100
17. Mṛgaśīrṣa	(182-184)	101
18. Siṃhamukha	(185-186)	102

		Verses	Page No.
19.	Kāṅgula (Lāṅgula)	(187-188)	103
20.	Alapadma	(189-191)	104
21.	Catura	(192-194)	105
22.	Bhramara	(195-196)	106
23.	Haṃsāsya	(197-199)	107
24.	Haṃsapakṣa	(200-201)	108
25.	Sandamśa	(202-203)	109
26.	Mukula	(204-206)	110
27.	Tāmracūḍa	(207-208)	111
28.	Triśūla	(209)	112
29.	Vyāghra	(210)	112
30.	Ardhasūcī (Sūcika)	(211)	113
31.	Kaṭaka	(212-213)	114
32.	Palli	(214-215)	115
33.	Ūrṇanābha	(216-218)	116
34.	Bāṇa	(219-220)	117
35.	Saṃyama	(221)	118
36.	Mudra	(222-223)	118
37.	Ajāmukha	(224-225)	119
38.	Ardhamukula	(226-227)	120
39.	Brahmoktaṣukaṭuṇḍa	(228)	121
40.	Triliṅga		122
41.	Rekhāchandra		122
42.	Brahma śukatuṇḍa		122

		Verses	Page No.
	43. Ardha muśṭi		122
	44. Ḉilita bhramara		123
	45. Ḉilita kapitha		123
	46. Vardhamānaka		123
	47. Khadga		123
	48. Muśti muṛga		124
9.	**Saṃyuta Hastāḥ (24)**	(229-231)	125
	1. Anjali	(232-233)	126
	2. Kapota	(234)	127
	3. Karkaṭa	(235-236)	127
	4. Svastika	(237)	128
	5. Ḍola	(238)	129
	6. Puṣpapuṭa	(239)	129
	7. Utsaṅga	(240-241)	130
	8. Śivaliṅga	(242)	131
	9. Kaṭakāvardhana	(243-244)	132
	10. Kartarīsvastika	(245)	133
	11. Śakaṭa	(246)	133
	12. Śaṅkha	(247)	134
	13. Cakra	(248)	135
	14. Sampuṭa	(249)	135
	15. Pāśa	(250)	136
	16. Kīlaka	(251)	137
	17. Matsya	(252-253)	137

	Verses	Page No.
18. Kūrma	(254)	138
19. Varāha	(255)	139
20. Garuḍa	(256)	139
21. Nāgabandha	(257)	140
22. Khaṭva	(258-259)	141
23. Bheruṇḍa	(260)	142
24. Avahittha	(261)	142
25 Gajadanta	(262-263)	143
26 Saṃyāmi		144
27 Mukula bheda		144
28. Uttarabodhi		144
29. Vajra mānas		145
30. Kavaca		145
31. Hasta svastika		145
10. Deva Hastāḥ	(264)	146
1. Brahma		146
2. Śambhu	(265)	147
3. Viṣṇu		147
4. Sarasvatī	(266)	148
5. Pārvatī	(267)	149
6. Lakṣmī	(268)	149
7. Vighneśvara		150
8. Ṣaṇmukha	(269)	150
9. Manmatha	(270)	151

	Verses	Page No.
11. **Dikpāla Hastāḥ**		152
1. Indra	(271)	152
2. Agni	(272)	152
3. Yama		153
4. Nirṛti	(273)	154
5. Varuṇa		154
6. Vāyu	(274)	155
7. Kubera	(275)	155
8. Īśāna	(276)	156
12. **Daśāvatāra Hastāḥ**		157
1. Matsya	(277)	157
2. Kūrma	(278)	157
3. Varāha	(279)	158
4. Nṛsiṃha	(280)	159
5. Vāmana	(281)	159
6. Paraśurāma	(282)	160
7. Rāmacandra	(283)	161
8. Balarāma	(284)	161
9. Kṛṣṇa	(285)	162
10. Kalki	(286)	163
11. Buddha	(287)	163
13. **Varna Hastāḥ**	164	
1. Brāhmaṇa	(288)	164
2. Kṣatriya	(289)	164

		Verses	Page No.
	3. Vaiśya	(290)	165
	4. Śūdra	(291)	166
14.	**Bāndhava hastāḥ**		167
	1. Dampati	(292)	167
	2. Mātṛ	(293-294)	168
	3. Pitṛ	(295-296)	169
	4. Śvaśrū	(297)	170
	5. Śvaśura	(298)	171
	6. Bhartṛbhrātṛ	(299)	172
	7. Nanāndṛ	(300)	172
	8. Jyeṣṭhakaniṣṭha bhrātṛ	(301)	173
	9. Putra	(302)	174
	10. Snuṣā	(303)	175
	11. Bhartṛ	(304)	175
	12. Sapatnī	(305)	176
15.	**Navagraha hastāḥ**		178
	1. Sūrya	(306)	178
	2. Candra	(307)	178
	3. Angāraka	(308)	179
	4. Budha	(309)	180
	5. Brahaspati	(310)	181
	6. Śukra	(311)	181
	7. Śani	(312)	182
	8. Rāhu	(313)	183
	9. Ketu	(314)	183

	Verses	Page No.
16. Rāja hastāḥ		185
17. Samudra hastāḥ	(315)	187
1. Lavaṇa	(316)	187
2. Ikṣu	(317)	188
3. Sūrā	(318)	189
4. Sarpi		189
5. Dadhi	(319)	190
6. Kṣīra	(320)	190
7. Jala	(321)	191
18. Nadi hastāḥ	(322-324)	192
19. Loka hastāḥ		194
9. Ūrdhvalokāḥ	(325-326)	194
10. Adholokāḥ	(327-328)	195
20. Nṛtta Hastāḥ (13)	(329-333)	196
21. Pāda Bhedāḥ (4)	(334-335)	198
22. Maṇḍala Bhedāḥ (10)	(336)	199
1. Sthānaka	(337	200
2. Āyata	(338)	200
3. Ālīḍha	(339-340)	201
4. Pratyālīḍha	(341)	202
5. Preṅkhaṇa	(342)	203
6. Prerita	(343-344)	204
7. Svastika	(345)	205
8. Mōṭita	(346)	206

		Verses	Page No.
	9. Samasūcī	(347)	207
	10. Pārśvasūcī	(348)	208
23.	**Sthānaka Bhedāḥ (6)**		209
	1. Samapāda	(351)	210
	2. Ēkapāda	(352)	211
	3. Nāgabandha	(353)	212
	4. Aindra	(354)	213
	5. Garuḍa	(355)	214
	6. Brahma	(356)	215
24.	**Utplavana Bhedāḥ (5)**	(357-358)	216
	1. Alagotpalavanaṃ	(359)	217
	2. Utplavanakartarī	(360)	218
	3. Aśvotplavanaṃ	(361)	219
	4. Moṭitotplavanaṃ	(362)	220
	5. Kṛpālagotplavanaṃ	(363)	221
25.	**Bhramarī Bhedāḥ (7)**	(364-366)	222
	1. Utpluta	(367)	223
	2. Cakra	(368)	224
	3. Garuḍa	(369)	226
	4. Ēkapāda	(370)	227
	5. Kuñcita		227
	6. Ākāśa	(371)	228
	7. Aṅga	(372)	229

	Verses	Page No.
26. Cāri Bhedāḥ (8)	(373-375)	230
1. Calana		231
2. Caṅkramaṇa	(376)	231
3. Saraṇam	(377-378)	232
4. Veginī	(379)	233
5. Kuṭṭanam	(380)	234
6. Luṭhitam	(381)	234
7. Lolitam	(382)	235
8. Viṣamasañcaraḥ	(383)	236
27. Gati Bhedāḥ (10)	(384-385)	237
1. Haṃsī	(386)	238
2. Mayūrī	(387)	239
3. Mṛgī	(388)	239
4. Gajalīlā	(389)	240
5. Turaṅgiṇī	(390-391)	241
6. Siṃhī	(392)	242
7. Bhujaṅgī	(393)	242
8. Maṇḍūkī	(394)	243
9. Vīrā	(395)	244
10. Mānavī	(396-399)	245
28. Vṛkṣa Hastāḥ (31)		247
1. Aśvatthaḥ		247
2. Kadalai	(400)	247
3. Nāraṅga		248

		Verses	Page No.
4.	Likuca		248
5.	Panasa	(401)	248
6.	Bilvā	(401)	248
7.	Punnāga		249
8.	Mandāra	(402)	249
9.	Vakula	(402)	249
10.	Vaṭa		
11.	Arjunaḥ		250
12.	Pāṭali	(403)	251
13.	Hiṇṭalā	(403)	251
14.	Phūga		251
15.	Campaka	(404)	252
16.	Khadira		252
17.	Śamī	(405)	253
18.	Aśokaḥ	(406)	253
19.	Siṅduvāra	(407)	254
20.	Amalakā	(408)	254
21.	Kuravaka	(409)	255
22.	Kapittha		255
23.	Ketakī	(410)	256
24.	Śiṃśapā	(411)	256
25.	Nimba		257
26.	Sāla		257
27.	Pārijāta	(412-413)	257

	Verses	Page No.
28. Tintriṇī		258
29. Jambu		258
30. Pālāśa	(414)	259
31. Rasāla	(414)	259
29. Mṛga Hastāḥ (22)		260
1. Siṃha	(415)	260
2. Vyāghra	(416)	261
3. Sūkara	(417)	261
4. Kapi	(418)	262
5. Bhallūka	(419-420)	263
6. Mārjāra	(421)	263
7. Camarī	(422)	264
8. Godhā	(423)	265
9. Śalya	(424)	266
10. Kuraṅga	(425)	266
11. Kṛṣṇasāra	(426)	267
12. Gokarṇa		267
13. Mūśika	(427)	268
14. Girika	(428)	269
15. Śaśa	(429)	270
16. Vṛścika		270
17. Śunaka	(430)	271
18. Uṣṭra	(431-432)	271
19. Aja		272

		Verses	Page No.
	20. Gārdabha	(433)	273
	21. Vṛṣabha	(434-435)	273
	22. Dhenu	(436)	274
30.	**Pakṣi Hastāḥ (21)**		275
	1. Pārāvata		275
	2. Kapota	(437)	275
	3. Śaśādana		276
	4. Ulūka	(438)	276
	5. Gaṇḍabheruṇḍa	(439-440)	277
	6. Cātaka		278
	7. Kukkuṭa	(441)	278
	8. Kokila		279
	9. Vāyasa	(442-443)	279
	10. Kurara		280
	11. Śuka	(444)	281
	12. Sārasa	(445)	281
	13. Baka	(446-447)	282
	14. Krauñca	(448)	283
	15. Khadyota	(449)	284
	16. Bhramara		284
	17. Mayūra	(450)	285
	18. Haṃsa		285
	19. Cakravāka	(451)	286
	20. Koyaṣṭika	(452)	286

	Verses	Page No.
31. Jalājantu Hastāḥ (22)		287
1. Bheka	(453-454)	287
2. Kulīra	(455)	288
3. Raktapāyi	(456)	289
4. Nakra	(457)	289
5. Ḍuṇḍubha	(458)	290
6. Vyālī	(459-460)	291
Legacy of Change		292
References		294

Foreword - 1

ABHINAYA DARPANAM
AN ILLUSTRATED TRANSLATION

The dance program at the University of Hawaii at Manoa is noted for its breadth of Asian and Pacific dance offerings. We recently had the good fortune of having an exhilarating semester-long guest artist residency with Dr. Anita Vallabh. She is renowned not only for her outstanding research but also for her years as an international Bharatanatyam performer. She is a role model for university dance students everywhere as she demonstrates an essential combination of experience that spans theory and practice; she is truly an artist and a scholar.

In her UHM course she included not only the requisite physical postures and movement of the dance, but also a comprehensive introduction to a centuries-long art form that included the history, scholarship, and ever-evolving development of a compelling tradition of a dance not always appreciated nor understood by Western audiences.

Her monograph, *Abhinaya Darpanam : An Illustrated Translation*, similarly bridges intellectual rigor and the essentials of gestures and postures used in the performance of this dance form. This book is comprehensive in its overview yet not overwhelming, intellectually interesting yet still compelling and straight forward.

This is an excellent text for western readers interested in learning about the myriad possibilities that Bharatanatyam postures represent and the contexts in which they might be used. She succinctly discusses the philosophical, practical, and artistic aspects of dance in general and Bharatanatyam specifically in the introduction plunges into the history of the form, which prepares the reader for a concise explanation of basic concepts, and concludes with descriptions of movements of the hands and various possible meanings, plus axial and locomotor possibilities of the lower body.

For anyone interested in an articulate and beautifully illustrated introduction to Bharatanatyam, this text should be an essential part of your library.

Gregg Lizenbery
Director and Graduate Chair of Dance
University of Hawaii at Manoa

Foreword - 2

Indian dramaturgy has had documented history of more than two thousand years. The earliest available treatise to this day is Bharata's Natyasastra. There have been many works on dance and drama after Bharata. All of them invariably followed the tenets of Natyasastra. While treatises of dance or dramaturgy have also included chapters of music in their content, treatises on music have included chapters on dance showing how dance and music have always been inseparable. In fact the body of a dancer is viewed as another music instrument with gestures and movements to embellish music. These nuances have lead to many more works dealing with various components of music and dance highlighting their interdisciplinary affiliations.

Then came a time when it was essential to author a treatise just confined to the movements and gestures in dance. Works like Hasta Lakshana Deepika, Hasta Muktavali are texts dealing with various hand gestures. Abhinaya Darpana occupies a very unique position among such focussed works dealing with abhinaya. There have been translations and commentaries to this work in many Indian languages with regional emphases. With the advent of technology and with many non- Indian students learning Indian Classical dances, there is a need for a practice oriented theory book by a teacher and a dancer.

Anita more than just fits into this slot being herself a performing artiste, a teacher, a choreographer, a researcher and above all as one who has been teaching foreign students. The fact that this book is in its second edition is in itself a proof of its usefulness. The second, revised and updated edition of Message in Movements is an Illustrated Translation of the Abhinaya Darpanam. What Anita has been doing is to find ways to improve upon her first edition based on the feed back she received from various sources and based on what she herself felt could make it more useful.

In this book I find a genuine urge of the author to make it the book for reference to students and teachers of dance. The most interesting aspect of this book lies in its simplicity, lucidity and sincerity.

I am sure Anita will write many more such book to help the student and teacher community.

Pappu Venugopala Rao

Acknowledgement

Ajñāna Timirāndhasya Jñānānjana Śalākayā |
Cakṣur Unmīlitam Yena Tasmai Śrī Gurave Namaḥ ||

To my spiritual master, Who with the torch of knowledge
Opened my eyes closed in ignorance, I offer my respectful obeisance.

As ever, I remain indebted to my Gurus, the Dhananjayans for their blessings in all my creative endeavors, and my love for dance. I acknowledge a debt of gratitude to Dr. Pappu Venugopala Rao for his immense scholarship and intellectual stimulation.

I owe much to V.A.K. Rango Rao for his critical remarks and corrections in the content matter of my first book "Message in Movements". In this too his corrections have been invaluable.

I remain grateful to my ever thoughtful, artistic friend Madhu Krishna for his sustaining presence and for his administrative and creative support. The work was immeasurably enriched by the support of my dear friend Rajam Raghunathan, Assistant Professor, Department of Philosophy, University of Hawaii, whose patience and enthusiasm for life and learning helped me through the innumerable details of correcting the manuscript. I thank my Research Assistant Chitra Rajaram for her gracious dispatch of everything from photocopying, proof reading, research, and seeing it through its long developmental process.

I owe a debt of gratitude to the Dance faculty of the Theatre and Dance Department of the University of Hawaii, especially Kara Miller for sharing her books and passion for dance and to Gregg Lizenbery, my hero. Much of the material for the introduction was procured from the amazing collection at the South Asia Library of the University of Hawaii. I thank my dear friend Monica Ghosh, the South Asian Librarian and Linda Laurence, Asia Collection Technician for their valuable assistance.

I extend my thanks to Singara Vel of Signet Designs for his administrative support. My thanks to P.T. Narendra and Renjit Babu for the photographs on which the illustrations of the movements of the feet are based. My heartfelt gratitude to Venkatesh and A.Selvaraj for the illustrations in the book. I am grateful to Bhavani Gangadhar of CEE GEE graphics for typesetting the contents of this book and to Sri Praveen and Neeraj Mittal of B.R. Rhythms for the printing of this book.

My life is perennially enriched by the abiding love of my family, my mother Aruna Murthy, husband Sagar Vallabh and our children.

AN EXPRESSION OF FAITH

The importance of Abhinaya Darpanam (Mirror of Gestures) to present day Indian dance traditions in general and Bharatanāṭyam in particular can never be overstated. For every dancer, teacher and choreographer crafting their experience in the artistic expression, it continues to provide new perceptions of movement and mime, new ways of presenting and imagining movement possibilities and enlarges the frame of performance by providing the material for reformulating and re-envisioning our insights of the fundamental units that constitute the dance form.

This second edition of 'Message in Movements' took a considerable period of time to realize its present form for two main reasons. Firstly, the process of illustrating and positioning the gestures with reference to its real life representation was overwhelming in its significance and potential usage across disciplines. I hence sustained the intellectual stimulation of aesthetic possibilities for a longer period than anticipated. Secondly, my experience of teaching in the Theatre and Dance department of the South Asian Pacific Studies, University of Hawaii during the fall semester 2011 opened my mind to renegotiate my traditionally privileged understanding of movement and aesthetics.

I briefly sketch my experience that enriched and reshaped my understanding of the scope of Abhinaya Darpanam in general and the capability of the body in informing a dance regardless of its familiarity.

As the learners (some trained classical dancers) assembled in class I was struck by their diverse representation (Asian, Hawaiian, American, and Afro- American) and soon apprehensive of the teaching methodology I had prepared prior to this encounter. Naively, in my preparation I had not considered their embodied cultural representation; the different manner in which they held the body, used gestures, and understood concept of time and moving space. We commenced our classes with adavus and the manner of its execution gave me an insight into redesigning the curriculum and teaching methodology to increase its scope (I had the students read poems of Rabindranath Tagore, choose those that inspired them and sequence the lines culled from different poems using gestures and adavu movement patterns), contextualize their work (the poems were based on the theme of love, following a discussion of their own life experiences), and weave together elements of word, movement and song in a sequential manner. Highly enthusiastic and dedicated, the students choreographed the movement patterns. Using their understanding of adavus and hand gestures (saṃyuta and asaṃyuta) they translated the poetry into movement. At that point in time my first book 'Message in Movements' containing hand gestures and feet movement proved a useful guide for the students in creating movement patterns.

As we worked together I realized that I had at the beginning, unfairly viewed them with comparatively less exacting, intellectual and physical scrutiny because of my bias that the aesthetic quality of Bharatanāṭyam is best constituted and expressed in a body that is imbued in Indian culture. It felt to me that this art was historically reserved as a cultural heritage for those born and raised in the country. It did not occur to me until I saw that in their intense engagement with the dance form and immense involvement in the creative process, beneath the group dynamics of agreements, disagreements, and reconciliations, they were experiencing the aesthetic quality of the art form, the joy of movement and expression. I learnt well within the semester of teaching that by initially denying them their somatic identity (experience of physicality) I had undervalued their dancing self. By disengaging their sphere of description/representation and denying them the exultant physical experience I had done a disservice to myself, and to them.

I now believe that while the body is inherently inscribed by the social practices of its culture, through daily practice the embodied experience actively creates a unique physical identity that represents the dancer's process of 'becoming' (a quality of harmony that is a result of a deep awareness of the sentient self) that is central to dance learning and the very essence of why we dance. The journey that will reveal to us our sentient self, its immense potential and capabilities begins at first with an awareness of the tenets of its practice.

This paradigm shift motivated me to present this illustrated and detailed version of the Abhinaya Darpanam that I hope will be useful for dancers across cultures in providing an imagery of our rich vocabulary, and in informing their creative endeavors. It is my humble belief that every few years, practitioners of the art must re-interpret the text, adding a layer every time so others may build upon it.

I hope this book will renew our awareness of the immense potential of the text to reveal to dedicated practitioners the body's kinesthetic intelligence and the power of sentient self to suggest, evoke a sense of life itself as it were, as it is and as it will be.

WHAT IS BHARATANĀṬYAM?

On the global stage Bharatanāṭyam in performance and choreography has evolved a transnational character merging 'innovation' and 'tradition'. With every performance dancers continue to redefine parameters of innovation, eschewing, embracing and rearticulating elements to create an aesthetic based on movement and/or emotion oriented lexicon (O'Shea, 2009).

Regardless of a dancer's orientation, strategy of form and, affiliation to stylistic traditions I offer an extended definition of Natya in general (referring to all the dance traditions of India), and classical Bharatanāṭyam in particular that inheres an aesthetic that to me is fundamental to Indian tradition.

Elaborating upon the definition offered by Judith Lynne Hanna (1979) who defines dance as 'human behavior composed from the dancers' perspective, of 1. Purposeful, 2. Intentionally rhythmical, and 3. Culturally patterned sequences of 4.a) non-verbal body movements 4.b) other than ordinary motor activities, 4.c) the motion having inherent aesthetic value,' and explanding the term 'Bharata' as an acronym denoting the three aspects of Bhāva, Rāga and Tāla, I now define Bharatanāṭyam/Nāṭyam as :

A culturally patterned sequences of intended movement, with inherent aesthetic value that aims at embodying the spiritual experience of Reality in its elements of 1) Bhāva, manifestation of feeling through bodily expressions, 2) Rāga, distinctive composition of musical notes that suggest an emotional state, and 3) Tāla, the rhythmic, metrical cycle measured within a unit of time, that intrinsically create a unique physical identity and a deep awareness of the sentient self.

SCOPE AND OBJECTIVE OF ABHINAYA DARPANAM

The Abhinaya Darpanam written by Nandikesvara is till today the mandatory text for every Bharatanāṭyam dancer, the first step towards methodical teaching, learning and practice. It is the veritable foundation on which the technique of Nāṭya is constantly evolving and which contains reference to all aspects of life to accommodate diverse perceptions and interests of the learners.

The scope of the text extends from a progressive understanding of the basic tenets of dance practice to executing combinations of adavu, chāri, maṇdala and, the vocabulary of gestures with kinesthetic awareness (ability to sense movement). The ability to sense movement comes with 'seeing' the movement in the mind and using that image to define the extent of pressure and tension required in the joints and muscles at every point of body positioning during execution of adavus. This will introduce some, re-educate others to perceptions of imagery at different levels of learning. For example, the experience of a movement can be described as an image or as evoking an image of a stalk gently swaying in the wind etc. This image is the student's initiation, albeit momentarily, into an experience of his/her dancing self from where he/she develops his 'intuitive imagery' and thereupon conceives of an authentic, creative sequential movement patterns (Franklin, 2004). Repeated practice will allow a graceful flow of movements executed at varying speed with increased precision.

Another area where the text informs the dancing body is in the realm of conditioning and avoidance of injury that is the bane of many dancers. An illustration of basic positions encourages movement analysis for body positioning, detailing of the line of gravity and centre of mass for better posture, alignment and balance. A studied understanding of these features will allow the dancer to exert the right amount of force to the required muscles without creating tension in other areas. Accordingly warm-ups can be structured with sequences ranging from less challenging to more challenging, depending on age, ability etc.

Besides focus on movement and kinesthetic awareness I hope the illustrations will generate an avid interest in tracing the genesis, purpose and the many functions of mudras across diverse cultural and religious traditions, curiosity in the inclusion of medicinal plants in the text, comparison of mythology across cultures in the astral world etc. In the course of my study I was particularly enamored by the representation of freshwater, terrestrial and ocean ecosystems within the framework of an earth-centered conception of cosmology, connecting our empirical/physical life to a transcendental reality.

At an introductory level this book is meant for students at all levels of learning and can be understood along with practical training either progressively in stages, or in levels of complexity. The text and illustrations are provided to engage the learners, simplify learning and introduce the learner to the concept of using imagery as a choreographic tool.

At this level and the intermediary level, teachers can also support the learning process by adapting the text with discretion to assess students in areas of:

1. 'Kinesthetic awareness' (inherent beauty in the composition of adavus, use of gestures)

2. 'Aesthetic awareness' (focused awareness and contemplation of the sentient self as a process in the experience of movement)

3. 'Cognitive awareness' (the communicative efficacy of dance as a non-verbal language due to its facility to fully engage the dancer at the physical-mental and spiritual levels of being)

4. 'Psychological awareness' (to use movement as a process of coping with known tension, aggression, bereavement etc)`(Mcutchen, 2006)

5. 'Cultural awareness' (using myth to teach values, customs which in turn determine the conceptualization of the style, structure, content and performance)

At a higher level of academic and practical learning, if we could allow in our teaching methodology a scope for rethinking the experience of the dancing body, we can negotiate between the objective understanding of the dance and it's subjective experience, engage with the cultural differences of the body and enlarge the scope of our understanding of 'how social identities are signaled, formed and negotiated though bodily movement' (Desmond Jane 1993-1994, p.34).

By thus understanding and placing the embodied dance on the center stage we can:

1. Foreground theoretical concerns based on the ideological underpinnings of dance practice (tracing the history, the changes that occur in its form and structure, the appropriations and assimilations, its transmission across geographical boundaries and its reinstatement in the new socio-cultural context).

2. Develop an intensive dance curriculum that addresses the entire gamut of dance learning, process and performance. I quote from 'Teaching Dance as Art in Education' by Mcutchen (2006) the six defining features for designing educational dance curriculum:

Comprehensive (broad in scope)

Substantive (challenging and significant)

Sequential (ordered and incremental)

Aesthetically driven (seeking fine quality)

Contextually coherent (relevant and related)

Inquiry based (participatory and investigative)

3. Understand how by contesting or accepting socio-political ideologies the body through practice creates its own representation that goes beyond its kinesthetic facility, physical properties and emotive capability.

4. Contribute to critical scholarly discourses on inter disciplinary approaches of dance and Cultural studies (history, philosophy, feminist theories, evolve crucial bodily discourse on cultural identities such as representations of gender, race, color, ability, Sociology (institutions, art management), Anthropology (social customs and beliefs of a community that informs the dance, cultural development, ethnography) and Literature (particularly post-modern theories on linguistics).

5. Engage in cross-cultural dialogues that will inform the subject matter of dance.

ABOUT THE BOOK

This version of the Abhinaya Darpanam is a reconciliation of P.S.R.Appa Rao's translation of Nandikesvara's Abhinaya Darpanam, and Manmohan Ghosh's edited and translated version of Nadikesvara's Abhinayadarpanam. I have chosen the above two texts for the reason that while Manmohan Ghosh's version is established as the mandatory text for Bharatanāṭyam dancers, P.S.R.Appa Rao's version is a reconciliation of Sriman. Tiruvenkatacharya's version of Abhinaya Darpanam (1887), Manmohan Ghosh's version and additional information based on other sources. The main focus of the present version however, is on the content of the Abhinaya Darpanam without tracing its history to an arbitrarily distant past (Manmohan Ghosh in his 1934 edited version affixed a tentative date around 1210 A.D), and commenting/comparing the different versions.

This version of Abhinaya Darpanam has 31 chapters divided and presented in the same manner as Appa Rao's version. However the granthāntara bhedas (text from other sources) have been excluded primarily because most are either movements in transition or similar to the established one. For example, in the dṛṣṭi bhedas, kuncita drishti is described by Appa Rao as 'the glance in which the eyelids, along with the eyelashes are slightly curved and the eyeballs are lowered,' and ākāsha dṛṣṭi as 'the glance in which the pupils are fully directed towards the sky'. While the first is rather obscure, the second is similar to Ullokita dṛṣṭi that is described in the main text. In the hand gestures I have however added based on my experience as a dancer, a few saṃyuta and asaṃyuta hastas that we now often use but are not specifically identified in either of the above versions.

Chapter 1 : The text of Abhinaya Darpanam begins with the prayer 'Āngikam Bhuvanam' to Lord Shiva who signifies auspiciousness and embodies the four ways of expressing. Āngika (aṅga =limb), expression through the movement of limbs, gestures and actions, Vāchika (vāk = speech) using words, language, Ahārya (adornment) expressing through make-up and costume, and Sāttvika (satta=omnipotent) expressing intense emotional states.

The ensuing dialogue between Nandikesvara and Devendra is not mentioned in Manmohan Ghosh's version of Abhinaya Darpanam perhaps because of its rather dubious assertion of the Abhinaya Darpanam to be an abridged version of the Bharatārnava. It does however find mention in Appa Rao's and Tiruvenkatacharya's version.

Chapter 2 : The second chapter contains the mythology of the origin of Nātya, its categorization into Nātya, Nṛtya and Nṛtta, the time of performance, characteristics of the assembly, characteristics of the chief of the sabha, the minister's qualities, arrangements of the sabha and orchestra, characteristics that determines the physical, emotional and artistic quality of the dancer, nature of the bells, quality of the male actor/dancer, the preliminary rituals and the definition and importance of abhinaya. Verses that described the outer aspects of a dancer and the characteristics of an actor have been taken from Appa Rao and marked by an asterisk.

Chapters 3 to 6 introduce the classification of Āngika Abhinayam. In describing the movements of the eye, eyebrow, neck and head, I have attempted to capture the explanations of each classification into illustrations at the point when the mood is best conveyed.

The movement and position of the hands are described in chapter 7 as the 12 Hasta Pranās. In this context the Naṭyashastra (chapter 9) mentions 'Keeping in view the form, action/activity, sign and nature of the objects/things/persons, and after carefully deciding what is appropriate, wise men should do Hasta Abhinaya. There is nothing in the world which cannot be represented by the hastas.'

Chapters 8 & 9 of Hasta mudras are similar in content to those of the first book 'Message in Movements.' However, I have included five more to facilitate cross reference while studying the later chapter on birds and animals.

The 48 single hand gestures and the 31 double hand gestures (Abhinaya Darpanam) mentions 28 and 24 respectively) have been taken from the following sources:

Non-combined hand gestures in Manmohan Ghosh's edition of Abhinaya Darpanam (1975)

(1) Patāka, (2) Tripatāka, (3) Ardhapatāka, (4) Kartarīmukha, (5) Mayūra, (6) Ardhacandra, (7) Arāla, (8) Śukatuṇḍa, (9) Muṣṭi, (10) Śikhara, (11) Kapittha, (12) Kaṭakāmukha, (13) Sūcī, (14) Candrakalā, (15) Padmakośa, (16) Sarpaśira, (17) Mṛgaśīrṣa, (18) Siṃhamukha, (19) Kāṅgula ,(20) Alapadma, (21) Catura, (22) Bhramara, (23) Haṃsāsya, (24) Haṃsapakṣa, (25) Sandaṃśa, (26) Mukula, (27) Tāmraçūḍa, (28) Triśūla, (29) Vyāghra, (30) Ardhasūcī, (31) Kaṭaka, (32) Palli.

Appa Rao's edition of Abhinaya Darpanam (1997)

(33) Ūrṇanābha, (34) Bāṇa, (35) Saṃyama, (36) Mudra, (37) Ajāmukha, (38) Ardhamukula, (39) Brahmoktaṣukaṭuṇḍa.

Mahābharata Chūdāmani (1952)

(35) Trilinga, (36) Rekhāchandra, (37) Brahmaśukatunda, (38) Ardhamuśṭi, (39) Cilitabrahmara, (40) Cilitakapittha.

Hasta Lakshana Dipika (1925)

(41) Vardhamānaka.

Mudra in Hindu and Budhist Practices - An Iconic Consideration (2005)

(42) Khadga, (43) Muśti-mṛga.

Combined hand gestures in Manmohan Ghosh's edition of Abhinaya Darpanam (1975)

(1) Añjali, (2) Kapōta, (3) Karkaṭa, (4) Svastika, (5) Ḍōla, (6) Puṣpapuṭa, (7) Utsaṅga, (8) Śivaliṅga, (9) Kaṭakāvardhana, (10) Kartarīsvastika, (11) Śakaṭaṃ, (12) Śaṅkha, (13) Çakra, (14) Sampuṭa, (15) Pāśa, (16) Kīlaka, (17) Mastya, (18) Kūrma, (19) Varāha, (20) Garuḍa, (21) Nāgabandha, (22) Khaṭva, (23) Bhēruṇḍa.

Appa Rao's edition of Abhinaya Darpanam (1997)

(24) Avahittha.

Mahābharata Chūdāmani (1952)

(25) Gajadanta, (26) Saṃyāmi.

Hasta Lakshana Dipika

(27) Mukula Bhēda.

Mudras in Buddhist and Hindu Practices - An Iconographic Consideration (2005)

(28) Uttarabodhi (29) Vajramānasa, (30) Kavaçaya, (31) Hastasvastika.

It is important to note that according to the Nātyaśāstra chapter IX "All these hand gestures are to be employed in performances along with action of eyes, brows, face etc., suggestive of various emotions. The wise should perform the actions of the hand as evident from the practices of the world in action, place, movements and nature".

Chapter 10 and 11 describe the gestures for the various gods and the lords of the eight cardinal directions. Their propitiation during the construction of the playhouse is well explained in the second chapter of the Nāṭyaśāstra. The associated mudra representing a lord is based either on their weapon or a characteristic feature. Find below the planet associated with each direction, the governing lord and their weapons for an analysis of the genesis of the mudra.

Name	Direction	Weapon	Graha (Planet)
Indra	East	Vajra (thunderbolt)	Sūrya (Sun)
Agni	South-east	Śūla (Spear)	Śukra (Venus)
Yama	South	Daṇda(staff)	Maṇgala (Mars)
Nirṭti	South-west	Khaḍga (sword)	Rāhu (North Lunar Node)
Varuṇa	West	Pāśa (noose)	Śani (Saturn)
Vāyu	North-west	Aṇkuśa (goad)	Chandra (Moon)
Kubera	North	Gadā (mace)	Budha (Mercury)
Īśāna	North-east	Triśūla (trident)	Brihaspati (Jupiter)

Chapter 12 describes the gestures for the eleven instead of ten reincarnations of Vishnu. Textually and according to individual belief the incarnations of Krishna and Buddha are included alternatively. The Abhinaya Darpanam mentions Krishna and not Buddha. The two have been included in the chapter.

Chapter 13 describes the gestures for the four varnās. The four fold division was created to facilitate efficient functioning of the society and although the Nāṭyaśāstra does not mention the gestures of the varna hastās, the second chapter mentions the importance of erecting the four pillars (after laying the foundation), each representing the Brahmin, Kṣatriya, Vaiśya and Śūdra to the chanting of prayers.

Chapters 14, 15 and 16 enumerate the gestures for relatives, nine planets, and kings respectively.

In chapter 17, while describing the seven hastas for the oceans the view of six Ācāryās, Brihaspati, Sukra, Ānjaneya, Dattila, Narada and Kohala. These Ācāryās are known to have written treatises on dance and perhaps the description of mudras is taken from their individual texts.

This chapter is followed by the delineation of rivers in chapter 18. Chapter 19 very briefly describes the seven upper and seven lower worlds and their representation using Patāka hasta moved in different ways.

The 20th chapter on Nṛtta hastās mentions five types of movements, upward, downward, left, right and in front. These are similar to the three types of hasta pracāra of

Nāṭyaśāstra (chapter.9). The difference between chapter 20 and chapter 6 lies in the movement. While chapter 20 describes the position of the palm, chapter 6 describes the movement of the arm/hand.

Chapters 21 to 27 describe the movements of the feet a few of which are repeated from the first edition of 'Message in Movements'. The Nāṭyaśāstra (Chapter VI) describes the cāris and maṇdalas thus, "The simultaneous movements of the limbs like feet, shanks, thighs, and lips are technically referred to as cari. This is called vyāyāma (exercise) when the movements are governed by appropriate rules and the limbs are in concordance with each other in their activity. The movement involving a single feet is designated as Cāri. A dance is initiated by Cāri movements, and all movements proceed from Cāris, they are necessary for the representation of fight (on the stage)". These movements are used to depict the discharge of weapons. Interestingly, while the hand gestures have their usages mentioned, the uses of the various movements of the feet and their composition is left to the discretion of the teacher.

Chapters 28 to 31 describing the hastas for trees and birds, provide interesting material for research. The trees described in chapter 28 are known medicinal plants, revered and sacred. Trees such as the Aśvattha known as the milk tree is venerated as sacred, the Aśoka tree, named after king Aśoka is considered sacred to Shiva, the sal tree is considered sacred to Viṣnu and the Nimba tree is known for its medicinal properties. Some of the birds mentioned are those associated with the emotion of love in mythology. The famous Chakora bird is said to look up to the moon and soak in its rays, a pair of Chakravāka birds are said to be two lovers separated, and the crane is a symbol of devoted love.

NOTE ON TRANSLATION

1. The Shlokas of the Abhinaya Darpanam have been translated and transliterated from Manmohan Ghosh's version. Those not found in Ghosh are taken from Appa Rao's version and marked with an asterisk (*). Some of the hasta mudras have been taken from sources mentioned above and denoted by an asterisk.

2. The translation is to be taken as contextual and not textual. It is a free translation and therefore the passages that describe the gesture and their usages textually in the locative (Saptami Vibhakti) for example, 'in denoting the clouds' is translated contextually in the Nominative (Prathama Vibhakti) as 'cloud.'

3. In chapters 8 and 9, some of the gestures are associated with more than one meaning. While I have chosen one of the meanings, it is imperative that dancers depict the movement suggested by their chosen interpretive meaning.

4. The conjunctions and particles are put in brackets or shown with the word without their literal translation in every verse. I mention them here for reference:

Ca = and
Tathā = likewise
Tu = but
Evam = thus
Ata = now

Api = also, but, although
Ataḥ = thus, then
Eva = only
Iti = like that, thus
Tataḥ = therefore.

5. There are many translations of the Natyasastra and the verses are numbered differently in each. Throughout the text of this version any mention of the same is to be referenced with Dr. C.P. Unni's translation.

6. The sign of hyphen in the transliteration and translation between compound words is to facilitate correct reading.

7. In describing the application of the various hand gestures, following the general classroom teaching methodology, only the word to word meaning is given and not the general meaning as in other chapters. This has been done to allow an easy reading of the uses along with the Sanskrit words for students.

8. In chapter 12 of Varna hasta, Manmohan Ghosh's edition begins with rakshasa hasta. As this classification is not part of the four economic divisions of Brahmana, Ksatriya, vaisya and Sudra, following Appa Rao's version I have also not included Rakshasa hasta which is thesame as Śakaṭa hasta in page 133.

9. This text can be interpreted in different ways and i have chosen to base much of my understanding from my learning and observation of other stylistic traditions.

10. In the chapters on the movement of the feet, the position of the hands are based on their most common usage in relation to the feet movement and not always depicted as described in the verse.

Transliteration of Sanskrit words in English :

अ	a	--	Cut
आ	ā	--	Aunty
इ	i	--	Pink
ई	ī	--	heat
उ	u	--	pull
ऊ	ū	--	cool
ऋ	ṛ	--	sharp
ए	e	--	fame
ऐ	ai	--	fight
ओ	o	--	roll
औ	au	--	round
अं	aṃ	--	thumb/
अः	aḥ	--	aha
क	ka	--	comfort
ख	kha	--	khadi
ग	ga	--	gun
घ	gha	--	ghee
ङ	ṅa	--	thing

च	ca	-- chat
छ	cha	-- stitch
ज	ja	-- jug
झ	jha	-- hedge
ञ	ṅa	-- pinch
ट	ṭa	-- ton
ठ	ṭha	-- better
ड	ḍa	-- dumb
ढ	ḍha	-- goddess
ण	ṇa	-- fun
त	ta	-- thin
थ	tha	-- thump
द	da	-- brother
ध	dha	-- buddha
न	na	-- numb
प	pa	-- pun
फ	pha	-- loop-hole
ब	ba	-- bun

भ	bha	--	abherrent
म	ma	--	money
य	ya	--	yacht
र	ra	--	rumble
ल	la	--	lump
व	va	--	won
श	śa	--	shrine
ष	ṣ	--	shall
स	sa	--	Sun
ह	ha	--	hunter
क्ष	kṣa	--	moksha
त्र	śra	--	shred
ज्ञ	jña	--	magnum

Chapter 1

अभिनय दर्पणम्

Abhinaya Darpaṇam

नमस्क्रिया

Namaskriyā

आङ्गिकं भुवनं यस्य वाचिकं सर्ववाङ्मयम् ।
आहार्यं चन्द्रतारादि तं नुमः सात्विकं शिवम् ।।1।।

Transliteration:

Āṅgikaṃ bhuvanaṃ yasya vācikaṃ sarvavāṅmayam |
Āhāryaṃ candratārādi taṃ numaḥ sātvikaṃ śivam ||

Meaning:

Yasya= for whom; āngikam bhuvanam = the movement of body is the universe; vācikam sarva vāṅmayam= whose speech is all literature; āhāryam candra-tārādi= jewels are the moon, stars, etc; tam numaḥ śivam = I bow to that Śiva; sātvikam- who is the embodiment of emotional expression.

I bow to Lord Śiva, who is the embodiment of emotional expression (sāttvika abhinaya), for whom the movement of body is the universe (āngika abhinaya), speech is all literature (vāchika abhinaya), and the moon and stars are adornments (āhārya ahinaya).

नन्दिकेश्वर देवेन्द्र संवादम्

DIALOGUE BETWEEN INDRA AND NANDIKEŚA

कल्याणाचल वासाय करुणारस सिंधवे ।
नमोस्तु नंदिकेशाय नाट्य शास्त्रार्थदायिने ।।2।।

Transliteration:

Kalayāṇācala vāsāya karuṇārasa sindhave |
Namostu nandikeśāya nāṭya śāstrārthadāyine ||

Meaning:

Kalayāṇa-acala-vāsāya = who dwells on the auspicious Kailāsa mountain; karuṇārasa sindhave = who is the ocean of compassion; nāṭya śāstra-arthadāyine = who reveals the meaning of Nāṭya Śāstra; Nandikeśāya = (to that) Nandikeśa; namah-astu = my obeisance.

I bow to Nandikeśa who resides on the auspicious Kailāsa mountain, who is the embodiment of compassion, and who (being an expert) reveals the meaning of Nāṭya Śāstra.

स्वागतं ते सुराधीश, कुशलं त्रिदिवौकसाम् ।
किमर्थ मागतम् ब्रूहि भवता मम सन्निधौ ।।3।।

Transliteration:

Svāgatam te surādhīsa, kuśalam tridivaukasām |
Kimartha māgatam brūhi bhavatā mama sannidhau ||

Meaning:

Surādhīsa = O Lord of Devas; swāgatam te = welcome to you; tridivoukasām kuśalam= are all the devas doing well; kimartham bhavata āgatam, mama sannidhou = what brings you here before me; brūhi = tell me.

Nandikeśa said: O Indra! Welcome to you. Are all the devas in heaven doing well? Tell me why you have come all the way to meet me.

त्वदीय कृपया पूर्वम् नाट्यशालां मलंकृताम् ।
त्वदीय नर्तकः सोऽयं त्वत्कृपामभिवांछति ।।4।।

Transliteration:

Tvadīya kṛpayā pūrvam nāṭyaśālām malaṅkṛtām |
Tvadīya nartakaḥ 'Śo'yaṃ tvatkṛpāmabhivāñchati ||

Meaning:

Pūrvam = earlier; tvadīya kṛpayā = through your kindness; alaṅkṛtam nāṭyaśālām = (O possess) well-decorated nāṭyaśāla (theatre); sah ayam twadīya nartakaḥ = (and) I, your dancer; abhivāñchati twat kṛpaṃ = (further) seek your kindness.

Indra replied; Through your kindness I already possess a well decorated and fully equipped theatre. I being the owner of that theatre, further request you for a favor.

मया विधेयम् किम् तस्य वद वासव तत्त्वतः।

Transliteration:

Mayā vidheyam kim tasya vada vāsava tattvataḥ |

Meaning:

Vāsava = O Indra ! tasya = for him (i.e., for yourself); kim mayā vidheyam = what is to be done by me; vada tattvataḥ = tell me truly and fully.

Nandikeśa : O Indra ! Tell me clearly what I can do for you.

दैतेय नाट्यशालायाम् नर्तको नटशेखरः ।।5।।
तम् विजेतुं अयम् नाट्यविनोदैः क्रमवेदिभिः ।
भवद्विरचितम् ग्रंथं भरतार्णव मिच्छति ।।6।।

Transliteration:

Daiteya nāṭyasālayām nartako naṭaśekharaḥ ||
Tam vijetuṃ ayam nāṭyavinodaiḥ kramavedibhiḥ |
Bhavadviracitam grandhaṃ bharatārṇava micchati ||

Meaning:

Daiteya nāṭyasālayām = in the theatre of the Daityas (demons); narṭako naṭaśekharaḥ = there is a dancer by name 'Nāṭaśekharaḥ' (or Master actor/dancer); ayam - this person (ie.Indra); kramavedibhiḥ nāṭyavinodaiḥ = wish to regularly learn the art of nāṭya; Vijetuṃ tam = to conquer him i.e., naṭaśekharaḥ; icchati bhavat-viracitam bharatārṇava grandhaṃ = desire to learn the treatise called 'Bharata-arṇavam" written by you.

Indra replied; In the theatre of the demons, there is one dancer called Nāṭaśekhara. I wish to conquer him by acquiring competence in dance and for this purpose I request you to teach me the treatise called Bharatārṇava, composed by you.

चतुस्सहस्त्र संख्याकैः ग्रंधैश्च परिपूरितम् ।
भरतार्णव शास्त्रं तु सुमते श्रृणु सादरम् ।।7।।

Transliteration:

Catussahasra saṅkhyākaiḥ grandhaiśca paripūritam |
Bharatārṇava śāstraṃ tu sumate śṛṇu sādaram ||

Meaning:

Sumate = O wiseman (O Indra!); Bharatārṇava śāstraṃ Catussaṅkhyākai grandhaiśca paripūritam = the treatise Bharatārṇava contains 4000 verses; sādaram śṛṇu = listen with reverance.

Nandikeśa replied : O Indra! I shall teach you Bharatārṇvam containing 4000 verses; listen carefully.

नंदिकेश! दयामूर्ते! विस्तारं संविहाय मे ।
संक्षिप्य नाट्यशास्त्रार्थम् क्रमपूर्व मुदाहर ।।8।।

Transliteration:

Nandikeśa! dayāmūrte! vistāraṃ samvihāya me |
Saṅkṣipya nāṭyaśāstrārtham kramapūrva mudāhara ||

Meaning:

Dayāmūrte, Nandikeśa = Kindhearted Nandikeśa; vistāraṃ samavihāya = without going into the full details; Saṅkṣipya = abridge the same; nāṭya śāstrārtham = the nuances of nāṭya śāstrā, kramapūrva mudāhara = teach me in the proper order.

Indra prayed : O kind hearted Nandikeśa! Without going into the full details, please abridge the same and teach me a concise version in a proper order without omitting the essential aspects.

वदामि सुमते देव संक्षिप्य भरतार्णवम् ।
दर्पणाख्य मिदं सूक्ष्म मवधारय सादरम् ।।9।।

Transliteration:

Vadāmi sumate deva saṅkṣipya bharatārṇavam |
Darpaṅākhya midaṃ sūkṣma mavadhāraya sādaraṃ ||

Meaning:

Sumate devā = O wise Indra! ; Vadāmi bharatārṇavam saṅkṣipya = (as desired by you) I shall teach you the abridged version of bharatārṇavam; sūkṣma idam Darpaṇam = essence of Abhinaya Darpaṇam; sādaraṃ avadhāraya = listen carefully.

Nandikeśa replied : O wise Indra ! I shall teach you, now, the abridged version of bharatārṇavam. titled 'Abhinaya Darpaṇam', Listen with concentration.

Chapter 2

नाट्योत्पत्तिः

Nāṭyōtpattiḥ (Origin of Nāṭya)

नाट्यवेदं ददौ पूर्वं भरताय चतुर्मुखः ।
ततश्च भरतः सार्धं गन्धर्वाप्सारसां गणैः ।।10।।
नाट्यं नृत्तं तथा नृत्यमग्रे शम्भोः प्रयुक्तवान् ।

Transliteration:

Nāṭyavedaṃ dadau pūrvaṃ bharatāya caturmukhaḥ |
Tataśca bharataḥ sārdhaṃ gandharvāpsārasāṃ gaṇaiḥ ||
Nāṭyaṃ nṛttaṃ tathā nṛtyamagre śambhoḥ prayuktavān |

Meaning:

Pūrvaṃ = long ago; caturmukhaḥ bharatāya nāṭyavedaṃ dadau = the four faced Brahma, gave to Nāṭya Vedaṃ to Bharata; bharataḥ = (then) Bharata; gandharvāpsārasāṃ gaṇaiḥsārdhaṃ = with his troupe consisting of Gandharvas and Apsaras; śambhoḥ agre = in the presence of Śiva; nāṭyaṃ-nṛttaṃ nṛtyam prayuktavān = presented Nāṭyaṃ-nṛttaṃ nṛtyam.

Long ago, Brahma created Nātya and entrusted it to sage Bharata, who with his troupe consisting of Gandharvas and Apsaras, presented Nātya, Nṛtta and Nṛtya, in the presence of Lord Śiva.

प्रयोगमुद्धतं स्मृत्वा स्वप्रयुक्तं ततो हरः ।।11।।
तण्डुना स्वगणाग्रण्या भरताय न्यदीदिशत् ।
लास्यमस्यातः प्रीत्वाः पार्वत्या समदीदिशत् ।।12।।

Transliteration:

Prayogamuddhataṃ smṛtvā svaprayuktaṃ tato haraḥ ||
Taṇḍunā svagaṇāgraṇyā bharatāya nyadīdiśat |
Lāsyamasyātaḥ prītvāḥ pārvatyā samadīdiśat ||

Meaning:

Tato haraḥ = then Lord Śiva; smṛtvā uddhataṃ prayogaṃ svaprayuktaṃ = remembering the virile form of dance performed by Himself; swagaṇa-agraṇyā taṇḍunā = through Taṇḍu the leader of his attendants; bharatāya samadīdiśat = got Bharata instructed; asyam-asyātaḥ = earlier to this (instruction); prītvāḥ = with affection towards Bharata; pārvatyā lāsyam samadīdiṣat = got him instructed in Lāsya through Pārvati.

Witnessing the performance presented by Bharata, Lord Śiva remembered the virile dance He performed, and through Taṇḍu, the leader of his attendants, taught Bharata the virile dance and requested Parvati to teach the graceful aspect of Lāsya.

बुद्धवाऽथ ताण्डवं ताण्डोर्मर्त्येभ्यो मुनयोऽवदन् ।
पार्वती त्वनुशास्ति स्म लास्यं बाणात्मजामुषाम् ।।13।।
तया द्वारवतीगोप्यस्ताभिः सौराष्ट्रयोषितः ।
ताभिस्तु तत्तद्देशीयास्तदशिष्यन्त योषितः ।।14।।
एवं परम्पराप्राप्तमेत्तल्लोके प्रतिष्ठितम् ।

Transliteration:

Buddhavā'tha tāṇḍavaṃ tāṇḍormartyebhyo munayo'vadan |
Pārvatī tvanuśāsti sma lāsyaṃ vāṇātmajāmuṣām ||
Tathā dvāravatīgopyastābhiḥ saurāṣṭrayoṣitaḥ |
Tābhistu tattaddeśīyāstadaśiṣyanta yoṣitaḥ ||
Evaṃ paramparāprāptamettalloke pratiṣṭhitam |

Meaning:

Atha = then; munayaḥ = the sages; tāṇḍoh tāṇḍavam buddhavā = having learned tāṇḍavam taught by Taṇḍu; martyebhyaḥ avadam = told (taught) tāṇḍavam to humans; Pārvati (tu) = Pārvati too; lāsyaṃ, bāṇātmajām, uṣām, anuśāsti sma = taught lāsya to Uṣa, the daughter of Bāṇāsura; tayā dvāravati gopyaḥ = from her (i.e. Uṣa) the gopis (i.e. cowherd women) of Dwārakānagara; tābhiḥ saurāṣṭra yoṣitaḥ = from them (i.e. gopis), the women of Sourāṣṭra; tābhih (tu) = and from them (i.e. women of Sourāṣṭra); tat-tat-deśiṣyan yoṣitaḥ = the women of various regions; tat asiṣyantaḥ = learned that dance; evaṃ param parāprāptam = thus, having passed on from region to region (or from generation to generation); ettalloke pratiṣṭhitam = thus this (the art of dance) was established and became popular in this world.

The sages, taught people the tāṇḍavam that they learned from Taṇḍu. Pārvati too, taught lāsya to Uṣa, the daughter of Bāṇāsura, who taught the gopis (i.e. cowherd women) of Dwārakānagara learn. The women of Sourāṣṭra learned from the gopis, who taught the women of various regions. Thus the art passed on from region to region and from generation to generation became established and popular in this world.

(नाट्य प्रशंसा)

(Nāṭya praśaṃsā)

ऋग्यजुः सामवेदेभ्यो वेदाच्चाथर्वणः क्रमात् ।।15।।
पाठ्यं चाभिनयं गीतं रसान् संगृह्य पद्मजः ।
व्यरीरचच्छास्त्रमिदं धर्मकामार्थमोक्षदम् ।।16।।

Transliteration:

Ṛgyajuḥ sāmavedebhyo vedāccātharvaṇaḥ kramāt ||
Pāṭhyaṃ cābhinayaṃ gītaṃ rasān saṅgṛhya padmajaḥ |
Vyarīracacchāstramidaṃ dharmakāmārthamokṣadam ||

Meaning:

Ṛk - yajus - sāmavedebhyaḥ = from Ṛgveda, Yajurveda and Sāmaveda; atharvaṇa vedāt ca = from Atharvaṇaveda as well; kramāt saṅgṛhya = having extracted respectively; pāṭhyaṃ ca, abhinayam, gītaṃ rasān = speech, abhinayam (acting), song and rasas; idaṃ śāstram vyarīracat = composed this Śāstra i.e. Nātya śāstra.; dharma - kāma - artha - mokṣadam = (this śāstra helps) to attain dharma (righteous conduct), kāma (desires), artha (wealth), and mokṣa (beatitude/liberation).

Brahma extracted speech from Ṛgveda, abhinayam from Yajurveda, gītaṃ from Sāmaveda and rasā from Atharvaṇaveda and composed the Nātya Śāstra, which bestows Dharma (righteous conduct), kāma (desires), Artha (wealth), and Mokṣa (beatitude/liberation), the four principal objectives of human existence.

कीर्तिप्रागल्भ्यसौभाग्यवैदग्ध्यानां प्रवर्धनम् ।
औदार्यस्थैर्यधैर्याणां विलासस्य च कारणम् ।।17।।
दुःखार्तिशोकनिर्वेदखेदविच्छेदकारणम् ।
अपि ब्रह्मपरानन्दादिदमभ्यधिकं मतम् ।।18।।
जहार नारदादीनां चित्तानि कथमन्यथा ।

Transliteration:

Kīrtiprāgalbhyasaubhāgyavaidagdhyānāṃ pravardhanam |
Audāryasthairyadhairyāṇāṃ vilāsasya ca kāraṇam ||
Duḥkhārtiśokanirvedakhedavicchedakāraṇam |
Api brahmaparānandādidamabhyadhikaṃ matam ||
Jahāra nāradādīnāṃ cittāni kathamanyathā |

Meaning:

Kīrti-prāgalbhaya-saubhāgya-vaidagdhyānām pravardhanam = (this art i.e. the dance) promotes fame, expertise, prosperity and intelligence; oudārya-sthairya-dhairya- vilāsasya (ca) kāraṇam = causes nobility, steadfastness, bravery and luxury; duḥkha - ārti - śoka - nirweda - kheda, viccheda kāraṇam = it is means to overcome sorrow, misfortune, affliction, disappointment and despondency; idam brahmaparānandat api abhyadhikam matam = this (i.e. the pleasure of bliss derived from this art) is considered greater or higher than even the Supreme Bliss; anyathā = otherwise; katham nāradādīni cittāni jahāra = how else can it attract the minds of sages like Narada?

This Nātya Śāstra - promotes fame, expertise, prosperity and intelligence; causes nobility, steadfastness, bravery and luxury; it is a means to overcome sorrow, misfortune, affliction, disappointment and despondency. The pleasure of bliss derived from this art is considered greater or higher than even the Supreme Bliss. Otherwise it could not have attracted the minds of sages like Narada.

नटनभेदाः
Naṭanabhedāḥ

Nāṭya - Nṛtta - Nṛtya

एतच्चतुर्विधोपेतं नटनम् त्रिविधम् स्मृतम् ।।19।।
नाट्यं नृत्तं नृत्यमिति मुनिभिर्भरतादिभिः ।

Transliteration:

Etaccaturvidhopetaṃ naṭanam trividham smṛtam ||
Nāṭyaṃ nṛttaṃ nṛtyamiti munibhirbharatādibhiḥ |

Meaning:

Etat naṭanam, catuḥ-vidha-upetam = this naṭanam (i.e. acting or act of communication) is fourfold; trividhama smṛtam = (it is) again of three types - Nāṭyaṃ - Nṛttaṃ - Nṛtyam; iti bharata - adibhiḥ - munibhiḥ = thus naṭana was categorised by sages like Bharata.

Naṭanam (i.e. acting or act of communication) is four-fold (Āngikam, etc.), which is again of three types - Nāṭyaṃ - Nṛttaṃ - Nṛtyam, as was categorised by sages like Bharata.

नटन प्रयोग कालः

Naṭana Prayoga Kālaḥ

(Proper times for the performance of Dance)

द्रष्टव्ये नाट्यनृत्ये च पर्वकाले विशेषतः ।।20।।
नृत्यं तत्र नरेन्द्रणामभिषेके महोत्सवे ।
यात्रायां देवयात्रायां विवाहे प्रियसङ्गमे ।।21।।
नगराणामगराणां प्रवेशे पुत्रजन्मनि ।
शुभार्थिभिः प्रयोक्तव्यं माङ्गल्यं सर्वकर्मभिः ।।22।।

Transliteration:

Draṣṭavye nāṭyanṛtye ca parvakāle viśeṣataḥ ||
Nṛtyaṃ tatra narendraṇāmabhiṣeke mahotsave |
Yātrāyāṃ devayātrāyāṃ vivāhe priyasaṅgame ||
Nagarāṇāmagarāṇāṃ praveśe putrajanmani |
Śubhārthibhiḥ prayoktavyaṃ māṅgalyaṃ sarvakarmabhiḥ ||

Meaning:

Nāṭya nṛtye (ca), draṣṭavye, parvakāle viśeṣataḥ = Nāṭya and Nṛtta should be witnessed, during festivals particularly; tatra Nṛtyaṃ - that Nṛtyaṃ; narendraṇām abhiṣeke, mahotsave, yātrāyāṃ vivāhe, priyasaṅgame devayātrāyām - nagarāṇām - agarāṇāṃ praveśe putrajanmami = at the time of coronation of kings, a great festival, pilgrimage or procession, temple festival (procession with an image of god), marriage, reunion of friends or beloveds, entering the city, entering a (new) house, birth of a son; śubha arthibhiḥ, prayoktavyaṃ = has to be arranged by those who are desirous of prosperity; maāṅgalyaṃ sarvakarmabhiḥ = this is auspicious on all occasions;

Nāṭya and Nṛtta should be witnessed particularly during festivals. Those who are desirous of prosperity have to arrange them as they are auspicious for all occasions . Nṛtyaṃ has to be witnessed at the time of coronation of kings, a great festival, pilgrimage or procession, temple festival (procession with an image of god), marriage, reunion of friends or beloveds, entering the city, entering a (new) house, birth of a son.

नाट्यम्
Nāṭyam

नाट्यं तन्नाटकम् चैव पूज्यं पूर्वकथायुतम् ।

Transliteration:

Nāṭyaṃ tannāṭakam caiva pūjyaṃ pūrvakathāyutam |

Meaning:

Tat nāṭyaṃ = that Nāṭya; nāṭakam ca eva = is Nāṭaka (Rūpaka i.e. play) and also; pūjyaṃ pūrvakathāyutam = (it is) full of enchanting ancient stories.

Nāṭya is only Nāṭaka (Rūpaka i.e. play). It is full of enchanting ancient stories.

नृत्तम्
Nṛttam

भावाभिनयहीनं तु नृत्तमित्यभिधीयते ।।23।।

Transliteration:

Bhāvābhinayahīnaṃ tu nṛttamityābhidhīyate ||

Meaning:

Nṛttam, bhāva - ābhinaya-hīnaṃ (tu) iti abhinaye = nṛttam is said to be without emotion and expression.

Nṛttam is said to be without emotion and expression.

नृत्यम्
Nṛtyam

रसभाव्यञ्जनादियुक्तं नृत्तमित्तीर्यते ।
एतन्नृत्यं महाराजसभायां कल्पयेत् सदा ।।24।।

Transliteration:

Rasabhāvyañjanādiyuktaṃ nṛttamittīryate |
Etannṛtyaṃ mahārājasabhāyāṃ kalpayet sadā ||

Meaning:

Nṛtyam, Rasa bhāva vyañjana - ādiyuktam, iti īryate = Nṛtyam is said to be exposition of Rasa, Bhāvās and other aspects.

Nṛtyam is said to be exposition of Rasā, Bhāva and other aspects.

***एतत् त्रयम् द्विधाभिन्नम् लास्य-ताण्डव सौज्ञकम् ।**
सुकुमाराम् तु तल्लास्यम् उद्धतम् ताण्डवम् विदुः ।।25।।

Transliteration:

Etat trayam dvidhābhinnam lāsya-tāṇḍava saujñakam |
Sukumārām tu tallāsyam uddhatam tāṇḍavam viduḥ ||

Meaning:

Etat trayam = these three (i.e. Nāṭyaṃ, Nṛtta and Nṛtya); dvidhābhinnama, lāsya-tāṇḍava saujanakam = are of two types, namely Lāsya-Tāṇḍava; tat lāsya (tu) sukumāram - that Lāsya is graceful and dainty; tāṇḍava uddhatam viduḥ = Tāṇḍavam is known to be bold and awe inspiring.

Nāṭyaṃ, Nṛtta and Nṛtya are again of two types - Lāsya and Tāṇḍava. Lāsya is graceful and dainty (sukumāram) and Tāṇḍavam is known to be bold and awe-inspiring (uddhatam).

सभापतिलक्षणम्
Sabhāpatilakṣaṇam
(Characteristics of the chief of the assembly)

श्रीमान् धीमान् विवेकी वितरणनिपुणो गानविद्याप्रवीणः ।
सर्वज्ञः कीर्तिशाली सरसगुणयुतो हावभावेष्वभिज्ञः ।।26।।
मात्सर्यद्वेषहीनः प्रकृतिहितसदाचारशीलो दयालु ।
धीरोधाथः कलावानभिनयचतुरो-सौ सभानायकः स्यात् ।।27।।

Transliteration:

Śrīmān dhīmān vivekī vitaraṇanipuṇo gānavidyāpravīṇaḥ |
Sarvajñaḥ kīrtiśālī sarasaguṇayuto hāvabhāveṣvabhijñaḥ ||
Mātsaryadveṣahīnaḥ prakṛtihitasadācāraśīlo dayālu |
Dhīroddātaḥ kalāvānabhinayacaturo-sau sabhānāyakaḥ syāt ||

Meaning:

Śrīmān = wealthy; dhīmān = wise; vivekī = discriminating; vitaraṇanipuṇaḥ = expert in providing succour to the needy; gānavidyāpravīṇaḥ = versed in music lore; Sarvajñaḥ all-knowing; kīrtiśālī =

renowned; sarasaguṇayutaḥ = of charming dispostition; hāva bhāveṣhu abhijñaḥ = knowledgeable of expression; mātsarya - ādyaih vihīnaḥ = devoid of jealousy and the like; prakṛti hitaḥ = favourite to the followers; sadācāraśīlaḥ = familiar with customary etiquette; dayāluḥ = sympathetic; Dhīroddāttaḥ = magnanimous and courageous; kalāvān = interested in all the arts; abhinaya caturaḥ = clever in the art of abhinayam; asou sabhānāyakaḥ syāt = a person possessing the above qualities should be the chief of the Sabha (Sabhānāyaka = Sabhāpati).

The leader of the Sabha should possess the following qualities: he should be wealthy, wise, discriminating, one who is expert in providing succour to the needy, well versed in music lore, all-knowing, renown, of charming disposition, knowledgeable of expressions, devoid of jealousy and the like, liked by the followers, familiar with customary etiquette, sympathetic, magnanimous and courageous, interested in all the arts and clever in the art of abhinayam.

मन्त्रिलक्षणम्

Mantrilakṣaṇam

(Characteristics of the minister)

मेधासुस्थिरभाषणागुणपराः श्रीमद्यशोलम्पटा ।
भावज्ञा गुणदोषभेदनिपुणाः श्रृङ्गारलीलायुताः ।।28।।
मध्यस्था नयकोविदाः सहृदयाः सत्पण्डिता भान्ति ते ।
भाषाभेदविचक्षणाः सुकवयश्चास्य प्रभोर्मन्त्रिणाः ।।29।।

Transliteration:

Medhāsusthirabhāṣaṇāguṇaparāḥ śrīmadyaśolampaṭā |
Bhāvajñā guṇadoṣabhedanipuṇāḥ śrṛṅgāralīlāyutāḥ ||
Madhyasthā nayakovidāḥ sahṛdayāḥ satpaṇḍitā bhānti te |
Bhāṣābhedavicakṣaṇāḥ sukavayaścāsya prabhormantriṇāḥ ||

Meaning:

Medhā, susthirabhāṣiṇāḥ = wise, men of their word; guṇaparāḥ = discerning of good qualities ; śrīmat - yaśaḥ lampaṭaḥ = wealthy, renowned; bhāvajñaḥ = learned in bhāvas; guṇadoṣabhedanipuṇāḥ = knowing good from evil; śṛṅgāralīlāyutāḥ = knowing erotics; madhyasthaḥ = impartial; nayakovidāḥ = versed in state craft; sahṛdayāḥ = cultured; satpaṇḍitā = learned; Bhāṣābhedavicakṣaṇāḥ = who can distinguish the various nuances of the language or dialects; sukavayaḥ = good poet; yasya prabhoh, mantriṇaḥ = the king's ministers who have all the above qualities; bhanti te = will shine.

The king (i.e. the chief of the Sabha) will shine only when his ministers possess the following qualities: they should be wise, men of their word, discerning of good qualities, wealthy, renowned, learned in bhāvas, knowing good from evil, knowing erotics, impartial, versed in state craft, cultured, knowledgeable, those who can distinguish the various nuances of the language or dialects and be good poets.

सभा लक्षणम्

Sabhā Lakṣaṇam

(Characteristics of the Assembly)

सभाकल्पतरुर्भाति वेदशाखोपजीवितः ।
शास्त्रपुष्पसमाकीर्णो विद्वद्भ्रमरशोभितः ।।30।।

Transliteration:

Sabhākalpatarurbhāti vedaśākhopajīvitaḥ |
Śāstrapuṣpasamākīrṇo vidvadbhramaraśobhitaḥ ||

Meaning:

Sabhākalpatarurḥ bhāti = the Assembly shines like the Kalpataru (which bestows boons); vedaśākha-upaśobhitam = Vedas are its branches; Śāstra-puṣpa samākīrnah = treatises on various arts are its flowers; vidvadbhramaraśobhitam = learned men (i.e. scholars) are its bees.

The Sabha/Assembly is compared to Kalpataru, a tree in the heaven which bestows boons- Vedas are its branches, treatises on various arts are its flowers, learned men (i.e. scholars) are its bees. The Sabha thus shines like the Kalpataru.

सत्याचारसभा गुणोज्ज्वाल सभा सद्धर्मकीर्तिः सभा ।
वेदालंकृतराजपूजित सभा वेदांतवेद्या सभा ।।31।।
वीणावाणि विशेष लक्षित सभा विख्यात वीर सभा ।
राजर्दाज कुमार शोभित सभा राजत्प्राकांतिसभा ।।32।।
विद्वांसः काव्यो भत्तः गायकः परिहासकः ।
इतिहास - पुराणज्ञः सभा सप्तांगलक्षणं ।।33।।

Transliteration:

Satyācārasabhā guṇojjvāla sabhā saddharmakīrtiḥ sabhā |
Vedālaṅkṛtarājapūjita sabhā vedāntavedyā sabhā ||
Vīṇāvāṇi viśeṣa lakṣita sabhā vikhyāta vīra sabhā |
Rājardāj kumāra śobhita sabhā rājatprākāntisabhā ||
Vidvāṃsaḥ kāvyo bhattaḥ gāyakaḥ parihāsakaḥ |
Itihāsa - purāṇajñaḥ sabhā saptāṅgalakṣaṇaṃ ||

Meaning:

Satyācārasabhā = the sabha is for men of integrity; guṇojjwāla sabhā = the sabha is shining with good qualities; saddharma kīrtiḥ sabhā = the sabha is famous for righteous conduct; veda - alaṅkṛta - rājapūjita sabhā = the sabha is adorned by Vedic scholars and honored by the kings; vedānta vedyā sabhā = Vedānta philosophy is expounded in the sabha; vīṇāvāṇi viśeṣa lakṣita sabhā = the sabha is distinguished by the sound of Vīṇā and literature; vikhyāta vīra sabhā = the sabha possesses renowned heroes; rājart - rāja kumāra śobhita sabhā = the sabha is ornamented by resplendent princes; and rājat prākānti sabhā = the sabha is shining with royal splendor. Vidvāṃsaḥ = scholars; kāvyaḥ = poets; bhattaḥ = heralds; gāyakaḥ = musicians; parihāsakaḥ = jesters (vidūṣakas); itihāsa - purāṇajñaḥ = those who are familiar with the epics, and mythology; sabhā saptāṅgalakṣaṇaṃ = thus the Sabha has seven limbs i.e. when the above seven types of men are there, then only it is called a Sabha.

The Sabha is for men of truth, shining with good qualities, famous for righteous conduct, adorned by Vedic scholars and honored by the kings. Vedānta philosophy is expounded in the sabha and it is distinguished by the sound of Vīṇā and literature. It has famous heroes and is ornamented by resplendent royal princes. The sabha has scholars, poets, heralds, wise men, musicians, jesters and those who are familiar with itihāsa (history) and purāṇa (mythology).

सभारचना Sabhāracanā

(Arrangement of the Sabha and Orchestra)

एवंविधः सभानाथः प्राङ्मुखो निविशेन् मुदा ।
वर्तेरन् पार्श्वयोस्तस्यकविमन्त्रिसुहृजनाः ।।34।।
तदग्रे नटनं कुर्यात् तत् स्थलं रङ्ग उच्यते ।

Transliteration:

Evaṃvidhaḥ sabhānāthaḥ praṅmukho niviśen mudā |
Varteran Pārśvayostasyakavimantrisuhṛjanāḥ ||
Tadagre naṭanaṃ kuryāt tat sthalaṃ raṅga ucyate |

Meaning:

Evaṃvidhaḥ, sabhānāthaḥ = the chief of the Sabha, possessing the qualities described above; prāṅmukḥ niviśen mudā = should sit comfortably, facing east; tasya pārśvayoḥ, kavi-mantri-suhṛjanāḥ varteran = on his both sides, poets, ministers and cultured people or friends are to be seated; tadagre naṭanaṃ kuryāt = then naṭana (dance) has to begin in front of sabhāpati; tat sthalam raṅgaḥ ucyate = the place where the dance begins is called Ranga (the stage).

The chief of the Sabha, possessing the qualities already described, should sit comfortably facing east. Poets, ministers and cultured people and friends are to be seated on both sides of the Sabhānātha. The naṭana (dance) has to begin in front of the Sabhāpati and that place is called 'Ranga'.

रङ्गमध्ये स्थिते पात्रे तत्समीपे नटोत्तमः ।।35।।
दक्षिणे तालधारी च पार्श्वद्वन्द्वे मृदङ्गकौ ।
तयोर्मध्ये गीतकारी श्रुतिकारस्तदन्तिके ।।36।।
एवं तिष्ठेत् क्रमेणैव नाट्यादौ रङ्गमण्डलो ।

Transliteration:

Raṅgamadhye sthite pātre tatsamīpe naṭottamaḥ ||
Dakṣiṇe tāladhārī ca pārśvadvandve mṛdaṅgakau |
Tayormadhye gītakārī śrutikārastadantike ||
Evaṃ tiṣṭhet krameṇaiva nāṭyādau raṅgamaṇḍalo |

Meaning:

Pātre raṅgamadhye sthite = while the dancer stands at the centre of the stage; tat samīpe naṭottamaḥ = the best dancer or the dance master sits near her; Dakṣiṇe tāladhārī = on her right the cymbalist; pārśwadvandve mṛdaṅgakau = on both sides the two mṛdangists; Tayoḥ rmadhye gītakārī = the vocalist in between them; tat-antike śrutikāraḥ = the one who keeps sruti, a little behind; Evaṃ raṅgamaṇḍalī nāṭya - adou tiṣthet = in the above order, the members of the troupe (i.e. orchestra) should occupy their positions on the stage before the dance begins.

Before the dance begins- the dancer stands at the centre of the stage; the naṭottama or the dance master sits near her. On her right the cymbalist, on both the sides the two mṛdangists, the vocalist in between them, and a little behind the srutikara have to be seated.

पात्रलक्षणम्

Pātralakṣaṇam

(Characteristics of Dancer)

तन्वी रूपवती श्यामा पीनोन्नतपयोधरा ।।37।।
प्रगल्भा सरसा कान्ता कुशला ग्रहमोक्षयोः ।
चारी ताल लयाभिज्ञा मंडल-स्थानपंडिता ।।38।।
हस्तांगस्थान निपुणा करणेसु विलासिनी ।
विशाललोचना गीतवाद्यतालानुवर्तिनी ।।39।।
परार्ध्यभूवासम्पन्ना प्रसन्नमुखपङ्कजा ।
एवंविधगुणोपेता नर्तकी समुदीरिता ।।40।।

Transliteration:

Tanvī rūpavatī śyāmā pīnonnatapayodharā ||
Pragalbhā sarasā kāntā kuśalā grahamokṣayoḥ |
Cārī tāla layābhijñā maṇḍala-sthānapaṇḍitā ||
Hastāṅgasthāna nipuṇā karaṇesu vilāsinī |
Viśālalocanā gītavādyatālānuvartinī ||
Parārdhyabhūvāsampannā prasannamukhapaṅkajā |
Evaṃvidhaguṇopetā nartakī samudīritā ||

Meaning:

Tanvī = of proper stature; rūpavatī = charming; śyāmā = dun colored; pīna-unnata payodharā = with full-rounded breasts; Pragalbhā = self confident; sarasā = playful; kāntā = agreeable; kuśalā graha-mokṣayoḥ kuśalā = expert in beginning and ending critical passages (the dancer should not be swayed away by impulse but perfectly be self-possessed); Cāri tāla layābhijña = skilled in cāri movements, tāla and laya; maṇḍala-sthāna paṇḍitā = skilled in mandalas; Hast aṅga sthāna nipuṇa = expert in using hastas, various limbs or aṅgarasa and sthānakas; karaṇesu vilāśinī = graceful in handling karaṇas; viśāla locanā = wide eyes; gīta-vādya-tāla-anuvartinī = able to follow the song being rendered along with instruments and tāla; para-arthya-bhūvāsampannā = adorned with best jewels; prasanna mukha paṅkajā = charming with lotus like face; evaṃ-vidhaguṇopetā nartakī samudīritā = when one possesses all the above qualities, then only she is considered as a Nartaki.

A woman is considered a Nartaki if she possesses the following qualities: proper stature, charming, dun colored, with full-rounded breasts, self confident, playful, agreeable, expert in beginning and ending critical passages, skilled in cāri movements, rhythm and laya, skilled in mandalas, expert in using hastas, various limbs or aṅgarasa and sthānakas, graceful in handling karaṇas, has large eyes, able to follow the song being rendered along with instruments and tāla, adorned with best jewels, and charming with lotus like face,

वर्जनीयपात्राणि

Varjanīyapātrāṇi

(Women not fit for Dance)

पुष्पाक्षी केशहीना च स्थूलोष्ठी लम्बितस्तनी ।
अतिस्थूलाप्यतिकृशा अत्युच्चाप्यतिवामना ।।41।।
कुब्जा च स्वरहीना च दशैता नाट्यवर्जित ।

Transliteration:

Puṣpākṣī keśahīnā ca sthūloṣṭhī lambitastanī |
Atisthūlāpyatikṛśā atyuccāpyativāmanā ||
Kubjā ca svarahīnā ca daśaitā nāṭyavarjita |

Meaning:

Puṣpākṣī = who has opaque eyes; keśahīnā (ca) = whose hair is scanty; sthūla-oṣṭhī = whose lips are thick; lambitastanī = whose breasts are pendant; Atisthūla(api)-atikṛśā = who is very stout or who is very thin; ati-ucca(api)-ativāmana = who is very tall or who is very short; Kubjā = who is hunch-backed; svarahīnā (ca) = who does not have a good voice; etaḥ daśaḥ nāṭya varjitaḥ = these ten women are to be rejected i.e., they are not fit to be dancers.

The following ten types of women are not fit to dance:

(1) who has opaque eyes (2) whose hair is scanty (3) whose lips are thick (4) whose breasts are droopy (5) who is very stout (6) who is very thin (7) who is very tall (8) who is very short (9) who is hunch backed (10) who does not have a good voice.

पात्रस्य प्राणाः

Pātrasya Prāṇāḥ

(Inner aspects of the life of a Dancer)

जवः स्थिरत्वं रेखा च भ्रमरी दृष्टिरश्रमः ।।42।।
मेधा श्रद्धा वचो गीतं पात्रप्राणा दश स्मृताः ।
एवंविधेन पात्रेण नृत्यं कार्यं विधानतः ।।43।।

Transliteration:

Javaḥ sthiratvaṃ rekhā ca bhramarī dṛṣṭiraśramaḥ ||
Medhā śraddhā vaco gītaṃ pātraprāṇā daśa smṛtāḥ |
Evaṃvidhena pātreṇa nṛtyaṃ kāryaṃ vidhānataḥ ||

Meaning:

Javaḥ = swiftness; sthiratvaṃ = composure; rekhā = symmetry; bhramarī = graceful execution of bhramaris; dṛṣṭiḥ = good looks; asramaḥ = ease; medhā = intelligence or retentive faculty; śraddhā = devotion or concentration; vacaḥ = well spoken; gītaiḥ = (the) song; antaḥ prāṇāḥ daśa smṛtāḥ = these ten are considered as the aspects of inner life of a nartaki; Evaṃ vidhena pātreṇa nṛtyaṃ kāryaṃ vidhānataḥ = as detailed so far and according to the rules the dancer has to proceed with the presentation of dance.

The following are the ten inner aspects of the life of a dancer:

Swiftness, composure, symmetry, graceful execution of bhramaris, good looks, ease, intelligence or retentive faculty, devotion or concentration, well spoken and a singer, The dancer having these ten inner aspects has to proceed with the presentation of dance. according to the rules laid down by the treatises.

*पात्र बहि प्राणः

Pātra bahi Prāṇaḥ

(Outer-aspects of the life of a Dancer)

मृदङ्गश्च सुतालौ च वेणुः गीतिः ततः श्रुतिः ।।44।।
एकवीणा किंकिणी च गायकाश्च सुविश्रुतः ।
इत्येवम् अन्वयज्ञैश्च पात्र प्राणाः बहिः स्मृतः ।।45।।

Transliteration:

Mṛdaṅgaśca sutālau ca veṇuḥ gītiḥ tataḥ śrutiḥ ||
Ekavīṇā kiṅkiṇī ca gāyakāśca suviśrutaḥ |
Ityevam anvayajñaiśca pātra prāṇāḥ bahiḥ smṛtaḥ ||

Meaning:

Mṛdaṅgaḥ (ca) = the Mṛdaṅgam; sutālaou (ca) = two cymbals of good tone; veṇuḥ = flute; gītiḥ song; (tataḥ) śrutiḥ = the drone; ekavīṇā = ekaveena (name of an instrument); kiṅkiṇī (ca) = the bells; uviśrutāḥ gāyakāḥ (ca) = male singer of good vocal range; Iti evam patra bahiḥ prāṇāḥ anvayajñaiḥ ca) patra prāṇāḥ bahiḥ smṛtaḥ = these eight aspects are considered by the traditionalists, as the outer external) aspects of the life of a dancer.

The traditionalists consider the following eight aspects as the outer aspects of the life of a dancer- ṛdaṅgam, two cymbals of good tone, flute, song, the drone, ekaveena, the bells and a male singer with ood vocal range.

किङ्किणीलक्षणम्
Kiṅkiṇīlakṣaṇam
(The Nature of the Bells)

सुखराश्च सुरूपाश्च सूक्ष्मा नक्षत्रदेवताः ।
किङ्किण्यः कांस्यरचिता एकैकाङ्गुलिकान्तरम् ।।46।।
बध्नीयान्नीलसूत्रेण ग्रन्थिभिश्च दृढं पुनः ।
शतद्वयं शतं वापि पादयोर्नाट्यकारिणी ।।47।।

Transliteration:

Sukharāśca surūpāśca sūkṣmā nakṣatradevatāḥ |
Kiṅkiṇyaḥ kāṃsyaracitā ekaikāṅgulikāntaram ||
Badhnīyānnīlasūtreṇa granthibhiśca dṛḍhaṃ punaḥ |
Śatadvayaṃ śataṃ vāpi pādayornāṭyakāriṇī ||

Meaning:

Sukharāś (ca) = should be sweet-toned; surūpāś (ca) = well shaped; sūkṣmā = dainty; nakṣatra devatāḥ = with the asterisms of their presiding deities; Kiṅkiṇyaḥ kāṃsyaracitā = the tiny bells should be made of bronze; eka-eka-aṅgulika-antaram = there should be one anguli (finger) gap between two bells; punaḥ nāṭyakāriṇī pādayoḥ = then, on the feet of the dancer; Śatadvayaṃ śataṃ vā = two hundred and/or one hundred bells; nīlasūtreṇa = with blue string; granthibhiḥ dṛḍhaṃ badhnīyat = should be tied firmly with firm knots.

The bells should be sweet-toned, well shaped, dainty, with the asterisms of their presiding deities and should be made of bronze. There should be one anguli (finger) gap between two bclls. At the time of dancing, two hundred or/and one hundred of such bells should be tied firmly on the feet of the dancer, with firm knots using blue string.

*नट/नर्तक लक्षणम्

Naṭa/Nartaka Lakṣaṇam
(Qualities of an Actor/Dancer)

रूपवान मधुरभाषि कृती वाग्मी पटुः तथा ।
कुलांगनासुतश्चैव शास्त्रज्ञो मधुरस्वरः ।।48।।
गीतवाद्यादि नृत्यज्ञो सिद्धकः प्रतिभानवान् ।
एतादृश गुणैः युक्तो नट इत्युच्यते बुधैः ।।49।।

Transliteration:

Rūpavān madhurabhāṣi kṛtī vāgmī paṭuḥ tathā |
Kulāṅganāsutaścaiva śāstrajño madhurasvaraḥ ||
Gītavādyādi nṛtyajño siddhakaḥ pratibhānavān |
Etādṛśa guṇaiḥ yukto naṭa ityucyate budhaiḥ ||

Meaning:

Rūpavān = handsome/charming; madhurabhāṣi= speaks sweetly; kṛtī= learned; vāgmī = eloquent; tathā patuḥ = steady; kulāṅgana-sutaḥ (ca-eva) = son of a woman of high birth; śāstrajñaḥ = learned in the treatises on arts; madhurāsvaraḥ = of sweet voice; gīta-vādya-ādi nṛtyajñaḥ= versed in song, instruments etc. pertaining to dance; siddhakaḥ= self-confident; pratibhānavān = having ready-wit; etadṛśa gunaiḥ yuktaḥ = one who possesses the above qualities; naṭaḥ iti budhaiḥ ucyate = will be called naṭa by the wise.

A person to be considered as a Naṭa by the wise should have the following qualities: handsome/charming, one who speaks sweetly, learned, eloquent, steady, son of a woman of high birth, versed in the treatises on arts, of sweet voice, versed in song, instruments etc. pertaining to dance, self-confident and having ready-wit.

*पूर्वरङ्गम्

Pūrvaraṅgam

(Preliminary rituals)

अकृत्व प्रार्थनम् पात्र माचरेत् यदि नाट्यकम् ।
तन्नाट्यम् नीच मित्याहुः नाट्यशास्त्र विचक्षणाः ।।50।।
नीचपात्र कृतम् नाट्यम् यदि पश्यन्ति मानवः ।
पुत्रहीन भविष्यन्ति जायन्ते पशुयोनिषु ।।51।।

तस्मात्सर्वम् समालोच्य पूर्वकैः यदुदाहृतं ।
देवता प्रार्थनादीनि कृत्व नाट्य मुपक्रमेत् ।।52।।

Transliteration:

Akṛtva prārthanam pātra mācaret yadi nāṭyakam |
Tannāṭyam nīca mityāhuḥ nāṭyaśāstra vicakṣaṇāḥ ||
Nīcapātra kṛtam nāṭyam yadi paśyanti mānavaḥ |
Putrahīna bhaviṣyanti jāyante paśuyoniṣu ||
tasmātsarvam samālocya pūrvakaiḥ yadudāhṛtaṃ |
Devatā prārthanādīni kṛtva nāṭya mupakramet ||

Meaning:

Yadi pātram akṛtvā prārthanam nāṭyakam ācaret = if the dancer begins to dance without offering prayers; nāṭya vicakṣaṇaḥ tat-nāṭyam nīcam iti āhuḥ = experts on the science of dance consider that dance as low; yadi nīcapātra-kṛtam nāṭyam paśyanti mānavaḥ = if people witness the dance of such a vulgar dancer; putrahīna bhaviṣyanti jāyante paśuyoniśu = will not have sons and will be reborn in the wombs of animals; tasmāt pūrvakaiḥ yat udāhṛtaṃ tat-sarvam samālocya = so, after carefully observing the rules laid down by our ancestors; Devatā prārthana-āndīni kṛtva, nāṭyam upakramet = and after offering prayers to Gods the dance has to begin.

If the dancer begins to dance without offering prayers, experts on the science of dance consider that dance low. People who witness that nāṭyam will not have sons and will be reborn in the wombs of animals. Therefore, the dance has to begin after carefully observing the rules for dancing and after offering prayer to gods.

प्रार्थनादिकम्
Prārthanādikam

विघ्नेशं मुरजाधिपं च गगनं स्तुत्वा महीं प्रार्थयेत् ।
तत्तद्वाद्यकदम्बकस्य विधिना पूजाविधानमयेत् ।।53।।
आलप्यातिमनोहरान् बहुविधीन् संपाद्य भूयस्तथा ।
गुर्वाज्ञामवलम्ब्य पात्रमुचितं श्रृङ्गारमेवारभेत् ।।54।।

Transliteration:

Vighneśaṃ murajādhipaṃ ca gaganaṃ stutvā mahīṃ prārthayet |
Tattadvādyakadambakasya vidhinā pūjāvidhānamayet ||
Ālapyātimanoharān bahuvidhīn sampādya bhūyastathā |
Gurvājñāmavalambya pātramucitaṃ śrṛṅgāramevārabhet ||

Meaning:

Murajādhipaṃ vighneśaṃ (ca), gaganaṃ stutvā = after praising vighneśa, the patron deity of mṛdangam, and the sky; mahīṃ prārthayet = the earth has to be praised; vidhinā tat-vādya kadambakasya pūjā-vidhām anayet = then, according to the rules, the orchestra has to be worshipped; atimanoharān ālapya = after captivating musical introduction; tathā bahuvidhīnam bhūyaḥ sampādya = (and) various rituals are performed; guruḥ-ajñām avalambya = next, obtaining the permission of the guru i.e., Nāṭyācārya; pātram ucitaṃ śṛṅgāram eva ārabhet = the dancer has to begin with appropriate Sṛṅgāra (amorous) abhinayam.

Before the dance begins, the patron deity of Mṛdangam (Vighneśa), the sky and the earth have to be offered prayers. Then, according to the rules the orchestra has to be worshipped. Next, after the captivating musical introduction, various rituals are to be performed. Then obtaining the permission of the guru i.e., Nāṭyācārya, the dancer has to begin with the appropriate Sṛṅgāra (amorous) movement.

रङ्गाधिदेवतास्तुतिः
Raṅgādhidevatāstutiḥ

भरतकुलभाग्यकलिके भावरसानन्दपरिणताकारे ।
जगदेकमोहनकले जय जय रङ्गाधिदेवते देवि ।।55।।

Transliteration:

Bharatakulabhāgyakalike bhāvarasānandapariṇatākāre |
Jagadekamohanakale jaya jaya raṅgādhidevate devi ||

Meaning:

Devi raṅg-ādhidevate = O Goddess, the presiding deity of the stage; Bharatakula bhāgya kalike = O Goddess of fortune of the profession of the actors/dancers; bhāvarasa-ānanda pariṇata-ākāre = who transforms the bhāvas into rasānanda (i.e., aesthetic pleasure); Jagat eka mohana kale = who alone can charm the entire world; jaya jaya = victory to thee.

O Goddess! The presiding deity of the stage. O Goddess of fortune of the profession of the actors/ dancers. The one who transforms the emotions into aesthetic pleasure and the one who alone can charm the entire world. victory to thee.

पुष्पाञ्जलिः
Puṣpāñjaliḥ

विघ्नानां नाशनं कर्तुं भूतानां रक्षणाय च ।
देवानां तुष्टये चापि प्रेक्षकाणां विभूतये ।।56।।

श्रेयसे नायकस्यात्र पात्रसंरक्षणाय च ।
आचार्यशिक्षासिद्ध्यर्थं पुष्पाञ्जलिमथारभेत् ।।57।।

Transliteration:

Vighnānāṃ nāśanaṃ kartum bhūtānāṃ rakṣaṇāya ca |
Devānāṃ tuṣṭaye cāpi prekṣakāṇāṃ vibhūtaye ||
śreyase nāyakasyātra pātrasaṃrakṣaṇāya |
Ācāryaśikṣāsiddhyarthaṃ puṣpāñjalimathārabhet ||

Meaning:

Vighnānāṃ nāśanaṃ kartum = to destroy obstacles; bhūtānāṃ rakṣaṇāya (ca) = to protect living beings; devānāṃ tuṣṭaye (ca-api) = to please the gods; prekṣakāṇāṃ vibhūtaye = to bring prosperity to the spectators; nāyakasya śreyase = for the safety of the sabhānāyaka; (atra) pātra saṃrakṣaṇāya = for the protection of the dancer; Ācārya śikṣā-siddhi-arthaṃ = for the success of the training given by the Ācārya (i.e. Guru); (atha) puṣpāñjalim ārabhet = now Puṣpāñjali (offering of flowers) should begin.

Puṣpāñjali (offering of flowers) should begin then, to destroy the obstacles, to protect the living beings, to please the gods, to bring prosperity to the spectators, for the safety of the sabhānāyaka, for the protection of the dancer and for the success of the training given by the Ācārya.

नाट्यक्रमः
Nāṭyakramaḥ

एवं कृत्वा पूर्वरङ्गं नृत्यं कार्यं ततः परम् ।
नृत्यं गीताभिनयनं भावतालयुतं भवेत् ।।58।।

Transliteration:

Evaṃ kṛtvā pūrvaraṅgaṃ nṛtyaṃ kāryaṃ tataḥ param |
Nṛtyaṃ gītābhinayanaṃ bhāvatālayutaṃ bhavet ||

Meaning:

Evaṃ pūrvaraṅgaṃ kṛtvā = thus completing the pūrvaraṅgaṃ; tataḥ param nṛtyaṃ kāryaṃ = next, nṛtyaṃ should begin; Nṛtyaṃ gītābhinayanaṃ bhāvatālayutaṃ bhavet = Nṛtyaṃ is abhinayam for the gītam (i.e. songs) accompanied by tāla and expression of bhāvas.

Thus completing the pūrvaraṅgaṃ, nṛtyaṃ should begin. Nṛtyaṃ is abhinayam for the gītam (i.e. songs) accompanied by tāla and bhāva.

आस्येनालम्बयेद् गीतं हस्तेनार्थं प्रदर्शयेत् ।
चक्षुर्भ्यां दर्शयेद् भावं पादाभ्यां तालमाचरेत् ।।59।।
यतो हस्तस्ततो दृष्टिर्यतो दृष्टिस्ततो मनः ।
यतो मनस्ततो भावो यतो भावस्ततो रसः ।।60।।

Transliteration:

Āsyenālambayet gītaṃ hastenārthaṃ pradarśayet |
Cakṣurbhyāṃ darśayed bhāvaṃ pādābhyāṃ tālamācaret ||
Yato hastastato dṛṣṭiryato dṛṣṭistato manaḥ |
Yato manastato bhāvo yato bhāvastato rasaḥa ||

Meaning:

Āsyena alambayet gītaṃ = the song should be sustained in the throat i.e., the song should be sung by the dancer herself; hastena arthaṃ pradarśayet = the meaning of the song should be expressed by the hands; bhāvaṃ cakṣurbhyāṃ darśayet = emotion should be expressed by the eyes i.e., dṛṣṭis; tālam pādābhyāṃ ācaret = and rhythm should be marked by the feet.

Hastaḥ yataḥ tataḥ dṛṣṭiḥ= wherever the hand moves, the glance should follow; dṛṣṭiḥ yataḥ, tataḥ manaḥ= where the glances are pointing, the mind should follow; manaḥ yataḥ, tataḥ bhāvaḥ= where the mind is fixed, there expression should follow; bhāvaḥ yataḥ, tataḥ rasaḥ= when bhāva is expressed, there is rasa.

During the dance, the dancer should render the song herself, should express the meaning of the song through the hastas, should express the emotions through the dṛṣṭis and should mark rhythm with the feet.

अभिनयः

Abhinayaḥ

तत्र त्वभिनयस्यैव प्राधान्यमिति कथ्यते ।
आङ्गिको वाचिकस्तद्वदाहार्यः सात्विकोऽपरः ।।61।।
चतुर्धाभिनयस्-

Transliteration:

Tatra tvabhinayasyaiva prādhānyamiti kathyate |
Āṅgiko vācikastadvadāhāryaḥ sātviko-paraḥ ||
Caturdhābhinayas-

Meaning:

Tatra tu abhinayasy eva prādhānyamiti kathyate = the importance of abhinayam in dance is now being explained. Caturdhābhinayaḥ = Abhinayam is fourfold; Āṅgikaḥ, vācikaḥ, (tadvat), āhāryaḥ (aprah) sātvikaḥ = (1) Āṅgikam (bodily movements, gestures, postures and actions), (2) vācikam (voice and speech), (3) Āhāryam (make-up and costume); and (4) sātvikam (emotional responses);

The importance of abhinayam in dance is now being explained.

Abhinayam is fourfold: (1) Āṅgikam (bodily movements, gestures, postures and actions), (2) Vācikam (vocal i.e. song, and speech), (3) Āhāryam (makeup,costume and stage decoration); and (4) Sātvikam (emotional responses).

आङ्गिको अभिनय
Āṅgiko Abhinaya

तत्र आङ्गिकोऽङ्गैर्निदर्शितः ।

Transliteration:

Tatra āṅāgiko-ṅgairnidarśitaḥ |

Meaning:

Tatra (ca) = in the above; angaiḥ nidarsitaḥ āngikaḥ = that which is expressed by the body and its limbs is called Āṅgika abhinayam.

That which expresses sāttavika bhāvas is called Sāttavika abhinayam by the experts on bhāvas.

वाचिकाभिनयः
Vācikābhinayaḥ

वाचा विरचितः काव्यनाटकादि तु वाचिकः ।।62।।

Transliteration:

Vācā viracitaḥ kāvyanāṭakādi tu vācikaḥ ||

Meaning:

Vācikaḥ = the speech which constitutes the kāvyas and plays is called vācikaḥ abhinayam

The speech which constitutes the libretto is called vācika abhinayam.

आहार्याभिनयः
Āhāryābhinayaḥ

आहार्यो हारकेयूरवेषादिभिरलंकृतिः ।

Transliteration:

Āhāryo hārakeyūraveṣādibhiralaṅkṛtiḥ |

Meaning:

Hāra-keyūra-veṣha-ādibhiḥ alamkṛtaḥ āhāryāḥ = that which decorates the body with garlands, makeup etc., is called āhārya abhinayam.

That which decorates the body with garlands, makeup etc., is called āhārya abhinayam.

सात्त्विकाभिनयः
Sāttvikābhinayaḥ

सात्त्विकः सात्त्विकैर्भावज्ञेन विभावितः ।।63।।
स्तम्भः स्वेदाम्बु रोमाञ्चः स्वरभङ्गोऽथ वेपथुः ।
वैवर्ण्यमश्र प्रलय इत्यष्टौ सात्त्विकाः स्मृताः ।।64।।

Transliteration:

Sāttvikaḥ sāttvikairbhāvajñena vibhāvitaḥ ||
Stambhaḥ svedāmbu romāñcaḥ svarabhaṅgo'tha vepathuḥ |
Vaivarṇyamaśra pralaya ityaṣṭau sāttvikāḥ smṛtāḥ ||

Meaning:

Sāttvikaiḥ bhāviaḥ, bhāvajñena vibhāvitaḥ sāttvikaḥ = that which expresses sāttvika bhāvas is called sāttvika abhinayam by the experts on bhāvas : Stambhaḥ = paralysis / stupefaction / immobility of the body; svedāmbu = sweating / perspiration; romāñcaḥ = horripilation; svarabhaṅgaḥ (svarabhedaḥ / vaisvaryam) = distortion of voice; vepathuḥ / kampam = trembling tremor; Vaivarṇyama = change of color / paleness; asuraḥ = tears / weeping; pralayaḥ = fainting / swoon/unconsciousness (loss of consciousness); iti-aṣṭou sāttvikāḥ smṛtāḥ. = thus, the eight sāttvikabhāvās have been named.

That which expresses sāttvika bhāvās is called sāttvika abhinayam by the experts on bhāva. The eight sāttvikabhāvās are: paralysis / stupefaction / immobility of the body, sweating / perspiration, horripilation, distortion of voice, trembling tremor, change of color / paleness, tears / weeping/ fainting / unconsciousness (loss of consciousness).

आङ्गिकाभिनयसाधनानि
Āṅgikābhinayasādhanāni

तत्राङ्गिकोङ्गप्रत्यङ्गोपाङ्गैस्त्रेधा प्रकाशतः ।

Transliteration:

Tatrāṅgikoṅgapratyaṅgopāṅgaistredhā prakāśataḥ |

Meaning:

Tatrāṅgiko aṅga-pratyaṅga-upāṅgaiḥ, tredhā prakāśataḥ = among the four abhinayas, Āṅgikābhinayam is three fold : (1) Aṅga (major limbs); (2) Pratyaṅgas (subsidiary limbs) and (3) Upāṅga (minor limbs).

Among the four types of abhinaya, Āṅgikābhinayam is three fold containing - (1) Aṅga (major limbs); (2) Pratyaṅga (subsidiary limbs) and (3) Upāṅga (minor limbs).

अङ्गानि
Aṅgāni

अङ्गान्यत्र शिरो हस्तौ वक्षः पार्श्वौ कटीतटौ ।।65।।
पादाविति षडुक्तानि ग्रीवामप्यपरे जगुः ।

Transliteration:

Aṅgānyatra śiro hastau vakṣaḥ pārśvau kaṭītaṭau ||
Pādāviti ṣaḍuktāni grīvāmapyapare jaguḥ |

Meaning:

Atra aṅgāni-śiraḥ, hastau vakṣaḥ pārśvau kaṭītaṭau, pādou-iti = among these, angas are six: (1) śiraḥ (head); (2) hastou (the two palms); (3) vakṣah (chest); (4) pārśvau (the two sides); (5) kaṭītaṭau (the two sides of the waist) and; (6) pādou (the two feet); iti ṣat-uktāni - these six are considered as aṅgas; apare grīvāma api jaguḥ. = some others consider neck also as an aṅga.

Among these, aṅgas are six: (1) śiraḥ (head); (2) hastou (the two palms); (3) vakṣah (chest); (4) pārśvau (the two sides); (5) kaṭītaṭau (sides of the waist) and; (6) pādou (feet). These six are considered as aṅga. some others consider neck also as an aṅga.

प्रत्यङ्गानि

Pratyaṅgāni

प्रत्यङ्गान्यथ च स्कन्धौ बाहु पृष्ठं तथोदरम् ।।66।।
ऊरु जङ्घे षडित्याहुरपरे मणिबन्धकौ ।
जानुनी कूर्परावेतत् त्रयमप्यधिकं जगुः ।।67।।
ग्रीवा स्यादप्य्

Transliteration:

Pratyaṅgānyatha ca skandhau bāhu pṛṣṭhaṃ tathodaram ||
Ūru jaṅghe ṣaḍityāhurapare maṇibandhakau |
Jānunī kūrparāvetat trayamapyadhikaṃ jaguḥ ||
Grīvā syādapya

Meaning:

Pratyaṅgāni (atha ca) ṣaṭa iti ahuḥ = pratyaṅgas are considered to be six; skandhe, bāhu pṛṣṭhaṃ (tatha) udaram, Ūru, jaṅghā = shoulders, arms, back, stomach, thighs and shanks; apare maṇibandhakau. Jānunī kūrparāvetat trayam api adhikaṃ jaguḥ = wrists, knees and elbows - these three are also pratyaṅgas according to some others; Grīvā Syādapy= to this, the neck also.

Pratyaṅgas are considered to be six: shoulders, the two arms, back, stomach, thighs and shanks. Some include the wrist, knees and elbows, and also the neck.

उपाङ्गानि

Upāṅgāni

उपाङ्गास्तु स्कन्ध एव जगुर्बुधाः।

दृष्टिर्भूपुटताराश्च कपोलौ नासिका हनू ।
अधरो दशना जिह्वा चुबुकं वदनं तथा ।।67।।
उपाङ्गानि द्वादशैव शिरस्यङ्गाम्तरेषु च ।
पार्णिगुल्फौ तथाङ्गुल्यः करयोः पादयोस्तले ।।68।।
एतानि पूर्वशास्त्रनुसारेणोक्तानि वै मया ।

Transliteration:

Dṛṣṭirbhūpuṭatārāśca kapolau nāsikā hanū |
Adharo daśanā jihvā cubukaṃ vadanaṃ tathā ||
Upāṅgāni dvādaśaiva śirasyaṅgāmtareṣu ca |
Pārṇigulphau tathāṅgulyaḥ karayoḥ pādayostale ||
Etāni pūrvaśāstranusāreṇoktāni vai mayā |

Meaning:

Dṛṣṭi, bhrū, puṭa, tārāḥ ca kapolau, nāsikā hanu, adharaḥ, daśanā jihvā, cubukaṃ tathā vadanaṃ =eyes, eyebrows, eyelids, pupils, cheeks, nose, jaws, lower lip, teeth, tongue, chin and face; dvādaśa eva Upāṅgāni śirasya-aṅgāmtareṣu ca = these twelve only are the Upāṅga in the aṅga called head; pārṇi gulphau, tathā karayoḥ aṅgulyaḥ pādayoḥ tale = heels, ankles, fingers of hands and the soles of feet; etāni pūrva śāstra-anusāreṇa, mayā uktāni vai = these have been included by me in Upāṅga keeping in view the ancient treatises.

Eyes, eyebrows, eyelids, pupils, cheeks, nose, jaws, lips, teeth, tongue, chin and face; these twelve only are the Upāṅga in the aṅga called head. Heels, ankles, fingers of hands and the soles of feet have been included by me in Upāṅga keeping in view the ancient treatises.

नृत्यमात्रोपयोगीनि कथ्यन्ते लक्षणैः क्रमात् ।।69।।
अङ्गानां चलनादेव प्रत्यङ्गोपाङ्गयोरपि ।
चलनं प्रभवेत्तस्मात् सर्वेषां नात्र लक्षणम् ।।70।।

Transliteration:

Nṛtyamātropayogīni kathyante lakṣaṇaiḥ kramāt ||
Aṅgānāṃ calanādeva pratyaṅgopāṅgayorapi |
Calanaṃ prabhavettasmāt sarveṣāṃ nātra lakṣaṇam ||

Meaning:

Nṛtya mātra-upayogyani kramāt lakṣaṇaiḥ kathyante = only those that are useful in dancing will be described now, in due order; Aṅgām calanāt eva pratyaṅga-upāṅgayo api Calanaṃ prabhavet = the movements of pratyaṅgas and upāṅgas depend on the movements of the aṅgas; tasmāt sarveṣāṃ lakṣaṇam atra na = that is why the nature and functions of all the limbs are not being described here.

The movements of pratyaṅgas and upāṅgas depend on the movements of the aṅgas. That is why the nature and functions of all the limbs are not being described here. Only those that are useful in dancing will be described now, in due order.

Chapter 3

शिरोभेदाः

Śirobhedāḥ

(Classification of head movements)

सममुद्वाहितमधोमुखमालोलितं धुतम् ।
कम्पितं च परावृत्तमुत्क्षिप्तं परिवाहितम् ॥71॥
नवधा कथितं शीर्षं नाट्यशास्त्रविशारदैः ।

Transliteration:

Samamudvāhitamadhomukhamālolitaṃ dhutam |
Kampitaṃ ca parāvṛttamutkṣiptaṃ parivāhitam ||
Navadhā kathitaṃ śīrṣaṃ nāṭyaśāstraviśāradaiḥ |

Meaning:

Samam, udvāhitam, adhomukham, ālolitaṃ dhutam = samam (level), udvāhitam (raised up), adhomukham (bent down), ālolitaṃ (rolling), dhutam (shaken = moved from left to right); kampitaṃ ca (nodding = moved up and down), parāvṛttam (turned away), utkṣiptaṃ (raised up from a side), parivāhitam(tossed on both the sides); śīrṣaṃ navadhā kathitaṃ nāṭya-śāstra viśāradaiḥ = thus, head movements are said to be nine fold by the experts of Nātya Śāstra.

Samam (level), udvāhitam (raised up), adhomukham (bent down), ālolitaṃ (rolling), dhutam (shaken = moved from left to right), kampitam (nodding = moved up and down), parāvṛttam (turned away), utkṣiptaṃ (raised up from a side), parivāhitam (tossed on both the sides)- these are the nine head movements according to the experts of Nātya Śāstra.

1. समशिरः

Samaśiraḥ

निश्चलं सममाख्यातं तन्नत्युन्नतिवर्जितम् ।।72।।

Transliteration:

Niścalaṃ samamākhyātaṃ tannatyunnativarjitam ||

Meaning:

Yat nati-unnati varjitam = without raising and lowering, niścalaṃ samam ākhyātam = keeping the head motionless is called Sama śiras.

When the head is neither bent nor raised, and is motionless, it is called Sama śiras.

विनियोगः (Application)

नृत्यारम्भे जपादौ च गर्वे प्रणयकोपयोः ।
स्तम्भने निष्क्रियत्वे च समशीर्षमुदाहृतम् ।।73।।

Transliteration:

Nṛtyārambhe japādau ca garve praṇayakopayoḥ |
Stambhane niṣkriyatve ca samaśīrṣamudāhṛtam ||

Meaning:

Nṛtya - ārambhe japādau ca garve, praṇaya - kopayoḥ = beginning of nṛtya, prayer etc., pride, affection, anger; stambhane, niṣkriyatve ca = paralysis, inaction; sama śīrṣam udāhṛtam = to denote the above, Sama śīrṣa is recommended.

Beginning of nṛtya, prayer etc., pride, affection, anger, paralysis, inaction- to denote the above, Sama śiras is recommended.

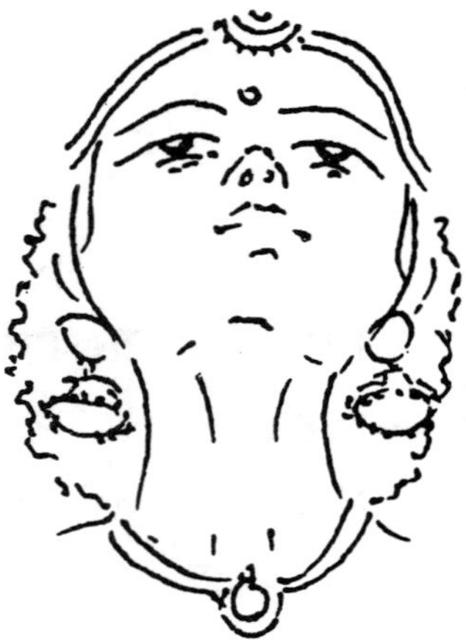

2. उद्वाहितशिरः
Udvāhitaśiraḥ

उद्वाहितशिरो ज्ञेयमूर्ध्वभागोन्नताननम् ।

Transliteration:

Udvāhitaśiro jñeyamūrdhvabhāgonnatānanam |

Meaning:

Ūrdhvabhāga- unnata - ānanam, Udvāhita śiraḥ jñeyam = when the head is raised up (looking up steadily), it is Udvāhita śiras.

When the head is raised up, it is Udvāhita śiras.

विनियोगः (Application)

ध्वजे चन्द्रे च गगने पर्वते व्योमगामिषु ।।74।।
तुङ्गवस्तुनि संयोज्यमुद्वाहितशिरो बुधैः ।

Transliteration:

Dhvaje candre ca gagane parvate vyomagāmiṣu ||
Tuṅgavastuni saṃyojyamudvāhitaśiro budhaiḥ |

Meaning:

Dhvaje, candre (ca), gagane, parvate, vyomagāmiṣu, tuṅgavastuni = flag, moon, sky, mountain, things in the air, tall objects; Udvāhita śiraḥ saṃyojyam budhaiḥ = to denote the above, Udvāhita śiras is used by the wise.

Flag, moon, sky, mountain, birds or things in the air, tall objects - to denote the above, Udvāhita śiras is employed by the wise.

3. अधोमुख शिरः
Adhomukha śiraḥ

अधस्तान्नमितं वक्त्र मधोमुखमीरितम् ।।75।।

Transliteration:

Adhastānnamitaṃ vaktra madhomukhamīritam ||

Meaning:

Adhastāt namitaṃ vaktram, adhomukham iritam = when the face is bent down, it is considered as Adhomukha śiras.

When the face is bent down, it is considered Adhomukha śiras.

विनियोगः (Application)

लज्जाखेदप्रणामेषु दुश्चिन्तामूर्छयोस्तथा ।
अधःस्थितार्थनिर्देशे युज्यतेऽम्बुनिमज्जने ।।76।।

Transliteration:

Lajjā-kheda-praṇāmeṣu duścintāmūrchayoḥ tathā |
Adhaḥsthitārthanirdeśe yujyate 'mbunimajjane ||

Meaning:

Lajjā-kheda-praṇāmeṣu, (tathā) duścintā - mūrchayoḥ, adhaḥsthita-arthanirdeśe, ambu-nimajjane = shyness or modesty, sorrow, bowing, evil thought, fainting, showing or looking at the objects on the earth, and a plunge into the water; yujyate to denote the above, Adhomukha śiras is used.

Shyness or modesty, sorrow, bowing, evil thought, fainting, showing or looking at objects on the earth, and a plunge into the water - to denote the above, Adhomukha śiras is used.

4. आलोलितशिरः
Ālolitaśiraḥ

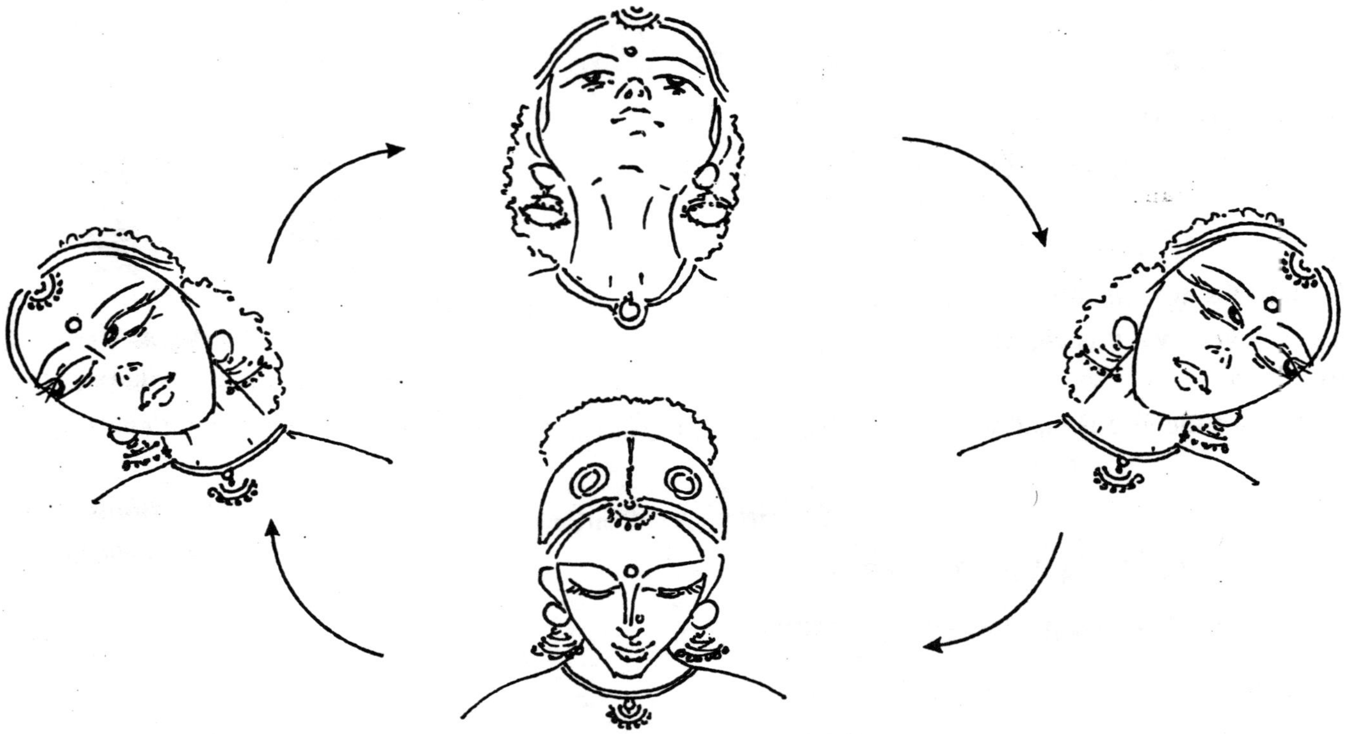

मण्डलाकारमुद्भ्रान्तमालोलितं शिरो भवेत् ।

Transliteration:

Maṇḍalākāramudbhrāntamālolitaṃ śiro bhavet |

Meaning:

Mandala-ākāram udbhrāntam, ālolitaṃ śiraḥ bhavet = when the head is moved in a circle, it is ālolita śiras.

When the head is moved in a circle, it is Ālolita śiras.

विनियोगः (Application)

निद्रोद्वेग ग्रहावेशमदमूर्छासु तन्मतम् ।।77।।
भ्रमणे विकटोद्दामहास्ये चालोलितं शिरः ।

Transliteration:

Nidrodvega grahāveśamadamūrchāsu tanmatam ||
Bhramaṇe vikaṭoddāmahāsye cālolitaṃ śiraḥ |

Meaning:

Nidrā - udvega, graha - āveśa, mada - mūrchāsu, tat-matam = this śiras is used to denote sleepiness, excitement, state of having been possessed by evil spirits, intoxication and fainting; bhramaṇe, vikaṭa-uddāma hāsye ca, ālolitaṃ śiraḥ = Ālolita śiras is also used to denote whirling about, unfair and uncontrollable laughter.

This śiras is used to denote sleepiness, excitement, state of having been possessed by evil spirits, intoxication and fainting. Ālolita śiras is also used to denote whirling about, unfair and uncontrollable laughter.

5. धुतशिरः
Dhutaśiraḥ

वामदक्षिणभागेषु चलितं तत् धुतमं शिरः ।।78।।

Transliteration:

Vāmadakṣiṇabhāgeṣu calitaṃ tat dhutaṃ śiraḥ ||

Meaning:

Vāma - dakṣiṇa bhāgeṣu calitaṃ, tat-dhutaṃ śiraḥ = when the head is turned from left to the right side, it is Dhuta śiras.

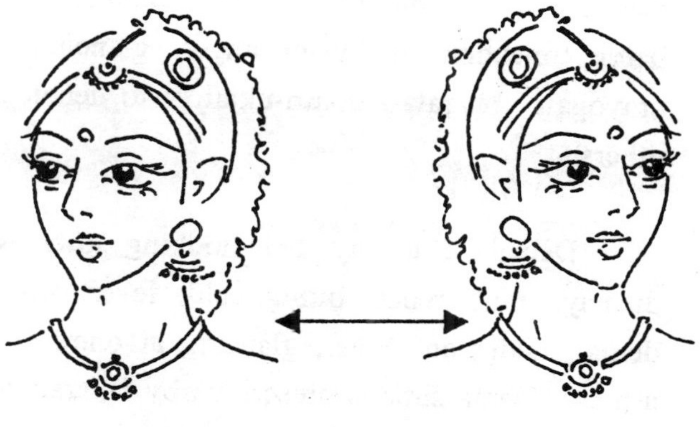

When the head is turned from left to right and from right to left, it is Dhuta śiras.

विनियोगः (Application)

नास्तीतिवचने भूयः पार्श्वदेशावलोकने ।
जनाश्वासे विस्मये च विषादे-नीप्सिते तथा ।।78।।
शीतार्ते ज्वरिते भीते सद्यःपीतासवे तथा ।
युद्धे यत्ने निषेधादावमर्षे स्वाङ्गवीक्षणे ।।80।।
पार्श्वाह्वाने च तस्योक्तः प्रयोगो भरतादिभिः ।

Transliteration:

Nāstītivacane bhūyaḥ pārśvadeśāvalokane |
Janāśvāse vismaye ca viṣāde-nīpsite tathā ||
Śītārte jvarite bhīte sadyaḥpītāsave tathā |
Yuddhe yatne niṣedhādāvamarṣe svāṅgavīkṣaṇe ||
Pārśvāhvāne ca tasyoktaḥ prayogo bharatādibhiḥ |

Meaning:

Nāsti - iti vacane, bhūyaḥ pārśvadeśa - avalokane, jana-āśvāse (ca), vismaye, ca anīpsite (tathā) = denial or to say 'No', looking towards sides repeatedly, empathizing with people, astonishment, dismay/ fear indifference; śītārte, jvarite, bhīte, tathā sadyaḥ-pīta-āsave = biting cold, fever, first stage of drinking liquor; yuddhe - yatne nisedhede ca amarṣe, sva-anga vikṣaṇe, pārśva-āhvāne ca = preparing for battle, rejection, indignant anger, glancing at one's own limbs, summoning from both sides; tasya prayogaḥ, bharata-ādibhiḥ-uktaḥ = to denote the above aspects, Dhuta śiras is prescribed by Bharata and others.

Denial or to say 'No', looking towards sides repeatedly, empathizing with people, astonishment, dismay, indifference, biting cold, fever, first stage of drinking liquor, preparing for battle, endeavour, denial, iindignant anger, glancing at one's own limbs, summoning from both sides- to denote the above aspects, Dhuta śiras is prescribed by Bharata and others.

6. कम्पितशिरः

Kampitaśiraḥ

ऊर्ध्वाधोभागचलितं तच्छिरः कम्पितं भवेत् ।।81।।

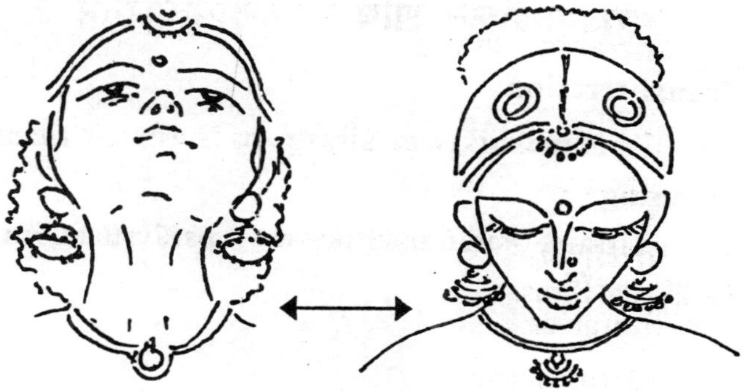

Transliteration:

Ūrdhvādhobhāgacalitaṃ tacchiraḥ kampitaṃ bhavet

Meaning:

Ūrdhva-adhobhāga calitaṃ, tat-śiraḥ kampitaṃ bhavet = shaking the head up and down is Kampita śiras.

Shaking the head up and down is Kampita śiras.

विनियोगः (Application)

रोषे तिष्ठेति वचने प्रश्ने संख्योपहूतयोः ।
आवाहने तर्जने च कम्पितं विनियुज्यते ।।82।।

Transliteration:

Roṣe tiṣṭheti vacane praśne saṅkhyopahūtayoḥ |
Āvāhane tarjane ca kampitaṃ viniyujyate ||

Meaning:

Roṣe, tiṣṭha-iti vacane ca = indignation / anger, asking to sit; praśne saṅkhyopahūtayoḥ āvāhane tarjane ca kampitaṃ viniyujyate = questioning, ennumerate, summoning, cautioning; Kampitam viniyujyate = to denote the above aspects, Kampita śiras is used.

Indignation, asking to sit, questioning, ennumerate, summoning, cautioning - to denote the above aspects Kampita śiras is used.

7. परावृतशिरः

Parāvṛtaśiraḥ

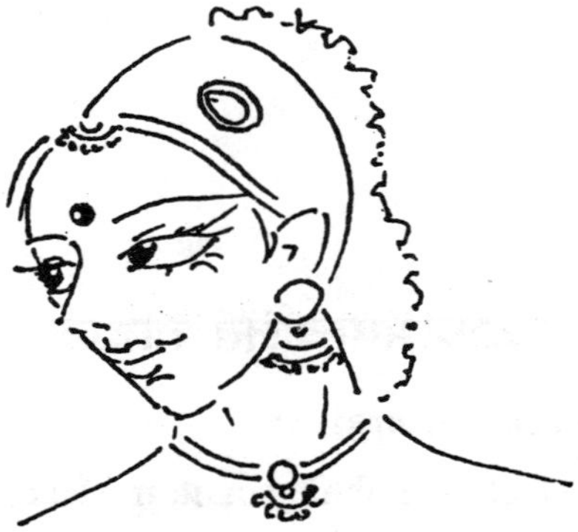

पराङ्मुखीकृतं शीर्षं परावृत्तमितीरितम् ।

Transliteration:

Parāṅmukhīkṛtaṃ śīrṣaṃ parāvṛttamitīritam |

Meaning:

Śīrṣaṃ, Parāṅmukhīkṛtaṃ parāvṛttam, iti, īritam = when the head is turned aside, it becomes Parāvṛtta Śiras.

When the head is turned aside, it becomes Parāvṛtta Śiras.

विनियोगः (Application)

तत् कार्यै कोपलज्जादिकृते वक्त्रापसरणे ।।83।।
अनादरै कचे तूण्यां परावृत्तशिरो भवेत् ।

Transliteration:

Tat kāryai kopalajjādikṛte vaktrāpasaraṇe ||
Anādarai kace tūṇyāṃ parāvṛttaśiro bhavet |

Meaning:

Tat kāryam, kopa-lajjā-adikṛte, vaktra - apasaraṇe, Anādarai, kace, tūṇyāṃ = to say 'that is to be done', expressing anger, shyness etc., to turn the face aside, aversion, to see one's own hair and quiver; parāvṛtta śiraḥ bhavet = to denote the above aspects, Parāvṛtta śiras is useful.

To say 'that is to be done', expressing anger, shyness etc., to turn the face aside, aversion, to see one's own hair and quiver- to denote the above aspects, Parāvṛtta śiras is useful.

8. उत्क्षिप्तशिरः

Utkṣiptaśiraḥ

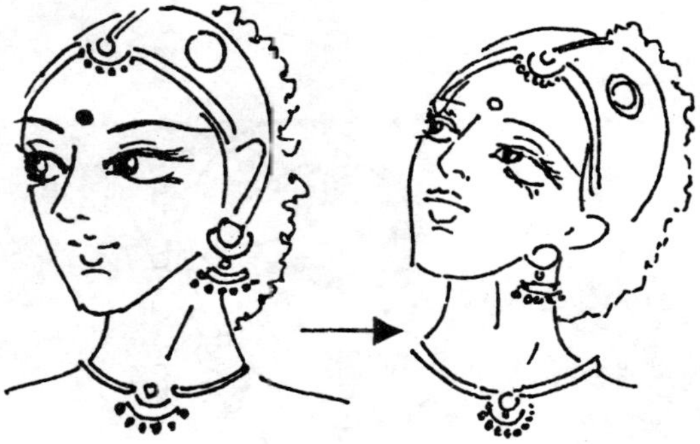

पार्श्वोर्ध्वभागचलितमुत्क्षिप्तं कथ्यते शिरः ।।84।।

Transliteration:

Pārśvordhvabhāgacalitamutkṣiptaṃ kathyate śiraḥ ||

Meaning:

Pārśva = ūrdhvabhāga calitam śiraḥ, utkṣiptaṃ kathyate = when the head is raised from a side, it is called utkṣipta śīras.

When the head is raised from a side, it is called utkṣipta śīras.

विनियोगः (Application)

गृहाणागच्छेत्याद्यर्थसूचने परिशोषणे ।
अङ्गीकारे प्रयोक्तव्यमुत्क्षिप्तं नाम शीर्षकम् ।।85।।

Transliteration:

Gṛhāṇāgacchetyādyarthasūcane pariśoṣaṇe |
Aṅgīkāre prayoktavyamutkṣiptaṃ nāma śīrṣakam ||

Meaning:

Gṛhāṇa- āgaccha - iti - adi - arthasūcane, pariśoṣaṇe, aṅgīkāre = saying 'take this', 'come here' etc., cheriṣing or supporting, to accept / agree / consent; utkṣiptam nāma śīrṣakam prayoktam = in denoting the above śiras called Utkṣiptam is to be used.

Saying 'take this', 'come here' etc., cherishing or supporting, assent - in denoting the above śiras called Utkṣiptam is to be used.

9. परिवाहितशिरः

Parivāhitaśiraḥ

पार्श्वयोश्चामरमिव ततं चेत् परिवाहितम् ।

Transliteration:

Pārśvayoścāmaramiva tataṃ cet parivāhitam |

Meaning:

Cāmaram-iva Pārśvayoḥ nataṃ cet parivāhitam = if the head is moved from side to side like a fan, it is considered as Parivāhita śīras.

If the head is moved from side to side like a fan, it is considered as Parivāhita śīras.

विनियोगः (Application)

मोहे च विरहे स्तोत्रे सन्तोषे चानुमांदने ।।86।।
विचारे च प्रयोक्तव्यं परिवाहितशीर्षकम् ।

Transliteration:

Mohe ca virahe stotre santoṣe cānumāndane ||
Vicāre ca prayoktavyaṃ parivāhitaśīrṣakam |

Meaning:

Mohe ca, virahe, stotre, santoṣe cā, anumāndane,Vicāre ca = passion, yearning for the beloved, praise, pleasure, gratification, sorrow or reflection; parivāhita śīrṣakam prayoktavyaṃ = in denoting the above, Parivāhita śiras is to be used.

Passion, yearning for the beloved, praise, pleasure, gratification, sorrow or reflection - in denoting the above, Parivāhita śiras is to be used.

Chapter 4

।। दृष्टिभेदाः ।।

Dṛṣṭi bhedāḥ

(Classification of Glances)

समालोकितं साची प्रालोकितनिमीलिते ।।87।।
उल्लोकितानुवृत्ते च तथा चैवावलोकितम् ।
इत्यष्टौ दृष्टिभेदाः स्युः कीर्तिताः पूर्वसूरिभिः ।।88।।

Transliteration:

Samamālokitam sācī prālokitanimīlite ||
Ullokitānuvṛtte ca tathā caivāvalokitam |
Ityaṣṭau dṛṣṭibhedāḥ syuḥ kīrtitāḥ pūrvasūribhiḥ ||

Meaning:

Samam - ālokitam, sācī, prālokita-nimīlite. Ullokita - ānuvṛtte (ca) (tathā-ca-evā), avalokitam = samam, ālokitam, sāci, prālokitam, nimīlitam, Ullokitam - ānuvṛttam and avalokitam; ityaṣṭau dṛṣṭibhedāḥ syuḥ kīrtitāḥ pūrvasūribhiḥ= thus there are eight dṛṣṭi bhedās as explained by ancient scholars.

Samam, ālokitam, sāci, prālokitam, nimīlitam, ullokitam, ānuvṛttam and avalokitam are eight dṛṣṭi bhedas as explained by ancient scholars.

1. समदृष्टिः

Samadṛṣṭiḥ

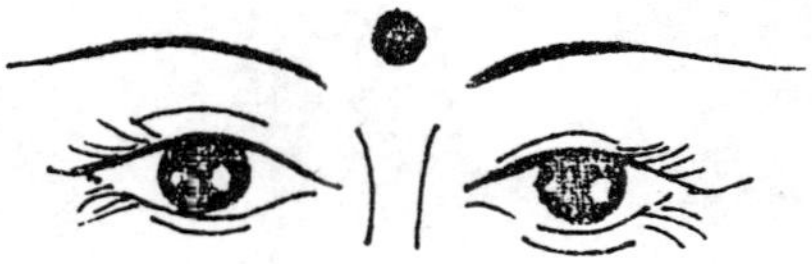

वीक्षणं सुरनारीवत् सानन्दं समवीक्षणम् ।।

Transliteration:

Vīkṣaṇaṃ suranārīvat sānandam samavīkṣaṇam ||

Meaning:

Sānandam suranārīvat vīkṣaṇaṃ sama vīkṣaṇam = gazing without winking and with pleasant face, like a celestial woman is Sama dṛṣṭi.

Gazing without winking and with pleasant face like a celestial woman is Sama dṛṣṭi.

विनियोगः (Application)

नाट्यारम्भे तुलायां चाप्यभ्यचिन्ताविनिश्चये ।।89।।
आश्चर्ये देवतारूपे समदृष्टिरुदादृता ।

Transliteration:

Nāṭyārambhe tulāyāṃ cāpyabhyacintāviniścaye ||
Āścarye devatārūpe samadṛṣṭirudāhṛtā |

Meaning:

Nāṭya-ārambhe, tulāyāṃ ca-api anya cintāviniścaye, āścarye, devatārūpe = beginning of dance, balancing, thinking of some other matter, surprise, image of god; sama dṛṣṭi udāhṛtā = in denoting the above, Sama dṛṣṭi is recommended.

Beginning of dance, balancing, thinking of some other matter, surprise, image of god- in denoting these, Sama dṛṣṭi is recommended.

2. आलोकितदृष्टिः
Ālokitadrstih

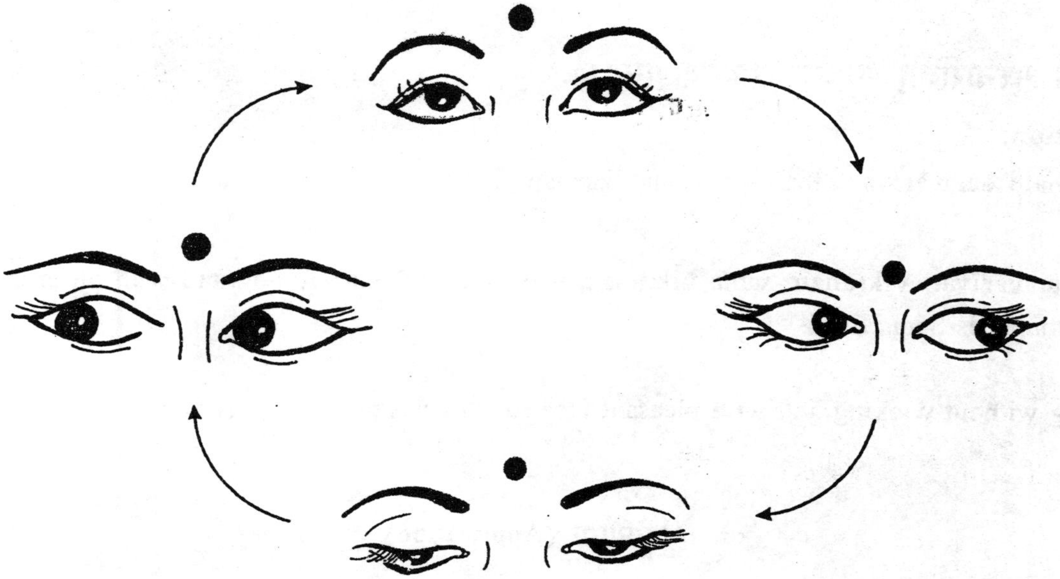

आलोकितं भवेदाशुभ्रमणं स्फुटवीक्षणम् ।।90।।

Transliteration:

Ālokitaṃ bhavedāśubhramaṇaṃ sphuṭavīkṣaṇam ||

Meaning:

Āśubhramaṇaṃ sphuṭa vīkṣaṇam ālokitaṃ bhavet = swiftly turning with a sharp glance is Ālokita dṛṣṭi.

Swiftly turning with a sharp glance is Ālokita dṛṣṭi.

विनियोगः (Application)

कुलालचक्रभ्रमणे सर्ववस्तुप्रदर्शने ।
याञ्चायां च प्रयोक्तव्यमालोकितनिरीक्षणम् ।।91।।

Transliteration:

Kulālacakrabhramaṇe sarvavastupradarśane |
Yāñcāyāṃ ca prayoktavyamālokitanirīkṣaṇam ||

Meaning:

Kulāla cakrabhramaṇe, sarvavastupradarśane, Yāñcāyāṃ (ca) = turning of potter's wheel, showing all objects around and begging; ālokitanirīkṣaṇam prayoktavyam = in denoting the above, Ālokita dṛṣṭi is used.

In denoting the turning of potter's wheel, showing all objects around and begging Ālokita dṛṣṭi is to be used.

3. साचीदृष्टिः
Sācīdṛṣṭiḥ

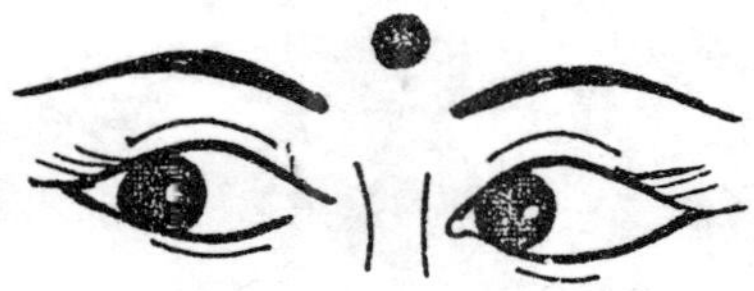

स्वस्थाने तिर्यगाकारमपाङ्गवलनं क्रमात् ।
साचीदृष्टिरिति ज्ञेया नाट्यशास्त्रविशारदैः ।।92।।

Transliteration:

Svasthāne tiryagākāramapāṅgavalanaṃ kramāt |
Sācīdṛṣṭiriti jñeyā nāṭyaśāstraviśāradaiḥ ||

Meaning:

Svasthāne, kramāt, tiryak-ākāra, mapāṅgavalanaṃ = looking out of the corners of the eyes obliquely without moving the head; Sācī dṛṣṭi iti nāṭya śāstra viśāradaiḥ jñeyā = it is to be considered as Sācī dṛṣṭi by the experts on Nātya Śāstra.

Sācīdṛṣṭi by the experts on Nātya Śāstra is looking out of the corners of the eyes obliquely without moving the head.

विनियोगः (Application)

इङ्गिते श्मश्रुसंस्पर्शे शरलक्ष्ये शुके स्मृतौ ।
सूचनायां च कार्याणां नाट्ये साचीनिरीक्षणम् ।।93।।

Transliteration:

Iṅgite śmaśrusaṃsparśe śaralakṣye śuke smṛtau |
Sūcanāyāṃ ca kāryāṇāṃ nāṭye sācīnirīkṣaṇam ||

Meaning:

Iṅgite, śmaśru saṃsparśe, śaralakṣye, smṛte, kāryāṇāṃ Sūcanāyāṃ ca nāṭye = intention, twirling the moustache, aiming an arrow, parrot, remembrance, suggesting the work to be done, and nāṭya; sāci nirīkṣaṇam = to denote the above aspects, Sācī dṛṣṭi is to be used.

In denoting intention, twirling the moustache, aiming an arrow, parrot, remembrance, suggesting the work to be done, and nāṭya Sācī dṛṣṭi is used.

4. प्रलोकितदृष्टिः

Pralokitadṛṣṭiḥ

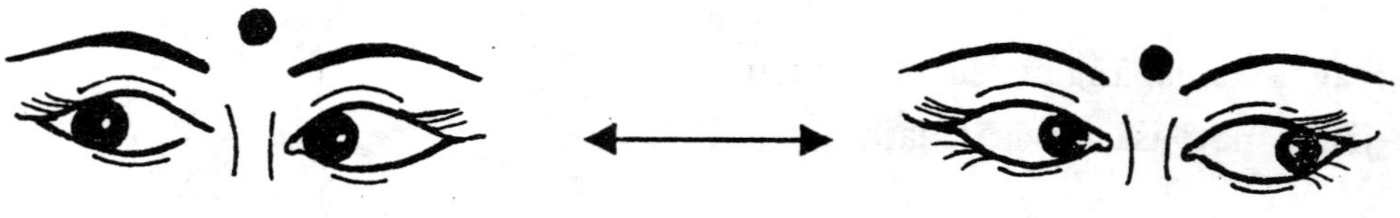

प्रलोकितं परिज्ञेयं चलनं पार्श्वभागयोः ।

Transliteration:

Pralokitaṃ parijñeyaṃ calanaṃ pārśvabhāgayoḥ |

Meaning:

Calanam pārśva bhāgayoḥ, Pralokitaṃ parijñeyam = when the glance turns form side to side, it becomes Pralokita dṛṣṭi.

When the glance turns form side to side, it becomes to denote Pralokita dṛṣṭi.

विनियोगः (Application)

उभयोः पार्श्वयोर्वस्तु निर्देशे च प्रसंजिते ।।94।।
चलने बुद्धिजाड्ये च प्रलोकितनिरीक्षणम् ।

Transliteration:

Ubhayoḥ pārśvayorvastu nirdeśe ca prasañjite ||
Calane buddhijāḍye ca pralokitanirīkṣaṇam |

Meaning:

Ubhayoḥ pārśvayoḥ rvastu nirdeśe, calane, buddhijāḍye ca = pointing objects on both sides, speaking about them, moving, and a mental affliction; pralokita nirīkṣaṇam = to denote the above, Pralokita dṛṣṭi is used.

In denoting pointing objects on both sides, speaking about them, moving, and a mental affliction, Pralokita dṛṣṭi is used.

5. निमीलितदृष्टिः
Nimīlitadṛṣṭiḥ

दृष्टेरर्धविकाशेन निमीलिता दृष्टिरीरिता ।।95।।

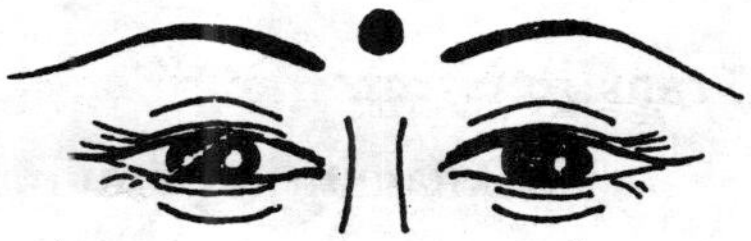

Transliteration:

Dṛṣṭerardhavikāśena nimīlitā dṛṣṭirīritā ||

Meaning:

Dṛṣṭeḥ - arardhavikāśe, nimīlitā dṛṣṭiḥ īritā = looking with the eyes half open, becomes Nimīlitā dṛṣṭi.

Looking with the eyes half open becomes Nimīlitā dṛṣṭi.

विनियोगः (Application)

आशीविषे पारवश्ये जपे ध्याने नमस्कृतौ ।
उम्मादे सूक्ष्मदृष्टौ च निमीलिता दृष्टिरीरिता ।।96।।

Transliteration:

Āśīviṣe pāravaśye jape dhyāne namaskṛtau |
Ummāde sūkṣmadṛṣṭau ca nimīlitā dṛṣṭirīritā ||

Meaning:

Āśīviṣe, pāravaśye, jape, dhyāne, namaskṛte, unmāde, sūkṣma dṛṣṭau = blessing, pleasurable self absorption, prayer, meditation, obeisance, madness and keen insight; nimīlitā dṛṣṭiḥ īritā= in denoting the above, Nimīlitā dṛṣṭi is prescribed.

In denoting blessing, pleasurable self absorption, prayer, meditation, obeisance, madness and keen insight, Nimīlitā dṛṣṭi is prescribed.

6. उल्लोकितदृष्टिः
Ullokitadṛṣṭiḥ

उल्लोकितमिति ज्ञेयमूर्ध्व भागे विलोकनम् ।

Transliteration:

Ullokitamiti jñeyamūrdhva bhāge vilokanam |

Meaning:

Ūrdhva bhāge vilokanam ullokitam iti jñeyam = looking up steadily is considered Ullokita dṛṣṭi.
Looking up steadily is Ullokita dṛṣṭi.

विनियोगः (Application)

ध्वजाग्रे गोपुरे देवमण्डले पूर्वजन्मनि ।।97।।
औन्नत्ये चन्द्रिकादावप्युल्लोकितनिरीक्षणम् ।

Transliteration:

Dhvajāgre gopure devamaṇḍale pūrvajanmani ||
Aunnatye candrikādāvapyullokitanirīkṣaṇam |

Meaning:

Dhvaja-agre, gopure, devamaṇḍale pūrvajanmani, aunnatye, candrika- ādau api = top of a flag, temple tower, realm of devatas, thinking of previous lives, height, moonlight etc.; ullokita nirīkṣaṇam = to denote the above, Ullokita dṛṣṭi is considered.

To denote the top of a flag, temple tower, realm of devatas, thinking of previous lives, height, moonlight etc. Ullokita dṛṣṭi is considered.

7. अनुवृत्तदृष्टिः
Anuvṛttadṛṣṭiḥ

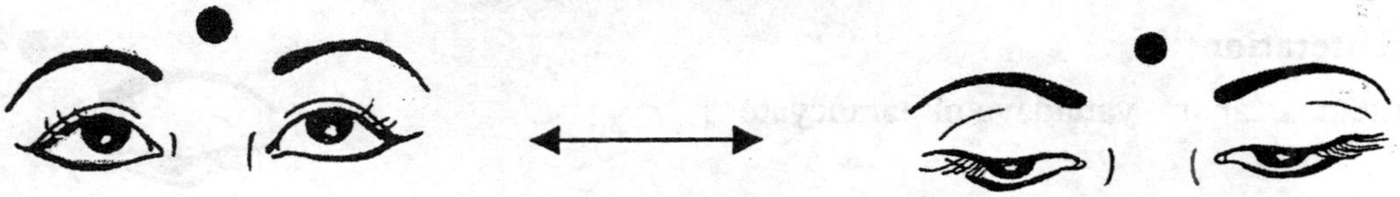

ऊर्ध्वाधो वीक्षणं वेगादनुवृत्तमितीरितम् ।।98।।

Transliteration:

Ūrdhvādho vīkṣaṇaṃ vegādanuvṛttamitīritam ||

Meaning:

Vegāt Ūrdhva- adho - nirīkṣaṇaṃ anuvṛttam iti, īritam = glancing quickly up and down is Anuvṛttadṛṣṭiḥ.

Glancing quickly up and down is Anuvṛttadṛṣṭiḥ.

विनियोगः (Application)

कोपदृष्टौ प्रियामन्त्रे अनुवृत्तनिरीक्षणम् ।

Transliteration:

Kopadṛṣṭau priyāmantre anuvṛttanirīkṣaṇam |

Meaning:

Kopadṛṣṭau, priya āmantre (api) anuvṛtta nirīkṣaṇam = Anuvṛtta dṛṣṭi is used in angry looks and friendly or affectionate invitation / greeting.

Anuvṛtta dṛṣṭi is used in angry looks and friendly or affectionate invitation / greeting.

8. अवलोकितदृष्टिः

Avalokitadṛṣṭiḥ

अधस्ताद्दर्शनं यत्तदवलोकितमुच्यते ।।99।।

Transliteration:

Adhastāddarśanaṃ yattadavalokitamucyate ||

Meaning:

Yat adhastāt darśanaṃ tat avalokitam ucyate = where there is looking downwards there is Avalokita dṛṣṭiḥ.

Where there is looking downwards there is Avalokita dṛṣṭi.

विनियोगः (Application)

छायालोके विचारे चर्यायां पठनश्रमे ।
स्वाङ्गावलोकने यानेऽप्यवलोकितमुच्यते ।।100।।

Transliteration:

Chāyāloke vicāre caryāyāṃ paṭhanaśrame |
Svāṅgāvalokane yāne 'pyavalokitamucyate ||

Meaning:

Chāya-āloke vicāre ca, caryāyāṃ, paṭhana śrame, Svāṅga- avalokane, yāne api = looking at a shadow, reflecting, working, fatigue due to study, looking at one's own body; avalokitam ucyate = in denoting the above aspects, Avalokita dṛṣṭi is prescribed.

Looking at a shadow, reflecting, working, fatigue due to study, looking at one's own body - in denoting the above aspects, Avalokita dṛṣṭi is prescribed.

Chapter 5

भ्रू भेदाः

Bhrū Bhedāḥ

(Classification of the movements of Eye-brows)

सहजा पतितोक्षिप्ता चतुरा रेचिता तथा ।
कुंचितेति षडेव-अत्र भ्रू चातुर्यवति क्रियाः ।।101।।

Transliteration:

Sahajā patitokṣipta caturā recitā tathā |
Kuñciteti śadeva'atra bhrū cāturyavati kriyāḥ ||

Meaning:

Sahajā patita-utkṣiptā caturā recitā (tathā), Kuñcitā = sahaja, patita, utkṣipta, caturā, recitā, kuñcita; śadeva, (atra), bhrū cāturyavati kriyāḥ = these are the six charming movements of the eye-brows.

The following are the six charming movements of the eye-brows: 1. Sahaja, 2. Patita, 3. Utkṣipta, 4. Catura, 5. Recita, 6. Kuñcita

1. सहज भ्रू

Sahaja Bhrū

सहजा स्यात् स्वभावभ्रूः विकार रहिता मुखे ।
सहजादिषु युज्येत इति भावविदो विदुः ।।102।।

Transliteration:

Sahajā syāt svabhāvabhıūḥ vikāra rahitā mukhe |
Sahajādiṣu yujyeta iti bhāvavido viduḥ ||

Meaning:

Mukhe vikāra-rahita, svabhāvabhrū, sahajā syāt = the natural eyebrow in a smooth face is Sahaja bhrū. Sahaja-ādiṣu, yujyeta, iti bhāvavidah viduḥ = experts on emotions know that this bhrū is to be used in denoting natural disposition.

The natural eyebrow in a smooth face is Sahaja bhrū. Experts on emotions know that this bhrū is to be used in denoting natural disposition.

2. पतित भ्रू
Patita Bhrū

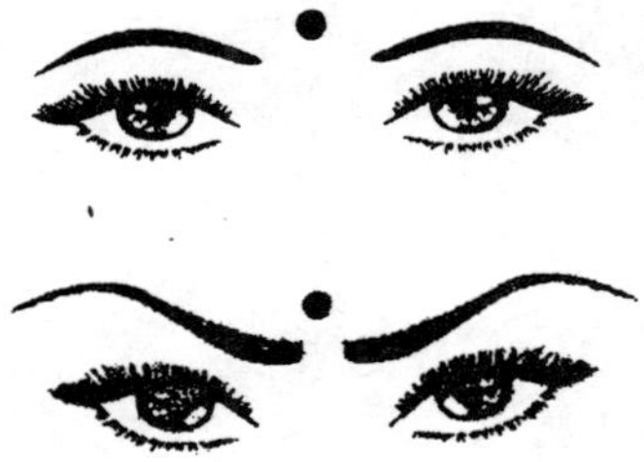

अचंचलभ्रूयुगं च पतनात् पतितमता ।
जुगुप्सायां विस्मये च असूयायां भवेदसौ ।।103।।

Transliteration:

Acañcalabhrūyugaṃ ca patanāt patitamatā |
Jugupsāyāṃ vismaye ca asūyāyāṃ bhavedasau ||

Meaning:

Acañcala - bhrū - yugaṃ (ca), patanāt, patitamatā = when the eyebrows being at rest are made to droop, then it is Patita bhrū.

Asou, Jugupsāyāṃ vismaye (ca), asūyāyāṃ bhāvet = this bhrū is used to denote disgust, astonishment and jealousy.

When the eyebrows are at rest and then droped, it is Patita bhrū. This bhrū indicates disgust, astonishment and jealousy.

3. उत्क्षिप्त भ्रू

Utkṣipta Bhrū

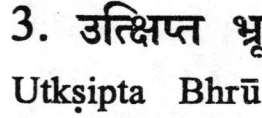

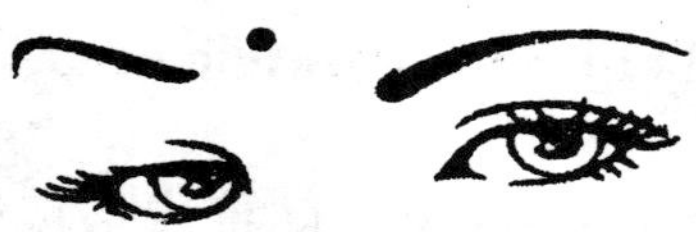

एकावा सा द्वितीया वा यदुक्षिप्त वतीतराम् ।
उत्क्षिप्ता सा भवेत स्त्रीणाम् कोपे सत्यवचस्यपि ।।104।।
श्रृंगार-भावे लीलायाम् भ्रूरेषा विनियुज्यते ।

Transliteration:

Ēkāvā sā dvitīyā vā yadukṣipta vatītarāṃ |
Utkṣiptā sā bhavet strīṇām kope satyavacasyapi ||
Śṛṅgāra-bhāve līlāyām bhrūreṣā viniyujyate |

Meaning:

Yat ekā vā sā dvitīyā vā, yadukṣipta vatītāraṃ, sā, utkṣiptā bhavet = when either one or both the eyebrows are raised up, it is Utkṣipta bhrū.

Strīṇāṃ kope, satyavacasya (api), śṛṅgāra-bhāve, līlāyām esha bhrū viniyujyate = women's anger, telling the truth, feelings of love and dalliance - to denote the above, this bhrū is used.

When either one or both the eyebrows are raised up, it is Utkṣipta bhrū. Women's anger, telling the truth, feelings of love and dalliance - to denote the above, this bhrū is used.

4. चतुर भ्रू
Catura Bhrū

द्वितीयसहिता स्तोका स्फुरिता मदमंतरा ।।105।।
चतुरा मुखसंस्पर्शे हृदानंदे च संभ्रमे ।

Transliteration:

Dvitīyasahitā stokā sphuritā madamantarā ||
Caturā mukhasaṃsparśe hṛdanānde ca saṃbhrame |

Meaning:

Dvitīyasahitā, stokā sphuritā madamantarā, Caturā = both the eyes, faintly quiver due to intoxication or cleverness - such a bhrū is called Catura bhrū.

Mukha- saṃsparśe, hṛda-anānde (ca) saṃbhrame = and this is used to denote touching one's face, heart's bliss and excitement.

Moving both the eyebrows in a pleasing manner is Catura bhrū.

This is used to denote the following : touching one's face, heart's bliss and excitement.

5. रेचित भ्रू
Recita Bhrū

लावण्य मधुराक्षिप्ता यद्येका रेचिता मता ।।106।।
रहस्य श्रवणे साधुकलने पदवीक्षणे ।

Transliteration:

Lāvaṇya madhurākṣiptā yadyekā recitā matā ||
Rahasya śravaṇe sādhukalane padavīkṣaṇe |

Meaning:

Ekā lāvaṇya-madhurā, ākṣiptā yadi, recitā matā = when one eyebrow is cast down with grace and sweetness, it is Recita bhrū.

Rahasya śravaṇe sādhu-kālane padavīkṣaṇe = this is used in listening to a secret, saying "well done" etc. and looking at a place.

When one eyebrow is cast down with grace and sweetness, it becomes Recita bhrū.

This bhru is used to denote the following : listening to a secret, saying sādhu (in appreciation) and looking as a particular place.

6. कुंचित भ्रू
Kuñcita Bhrū

एकावा सा द्वितीया वा कुंचिता कुंचिता मता ।।107।।
मोट्टायिते कुट्टमिते विलासे किलिकिंचिते ।

Transliteration:

Ēkāvā sā dvitīyā vā kuñcitā kuñcitā matā ||
Mottāyite kuttamite vilāse kilikiñcite |

Meaning:

Ēkā vā, dvitīyā vā, kuñcitā, sā kuñcitā matā = when one eyebrow or both the eye brows are arched (or bent), it becomes Kuñcita bhrū.

Mottāyite kuttamite vilāse kilikiñcite = this eyebrow is used to denote mottāyita (involuntary expression of affection of a woman towards an absent lover), kuttāmita (feigned displeasure of a lover's endearments or caress), vilāsa (pleasure at seeing the beloved) and kilikiñcite (hysterics).

When one eye brow or both the eye brows are arched/bent, it becomes Kuñcita bhrū.

This bhrū is used to denote involuntary expression of affection of a woman towards an absent lover, feigned displeasure of a lover's endearments or caress, pleasure at seeing the beloved, hysterics.

Chapter 6

ग्रीवाभेदाः

Grīvā Bhedāḥ

(Classification of the movements of neck)

सुन्दरी च तिरश्चीना तथैव परिवर्तिता ।।108।।
प्रकम्पिता च भावज्ञै ज्ञेया ग्रीवा चतुर्विधा ।

Transliteration:

Sundarī ca tiraścīnā tathaiva parivartitā ||
Prakampitā ca bhāvajñai jñeyā grīvā caturvidhā |

Meaning:

Sundarī (ca), tiraścīnā (tathā - eva), parivartitā, prakampitā (ca) = Sundari, tiraścīnā, Parivartitā and Prakampitā; bhāvajñai grīvā caturvidhā jñeyā = scholars of bhāvas know the Grīvā bhedas i.e. the movements of neck to be fourfold.

Scholars on bhāvas know the Grīvā Bhedas i.e. the movements of neck to be fourfold.1 Sundarī 2. Tiraścīnā, 3. Parivartitā and 4. Prakampitā.

1. सुन्दरी ग्रीवा

Sundarī Grīvā

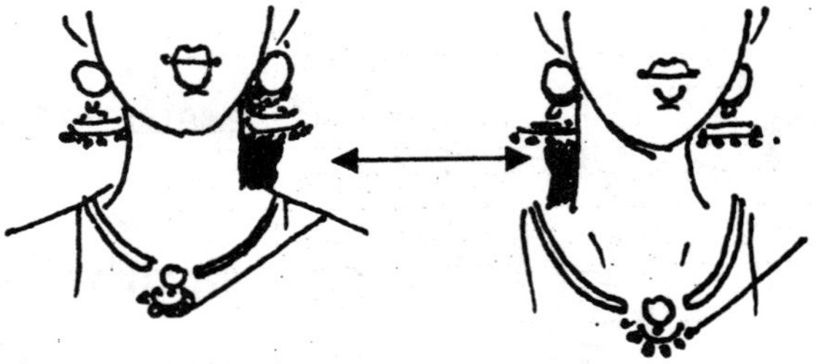

तिर्यक् प्रचलिता ग्रीवा सुन्दरीति निगद्यते ।।109।।

Transliteration:

Tiryak pracalitā grīvā sundarīti nigadyate ||

विनियोगः (Application)

स्नेहारम्भे तथा यत्ने सम्यगर्थेपि च स्मृतौ ।
सरसत्वे अनुमोदे च सा ग्रीवा सुन्दरी मता ।।110।।

Transliteration:

Snehārambhe tathā yatne samyagarthepi ca smṛtau |
Sarasatve anumode ca sā grīvā sundarī matā ||

Meaning:

Tiryak - pracalitā grīvā sundarī - iti, nigadyate = when the neck is moved obliquely (to and fro/ horizontally), it is known as Sundarī grīva.

Sneha-ārambhe (tathā), yatne, samyak arthe (api), smṛtou, SSarasatve, anumode (ca) = beginning of friendship, effort saying 'welldone', recollection, charm and approval; sā sundarī grīvā matā = in denoting the above aspects, Sundarī grīvā is useful.

When the neck is moved obliquely (to and fro/horizontally), it is known as Sundarī grīva. beginning of friendship, understanding, recollection, charm and feeling of pleasure from sympathy. In denoting the above aspects, Sundarī grīvā is useful.

तिरश्चीना ग्रीवा

Tiraścīnā grīvā

पार्श्वे द्वय ऊर्ध्वभागे तु चलिता सर्पयानवत् ।
सा ग्रीवा तु तिरश्चीनेत्युच्यते नाट्यकोविदैः ।।111।।

Transliteration:

Pārśva dvya ūrdhvabhāge tu calitā sarpayānavat |
Sā grīvā tu tiraścīnetyucyate nāṭyakovidaiḥ ||

विनियोगः (Application)

खड्गभ्रमे सर्पगत्यां तिरश्चीना प्रयुज्यते ।

Transliteration:

Khaḍgabhrame sarpagatyāṃ tiraścīnā prayujyate |

Meaning:

Pārśvaya-urdhvabhāge (tu), sarpayānavat calitā, sā grīvā tu tiraścīnagrīvā (tu) iti, nāṭyakovidaiḥ ucyate = an upward movement of the neck on both sides, like the gliding of a snake, is considered by the experts on nātya, as Tiraścīnā grīva.

Khaḍgabhrame sarpagatyāṃ tiraścīnā prayujyate = this grīva is used to denote brandishing of a sword and serpentine movement.

An upward movement of the neck on both sides, like the gliding of a snake is considered by the experts on nātya as Tiraścīnā grīva. This grīva is used to denote brandishing of a sword and serpentine movement.

3. परिवर्तिता ग्रीवा

Parivartitā grīvā

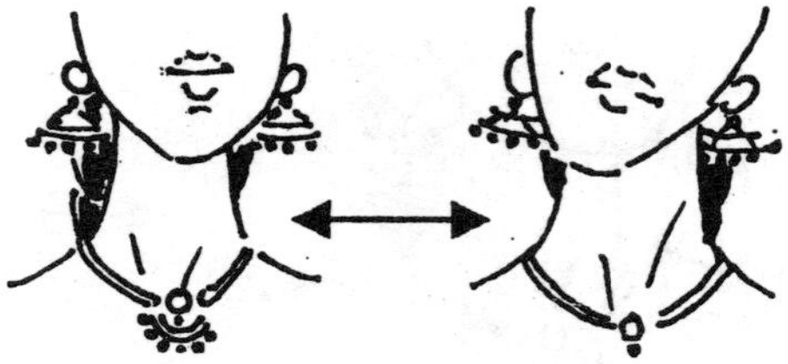

सव्यापसव्यचलिता ग्रीवा यत्रार्धच चन्द्रवत् ।।112।।
सा हि नाट्यकलाभिज्ञैः विज्ञेया परिवर्तिता ।

Transliteration:

Savyāpasavyacalitā grīvā yatnārdhacandravat ||
Sā hi nāṭyakalābhijñaiḥ vijñeyā parivartitā |

विनियोगः (Application)

श‍ृङ्गारनटने कान्ता कपोलद्वयचुम्बने ।।113।।
नाट्यतन्त्रविचारज्ञैः प्रयोज्या परिवर्तिता ।

Transliteration:

Śṛṅgāranaṭane kāntā kapoladvayacumbane ||
Nāṭyatantravicārajñaiḥ prayojyā parivartitā |

Meaning:

Yatra, ārdhacandravat, savya-apasavya calitā. sā, nāṭyakalā-bhijñaih, Parivartitā grīvā vijñeyā = neck moving to right to left suggesting half moon, is known as Parivartitā grīvā by the experts on the art of nātya.

Śṛṅgāra-naṭane, kānta-kapoladvaya-cumbane, nāṭyatantra-kalābhijñairvijñeyā prayojyā parivartitā prayojyā = in erotic dances and in kissing both cheeks of the charming beloved, Parivartitā grīvā is prescribed by the experts on nātya.

Neck moving to right to left suggesting half moon, is known as Parivartitā grīvā. In erotic dances and in kissing both cheeks of the charming beloved, Parivartitā grīvā is prescribed by the experts on nātya.

4. प्रकम्पिता ग्रीवा

Prakampitā Grīvā

पुरः पश्चात् प्रचलनात् कपोती कण्ठ कम्पवत् ।।114।।
प्रकम्पितेति सा ग्रीवा नाट्यशास्त्रे प्रशस्यते ।

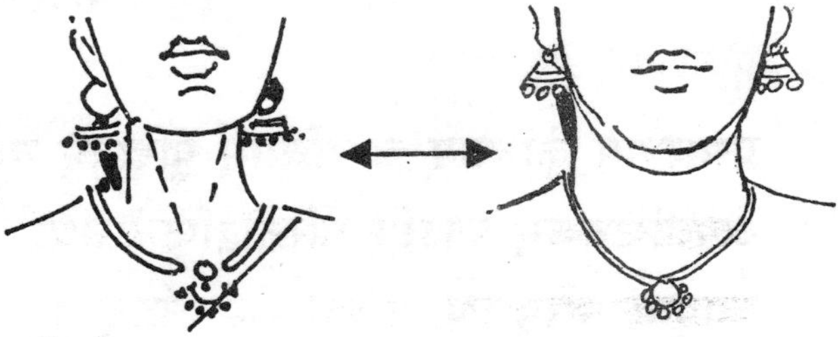

Transliteration:

Puraḥ paścāt pracalanāt kapoti kaṇṭha kampavat ||

Prakampiteti sā grīvā nāṭyaśāstre praśasyate |

विनियोगः (Application)

युष्मदस्मदिति प्रोक्ते देशीनाट्ये विशेषतः ।।115।।
डोलायां मणिते चैव प्रयोक्तव्या प्रकम्पिता ।

Transliteration:

Yuṣmadasmaditi prokte deśīnāṭye viśeṣataḥ ||
Dolāyāṃ maṇite caiva prayoktavyā prakampitā |

Meaning:

Kapoti kanthvat, puraḥ paścāt pracalanāt, sā grīvā , prakampitā iti, nāṭyaśāstre praśasyate = when the neck moves forward and backward like that of a she-pigeon, it is recognised in Nāṭyaśāstra as Prakampitā Grīvā.

Yuṣmat-asmat-iti- prokte, viśeṣataḥ deśīnāṭye, prayoktavyā = saying 'you and I' especially in Deśīnāṭya;

dolāyāṃ, maṇite (ca-eva), prakampitā = swinging and inarticulate murmuring / cooing produced as if in sexual ecstasy - to denote the above aspects, this Grīvā has to be used.

When the neck moves forward and backward like that of a she-pigeon, it is recognised in Nāṭyaśāstra as Prakampitā Grīvā. Saying 'you and I' especially in Deśīnāṭya; swinging and inarticulate murmuring / cooing produced as if in sexual ecstasy - to denote the above aspects, this Grīvā has to be used.

Chapter 7

द्वादश हस्त प्राणाम्

Dvādaśa Hasta Prāṇām

(12 movements of Hands)

प्रसारणम् कुंचितम् च रेचितम् पुंखितम् तथा ।
अपवेष्टितकम् चाऽपि प्रेरितोद्वेष्टिते तथा ।।116।।
व्यावृतः परिवृत्तश्च संकेतः तडनमंत्रम् ।
चिह्नं पदार्थटीक प्राणा द्वादश हस्तजाः ।।117।।

Transliteration:

Prasāraṇam kuñcitam ca recitaṃ puṅkhitaṃ tathā |
Apaveṣṭitakaṃ cāpi preritodveṣṭite tathā ||
Vyāvṛtaḥ parivṛttaśca saṅketaḥ taḍanamantram |
Cihnaṃ padārthatīka prāṇā dvādaśa hastajāḥ ||

Meaning:

Prasāraṇam kuñcitam (ca), recitaṃ, puṅkhitaṃ, (tathā) apaveṣṭitakaṃ (ca api) preritodveṣṭite (tathā), vyavṛtaḥ, parivṛttaḥ (ca), saṅketaḥ (tat-anamantram), cihnaṃ, padārthika-iti, prāṇā dvādasā hastajāḥ = the lives or movements of the hastas are twelve. 1. Prasāraṇam, 2. Kuñcitam, 3. Recitaṃ, 4. Puṅkhitaṃ, 5. Apaveṣṭita(ka)ṃ 6. Parivṛttaḥ, 7. Udveṣṭitam, 8. Vyavṛttam, 9. Parivṛttam, 10. Saṅketam, 11. Cihnaṃ, 12. Padārthatīka.

The lives or movements of the hastas are twelve. 1. Prasāraṇam, 2. Kuñcitam, 3. Recitaṃ, 4. Puṅkhitaṃ, 5. Apaveṣṭita(ka)ṃ 6. Parivṛttaḥ, 7. Udveṣṭitam, 8. Vyavṛttam, 9. Parivṛttam, 10. Saṅketam, 11. Cihnaṃ, 12. Padārthatīka.

1. प्रसारणम्
Praśaraṇam

प्रसरणामिति ज्ञेय-मंगुलिनाम् प्रसारणात् ।

Transliteration:

Prasaraṇāmiti jñeya-maṅgulinām prasāraṇāt |

Meaning :

Angulinām prasāraṇāt, prasāraṇam, iti jñeyam = extending/stretching the fingers is Prasāranam.

When the fingers are extended, it is Prasāraṇam.

2. कुंचितम्
Kuñcitam

कुंचना-दंगुलीनाम् (च) कुंचितम् समुद्रितं ।।118।।

Transliteration:

Kuñcana-daṅgulīnām (ca) kuñcitam samudritaṃ ||

Meaning :

Angulinām (ca), kuncanāt, kuñcitam samudritam =bending the fingers (towards palm) is said to be kuñcitam.

Bending the fingers towards palm is kuñcitam.

3. रेचितम्

Recitam

अंगुलीनाम् प्रचालनात् रेचितम् परिकीर्तितम् ।

Transliteration:

Aṃgulīnām pracālanāt recitam parikīrtitam |

Meaning :

Aṃgulīnām pracālanāt, recitam, parikīrtitam = quick movement or separation or fingers is Recitam. Quick movement or separation of fingers is Recitam.

4. पुंखितम्

Puṃkhitam

पुरोभागे कुंचितो वा रेचितो वा प्रसारितः ।।119।।
यो हस्तस्तु पताकादिः नाम्ना-असौ पुंखितो भवेत् ।

Transliteration:

Purobhāge kuñcito vā recito vā prasāritaḥ ||
Yo hastastu patākādiḥ nāmnā-asau puṃkhito bhavet |

Meaning :

Yah, patāka - ādihastāh (tu) purobhāge, kuncitah vā, recitah vā, prasāritah, asou, pumkhitah, nāmna, bhavet = When Patāka hasta bends or moves quickly or stretches forward, it is known as Pumkhitam.

When Patāka hasta bends or moves quickly or stretches forward, it is pumkhitam.

5. अपवेष्ठित(क)म्
Apaveṣṭhita(ka)ṃ

अधस्तात गमनम् यस्य हस्तस्य नाम्ना अपवेष्ठितः ।।120।।

Transliteration:

Adhastāt gamanam yasya hastasya nāmnā apaveṣṭhitaḥ ||

Meaning :

Yashya hastasya adhastāt, gamanam, nāmnā apaveṣṭhita(ka)m = when the hand is directed downwards, it is apaveṣṭhita(ka)m.

When the hand is stretched downwards, is it Apaveṣṭhitakam.

6. प्रेरितम्
Preritaṃ

पश्चात्-भागे कुंचितो वा रेचितो वा प्रसारितः ।
यो हस्तः कथितः सोऽयम प्रेरितः पूर्वासूरिभिः ।।121।।

Transliteration:

Paścāt-bhāge kuñcito vā recito vā prasāritaḥ |
Yo hastaḥ kathitaḥ so'ayama preritaḥ pūrvāsūribhiḥ ||

Meaning :

Yah hastah, pascāt-bhāge, kuñcitah, va, recitah, vā, prasāritah, sah, ayam, purvarūribhih preritah kathitah = when the hand, at the back, bends or moves quickly or is stretched it is recognised as Preritam by the ancient scholars.

If the hand placed at the back, bends or moves quickly or is stretched it is considered as preritam.

7. उद्वेष्टितम्

Udveṣṭitaṃ

हस्ताना-मूर्द्ध्वभागे यदगमनम् चास्ति नर्तने ।
तदुद्वेष्टिट मित्याहुः भरतागम वेदितः ।।122।।

Transliteration:

Hastānā-mūrddhvabhāge yadagamanam cāsti nartane |
Tadudveṣṭiṭa mityāhuḥ bharatāgama veditaḥ ||

Meaning :

Nartane, hastānām ūrdhvabhāge, yet gamanam (ca), asti, tat-udveshtitam-iti bharata-āgama-veditaḥ ahuh = in dance, when the hand is directed upwards, it is known, by the experts on Nāṭya as Udveshtitam.

If the hand, is directed upwards in Nāṭya, it is Udveshtitam.

8. व्यावृत्त(क)म्

Vyāvṛtta(ka)m

उदग्रतः पार्श्वभागे हस्तो व्यावृत्तको भवेत् ।

Transliteration:

Udagrataḥ pārśvabhāge hastọ vyāvṛttako bhavet |

Meaning :

Hastah, pārsvabhāge Udagrataḥ, vyāvṛttakah bhavet = when the hand is raised up from a side, it is Vyāvṛtta(ka)m.

When the hand is raised up from a side, it is Vyāvṛtta(ka)m.

9. परिवृत्तम्
Parivṛttaṃ

पार्श्वभ्याम् च पुरोभागे यो हस्तो नटने कृतः ।।123।।
परिवृत्तः समाख्यातः नाम्ना हस्तविशारदैः ।

Transliteration:

Pārśvabhyām ca purobhāge yo hasto naṭane kṛtaḥ ||
Parivṛttaḥ samākhyātaḥ nāmnā hastaviśāradaiḥ |

Meaning :

Natane, pārsvābhyām, purobhāge, yah hastah kṛtaḥ, nāmnā, Parivṛttaḥ, hasta-vIśāradaiḥ, samākhyātaḥ = in Nāṭya, when the hand is brought forward from the sides, it is considered as Parivrttam by the experts on hand movements.

If the hand is brought forward from the sides in Nāṭya, it is Parivṛttam.

10. संकेतम्
Saṃketaṃ

ऊहाविधान रचना वीना स्थूलोक्तिपूर्वकम् ।।124।।
यो हस्तो नियमम् प्राप्तः सः संकेतः उदाहृतः ।

Transliteration:

Ūhāvidhāna racanā vīnā sthūloktipūrvakam ||
Yo hasto niyamam prāptaḥ saḥ saṃketaḥ udāhṛtaḥ |

Meaning :

Yah hastah, sthūla-uktipūrvakam, ūhāvidhāna-racana vinā, niyamam prāptah, sah, samketah udāhrtah

= when the hand is able to communicate the meaning of a suggestion, without depending on the words, it is Saṃketam.

When the hand communicates the meaning of a suggestion, without depending on the words, it is Saṃketam.

11. चिह्नम्
Cihnaṃ

प्रत्यक्षाणाम् परोक्षाणाम् वस्तूनाम् नाट्यकर्मणि ।।125।।
स्थावरत्वम् जंगमत्व मीयूषामपि तदृषम् ।
तदाकार प्रकटनम् तन्मुखस्य निरीक्षणम् ।।126।।

तत्-स्थाना दर्शनम् च-अपि तत्-ध्वजानाम् च दर्शनाम् ।
तदायुध-प्रकटनम् तदग्रतार्थ निवेदनम् ।।127।।
तदव्याप्त दर्शनम् चापि तच्चेष्टा दर्शनम् तथा ।
अष्ट लक्षण मित्येच्चिह्न मित्याभिधीयते ।।128।।

Transliteration:

Pratyakṣāṇām parokṣāṇām vastūnām nāṭyakarmaṇi ||
Sthāvaratvam jaṅgamatva mīyūṣāmapi tadṛṣam |
Tadākāra prakaṭanam tanmukhasya nirīkṣaṇam ||

Tat-sthānā darśanam ca-api tat-dhvajānām ca darśanām |
Tadāyudha-prakaṭanam tadagratārtha nivedanam ||

Tadavyāpta darśanam cāpi taccesṭā darśanam tathā |
Asṭa laksana mityeccihna mityābhidhīyate ||

M : Nātya karmani = in the process of nātya/nrtya; pratyakshāṇām, parokshāṇām = whether visible or not; sthāvaratvam, jangamatvam vastūnām-iyushām, (api) tadrṣam = whether the objects are stationary or moving, and such other objects, to show/reveal/communicate :
tat-ākāra prakaṭanam = their form;
tat-mukhasya nirīkṣaṇam = their face;
tat-sthāna darśanam dhvajānām = their dwelling place;
tat-dhvajānām darśanam = their banners;
tat-āyudha prākaṭanam = their weapons ;
tat-agratārtha nivedana = their virtues;
tat-vyāpta darśanam = their range ;
tat-cesṭa darśanam = their actions;
asṭa lakṣanamiti, etat cinham, iti, abhidhīyate = that which is having the above eight characteristics is known as Cihnam.

The hasta prāna known as cihnam will depict the following eight aspects, in nātyam-nrtyam – whether the objects are visible or unseen, whether stationary or moving or such other objects: 1. their forms, 2. their faces, 3. their dwelling places, 4. their banners, 5. their weapons, 6. their virtues, 7. their ranges and 8. their actions.

12. पदार्थटीक

Padārthatīka

पदानाम् कठितानाम् स्यादर्थ निर्वाहता यदि ।
इयम् पदार्थटीकेति कथिता भरतादिभिः ।।129।।

Transliteration:

Padānām kaṭhitānām syādartha nirvāhatā yadi |
Iyam padārthatīketi kathiṭā bharatādibhiḥ ||

Meaning:

Kathitānām padānām, artha-nirvāhata syāt yadi = when the meanings of the words uttered are communicated through the hands; iyam pada-artha-tikā-iti, kathitā, bharata -ādibhiḥ = it is considered as padārthatīka by Bharata and other writers.

When the meanings of the libretto rendered are communicated through the hands, it is known as Padārthatīka.

हस्त भेदाः
Hasta Bhedāḥ

अथेदानीम् तु हस्तानाम् लक्षणम् प्रोच्यते मया ।
असंयुता संयुतश्च द्वेधा हस्ताः प्रकीर्तितः ।।130।।
तत्रासंयुता हस्तानामादौ लक्षण मुच्यते ।

Transliteration:

Athedānīm tu hastānām lakṣaṇam procyate mayā |
Asamyutāḥ samyutaśca dvedhā hastā prakīrtitaḥ ||
Tatrāsaṃyutā hastānāmādau lakṣaṇa mucyate |

Meaning :

Athedānīm tu hastānām lakṣaṇam procyate mayā = the two hastas Asamyuta and Samyuta; Asamyutāḥ samyutaśca dvedhā hastā prakīrtitaḥ = Hands are of two types, Asamyuta and Samyuta, Tatrāsaṃyutā hastānāmādau lakṣaṇa mucyate = Now, at first the characterstics of Asamyuta hastas will be described.

Atha-idanim (tu), hastānām, lakshanam, mayā, procyate = now, the characteristics of the hastas, will be described.

Chapter 8

असंयुतहस्ताः

Single Hand Gestures

पताकस्त्रिपताकोऽर्धपताकः कर्तरीमुखः।।131।।
मयूराख्योऽर्धचन्द्रश्च अरालः शुकतुण्डकः।
मुष्टिश्च शिखराख्यश्च कपित्थः कटकामुखः।।132।।
सूची चन्द्रकला पद्मकोशः सर्पशिरस्तथा।
मृगशीर्षः सिंहमुखः कांगुलश्चालपद्मकः।।133।।
चतुरो भ्रमरश्चैव च हंसास्यो हंसपक्षकः।
सन्दंशो मुकुलश्चैव ताम्रचूडस्त्रिशूलकः।।134।।
इत्यसंयुतहस्तानामष्टाविंशतिरीरिता।

Transliteration

Patākaḥ tripatāko-ardhapatākaḥ kartarīmukhaḥ ||
Mayūrākhyo-ardhacandraśca arālaḥ śukatuṇḍakaḥ |
Muṣṭiśca śikharākhyaśca kapitthaḥ kaṭakāmukhaḥ ||
Sūcī candrakalā padmakośaḥ sarpaśirastathā |
Mṛgaśīrṣaḥ siṃhamukhaḥ kāṅgula ścālapadmakaḥ ||
Caturo bhramaraścaiva ca haṃsāsyo haṃsapakṣakaḥ |
Sandaṃśo mukulaścaiva tāmracūḍaḥ striśūlakaḥ ||
Ityasaṃyuta hastānāmaṣṭāviṃśati-rīritā |

Meanings :

(1) Patāka, (2) Tripatāka, (3) Ardhapatāka, (4) Kartarīmukha, (5) Mayūra (6) Ardhacandra, (7) Arāla, (8) Śukatuṇḍa (9) Muṣṭi, (10) Śikhara, (11) Kapittha, (12) Kaṭakāmukha, (13) Sūcī, (14) Candrakalā, (15) Padmakośa, (16) Sarpaśira, (17) Mṛgaśīrṣa, (18) Siṃhamukha, (19) Kāṅgula, (20) Ālapadma, (21) Catura,

(22) Bhramara (23) Haṃsāsya, (24) Haṃsapakṣa (25) Sandaṃśa, (26) Mukula (27) Tāmracūḍa (28) Triśūla. These are the 28 single hand gestures.

पताक हस्तः

Patāka hasta (Flag)

अङ्गुल्यः कुञ्चिताङ्गुष्ठः संश्लिष्टाः प्रसृता यदि ।।135।।
स पताककरः प्रोक्तो नृत्य कर्म विशारदैः ।

Transliteration

Aṅgulyaḥ kuñcitāṅguṣṭhaḥ saṃśliṣṭāḥ prasṛtā yadi ||
Sa patākakaraḥ prokto nṛtya karma viśāradaiḥ |

Meanings :

When the thumb is bent and its tip is at the root of the forefinger and the palm and the four fingers are stretched, it becomes Patāka hasta.

विनियोगः (Application)

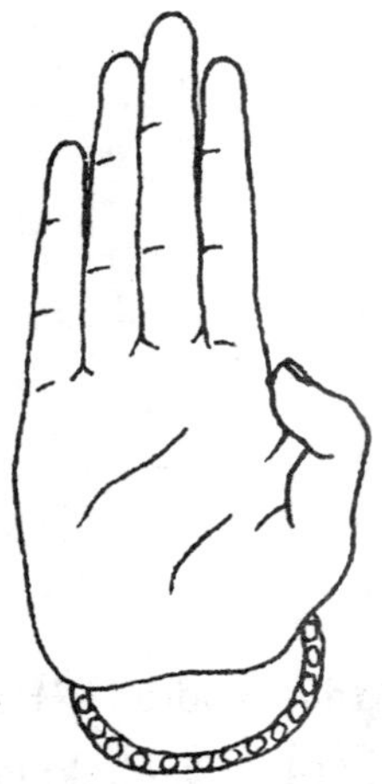

नाट्यारम्भे वारिवाहे वने वस्तुनिषेधने ।।136।।
कुचस्थले निशायां च नद्याम्मरमण्डले ।
तुरङ्गे खण्डने वायौ शयने गमनोद्यमे ।।137।।
प्रतापे च प्रसादे च चन्द्रिकायां घनातपे ।
कवाटपाटने सप्तविभक्त्यर्थे तरङ्गके ।।138।।
वीथिप्रवेशभावेऽपि समत्वे चाङ्गरागके ।
आत्मार्थे शपथे चापि तूष्णींभावनिदर्शने ।।139।।
तालपत्रे च खेटे च द्रव्यादिस्पर्शने तथा ।

आशीर्वादक्रियायां च नृपेश्रेष्ठस्य भावने ।।140।।
तत्र तत्रेति वचने सिन्धौ च सुकृतिक्रमे ।
सम्बोधने पुरोगेऽपि खड्गरूपस्य धारणे ।।141।।
मासे संवत्सरे वर्षदिने सम्मार्जने तथा ।
एवमर्थेषु युज्यन्ते पताकहस्तभावनाः ।।142।।

Transliteration

Nāṭyārambhe vārivāhe vane vastuniṣedhane ||
Kucasthale niśāyāṃ ca nadyām amaramaṇḍale |
Turaṅge khaṇḍane vāyau śayane gamanodyame ||
Pratāpe ca prasāde ca candrikāyāṃ ghanātape |
Kavāṭapāṭane saptavibhaktyarthe taraṅgake ||
Vīthipraveśabhāve'pi samatve cāṅgarāgake |
Ātmārthe śapathe cāpi tūṣṇīmbhāvanidarśane ||
Tālapatre ca kheṭe ca dravyādisparśane tathā |
Āśīrvādakriyāyāṃ ca nṛpeśreṣṭhasya bhāvane ||
Tatra tatreti vacane sindhau ca sukṛtikrame |
Sambodhane puroge'pi khaḍgarūpasya dhāraṇe ||
Māse saṃvatsare varṣadine sammārjane tathā |
Evamartheṣu yujyante patākahastabhāvanāḥ ||

Transliteration with meanings :

Nāṭyā-rambhe = begining of dance; vārivāhe = cloud; vane = forest; vastu niṣedhane = forbiding things, to say 'no'; kucasthale = breast, chest; niśāyāṃ (ca) = night; nadyām = river; amaramaṇḍale = heaven; turaṅge = horse; khaṇḍane = cutting; vāyau = wind; śayane = reclining; gamana-udyame = walking; pratāpe (ca) = prowess; prasāde (ca) = graciousness; candrikāyāṃ = moon light; ghana-ātape = radiant heat; kavāṭa-pāṭane = opening and closing the door; saptavibhakti-arthe = denoting the seven cases (of grammar); taraṅgake = ripples; vīthipraveśabhāve (api) = entering the street; samatve (ca) = equality; aṅgarāgake = anointing one's own body; applying sandalpaste etc.; ātmārthe = one's self; śapathe (ca-āpi) = taking an oath; tūṣṇīmbhāva-nidarśane = silence; tālapatre (ca) = palmyra leaf; kheṭe (ca) = shield; dravyādi-sparśane (tathā) = touching things; āśīrvāda kriyāyāṃ (ca) = benediction; nṛpa-śreṣṭtasya bhāvane = a good ideal king / emperor; tatra - tatra - iti vacane = saying there and there; sindhou (ca) = sea; sukṛtikrame = doing good deeds; sambodhane (tu) = addressing; puroge (api) = moving forward; khaḍga - rūpasyadhāraṇe = holding a sword; māse = month; saṃvatsare = year; varṣa dine = rainy day; sammārjane (tathā) = sweeping; evam artheṣu yujyante patāka hasta bhāvanāḥ = in denoting the above aspects, Patāka hasta is to be used.

त्रिपताक हस्तः

Tripatāka hasta (Tripartite flag)

स एव त्रिपताकः स्याद्वाक्रितानामिकाङ्गुलिः ।

Transliteration

Sa eva tripatākaḥ syādvākritānāmikāṅguliḥ |

Meanings :

When the ring finger of Patāka hasta is bent, it becomes 'Tripatāka hasta'.

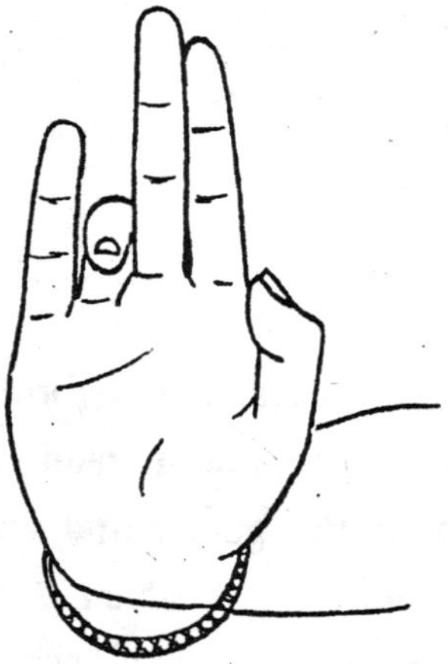

विनियोगः (Application)

मकुटे वृक्षभावेषु वज्रे तद्धरवासवे ।।143।।
केतकीकुसुमे दीपे वह्निज्वाला विजृम्भणे ।
कपोते/कपोले पत्रलेखायां बाणार्थे परिवर्तने ।।144।।
युज्यते त्रिपताकोऽयं कथितो भरतोत्तमैः ।

Transliteration

Makuṭe vṛkṣabhāveṣu vajre taddharavāsave ||
Ketakīkusume dīpe vahnijvālā vijṛmbhaṇe |
Kapote/kapole patralekhāyāṃ bāṇārthe parivartane ||
Yujyate tripatāko-yaṃ kathito bharatottamaiḥ |

Meanings :

Makuṭe = a crown; vṛkṣa-bhāveṣu = tree; vajre = thunderbolt, weapon of Indra; tat-dhara vāsave = the holder of the Vajra (Indra); ketakīkusume = screw-pine flower; dīpe = light (lamp); vahni-jvālā vijṛmbhaṇe = flames of fire; kapote = dove; kapole = cheek; patra lekhāyāṃ = writing letters, drawing patterns; bāṇa-arthe = arrow; parivartane = turning round; Yujyate tripatāko-yaṃ kathito bharatottamaiḥ = in denoting the above tripataka hasta is used, as described by Bharata.

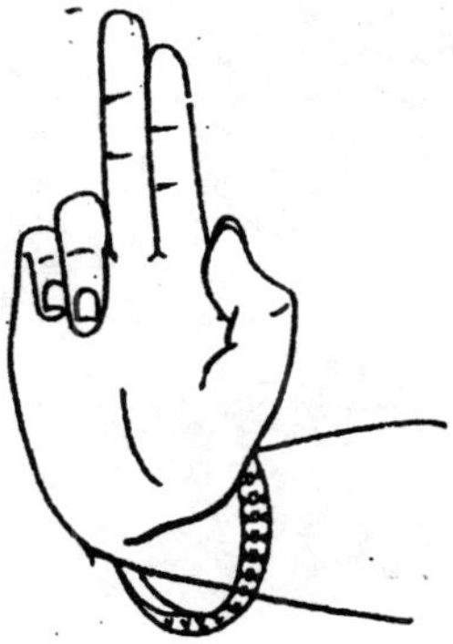

अर्धपताक हस्तः

Ardhapatāka hasta (Half flag)

त्रिपताके कनिष्टा चेद् चक्रिताऽर्धपताकिका ।।145।।

Transliteration

Tripatāke kaniṣṭā ced cakritā'rdhapatākikā ||

Meanings :

When the little finger of Tripatāka hasta is bent, it becomes Ardhapatāka hasta.

विनियोगः (Application)

पल्लवे फलके तीरे उभयोरिति वाचके ।
क्रकचे छुरिकायां च ध्वजे गोपुरश्रृङ्गयोः ।।146।।
युज्यतेर्धपताकोयं तत्तत्कर्मप्रयोगके ।

Transliteration :

Pallave phalake tīre ubhayoriti vācake |
Krakace churikāyāṃ ca dhvaje gopuraśṛṅgayoḥ ||
Yujyaterdhapatākoyam tattatkarmaprayogake |

Meanings :

Pallave = tender branch; phalake = writing or painting board; tīre = bank of river; ubhayoh - iti vācake = saying 'both'; krakace = saw; churikāyāṃ (ca) = knife; dhvaje = flag; gopura-śṛṅgayoh = temple tower and horn like structure atop a temple; yujyate = in denoting the above; ardhapatākoyaṃ; tat-taṭ-karma prayogake = according to their specific qualifies, Ardhapatāka is used.

कर्त्तरीमुख हस्तः

Kartarīmukha hasta (scissors' blade)

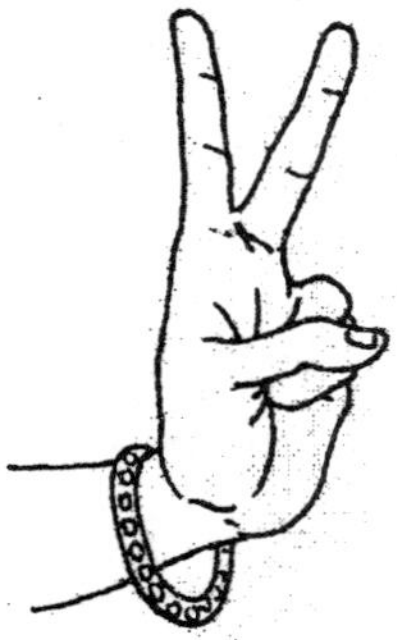

अस्यैव चापि हस्तस्य तर्जनी च कनिष्ठिका ।।147।।
बहिः प्रसारिते द्वे च स करः कर्तरीमुखः ।

Transliteration

Asyaiva cāpi hastasya tarjanī ca kaniṣṭhikā ||
Bahiḥ prasārite dve ca sa karaḥ Kartarīmukhaḥ |

Meanings :

When the forefinger and the little finger of Tripatāka hasta are extended back, it beomes Kartarīmukha hasta.

विनियोगः (Application)

स्त्रीपुंसयोस्तु विश्लेषे विपर्यासपदेऽपि वा ।।148।।
लुण्ठने नयनान्ते च मरणे भेदभावने ।
विद्युदर्थेऽप्येकशय्याविरहे पतने तथा ।।149।।
लतायां युज्यते यस्तु स करः कर्तरीमुखः ।

Transliteration

Strīpuṃsayostu viśleṣe viparyāsapade'pi vā ||
Luṇṭhane nayanānte ca maraṇe bhedabhāvane |

Vidyudarthe'ekaśayyāvirahe patane tathā ||
Latāyām yujyate yastu sa karaḥ kartarīmukhaḥ |

Meanings :

Strī - puṃsayoḥ (tu) viśleṣe = separation of woman and man; viparyāsapade (api-vā) = opposition; luṇṭhane = to twirl; nayana-ante (ca) = corner of an eye; maraṇe = death; bheda-bhāvane = disagreement, differences; vidyut-arthe = lightning; ekaśayyāvirahe = reclining alone with pangs of separation; patane (tathā) = falling; latāyām = creeper; yujyate yastu sa karaḥ kartarīmukhaḥ = Kartarīmukha hasta is used to denote the above.

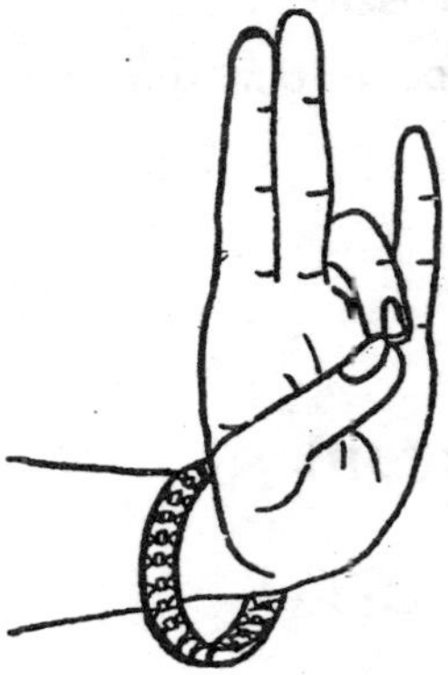

मयूर हस्तः

Mayūra hasta (Peacock)

अस्मिन्नामिकाङ्गुष्ठौ श्लिष्टौ चान्याः प्रसारिताः ।।150।।
मयूरहस्तः कथितः करटीकाविचक्षणैः ।

Transliteration

Asminnāmikāṅguṣṭhau śliṣṭau cānyāḥ prasāritāḥ ||
Mayūrahastaḥ kathitaḥ karaṭokāvicakṣaṇaiḥ |

Meanings :

If in Kartarīmukha hasta, ring finger and thumb are joined at the tips and other fingers are extended, it will be Mayūra hasta.

विनियोगः (Application)

मयूरास्ये लतायां च शकुने वमने तथा।।151।।
अलकस्यापनयने ललाटतिलकेषु च ।
नद्युदकस्य निक्षेपे शास्त्रवादे प्रसिद्धके ।।152।।
एवमर्थेषु युज्यन्ते मयूरकरभावनाः ।

Transliteration

Mayūrāsye latāyāṃ ca śakune vamane tathā ||
Alakasyāpanayane lalāṭatilakeṣu ca |
Nadyudakasya nikṣepe śāstravāde prasiddhake ||
Ēvamartheṣu yujyante mayūrakarabhāvanāḥ |

Meanings

Mayūra-āsye = peacock's beak; latāyāṃ (ca) = creeper; śakune = omen; vamane = vomiting; (tathā) alakasyā apanayane = stroking the hair; lalāṭa - tilakeṣu (ca) = applying decorative mark applied on forehead; nadyudakasya nikṣepe = sprinkling river water on the head; śāstra vāde = discussion on śāstras; prasiddhake = renowned; Evam-artheṣu yujyante mayūrakara bhāvanāḥ = mayūra is used in denoting the above.

अर्धचन्द्र हस्तः

Ardhacandra hasta (Half-moon)

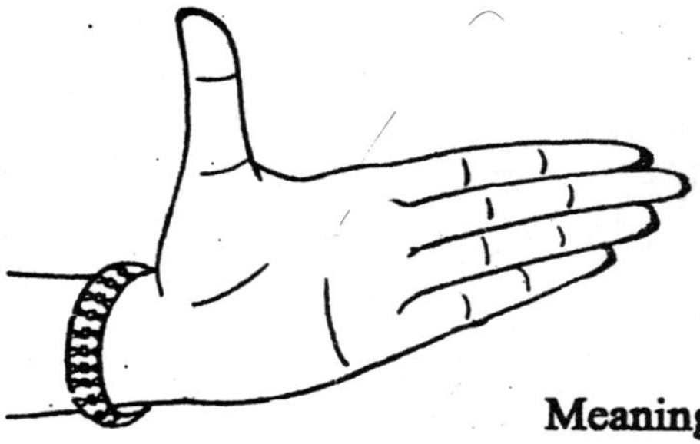

अर्धचन्द्रकरः सोऽयं पताकेऽङ्गुष्ठसारणात् ।।153।।

Transliteration

Ardhacandrakaraḥ so-yaṃ patāke-ṅguṣṭhasāraṇāt ||

Meanings :

If the thumb of the Patāka hasta is stretched out, it becomes Ardhacandra hasta.

विनियोगः (Application)

चन्द्रे कृष्णाष्टमीभाजि गलहस्तार्थकेऽपि च ।
भल्लायुधे देवतानामभिषेचनकर्मणि ।।154।।
भुक्पात्रे चोद्भवे कट्यां चिन्तायामात्मवाचके ।

ध्याने च प्रार्थने चापि अङ्गानां स्पर्शने तथा ।।155।।
प्राकृतानां नमस्कारे अर्धचन्द्रो नियुज्यते।

Transliteration

Candre kṛṣṇāṣṭamībhāji galahastārthake api ca |
Bhallāyudhe devatānāmabhiṣecanakarmaṇi ||
Bhukpātre codbhave kaṭyāṃ cintāyāmātmavācake |
Dhyāne ca prārthane cāpi aṅgānāṃ sparśane tathā ||
Prākṛtānāṃ namaskāre ardhacandro niyujyate |

Meanings :

Candre = moon; kṛṣṇāṣṭamībhāji = eighth day of new moon; gala - hastārthake (api-ca) = seizing the neck (with intension to throwout); bhalla-āyudhe = a spear; devatānām, abhiṣecana karmaṇi = consecrating an image of god; bhuk - pātre - (ca) = plate used for eating; udbhave = origin/birth; kaṭyāṃ = waist; cintāyām = contemplating on oneself; ātma vācake = talking of / to one's self or to show one's self; dhyāne - (ca) = meditation; prārthane (ca-api) = prayer; aṅgānāṃ sparśane (tatha) = touching the limbs; prākṛtanāṃ namaskāre = greeting common people / greeting by common people; ardha-candraḥ, niyujyate = in denoting the above ardhacandra hasta is used.

अराल हस्तः

Arāla hasta (Bent)

①

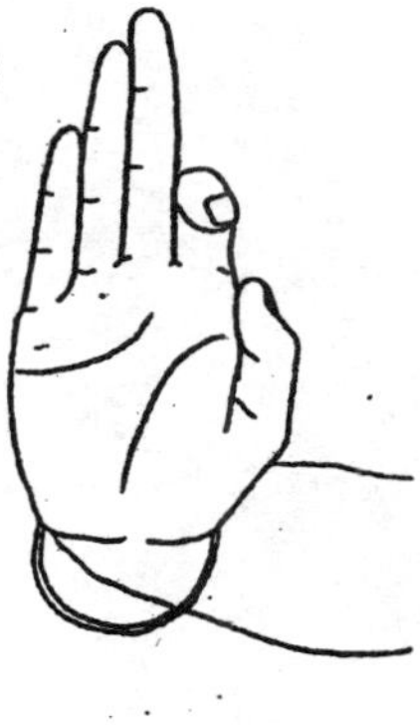

②

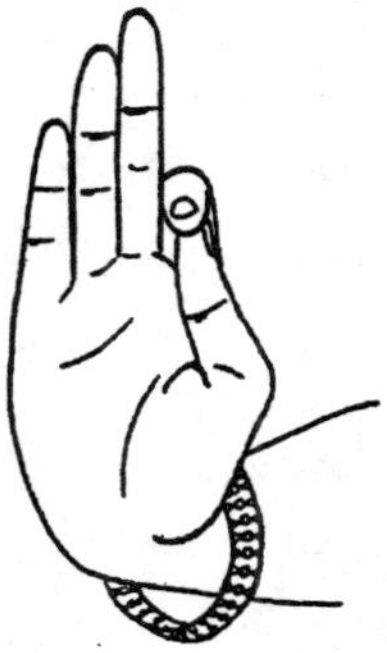

पताके तर्जनी चक्रा नाम्ना सोऽयमरालकः ।।156।।

Transliteration

Patāke tarjanī cakrā nāmnā so-yamarālakaḥ ||

Meanings :

(1) If the forefinger of Patāka hasta is bent, then it becomes Arāla hasta.

(2) Alternatively when the index finger is placed above the thumb it is *Arāla.*

विनियोग: (Application)

विषाद्यमृतपानेषु प्रचण्डपवनेऽपि च ।

Transliteration :

Viṣādyamṛtapāneṣu pracaṇḍapavane'api ca |

Meanings :

Visha - amṛta - ādi pāneshu = drinking poison, ambrosia etc; pracaṇḍa pavane-api-ca = violent wind.

शुकतुण्ड हस्त:

Śukatuṇḍa hasta (Parrot's beak)

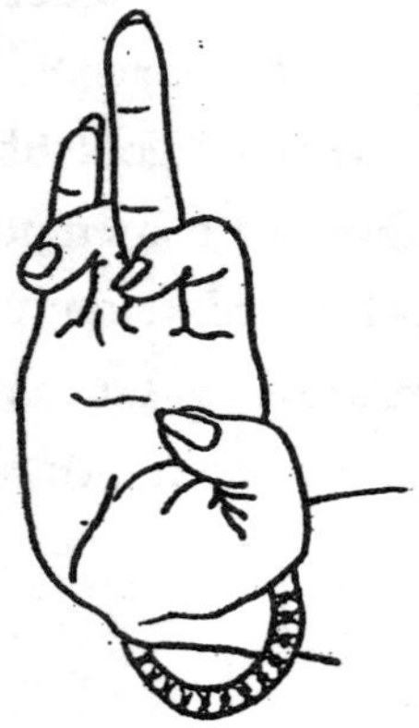

अस्मिन्नानामिका वक्रा शुकतुण्डकरो भवेत् ।।157।।

Transliteration

Asminnānāmikā vakrā śukatuṇḍakaro bhavet ||

Meanings :

When the ring finger in the Arala hasta is also bent (fore finger is already bent), it becomes Śukatuṇḍa hasta

विनियोग: (Application)

बाणप्रयोगे कुन्तार्थे वाऽऽलयस्य स्मृतिक्रमे ।
मर्मोक्त्यामुग्रभावेषु शुकतुण्डो नियुज्यते ।।158।।

Transliteration :

Bāṇaprayoge kuntārthe vālayasya smṛtikrame |
Marmoktyāmugrabhāveṣu śukatuṇḍo niyujyate ||

Meanings :

Bāṇaprayoge = shooting an arrow; kunta-ārthe = throwing a spear; ālayasya = past; **smṛtikrame** = to recall in proper order; marmoktyām = crptic word, ugrabhāveṣu = angry mood, **śukatuṇḍo niyujyate** = Śukatunda is used.

मुष्टि हस्तः

Muśṭi hasta (fist)

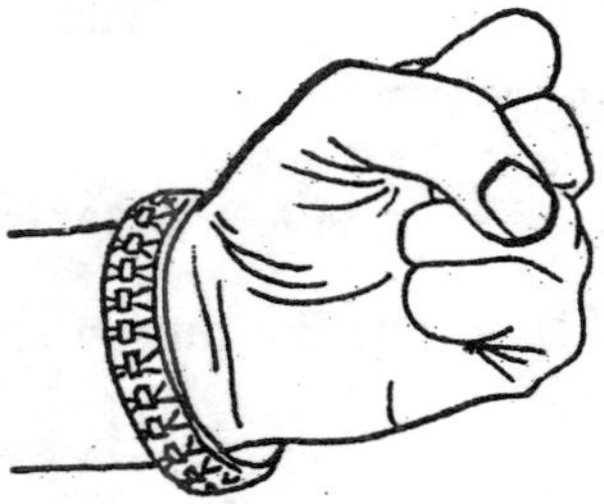

मेलनादङ्गलीनञ्च कुञ्चितानां तलान्तरे ।
अङ्गुष्टश्चोपरियुतो मुष्टिहस्तोयमीर्यते मिष्यते ।।159।।

Transliteration

Melanādaṅgalīnañca kuñcitānāṃ talāntare |
Aṅguṣṭaścopariyuto muṣṭihastoyamīryate ||

Meanings :

If the four fingers are bent and closely pressed towards the palm and thumb is placed upon them, the hand gesture is known to be *Muśṭi.*

विनियोगः (Application)

स्थिरे कचग्रहे दार्ढ्ये वस्त्वादीनां च धारणे ।
मल्लानां युद्धभावेऽपि मुष्टिहस्तोऽयमीर्यते ।।160।।

Transliteration :

Sthire kacagrahe dārḍhye vastvādīnāṃ ca dhāraṇe |
Mallānāṃ yuddhabhāve-api muṣṭihasto-ayamīryate ||

Meanings :

Sthire = steadiness; kaca grahe = grasping the hair; dārḍhye = valour; vastu - ādīnāṃ (ca) dhāraṇe = holding things etc.; mallānāṃ yuddha bhāve (api) = wrestlers thinking of a fight;

mushṭi - hastaḥ-ayamīryate = to denote the above muśṭi hasta is to be used.

शिखर हस्तः

Śikhara hasta (Peak)

चेन्मुष्टिरुन्नताङ्गुष्टः स एव शिखरः करः ।

Transliteration

Cenmuṣṭirunnatāṅguṣṭaḥ sa eva śikharaḥ karaḥ |

Meanings :

If in Muśṭi the thumb is raised upwards and held straight it is called *Śikhara.*

विनियोगः (Application)

मदने कार्मुके स्तम्भे निश्चये पितृकर्मणि ।।161।।
ओष्ठे प्रविष्टरूपे च रदने प्रश्नभावने ।
लिङ्गे नास्तीति वचने स्मरणेऽभिनयान्तिके।।162।।
कटिबन्धाकर्षणे च परिरम्भविधिक्रमे ।
घण्टानिनादे शिखरो युज्यते भरतादिभिः।।163।।

Transliteration :

Madane kārmuke stambhe niścaye pitṛkarmaṇi ||
Ōṣṭhe praviṣṭarūpe ca radane praśnabhāvane |
Liṅge nāstīti vacane smaraṇe'abhinayāntike ||
Kaṭibandhākarṣaṇe ca parirambhavidhikrame |
Ghaṇṭānināde śikharo yujyate bharatādibhiḥ ||

Meanings :

Madane = the God of love, Manmatha; kārmuke = bow; stambhe = pillar; niścaye = resolve; pitṛkarmaṇi = offering to gratify ancestors; oṣṭhe = lip; praviṣṭa rūpe (ca) = entering, pouring; radane = tooth; praśna bhāvane = questioning; liṅge = Sivalingam; nāsti-iti vacane = saying 'no'; smaraṇe = recollection; abhinaya-antike = to beckon expressively; kaṭi-bandha-ākarṣaṇe (ca) = to tie around waist; parirambha vidhikrame = embracing; ghaṇṭāninā̄de = sound of bell; śikharo yujyate bharatādibhiḥ = in denoting the above śikhara is to be used.

कपित्थ हस्तः

Kapittha (Woodapple)

अङ्गुष्ठमूर्ध्नि शिखरे वक्रिता यदि तर्जनी ।
कपित्थाख्यः करः सोयं कीर्तितो नृत्तकोविदैः ।।164।।

Transliteration

Aṅguṣṭhamūrdhni śikhare vakritā yadi tarjanī |
Kapitthākhyaḥ karaḥ soyaṃ kīrtito nṛttakovidaiḥ ||

Meanings :

Bending the forefinger of the Śikhara pose and placing it over the thumb in a pressing position, forms *Kapittha*.

विनियोगः (Application)

लक्ष्म्यां चैव सरस्वत्यां नटानां तालधारणे ।
गोदोहने-प्यञ्जने च लीलाकुसुमधारणे।।165।।
चेलाञ्चलादिग्रहणे पटस्यैवावगुण्ठने ।
धूपदीपार्चने चापि कपित्थः संप्रयुज्यते।।166।।

Transliteration :

Lakṣmyāṃ caiva sarasvatyāṃ naṭānāṃ tāladhāraṇe |
Godohane-pyañjane ca līlākusumadhāraṇe ||
Celāñjalādigrahaṇe paṭasyaivāvaguṇṭhane |
Dhūpadīpārcane cāpi kapitthaḥ samprayujyate ||

Meanings :

Lakṣmyāṃ (ca- eva) = Lakshmi; sarasvatyāṃ = Sarasvati; naṭānāṃ = of dancers; tāladhāraṇe = holding cymbals; godohane (api) = milking a cow; añjane (ca) = collyrium; līlā = graceful; kusuma = flower; dhāraṇe = holding (gracefully holding a flower); celāñcala-ādi-grahaṇe = grasping the edge of a robe; paṭasya-evā-vaguṇṭhane = covering the head with a veil; dhūpa-dīpa-arcane (ca-api) = offering incense, and light; kapitthaḥ, samprayujyate = to indicate the above kapittha hasta is used.

कटकामुख हस्तः

Kaṭakāmukha hasta (Half-closed fist, link in a bangle or chain)

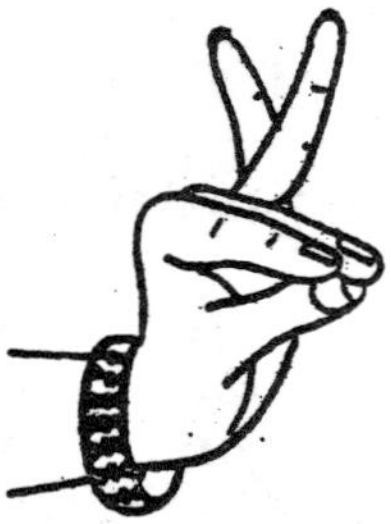

①

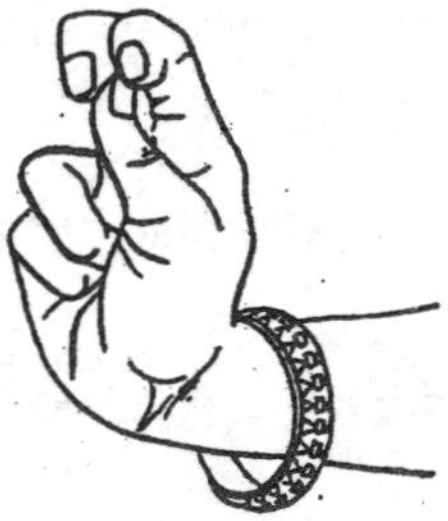

②

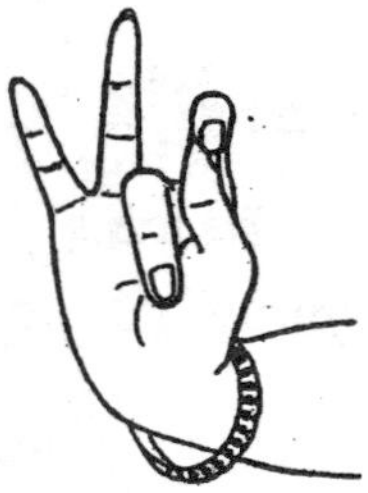

कपित्थे तर्जनी चोर्ध्वं मुछिताङ्गुष्ठमध्यमा ।
कटकामुखहस्तोऽयं कीर्तितो भरतागमैः ।।167।।

Transliteration

Kapitthe tarjanī cordhvaṃ muchitāṅguṣṭhamadhyamā |
Kaṭakāmukhahasto-yaṃ kīrtito bharatāgamaiḥ ||

Meanings :

In Kapittha hasta, if the tip of the forefinger touches the tips of the thumb and the middle finger, it becomes Kaṭakāmukha hasta (kaṭaka-mukha = link in a bangle or chain).

Kaṭakāmukha hasta is denoted by two other gestures.

(1) In *Kapittha* hasta, placing the middle finger on the thumb is *Kaṭakāmukha.*

(2) In *Kapittha* hasta, raising the ring and little finger is *Kaṭakāmukha.*

विनियोग: (Application)

कुसुमावचये मुक्तास्त्रग्दाम्नां धारणे तथा ।
शरमध्याकर्षणे च नागवल्लीप्रदानके ।।168।।
कस्तूरिकादिवस्तूनां पेषणे गन्धवासने ।
वचने दृष्टिभावेऽपि कटकामुख इष्यते ।।169।।

Transliteration :

Kusumāvacaye muktāsragdāmnāṃ dhāraṇe tathā |
Śaramadhyākarṣaṇe ca nāgavallīpradānake ||
Kastūrikādivastūnāṃ peṣaṇe gandhavāsane |
Vacane dṛṣṭibhāve'api kaṭakāmukha iṣyate ||

Meanings :

Kusuma-avacaye = plucking flowers; muktā-srag-dāmnāṃ dhāraṇe = wearing a pearl necklace or a garland of flowers; tathā śara-madhyākarṣaṇe (ca) = drawing the string of a bow with an arrow; nāgavallī pradānake = offering folded betel leaves; kastūri-ādi-vastūnāṃ = musk and other perfumes. peṣaṇe = mix; gandhavāsane = smell of sandal; vācane = speech; dṛṣṭi bhāve (api) = glancing; kaṭakāmukha iṣyate = in denoting the above, Kaṭakāmukha hasta is used.

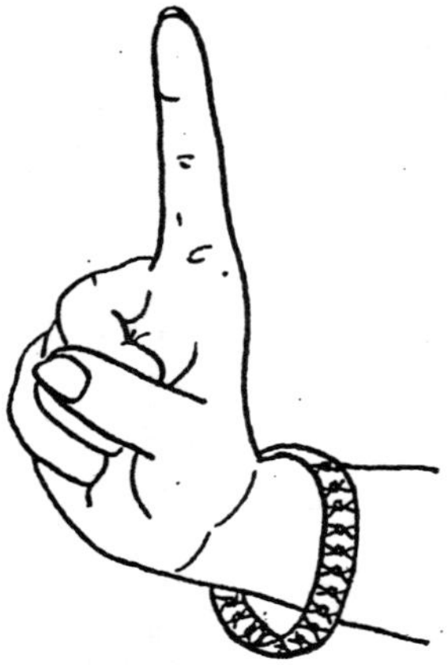

सूची हस्तः
Sūcī hasta (Needle)

ऊर्ध्वं प्रसारिता यत्न कटकामुखतर्जनी ।
सूचीहस्तः स विज्ञेयो भरतागमकोविदैः ।।170।।

Transliteration

Ūrdhvaṃ prasāritā yatna kaṭakāmukhatarjanī |
Sūcīhastaḥ sa vijñeyo bharatāgamakovidaiḥ ||

Meanings :

When the forefinger of the Kaṭakāmukha hasta is raised, it becomes Sūcī hasta (Sūcī=needle; Sūcimukha = needle point).

विनियोगः (Application)

एकार्थेऽपि परब्रह्मभावनायां शतेऽपि च ।
रवौ नगर्यां लोकार्थे तथेति वचनेऽपि च ।।171।।
यच्छब्देऽपि तच्छब्दे विजनार्थेऽपि तर्जने ।
कार्श्ये शलाके वपुषि आश्चर्ये वेणिभावने ।।172।।
छत्रे समर्थे पाणौ च रोमाल्यां भेरिवादने ।
कुलालचक्रभ्रमणे रथाङ्गमण्डले तथा ।।173।।
विवेचने दिनान्ते च सूचीहस्तः प्रकीर्तितः ।

Transliteration :

Ēkārthe-api parabrahmabhāvanāyāṃ śate-api ca |
Ravau nagaryāṃ lokārthe tatheti vacane-api ca ||

Yacchabde-api tacchabde vijanārthe-api tarjane |
Kārśye śalāke vapuṣi āścarye veṇibhāvane ||
Chatre samarthe pāṇau ca romālyāṃ bherivādane |
Kulālacakrabhramaṇe rathāṅgamaṇḍale tathā ||
Vivecane dinānte ca sūcīhastaḥ prakīrtitaḥ |

Meanings :

Ēka-arthe (api) = in the sence of one; parabrahma bhāvanāyāṃ = supreme being; śate (api-ca) = hundred; ravou = Sun; nagaryāṃ = city; loka-rthe = world; tathā-iti-vacane (api ca) - saying 'thus'; yat-śhabde (api) tat-śhabde = saying 'this' and 'that'; vijana-arthe (api) = deserted, solitude; tarjane = threatening; kārśye = emaciated; śalāke = twig/rod; vapushi = the body; āścarye = astonishment; veṇibhāvane = to braid hair; chatre = umbrella; samarthe = capability, pāṇou = hand; romālyāṃ = line of hair; bherivādane = beating the drum; kulāla cakra-bhramaṇe = turning of the potter's wheel; rathāngamaṇḍale (tathā) = circumference of a chariot wheel; vivecane = pondering; dina-ante (ca) = evening; sūcīhastaḥ, prakīrtitaḥ = in denoting the above, the use of Śucihasta is presrcibed.

चन्द्रकला हस्तः

Candrakalā hasta (Shape of a Crescent)

सूच्यामङ्गुष्ठमोक्षे तु करश्चन्द्रकला भवेत् ।।174।।

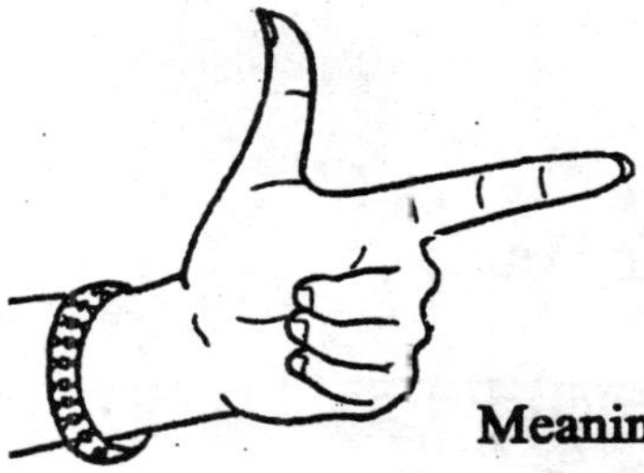

Transliteration

Sūcyāmaṅguṣṭhamokṣe tu karaścandrakalā bhavet ||

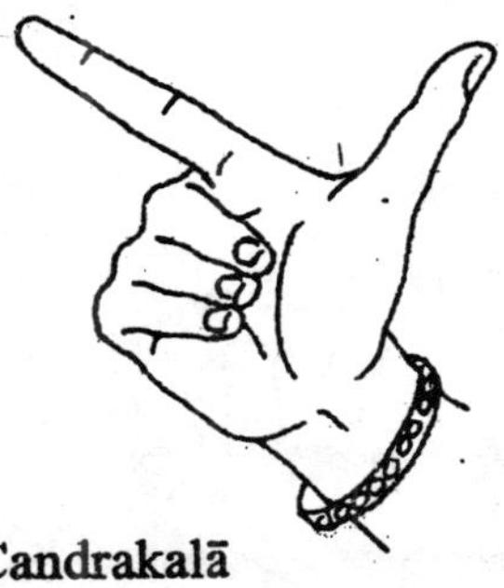

Meanings :

If the thumb of the Sūcī hasta is released wide apart, it becomes Candrakalā hasta (Candrakala = digit of the moon).

Candrakalā hasta is of two types;

(1) Stretching the thumb from *Sūcī* hasta is *Candrakalā*

(2) Stretching the middle finger, ring finger and little finger, perpendicular to index finger is *Candrakalā* hasta.

विनियोगः (Application)

चन्द्रे मुखे च प्रादेशे तन्मात्राकारवस्तुनि ।
शिवस्य मुकुटे गङ्गानद्यां च लगुडेऽपि च ।।175।।
एषां चन्द्रकला चैव विनियोज्या विधीयते ।

Transliteration :

Candre mukhe ca prādeśe tanmātrākāravastuni |
Śivasya mukuṭe gaṅgānadyāṃ ca laguḍe-api ca ||
Eṣām candrakalā caiva viniyojyā vidhīyate |

Meanings :

Candre = moon; mukhe = face; prādeśe = the distance between thumb and index finger; tanmātra-akāra vastuni = indicating a thing of the size between the tip of the forefinger and the thumb; śivasya mukuṭe = head ornament of śiva (half-moon); gaṅgānadyāṃ (ca) = river Ganga; laguḍe-(api ca) = cudgel; eshām, candrakalā (ca-êva), viniyojyā vidhīyate = to denote the above, the use of candrakalā hasta is prescribed.

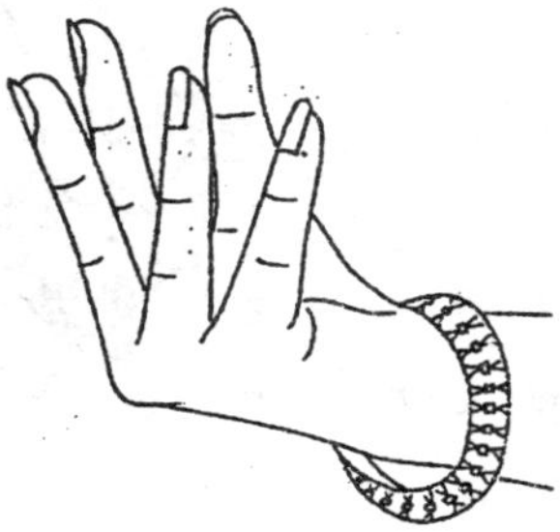

पद्मकोश हस्तः

Padmakośa hasta (Lotus bud)

अङ्गुल्यो विरला किञ्चित् कुञ्चितास्तलनिम्नगाः।।।176।।
पद्मकोशाभिधो हस्तस्तन्निरूपणमुच्यते ।।

Transliteration :

Aṅgulyo viralā kiñcit kuñcitāstalanimnagāḥ |
Padmakośābhidho hastastannirūpaṇamucyate ||

Meanings :

When all the five fingers are separated and slightly bent and the palm is hollow, it is Padmakośā hasta (Padmakośā = lotus bud).

विनियोगः (Application)

फले बिल्वकपित्थादौ स्त्रीणां च कुचकुम्भयोः ।।177।।
आवर्ते कन्दुके स्थाल्यां भोजने पुष्पकोरके ।
सहकारफले पुष्पवर्षे मञ्जरिकादिषु ।।178।।
जपाकुसुमभावे च घण्टारूपे विधानके ।।
वल्मीके कमलेऽप्यण्डे पद्मकोशो विधीयते।।179।।

Transliteration :

Phale bilvakapitthādau strīṇāṃ ca kucakumbhayoḥ |
Āvarte kanduke sthālyāṃ bhojane puṣpakorake ||
Sahakāraphale puṣpavarṣe mañjarikādiṣu |
Japākusumabhāve ca ghaṇṭārūpe vidhānake ||
Valmīke kamale-apyaṇḍe padmakośo vidhīyate |

Meanings :

Phale = fruit; bilva - kapittha - ādou = bel, woodapple etc; strīṇāṃ (ca) kuca - kumbhayoḥ = round breasts of women; āvarte = turning round or circular movement; kanduke = ball; sthālyāṃ = plate; bhojane = food; puṣpa - korake = flower bud; sahakāraphale = mango fruit; pushpavarshe = shower of flowers; mañjarika - ādishu = bouquet of flowers; japākusuma bhāve (ca) = hibiscus flower; ghaṇṭārūpe vidhānake = the shape of a bell; valmīke = snake - pit (anthill); kamale (api) = lotus; aṇḍe = egg; padmakośah vidhīyate = in denoting the above, padmakośa hasta is prescribed.

सर्पशीर्ष हस्तः

Sarpaśīrṣa hasta (Hood of a snake)

पताका नमिताग्रा चेत् सर्पशीर्षकरो भवेत् ।।

Transliteration :

Patākā namitāgrā cet sarpaśīrṣakaro bhavet ||

Meanings :

When the fingers of Patāka hand are bent at the tip, it is *Sarpaśīrṣa* hasta

विनियोगः (Application)

चन्दने भुजगे मन्द्रे प्रोक्षणे पोषणादिषु ।।180।।
देवस्योदकदानेषु आस्फाले गजकुम्भयोः ।
भुजस्थाने तु मल्लानां युज्यते सर्पशीर्षकः ।।181।।

Transliteration :

Candane bhujage mandre prokṣaṇe poṣaṇādiṣu |
Devasyodakadāneṣu āsphāle gajakumbhayoḥ ||
Bhujasthāne tu mallānāṃ yujyate sarpaśīrṣakaḥ |

Meanings :

Candane = sandal paste; bhujage = serpent; mandre = low tone; prokṣaṇe = sprinkling; poshaṇa - ādishu = nourishing or cherishing; devasya-udakadāneshu = offering of water to gods; āsphāle = pat; gaja - kumbhayoḥ = protuberance of elephant head; bhujasthāne = shoulders; (tu) mallānāṃ = wrestlers; sarpaśīrsha - karaḥ, yujyate = in denoting the above, sarpasīrśa hasta is used.

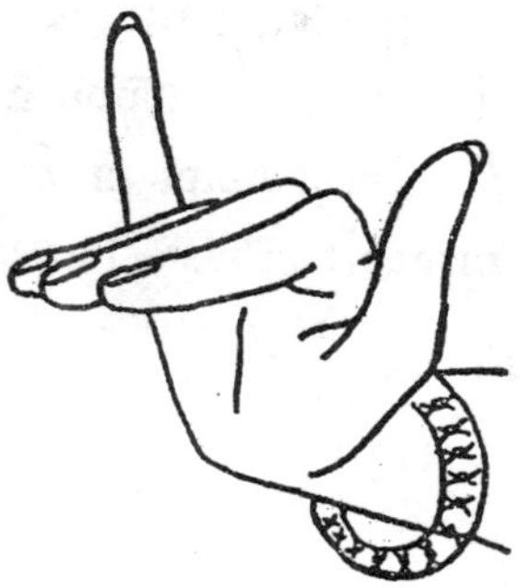

मृगशीर्ष हस्तः

Mṛgaśīrṣa hasta (Deer head)

अस्मिन् कनिष्ठिकाङ्गुष्ठे प्रसृते मृगशीर्षकः ।।182।।

Transliteration :

Asmin kaniṣṭhikāṅguṣṭhe prasṛte mṛgaśīrṣakāḥ ||

Meanings :

If the little and the thumb of the Sarpaśīrsha hasta are extended, it becomes mṛgaśīrsha hasta (mṛga-śīrsha = deer head).

विनियोगः (Application)

स्त्रीणामर्थे कपोले च चक्रमर्यादयोरपि ।
भीत्यां विवादे नेपथ्ये आह्वाने च त्रिपुण्ड्रके ।।183।।
मृगमुखे रङ्गवल्ल्यां पादसंवाहने तथा ।
सर्वस्वे मेलने काममन्दिरे छत्रधारणे।।184।।
सञ्चारे च प्रियाह्वाने युज्यते मृगशीर्षकः ।

Transliteration :

Strīṇāmarthe kapole ca cakramaryādayorapi |
Bhītyāṃ vivāde nepathye āhvāne ca tripuṇḍrake ||
Mṛgamukhe raṅgavallyāṃ pādasaṃvāhane tathā |
Sarvasammelane kāmamandire chatradhāraṇe ||
Sañcāre ca priyāhvāne yujyate mṛgaśīrṣakaḥ |

Meanings :

Strīṇām-arthe = to denote women; kapole (ca) = cheek; cakra = wheel; maryādayoh (api) = being courteous; bhītyāṃ = fear; vivāde = quarrel or argument; nepathye = background; āhvāne (ca) = welcoming; tripuṇḍrake - three lines of vibhūti (applied on forehead); mṛgamukhe = face of a deer; raṅgamallyām

= drawing patterns on the ground; pādasaṃvāhane (tathā) = massage of the feet; sarwasammelane = grouping all; kāma mandire = female reproductive organ; chatradhāraṇe = holding an umbrella; sañcāre (ca) =roaming; priya - āhvāne = to beckon a loved one; yujyate mṛgaśīrṣakaḥ = in denoting the above, mṛgaśīrṣa hasta has to be used.

सिंहमुख हस्तः

Simhamukha hasta (Lion-face)

मध्यमानामिकाग्राभ्यामङ्गुष्ठो मिश्रितो यदि ।।185।।
शेषौ प्रसारितौ यत्र स सिंहास्यकरो भवेत् ।

Transliteration :

Madhyamānāmikāgrābhyāmaṅguṣṭho miśrito yadi ||
Śeṣau prasāritau yatra sa siṃhāsyakaro bhavet |

Meanings :

When the tips of the middle finger and the ring finger are placed on the thumb and the rest are extended, it becomes Simhamukha hasta.

विनियोगः (Application)

होमे शशे गजे दर्भ चलने पद्मदामनि ।।186।।
सिंहानने वैद्यपाके शोधने संप्रयुज्यते ।

Transliteration :

Home śaśe gaje darbha calane padmadāmani ||
Siṃhānane vaidyapāke śodhane samprayujyate |

Meanings :

Home = sacrificial offering; śaśe = hare; gaje = elephant; darbha calane = movement of kusa grass; padmadāmani = lotus garland; siṃha - ānane = lion's face; vaidya - pāka sodhane = testing the preparation of medicine; samprayujyate = are the uses.

काङ्गुल हस्तः
Kāṅgula hasta (Long pepper)

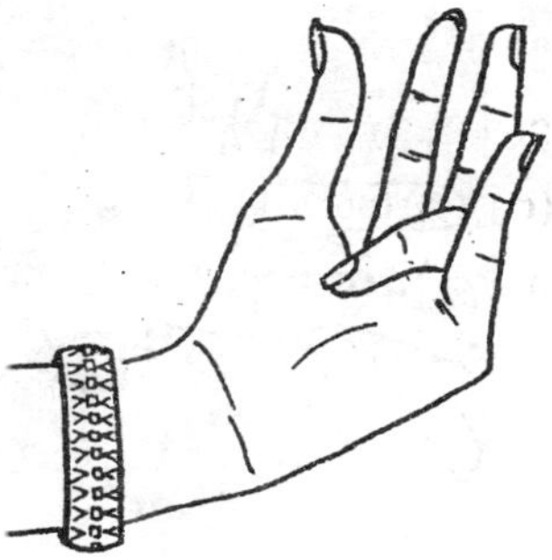

पद्मकोशेऽनामिका चेन्नभ्रा काङ्गुलहस्तकः ।।187।।

Transliteration :

Padmakośe'nāmikā cennabhrā kāṅgulahastakaḥ ||

Meanings :

If the ring finger of Padmakośa hasta is bent, it becomes Kāṅgula hasta.

विनियोगः (Application)

लकुचस्य फले बालकिंकिण्यां घण्टिकार्थके ।
चकोरे क्रमुके बालकुचे कह्लारके तथा ।।188।।
चातके नालिकेरे च काङ्गुलो युज्यते करः ।

Transliteration :

Lakucasya phale bālakiṅkiṇyāṃ ghaṇṭikārthake |
Cakore kramuke bālakuce kalhārake tathā ||
Cātake nālikere ca kāṅgulo yujyate karaḥ |

Meanings :

Lakucasya phale = bunch of grapes; bālakiṅkiṇyāṃ = little bells. ghaṇṭikārthake = ringing bell, cakore = Patridge; kramuke = betel-nut tree; bālakuce = bosoms of young maiden; kalhārake (tathā) = water lily; cātake = Sparrow; nālikere (ca) = coconut tree; kāṅgulo yujyate karaḥ = uses of kāṅgula hasta.

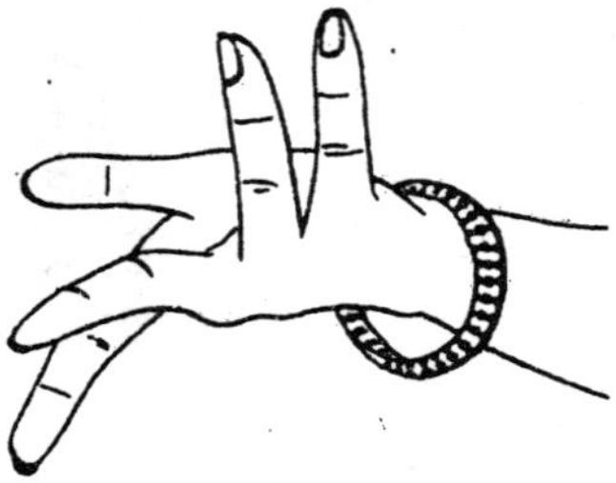

अलपद्म हस्तः
Alapadma hasta (Full bloomed lotus)

कनिष्ठाद्या वक्रिताश्च विरलाश्चालपद्मकः ।।189।।

Transliteration :

Kaniṣṭhādyā vakritāśca viralāścālapadmakaḥ ||

Meanings :

If all the fingers are separated and stretched towards the palm, it becomes Alapadma hasta (Alapadma or Solapadma=full-blown lotus).

विनियोगः (Application)

विकचाब्जे कपित्थआदिफले चावर्तके कुचे ।
विरहे मुकुरे पूर्णचन्द्रे सौन्दर्यभावने ।।190।।
धम्मिल्ले चंद्रशालायां ग्रामे चोद्धृतकोपयोः ।
तटाके शकटे चक्रवाके कलकलारवे।।191।।
श्लाघने सोऽलपद्मश्च कीर्तितो भरतागमे ।

Transliteration :

Vikacābje kapitthaādiphale cāvartake kuce |
Virahe mukure pūrṇacandre saundaryabhāvane ||
Dhammille candraśālāyāṃ grāme coddhṛtakopayoḥ |
Taṭāke śakaṭe cakravāke kalakalārave ||
Ślāghane so-alapadmaśca kīrtito bharatāgame |

Meanings :

Vikaca-abje = full blown lotus; kapittha-ādiphale = woodapple etc; āvartake = circular movement;

kuce = breast; virahe = yearning for the beloved; mukure = mirror; pūrṇa-candre = full-moon, saundaryabhāvane = thinking about beauty; dhammille = hair - knot; candraśālāyāṃ = marble pavilion/ moonlit tower; grāme (api) = village; uddhṛta kopayoḥ = bristling anger; taṭāke = lake; śakaṭe = cart; cakravāke = Chakravaka bird; kala kalā rave = cooing; ślāghane = praise; solapadmah (ca) kīrtito bharata āgame = in denoting the above, Alapadma hasta is prescribed by Bharata.

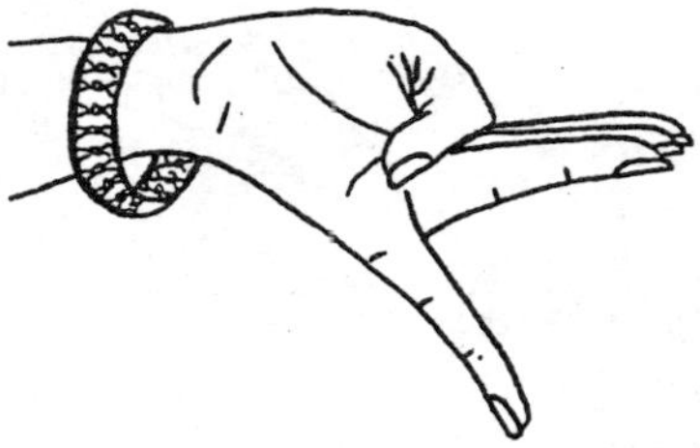

चतुर हस्तः

Catura hasta (square)

तर्जन्याद्यास्तत्र श्लिष्टाः कनिष्ठा प्रसृता यदि ।।192।।
अङ्गुष्ठोऽनामिकामूले तिर्यक् चेच्चतुरः करः।

Transliteration :

Tarjanyādyāstatra śliṣṭāḥ kaniṣṭhā prasṛtā yadi ||
Aṅguṣṭho-nāmikāmūle tiryak ceccaturaḥ karaḥ |

Meanings :

When forefinger, middle finger and ring finger are close to one another and stretched, the little finger is extended separately and the thumb is bent obliquely to touch the base of the ring finger, it becomes Catura hasta.

विनियोगः (Application)

कस्तूर्यां किञ्चिदर्थे च स्वर्णे ताम्रे च लोहके ।।193।।
आर्द्रे खेदे रसास्वादे लोचने वर्णभेदने ।
प्रमाणे सरसे मन्दगमने शकलीकृते ।।194।।
आनने घृततैलादौ युज्यते चतुरः करः।

Transliteration :

Kastūryāṃ kincidarthe ca svarṇe tāmre ca lohake ||
Ārdre khede rasāsvāde locane varṇabhedane |

Pramāṇe sarase mandagamane śakalīkṛte ||
Ānane ghṛtatailādau yujyate caturaḥ karaḥ |

Meanings :

Kastūryāṃ = musk; kincit - arthe = meaning a little; svarṇe - tāmre (ca) - lohake - gold, copper, iron and other metals; ārdre = compassion; khede = sorrow; rasa-āsvāde = experience of aesthetic pleasure; locane = eyes; varṇa-bhedane = differentiating colours or castes; pramāṇe = oath; sarase = playful, teasing; mandagamane = slow walking, śakalīkṛte = breaking to pieces; ānane = face; ghṛta - taila-ādou = ghee, oil, etc; caturaḥ karaḥ yujyate = in denoting the above, catura hasta is used.

भ्रमर हस्तः

Bhramara hasta (Bumblebee)

मध्यमाङ्गुष्ठसंयोगे तर्जनी वक्रिताकृतिः ।।195।।
शेषाः प्रसारिताश्चसौ भ्रमराभिधहस्तकः ।

Transliteration :

Madhyamāṅguṣṭhasaṃyoge tarjanī vakritākṛtiḥ ||
Śeṣāḥ prasāritāścāsau bhramarābhidhahastakaḥ |

Meanings :

When the middle finger and the thumb meet each other, the forefinger is bent and the ring finger and the little finger are stretched, it becomes Bhramara hasta.

विनियोगः (Application)

भ्रमरे च शुके पक्षे सारसे कोकिलादिषु ।।196।।
भ्रमराख्याश्च हस्तो-अयं कीर्तितो भरतागमे ।

Transliteration :

Bhramare ca śuke pakṣe sārase kokilādiṣu ||
Bhramarākhyāśca hasto'yaṃ kīrtito bharatāgame |

Meanings :

Bhramare (ca) = bumblebee; śuke = parrots; pakṣe = wings of a bird; sārase = cranes; kokila-ādiṣu = cuckoos etc; bhramara ākhyāśca hasto-ayaṃ = in denoting the above, this bhramara hasta; kīrtito bharata-āgame = is prescribed by Bharata.

हंसास्य हस्तः

Hamsāsya hasta (Swan face)

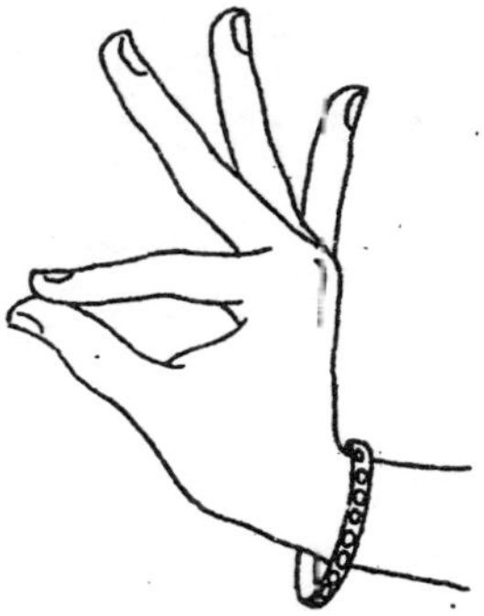

मध्यमाद्यास्त्रयोङ्गुल्यः प्रसृता विरला यदि ।।197।।
तर्जन्यङ्गुष्ठसंश्लेषात् करो हंसास्यको भवेत् ।

Transliteration :

Madhyamādyāstrayoṅgulyaḥ prasṛtā viralā yadi ||
Tarjanyaṅguṣṭhasaṃśleṣāt karo haṃsāsyako bhavet |

Meanings :

When the three fingers i.e. middle, ring and little finger are separated and extended, the tips of the forefinger and the thumb joined, then it becomes Haṃsāsya hasta.

विनियोगः (Application)

माङ्गल्ये सूत्रबन्धे च उपदेशविनिश्चये।।198।।
रोमाञ्चे मौक्तिकादौ च दीपवर्तिप्रसारणे ।
निकषे मल्लिकादौ च चित्रे तल्लेखने तथा।।199।।
दंशे च जलबन्धे च हंसास्यो युज्यते करः ।

Transliteration :

Māṅgalye sūtrabandhe ca upadeśaviniścaye ||
Romānce mauktikādau ca dīpavartiprasāraṇe |
Nikaṣe mallikādau ca citre tallekhane tathā ||
Daṃśe ca jalabandhe ca haṃsāsyo yujyate karaḥ |

Meanings :

Māṅgalye = auspicious; sūtrabandhe (ca) = tying a holy thread; upadeśa = advice; viniścaye = certainty; romānce = horripulation; mauktika-ādau (ca) = pearl etc dīpavarti - prasāraṇe = extending the wick of a lamp; nikashe = rubbing on the touch-stone; mallika - ādau (ca) = jasmine flower etc, citre = picture; tad-lekhane = painting of a picture; daṃśe (ca) = bite; jalabandhe (ca) = dam; haṃsāsya yujyate karaḥ = in denoting the above, Hamsāsya hasta is used.

हंसपक्ष हस्तः

Hamsapakṣa hasta (Swan's wing)

सर्पशीर्षकरे सम्यक् कनिष्ठा प्रसृता यदि ।।200।।
हंसपक्षः करः सोऽयं तन्निदृ पणमुच्यते ।

Transliteration :

Sarpaśīrṣakare samyak kaniṣṭhā prasṛtā yadi ||
Haṃsapakṣaḥ karaḥ so-yaṃ tannirūpaṇamucyate |

Meanings :

When the little finger of Sarpaśīrsha hasta is extended, it becomes Hamsapaksha (swan-wing) hasta.

विनियोगः (Application)

षट्संख्यायां सेतुबन्धे नखरेखाङ्कणे तथा ।।201।।
पिधाने हंसपक्षोऽयं कथितो भरतागमे ।

Transliteration :

Ṣaṭsaṅkhyāyāṃ setubandhe nakharekhāṅkaṇe tathā ||
Pidhaāne haṃsapakṣo-ayaṃ kathito bharatāgame |

Meanings :

Ṣaṭ-saṅkhyāyāṃ = number six; setubandhe = constructing a bridge; nakharekhāṅkaṇe (tatha) =

making marks with the nails; pidhāne = closed, haṃsapaksohyaṃ kathito bharatāgame = in denoting the above, Hamsapakṣa hasta has to be used, according to Bharata.

सन्दंश हस्तः

Sandaṃśa hasta (Pincers)

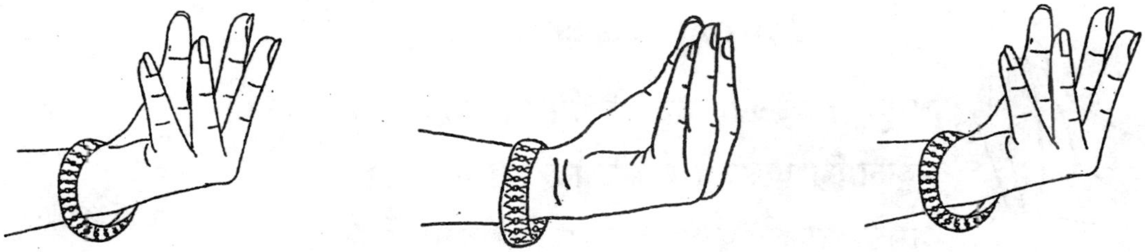

पुनः पुनः पद्मकोशः संश्लिष्टो विरलो यदि ।।202।।
सन्दंशाभिधहस्तोऽयं कीर्तितो नृत्यकोविदैः ।

Transliteration :

Punaḥ punaḥ padmakośaḥ saṃśliṣṭo viralo yadi ||
Sandaṃśābhidhahasto-ayaṃ kīrtito nṛtyakovidaiḥ |

Meanings :

When in the Padmakosa hasta, fingers close and open-up partly in a repeated manner, the gesture is described as *Sandamśa.*

विनियोगः (Application)

उदरे बलिदाने च व्रणे कीटे महाभये ।।203।।
अर्चने पञ्चसंख्यायां सन्दंशाख्यो नियुज्यते ।

Transliteration :

Udare balidāne ca vraṇe kīṭe mahābhaye ||
Arcane pañcasaṅkhyāyāṃ sandaṃśākhyo niyujyate |

Meanings :

Udare = stomach; balidāne (ca) = sacrificial offerings; vraṇe = a cyst; kīṭe = insect; mahābhaye = great fear; arcane = worship; pañca-saṅkhyāyāṃ = to denote the number-5; samdaṃśa-ākhyah, niyujyate = in denoting the above, sandamśa hasta is used.

मुकुल हस्तः

Mukula hasta (Bud)

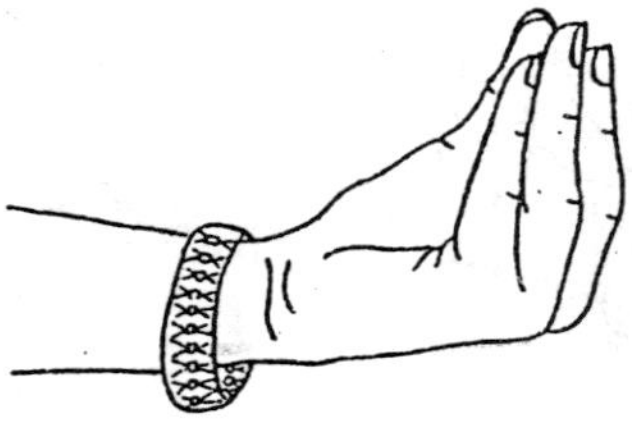

अङ्गुलीपञ्चकं चैव मेलयित्वा प्रदर्शने ।।204।।
मुकुलाभिधहस्तोऽयं कीर्त्यते भरतागमे ।
कुमुदे भोजने पञ्चबाणे मुद्रादिधारणे ।।205।।
नामौ च कदलीपुष्पे युज्यते मुकुलः करः ।

Transliteration :

Aṅgulīpañcakaṃ caiva melayitvā pradarśane ||
Mukulābhidhahasto-ayaṃ kīrtyate bharatāgame |
Kumude bhojane pañcabāṇe mudrādidhāraṇe ||
Nāmau ca kadalīpuṣpe yujyate mukulaḥ karaḥ |

Meanings :

When all the five fingers are joined together at the tips, it becomes Mukula hasta (mukula = bud).

विनियोगः (Application)

कुमुदे भोजने पञ्चबाणे मुद्रादिधारणे ।।206।।
नाभौ च कदलीपुष्पे युज्यते मुकुलः करः।

Transliteration :

Kumude bhojane pañcabāṇe mudrādidhāraṇe ||
Nābhau ca kadalīpuṣpe yujyate mukulaḥ karaḥ |

Meanings :

Kumude = water - lily; bhojane = eating; pañcabāṇe = five arrows/cupid; mudra - ādi- dhāraṇe = seal with symbol (or) holding or wearing the signet or seal (religious or ornamental); nābhau (ca) = navel; kadalī - puṣpe = plantain flower; mukuḷaḥ karaḥ yujyate = in denoting the above, mukula hasta is used.

ताम्रचूड हस्तः

Tāmracūḍa hasta (Rooster)

मुकुले ताम्रचूडः स्यात्तर्जनी चक्रिता यदि ।।207।।

Transliteration :

Mukule tāmracūḍaḥ syāttarjanī cakritā yadi ||

Meanings :

If the forefinger of Mukula hasta is curved it becomes Tāmracūḍa hasta.

विनियोगः (Application)

कुक्कुटादौ बके काके उष्ट्रे वत्से च लेखने।
युज्यते ताम्रचूडाख्यः करो भरतवेदिभिः।।208।।

Transliteration :

Kukkuṭādau bake kāke uṣṭre vatse ca lekhane |
Yujyate tāmraccūḍākhyaḥ karo bharatavedibhiḥ ||

Meanings :

Kukkuṭa-ādau = rooster etc; bake = crane; kāke = crow; ushṭre = camel; vatse (ca) = calf; lekhane = writing; yujyate tāmracūḍā (akhyah), karo bharatavedibhiḥ = in denoting the above, ṭāmracūḍa hasta is prescribed by Bharata.

त्रिशूल हस्तः

Triśūla hasta (Trident)

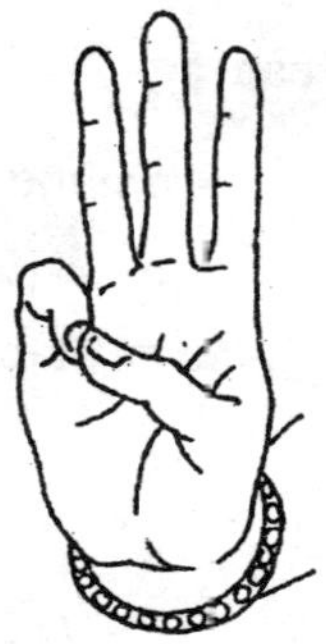

निकुच्चनयुताङ्गुष्ठकनिष्ठस्तु त्रिशूलकः ।

Transliteration :

Nikuccanayutāṅguṣṭhakaniṣṭhastu triśūlakaḥ |

If the thumb and the little finger of Patāka hasta are curved, it becomes Triśūla hasta (Triśūla = trident).

विनियोगः (Application)

बिल्वपत्रे त्रित्वयुक्ते त्रिशूलकर ईरितः।।209।।

Transliteration :

Bilvapatre tritvayukte triśūlakara īritaḥ ||

Meanings :

Bilva-patre = bilva leaf; tritva-yukte = number 3 or trinity, triśūlakara īritaḥ = in denoting the above, triśūla hasta is prescribed.

व्याघ्र हस्तः

Vyāghra hasta (Tiger)

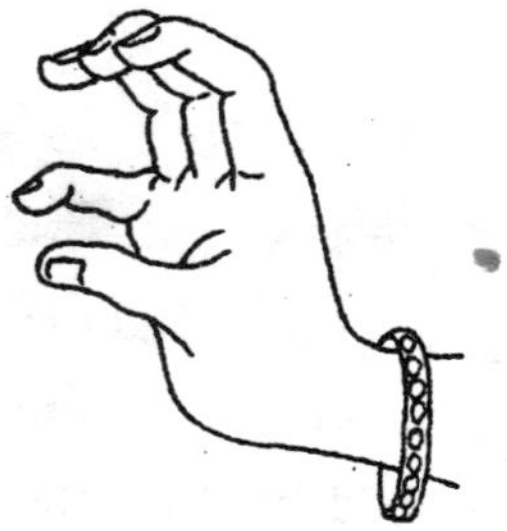

कनिष्टाङ्गुष्ठा नामाने मृगशीर् करे तथा ।
व्याघ्र हस्तः स विज्ञेयो भरतागम कोविदैः ।।210।।

Transliteration :

Kaniṣṭāguṣṭhā nāmāne mṛgaśīr kare tathā |
Vyāghra hastaḥ sa vijñeyo bharatāgama kovidaiḥ ||

Meanings :

When in the sarpaśirṣa mudra the little finger and thumb are brought forward it is *Vyāghra* hasta.

विनियोगः (Application)

व्याघ्रे भेके मर्कटे च शुक्तौ संयुज्यते करः ।

Transliteration :

Vyāghre bheke markaṭe ca śuktau saṃyujyate karaḥ |

Meanings :

Vyāghre = tiger; bheke = frog; markaṭe (ca) = monkey; śūkte = pearl shell; saṃyujyate karaḥ = in denoting the above; Vyāghra hasta is used.

अर्धसूची हस्तः

Ardhasūcī hasta (Half - needle)

कपित्थे तर्जनी ऊर्ध्वासरणेत्वार्धसूचिकः ।।211।।

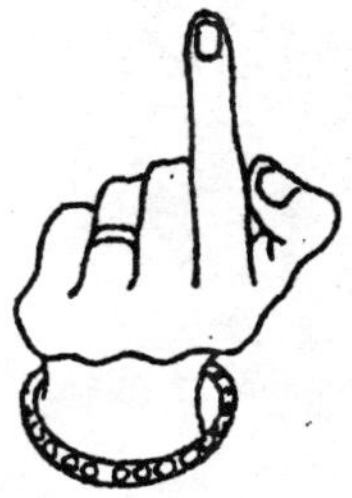

Transliteration :

Kapitthe tarjanī ūrdhvāsaraṇetvārdhasūcikaḥ ||

Meanings :

When the thumb in suci is placed in the middle of index finger, it is *Ardhasūcī* hasta.

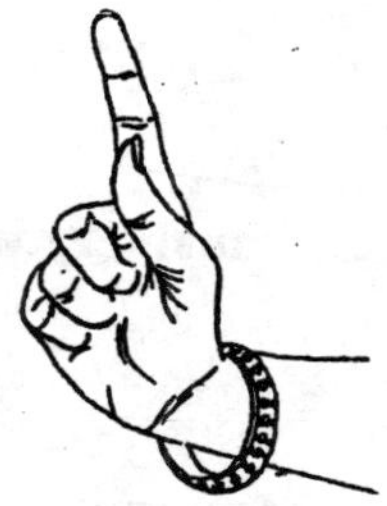

विनियोगः (Application)

अङ्कुरे पक्षिशावादौ बृहत्कीटे नियुज्यते ।

Transliteration :

Aṅkure pakṣiśavādau bṛhatkīṭe niyujyate |

Meanings :

Aṅkure = sprout; pakṣī - śāva - ādau = young bird etc; bṛhatkīṭe = large insect; niyujyate = to denote the above ardhasūcī hasta is used.

कटक हस्तः

Kaṭaka hasta (Bracelet)

संदंशेऽप्यूद्ध्वं भागे तु मध्यमानामिकान्वयात् ।।212।।
.... कटको हस्तो उच्यते ।

Transliteration :

Sandaṃśe-apyūrddhva bhāge tu madhyamānāmikānavāyāt |
.... kaṭako hasto ucyate ||

Meanings :

In the patāka hasta if the thumb, middle finger, and ring finger are bent and moved towards the palm it is known as *Kaṭaka.*

विनियोगः (Application)

एतस्य विनियोगस्तु...............दर्शने।।213।।
आह्वानभावचलने.........।

Transliteration :

Etasya viniyogastu...............darśane ||
Āhvānabhāva calane........... |

Meanings :

Etasya viniyogaḥ (tu)...............darśane āhvāne bhāva calane = it is used to denote seeing, calling a person and moving.

*The verse is left incomplete due to loss in the text of the original manuscript.

पल्लि हस्तः

Palli hasta (Small village)

मयूरे तर्जनीपृष्ठो मध्यमेन युतो यदि ।।214।।

Transliteration :

Mayūre tarjanīpṛṣṭho madhyamena yuto yadi ||

Meanings :

In Mayura hasta when the index finger is placed in front of the middle finger it is *Palli* hasta.

विनियोगः (Application)

पल्लिहस्तः स विज्ञेयः पल्ल्यर्थे विनियुज्यते।

Transliteration :

Pallihastaḥ saḥ vijñeyaḥ Pallyarthe viniyujyate |

Meanings :

It is used to denote a village or hut.

अभिनयवशादेशां संयुतत्वं प्रकीर्तित् ।
मार्गप्रदर्शनं तेषां क्रमाल्लक्ष्यानुसारतः ।।215।।

Transliteration :

Abhinayavaśādeśāṃ saṃyutatvaṃ prakīrtit |
Mārgapradarśanaṃ teṣāṃ kramāllakṣyānusārataḥ ||

Meanings :

The single hand gestures become double hand gestures depending on the necessity in abhinayam. Their essential characteristic will now be explained in order.

*ऊर्णनाभ हस्तः

Ūrṇanābha hasta (Spider)

पद्मकोषाङ्गुलीनाम च कुंचनात् ऊर्णनाभकः ।

Transliteration :

Padmakoṣāṅgulīnāma ca kuñcanāt ūrṇanābhakaḥ |

Meanings :

When all the fingers of Padmakoṣā hasta are curved it is *Ūrṇanābha* hasta.

हस्ताभ्याम् कुर्वतः पूर्वम् दैत्यवक्षो विदारणम् ।।216।।
नृसिंहात् ऊर्णनाभश्च जटः शार्दूलकोऋषिः ।
क्षत्रान्वयो रक्तकान्तिः आदिकूर्मो अधि देवता ।।217।।

Transliteration :

Hastābhyām kurvataḥ pūrvam daityavakṣo vidāraṇām ||
Nṛsiṃhāt ūrṇanābhaśca jaṭaḥ śārdūlakoṛṣiḥ |
Kṣatrānvayo raktakāntiḥ ādikūrmo adhi devatā ||

Meanings :

Ūrṇanābha hasta originated from Narasimha when he tore apart the chest of Hiraṇyakaśipu. It's sage is Śārdūla, it belongs to Kṣatriya race, its color is red and its presiding deity is Ādikūrma

विनियोगः (Application)

शीरः कन्दूयाने चौर्ये नरसिंम्हे मृगानने ।
हार्यक्षे वानरे कूर्मे कार्णिकारे कुचे भये ।।218।।
क्षत्रजातौ रक्तकांता-वूर्णनाभो नियुज्यते ।

Transliteration :

Śīrāḥ kandūyāne caurye narasimhe mṛganāne |
Hāryakshe vānare kūrme kārṇikāre kuce bhāye ||
Kshatrājātau raktakāntā-ūrṇanābho niyujyate |

Meanings :

Śīrāḥ kandūyāne = scratching the head; caurye = theft; narasimhe = Narasimha; mṛgānane = face of an animal; hāryakshe = lion; vānare = monkey; kūrme = tortoise; kārṇikāre = pericarp of a lotus; kuce = breast; bhaye = fear; kshatrajātaou = kshatriya race; rakta - kāntā = blood red; ūrṇanābho niyujyate = in denoting the above, ūrṇanābha hasta is used.

*बाण हस्तः

Bāṇa hasta (Arrow)

तर्जन्याद्याछ त्रयः श्लिष्टः किंचित् अङ्गुष्ठ पीडिताः ।।219।।
कनिष्ठिका च प्रसृता बाणः कथितः करः।

Transliteration :

Tarjanyādyācha trayaḥ śliṣṭaḥ Kiñcit aṅguṣṭha pīḍitāḥ ||
Kaniṣṭhikā ca prasṛtā bāṇaḥ kathitaḥ karaḥ |

Meanings :

In the muśṭi hasta when the little finger is stretched up, it is *Bāṇa* hasta.

विनियोगः (Application)

षट्संख्यायाम् नालनृत्ये बाणहस्तो नियुज्यते ।।220।।

Transliteration :

Shaṭsaṅkhyāyām nālanṛtye Bāṇahasto niyujyate ||

Meanings :

Shaṭ-saṅkhyāyām = number six; nālanṛtye = graceful sway of a lotus stalk; bāṇahasta, niyujyate = in denoting the above, Bāṇahasta is used.

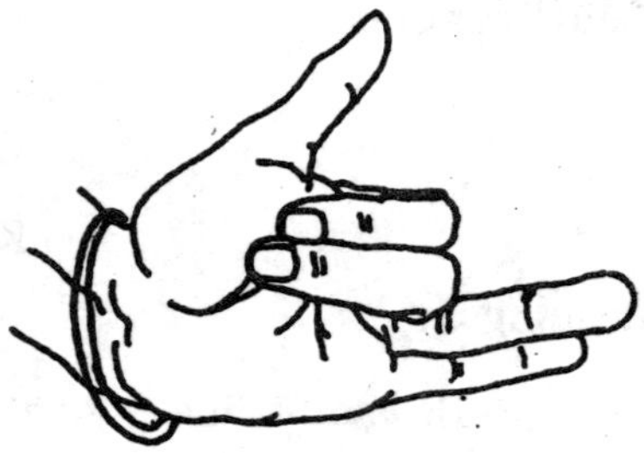

*संयम हस्त

Saṃyama hasta (Self Controlled)

तर्जनीमध्यमौ हस्त-तले नम्रीकृतौ यदि ।
इतरौ प्रसृतौ सोऽअयम् करः संयम्नामकः ।।221।।

Transliteration :

Tarjanīmadhyamau hasta-tale namrīkṛtau yadi |
Itarau prasṛtau so-ayam karaḥ saṃyamanāmakaḥ ||

Meanings :

If the forefinger and the middle finger are bent towards the palm and the other fingers are extended, it is samyama hasta.

विनियोगः (Application)

प्रणायामे महायोगे युज्यते च-आर्यभावने ।

Transliteration :

Praṇāyāme mahāyoge yujyate ca-āryabhāvane |

Meanings :

Praṇāyāme mahāyoge, āryabhāvane (ca) yujyate = in denoting prāṇāyāma, practice of yoga and saying 'the honorable', this hasta is used.

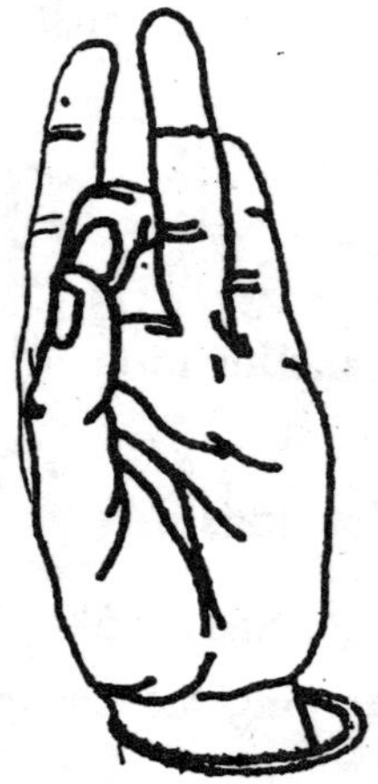

*मुद्र हस्त

Mudra hasta (Symbol)

कार्योः मध्य-माङ्गुष्ठे योगात मुद्राकरो भवेत् ।।222।।

Transliteration :

Kāryoḥ madhya-māṅguṣṭhe yogāt mudrākaro bhavet ||

Meanings :

When the thumbs and the middle fingers meet, in both hands, then it is Mudrā hasta.

अणौ तृणे गोमुखे च त्रोटीपुट निदर्शने ।
मुद्रा हस्तो युज्यतेऽसौ भरतागम कोविदैः ।।223।।

विनियोगः (Application)

Transliteration :

Aṇau tṛṇe gomukhe ca trotipuṭa nidarśane.
Mudrā hasto yujyate'asau bharatāgama kovidaiḥ ||

Meanings :

Kāryoḥ, madhya-māṅguṣṭha yogāt, mudrakaraḥ, bhavet = when the tips of the thumb and the middle finger are joined, in both hands, then it is Mudra hasta.

Anau, tṛṇe gomukhe (ca) troṭīpuṭa nidarśane = atom, grass, cow's face, beak of a bird; asou, mudrā hastaḥ, bharatāgama kovidaiḥ, yujyate = in denoting the above, Mudrā hasta is used by the experts on nāṭya śāśtra.

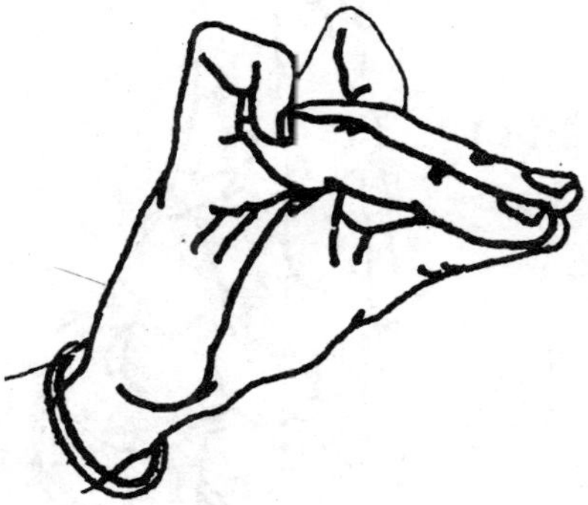

*अजामुख हस्त

Ajāmukha hasta (Goat Face)

सिंम्हाननाभिधकरे तर्जनी च कनिष्ठिका ।
मध्यमानामिका पृष्ठे योगात्-भूयात् अजामुखः ।।224।।

Transliteration :

Simmhānanābhidhakare tarjanī ca kaniṣṭhikā |
Madhyamānāmikā pṛṣṭhe yogāt-bhūyāt ajāmukhaḥ ||

Meanings :

When the forefinger and the little finger of Simhamukha hasta are placed at the back of the middle finger and the ring finger, respectively, it becomes Ajāmukha hasta.

विनियोग: (Application)

अजादिकानाम् वक्त्रेषु निर्विषाण मुखेषु च ।
गजकुम्भे मल्लयुद्धे अजवक्त्रो नियुज्यते ।।225।।

Transliteration :

Ajādikānām vaktreṣu nīrviṣāṇa mukheṣu ca |
Gajakumbhe mallayuddhe ajavaktro niyujyate ||

Meanings :

Aja-ādikānām vaktreshu, nīrviṣāṇa mukheṣu (ca), gajakumbhe, mallayuddhe = the faces of goat etc., the faces of animals without horns, elephant's kumbhasthalam, wrestling; ajāvaktraḥ niyujyate = in denoting the above, Ajāmukha hasta is used.

*अर्धमुकुल हस्त
Ardhamukula hasta

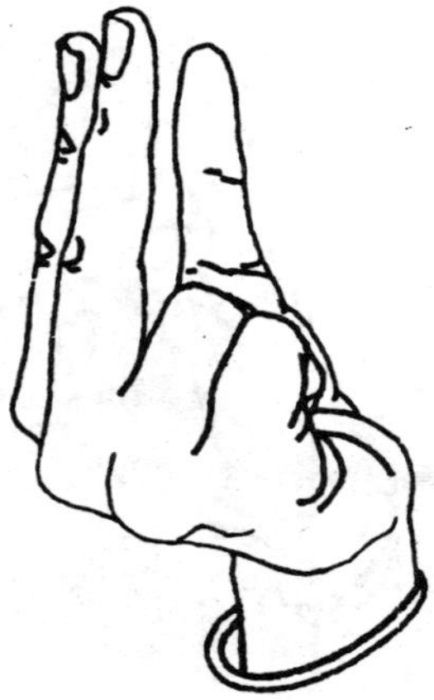

लांगूलाख्य करे संयक् कनिष्ठ वक्रिता यदि ।
प्रोक्तो-अर्धमुकुलाख्यो-असौ भरतागम वेदिभिः ।।226।।

Transliteration :

Lāṅgūlākhya kare saṃyak kaniṣṭha vakritā yadi |
Prokto-ardhamukulākhyo-asau bharatāgama vedibhiḥ ||

Meanings :

If the little finger of the Lāngūla hasta is bent well, then it becomes Ardhamukula hasta.

विनियोगः (Application)

लिकुचे शीलभवे चाप्युचितेऽअपि कुचेऽअपि च ।
लोभे मुकुलपद्मे च करणे विनियुज्यते ।।227।।

Transliteration :

Likuce śīlabhāve cāpyucite'api kuce'api ca |
Lobhe mukulapadme ca karaṇe viniyujyate ||

Meanings :

Likuce, śīlabhave (ca), (api) ucite, (api) kuce, (api-ca) lobhe, mukula padme (ca) karaṇe viniyujyate = in denoting likuca fruit, good character, appropriateness, breast, stinginess, lotus bud, tool - this hasta is used.

*ब्रह्मोक्तषुकटुण्ड हस्त
Brahmoktaṣukaṭuṇḍa hasta

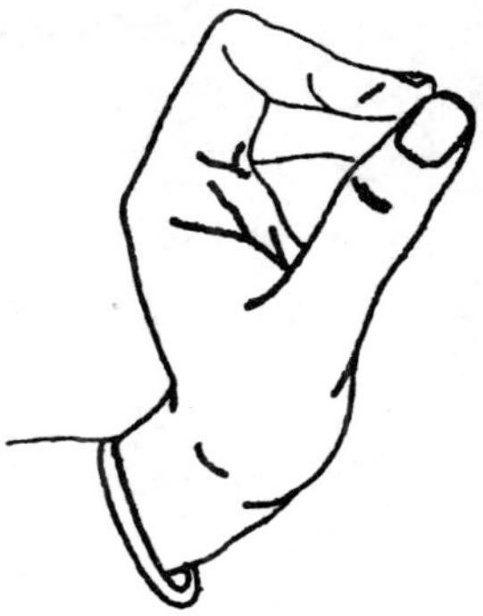

कपित्थे-अंगुष्ठ-तर्जन्यौ समानाग्रौ धृतौ यदि।
ब्रह्मोक्त शुकतुन्डः स्यात् गरुडार्थे नियुज्यते ।।228।।

Transliteration :

Kapitthe-aṃguṣṭha-tarjanyau samānāgrau dhṛtau yadi |
Brahmokta ṣukatunḍaḥ syāt garuḍārthe niyujyate ||

Meanings :

Yadi, kapitthe, aṃguṣṭha - tarjanyau, samāna - agrau, dhṛtau = if the tip of the thumb and the fore finger of Kapitha hasta are held on the same level; brahma-ukta ṣukatundhaḥ syāt = then it becomes Brahmokta ṣukatundha hasta.

Garuḍa-ārthe, niyujyate = this hasta denotes Garuḍa.

When the tips of the thumb and the forefinger of the Kapitha hasta are held on the same level, then it is Brahṃokta sukatundha hasta. This hasta denotes Garuḍa.

*त्रिलिंग हस्तः

Triliṇga hasta

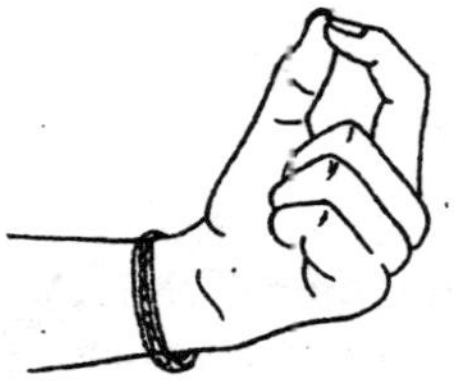

When the index finger and thumb join at the tip, and middle finger, ring finger and little finger fold into the palm, it is described as *Trilinga.*

*रेखाचंद्र हस्तः

Rekhācandra hasta (Rays of the moon)

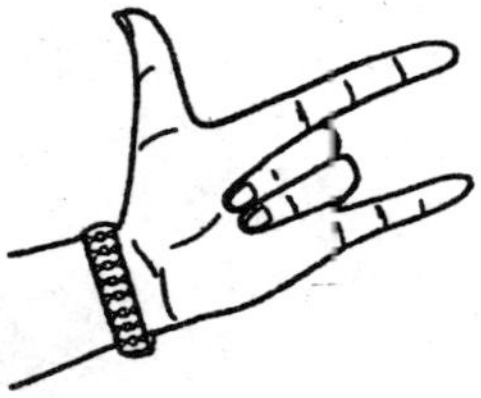

When the middle and ring finger of ardhacandra are folded towards the palm it is called *Rekhācandra* hasta.

*ब्रह्मशुकतुण्ड हस्तः

Brahma Śukatuṇda hasta

When the ḷittle finger and ring finger are pointed straight and the index finger and middle finger are folded towards the palm and over the thumb, it is *Brahma śukatuṇadam.*

*अर्ध मुष्ठी हस्तः

Ardha muśṭi hasta (Half fist)

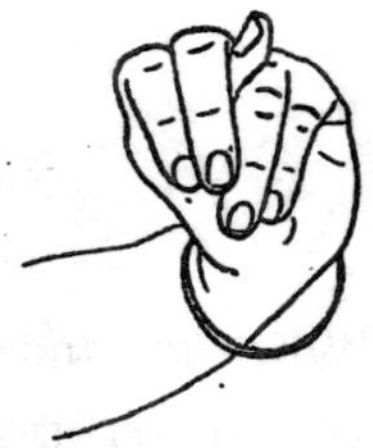

In the muśti hasta when the thumb is placed between the middle finger and the ring finger, it is *Ardha muśṭi.*

*चिलिट भ्रमर हस्तः

Ciliṭa bhramara hasta (Variation of bhramari)

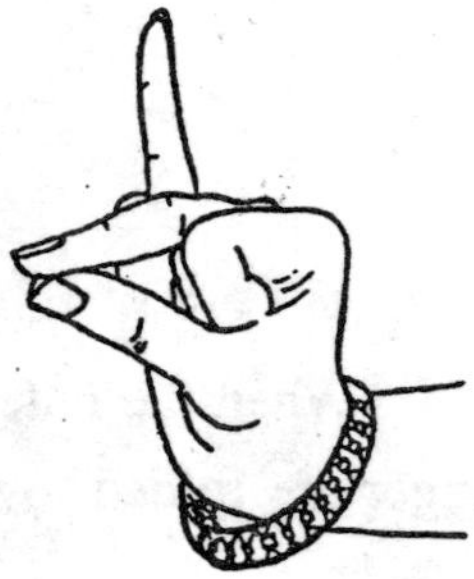

In the bhramara hasta when the ring finger is folded in towards the palm it is *Cilita bhramara.*

*चिलिट कपित्थ हस्तः

Ciliṭa kapittha hasta (Variation of kapittha)

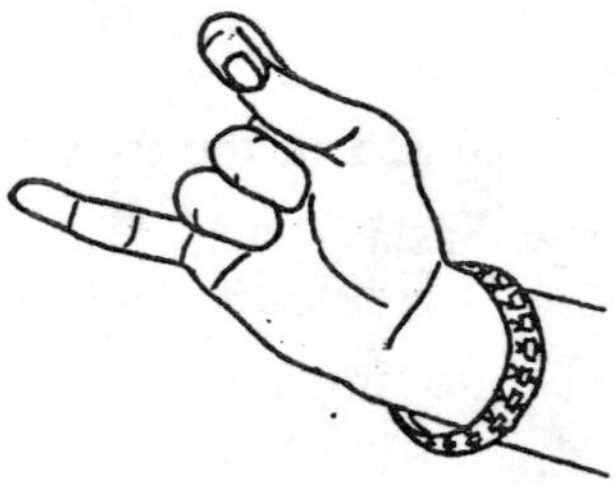

In kapittha hasta when the little finger is raised it is *Cilita Kapittham.*

*वर्धमानक हस्तः

Vardhamānaka hasta (Increasing)

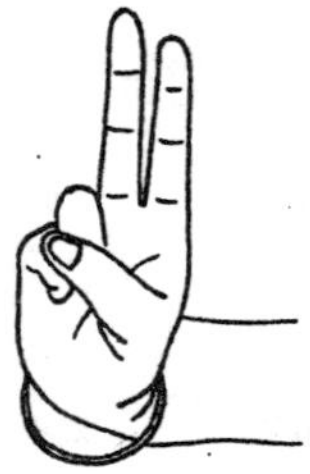

When the index finger is curved and place on the inside of the thumb to its middle and the middle finger, ring finger and little finger are curved and placed in a layered manner it is *Vardhamānaka* hasta.

*खड्ग हस्तः

Khadga hasta (Sword)

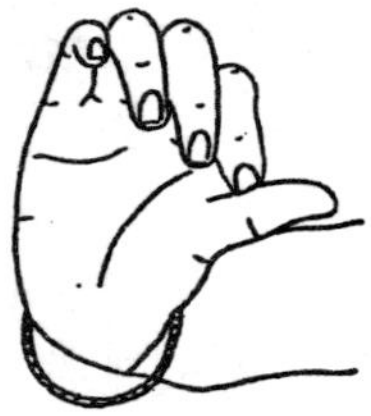

When the index and middle finger are pointed straight and the ring finger and little finger are folded towards the palm with the thumb over them, it is *Khadga* hasta.

*मुष्टि मृग हस्तः

Muśṭi mṛga hasta

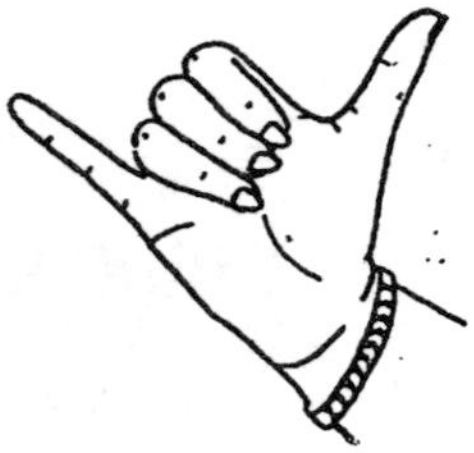

When in the muśṭi hasta, the little finger and thumb are stretched it is *Muśṭi mṛga* hasta.

Chapter 9

संयुत हस्तः

Combined Hand Gestures

अञ्जलिश्च कपोतश्च कर्कटः स्वस्तिकस्तथा ।
डोलाहस्तः पुष्पपुट उत्सङ्गः शिवलिङ्गकः ।।229।।
कटकावर्धनश्चैव कर्तरीस्वस्तिकस्तथा ।
शकटं शङ्खचक्रे च सम्पुटः पाशकीलकौ ।।230।।
मत्स्यः कूर्मो वराहश्च गरुडो नागबन्धकः ।
खट्वा भेरुण्ड इत्येते संख्याता संयुताः कराः ।।231।।
त्रयोविंशतिरित्युक्ताः पूर्वगैर्भरतादिभिः ।

Transliteration :

Añjaliśca kapotaśca karkaṭaḥ svastikastathā |
Ḍolāhastaḥ puṣpapuṭa utsaṅgaḥ śivaliṅgakaḥ ||
Kaṭakāvardhanaścaiva kartarīsvastikastathā |
Śakaṭaṃ śaṅkhacakre ca sampuṭaḥ pāśakīlakau ||
Mastyaḥ kūrmo varāhaśca garuḍo nāgabandhakaḥ |
Khaṭvā bheruṇḍa ityete saṅkheātā saṃyutātāḥ karāḥ ||
Trayoviṃśatirityuktāḥ pūrvagairbharatādibhiḥ |

(1) Añjali, (2) Kapota, (3) Karkaṭa, (4) Svastika, (5) Ḍola, (6) Puṣpapuṭa, (7) Utsaṅga, (8) Śivaliṅga, (9) Kaṭakāvardhana, (10) Kartarīsvastika, (11) Śakaṭaṃ, (12) Śaṅkha, (13) Cakra, (14) Sampuṭa, (15) Pāśa, (16) Kīlaka, (17) Mastya, (18) Kūrma, (19) Varāha, (20) Garuḍa, (21) Nāgabandha, (22) Khaṭva, (23) Bheruṇḍa, These are the 23 double hand gestures.

अञ्जलि हस्तः
Anjali hasta (Salutation)

पताकतलयोर्योगादञ्जलिः कर ईरितः ।।232।।

Transliteration :

Patākatalayoryogādañjaliḥ kara īritaḥ |

Meanings :

The joining of palms of two Paṭāka is called *Anjali.*

विनियोगः (Application)

देवतागुरुविप्राणां नमस्कारेष्वनुक्रमात् ।
कार्यः शिरोमुखोरस्थो विनियोगेऽञ्जलिर्बुधैः ।।233।।

Transliteration :

Devatāguruviprāṇāṃ namaskāreṣvanukramāt |
Kāryaḥ śiromukhorastho viniyoge-anjalirbudhaiḥ ||

Meanings :

Devatā = god, guru; viprāṇām namaskāreshu anukramāt = in bowing to gods, elders or gurus and brāhmins; śiro - mukha - urasthaḥ kāryaḥ = while doing that, Anjali hasta has to be on the head (for gods), before the face (for gurus) and on the chest (for brahmins), respectively; budhaiḥ anjalih, viniyojyaḥ = wise people thus use anjali hasta.

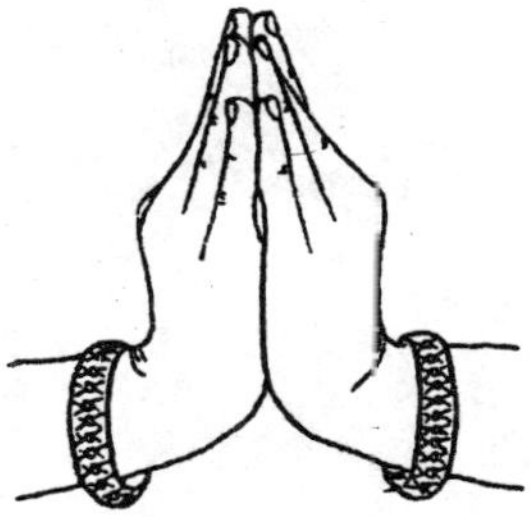

कपोत हस्तः

Kapota hasta (Dove)

कपोतोऽसौ करो यत्र श्लिष्टाऽऽमूलाग्रपार्श्वकः ।

Transliteration :

Kapoto'sau karo yatra śliṣṭā'mūlāgrapārśvakaḥ |

Meanings :

Kapota is that gersture wherein the two Patāka hands are joined and cupped towards the finger tips, sides and base of the palms.

विनियोगः (Application)

प्रणामे गुरुसम्भाषे विनयाङ्गीकृतेष्वयम् ।।234।।

Transliteration :

Praṇāme gurusambhāṣe vinayāṅgīkṛteśvayam ||

Meanings :

Praṇāme = obeisance/greeting; guru-sambhāśā = conversation with guru; vinaya - agīkṛteśvayam = agreeing with humbleness.

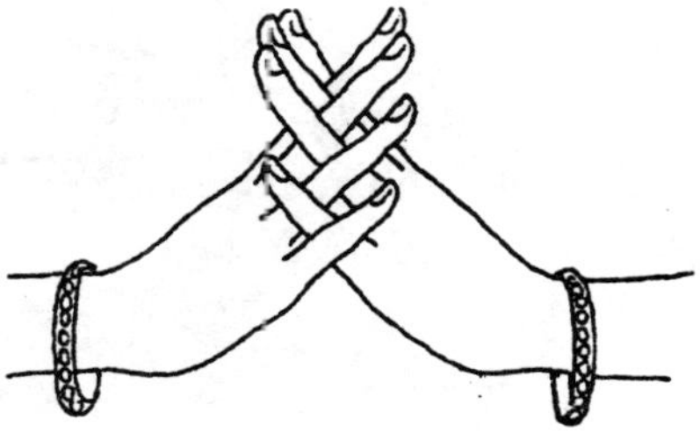

कर्कट हस्तः

Karkata hasta (Crab)

अन्योन्यास्यान्तरे यत्राङ्गुल्यो निःसृत्य हस्तयोः ।
अन्तर्बहिर्वा वर्तन्ते कर्कटः सोऽभिधीयते ।।235।।

Transliteration :

Anyonyāsyāntare yatrāṅgulyo niḥsṛtya hastayoḥ |
Antarbahirvā vartante karkaṭaḥ so'bhidhīyate ||

Meanings :

Karkata is the pose where the fingers of both hands are interlocked and stretched across.

विनियोगः (Application)

समूहागमने तुन्दर्शने शङ्खपूरणे ।
अङ्गानां मोटने शाखोन्नमने च नियुज्यते ।।236।।

Transliteration :

Samūhāgamane tundarśane śaṅkhapūraṇe |
Aṅgānāṃ moṭane śākhonnamane ca niyujyate ||

Meanings :

Samūha-āgamane = arrival of a group; tunda - darśane = seeing or showing the stomach; śaṅkhapūraṇe = blowing the conch; aṅgānāṃ moṭane = stretching or cracking the limbs; śākhā-unnamane (ca) = bending the bough of a tree; niyujyate = to denote the above, karkaṭa hasta is used

स्वस्तिक हस्तः
Svastika hasta (Crossing)

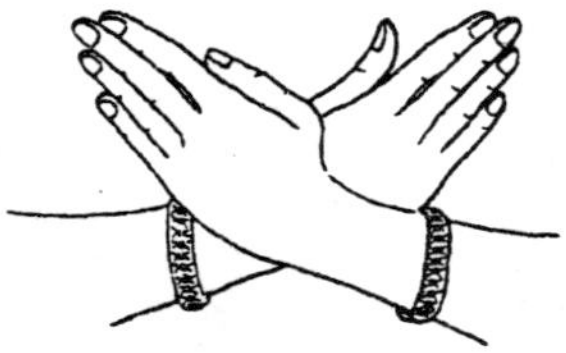

पताकयोः सन्नियुक्तः करयोर्मणिबन्धयोः ।
संयोगेन स्वस्तिकाख्यो मकरे विनियुज्यते ।।237।।

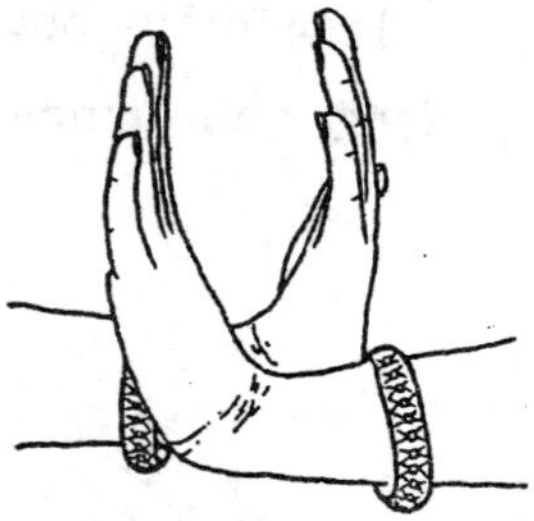

Transliteration :

Patākayoḥ sanniyuktaḥ karayormaṇibandhayoḥ |
Saṃyogena svastikākhyo makare viniyujyate ||

Meanings :

Svastika gesture is formed when two patāka hastās are held across at the wrist. It is used to denote a crocodile

डोला हस्तः

Ḍola hasta (Swing)

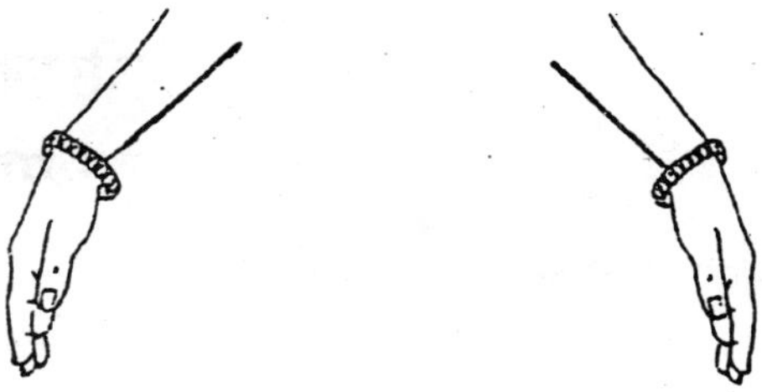

पताक ऊरदेशस्थे डोलाहस्तोऽयमिष्यते ।

Transliteration :

Patāka ūradeśasthe ḍolāhasto'amiṣyate |

Meanings :

When the Patāka gesture is placed along the sides of the thighs, the formation is called *Dolā.*

विनियोगः (Application)

नाट्यारम्भे प्रयोक्तव्य इति नाट्यविदो विदुः ।।238।।

Transliteration :

Nāṭyārambhe prayoktavya iti nāṭyavido viduḥ ||

Meanings :

Nāṭya-ārambhe prayoktavyaḥ, iti, nāṭya vido-viduḥ = experts on nātya know that Ḍola hasta has to be used at the beginning of nāṭya.

पुष्पपुट हस्तः

Puṣpapuṭa hasta (flower casket)

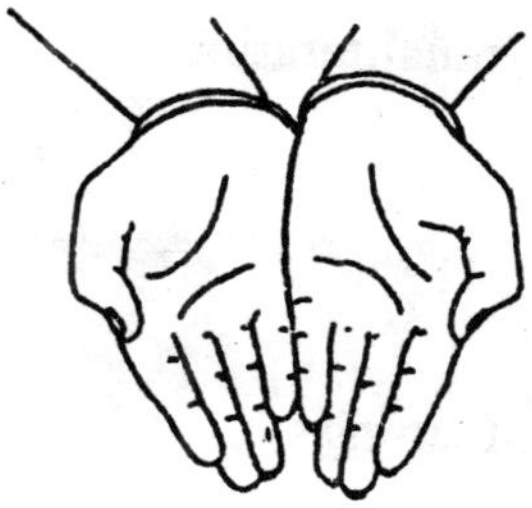

संश्लिष्टकरयोः सर्पशीर्षः पुष्पुपुटः करः ।

Transliteration :

Saṃśliṣṭakarayoḥ sarpaśīrṣaḥ puṣpupuṭaḥ karaḥ |

Meanings :

Puṣpapuṭa pose is formed when two sarpaśīrṣa hastas are held together.

विनियोगः (Application)

नीराजनाविधौ वारिफलादिग्रहणेऽपि च ।।239।।
सन्ध्यायामर्घ्यदाने च मन्त्रपुष्पे च युज्यते ।

Transliteration :

Nīrājanāvidhau vāriphalādigrahaṇe'api ca ||
Sandhyāyāmarghyadāne ca mantrapuśpe ca yujyate |

Meanings :

Nīrājana - vidhau = offering ārati, light; vāri - phala-ādi - grahaṇe (api ca) = receiving or collecting water, fruits etc. sandhyāyām, arghya-dāne (ca) = twilight offerings (to the Sun); mantra-puṣpe = at the time of chanting Mantrapushpa; niyujyate = Puṣpapuṭa hasta is used to denote the above aspects.

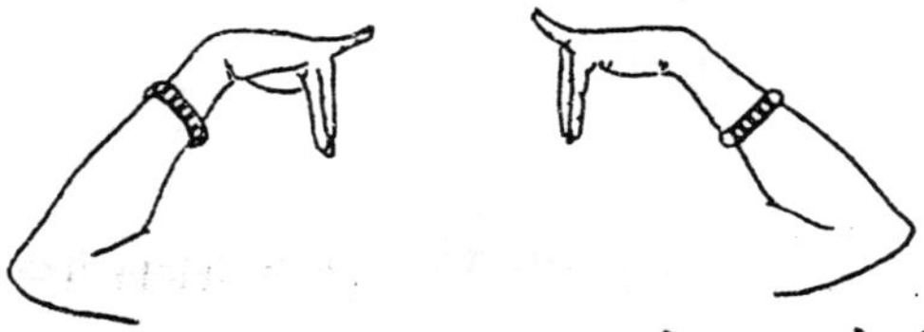

उत्सङ्ग हस्तः
Utsaṅga hasta (Threshold)

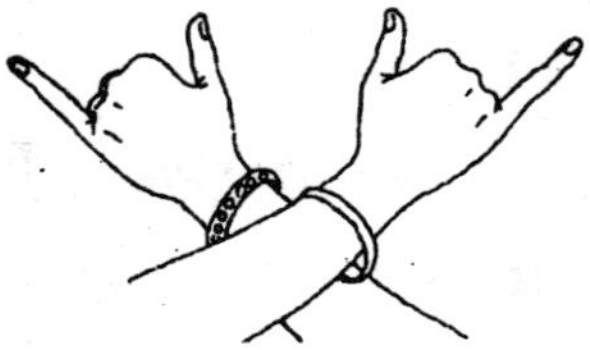

अन्योन्यबाहुदेशस्थौ मृगशीर्षकरौ यदि ।।240।।
उत्सङ्गहस्तः स ज्ञेयो भरतागमवेदिभिः ।

Transliteration :

Anyonyabāhudeśasthau mṛgaśīrṣakarau yadi ||
Utsaṅgahastaḥ sa jñeyo bharatāgamavedibhiḥ |

Meanings :

Utsaṅga is formed when two mṛgaśīrṣa gestures are placed on the shoulders or across on opposite sides.

विनियोगः (Application)

आलिङ्गने च लज्जायामङ्गदादिप्रदर्शने ।।241।।
बालानां शिक्षणे चायमुत्सङ्गो युज्यते करः ।

Transliteration :

Āliṅgane ca lajjāyāmaṅgadādipradarśane ||
Bālānāṃ śikṣaṇe cāyamutsaṅgo yujyate karaḥ |

Meanings :

Āliṅgane (ca) = embrace; lajjāyām = modesty or shyness; aṅgada-ādi pradarśane = showing armlets etc. bālānāṃ śikṣaṇe (ca) = educating or disciplining the children; utsaṅga karaḥ, yujyate = in denoting the above, utsaṅga hasta is used.

शिवलिङ्ग हस्तः
Śivaliṅga hasta

वामेऽर्धचन्द्रो विन्यस्तः शिखरः शिवलिङ्गकः ।।242।।

Transliteration :

Vāme'rdhacandro vinyastaḥ śikharaḥ śivaliṅgakaḥ ||

Meanings :

When śikhara gesture of right hand is placed over the ardhacandra gesture of left hand, the hasta is called *Śivaliṅga*.

विनियोगः (Application)

विनियोगस्तु तस्यैव शिवलिङ्गस्य दर्शने ।

Transliteration :

Viniyogastu tasyaiva śivaliṅgasya darśane |

Meanings :

Tasya viniyogaḥ (tu) śivaliṅga pradarśane, eva = it is used in depicting śivaliṅga only.

कटकावर्धन हस्तः

Kaṭakāvardhana hasta (Circle of a bracelet)

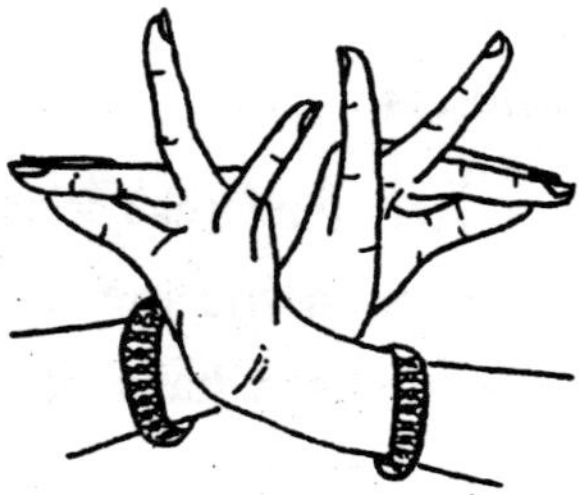

कटकामुखयोः पाण्योः स्वस्तिको मणिबन्धयोः ।।243।।
कटकावर्धनाख्यः स्यादिति नाट्यविदो विदुः ।

Transliteration :

Kaṭakāmukhayoḥ pāṇyoḥ svastiko maṇibandhayoḥ ||
Kaṭakāvardhanākhyaḥ syāditi nāṭyavido viduḥ |

Meanings :

When the two kaṭakāmukha gestures are crossed at the wrist, the hasta is called *kaṭakāvardhana.*

विनियोगः (Application)

पट्टाभिषेके पूजायां विवाहादिषु युज्यते ।।244।।

Transliteration :

Paṭṭābhiṣeke pūjāyāṃ vivāhādiṣu yujyate ||

Meanings :

Paṭṭābhiṣeke = coronation; pūjāyāṃ = ritual or worship; vivāha - ādiṣu = marriage; yujyate = in denoting the above aspects, kaṭakāvardhana hasta is used

कर्तरीस्वस्तिक हस्तः

Kartarīsvastika hasta (Crossing of two scissor's blades)

कर्तरी स्वस्तिकाकारा कर्तरीस्वस्तिको भवेत् ।

Transliteration :

Kartarī svastikākārā kartarīsvastiko bhavet |

Meanings :

When both hands with kartarīmukha hasta are held across at wrists, the gesture is called kartarīsvastika.

विनियोगः (Application)

शाखासु चाद्रिशिखरे वृक्षेषु च नियुज्यते ।।245।।

Transliteration :

Śākhāsu cādriśikhare vṛkṣeṣu ca niyujyate ||

Meanings :

Śākhāsu (ca) = branches of a tree; adri śikhare = the summit of a hill; vṛkṣeṣu (ca) = trees; niyujyate = this hasta is used to denote the above aspects.

शकट हस्तः

Śakaṭa hasta (Wheel)

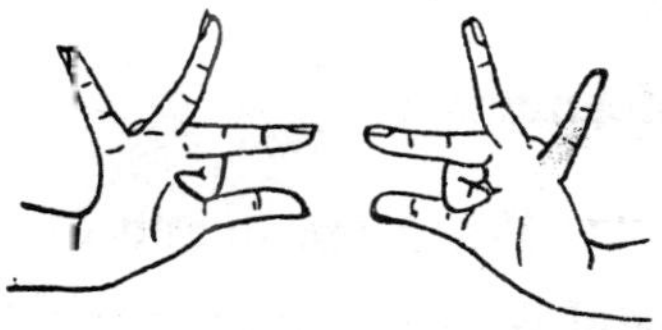

भ्रमरे मध्यमाङ्गुष्ठप्रसाराच्छकटो भवेत् ।।

Transliteration :

Bhramare madhyamāṅguṣṭhaprasārācchakaṭo bhavet ||

Meanings :

When both the middle fingers and the thumb are separated in Bhramara gesture, it is called *Śakaṭa hasta.*

विनियोगः (Application)

राक्षसाभिनये प्रायः शकटो विनियुज्यते ।।246।।

Transliteration :

Rākṣasābhinaye prāyaḥ śakaṭo viniyujyate ||

Meanings :

Prāyaḥ, rākṣasa - ābhinaye, śakaṭaḥ viniyujyate = often, śakaṭa hasta is used to denote the gestures of rākshasas.

शङ्‌ख हस्तः
Śaṅkha hasta (Conch)

शिखरान्तर्गताङ्गुष्ठ इतराङ्गुष्ठसङ्गतः ।
तर्जन्या युत आश्लिष्टः शङ्‌खहस्तः प्रकीर्तितः ।।247।।

Transliteration :

Śikharāntargatāṅguṣṭha itarāṅguṣṭhasaṅgataḥ |
Tarjanyā yuta āśliṣṭaḥ śaṅkhahastaḥ prakīrtitaḥ ||

Meanings :

When the thumb of the left hand is enclosed by the fingers of the right, and the thumb of the right hand is placed on the middle finger of the left, it is *Śaṅkha* hasta.

विनियोगः (Application)

शङ्खादिषु प्रयोज्योऽयमित्याहुर्भरतादयः ।

Transliteration :

Śaṅkhādiṣu prayojyo'ayamityāhurbharatādayaḥ |

Meanings :

Ayam, śaṅkhādiṣu prayojyaḥ, iti, bharata- ādayaḥ = Bharata and others say that this hasta is used in denoting conch etc.

चक्र हस्तः

Cakra hasta (Discus)

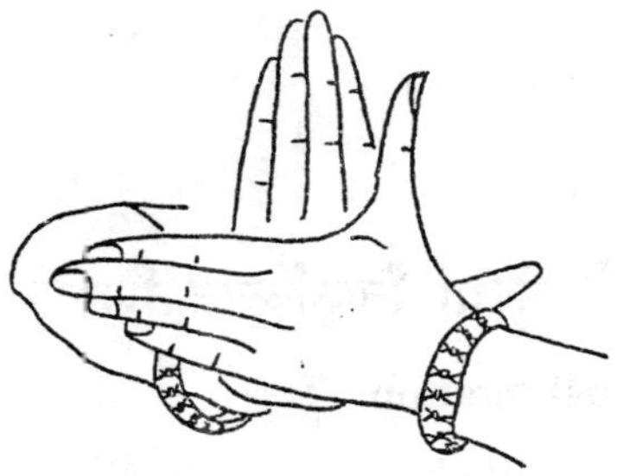

यत्नार्धचन्द्रौ तिर्यञ्चावन्योन्यतलसंस्पृशौ ।।248।।
चक्रहस्तः स विज्ञेयश् चक्रार्थ विनियुज्यते ।

Transliteration :

Yatnārdhacandrau tiryañcāvanyonyatalasaṃspṛśau ||
Cakrahastaḥ sa vijñeyaś cakrārtha viniyujyate |

Meanings :

When the palms of the archacandra touch one another with one hand vertical and the other placed horizontally over the other, it is *Cakra* hasta. This hasta is used to denote a discus.

सम्पुट हस्तः

Sampuṭa hasta (Casket)

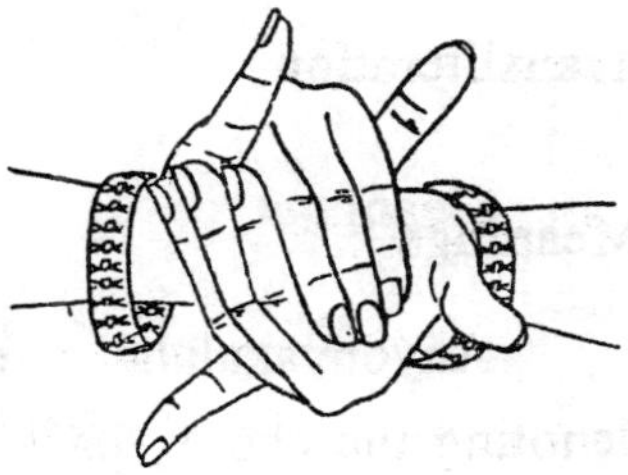

कुञ्चिताङ्गलयश्चके प्रोक्तः सम्पुटहस्तकः ।।249।।

Transliteration :

Kuñcitāṅgalayaścake proktaḥ sampuṭahastakaḥ ||

Meanings :

When the fingers of cakra hasta are curved one over the other, they form *Sampuṭa* hasta.

विनियोगः (Application)

वस्त्वाच्छादे सम्पुटे च सम्पुटः कर ईरितः ।

Transliteration :

Vastvācchāde sampuṭe ca sampuṭaḥ kara īritaḥ |

Meanings :

Vastu - ācchādane sampuṭe (ca), sampuṭaḥ karaḥ - in denoting concealment of things and a casket, sampuṭa hasta is prescribed.

पाश हस्तः

Pāśa hasta (noose)

सूच्यां निकुञ्चिते श्लिष्टे तर्जन्यौ पाश ईरितः ।।250।।

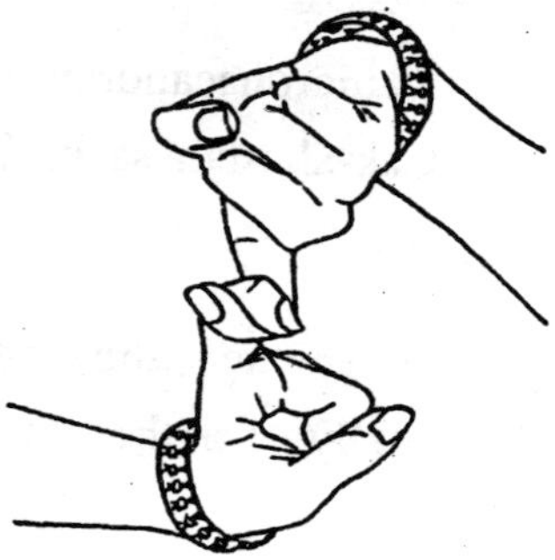

Transliteration :

Sūcyāṃ nikuñcite śliṣṭe tarjanyau pāśa īritaḥ ||

Meanings :

When the index fingers of sūcī are bent inwardly and joined, the gesture is called *Pāśa* hasta.

विनियोगः (Application)

अन्योन्यकलहे पाशे शृङ्खलायां नियुज्यते ।

Transliteration :

Anyonyakalahe pāśe śṛṅkhalāyāṃ niyujyate |

Meanings :

Anyonyakalahe = quarrel between people; pāśe = noose, śṛṅkhalāyāṃ = chain; niyujyate = in denoting the above, pāśa hasta is used.

कीलक हस्तः

Kīlaka hasta (Bond)

कनिष्ठे कुञ्चिते श्लिष्टे मृगशीर्षस्तु कीलकः ।।251।।

Transliteration :

Kaniṣṭhe kuñcite śliṣṭe mṛgaśīrṣastu kīlakaḥ ||

Meanings :

In the bāna hasta when the little fingers are inwardly bent and joined, they form *Kīlaka.*

विनियोगः (Application)

स्नेहे नर्मानुलापे च कीलको विनियुज्यते ।

Transliteration :

Snehe narmānulāpe ca kīlako viniyujyate |

Meanings :

Snehe = affection; narmānulāpe ca = veiled talk, being secretive, kīlako viniyujyate = these are the uses of Kīlaka hasta.

मत्स्य हस्तः

Matsya hasta (Fish)

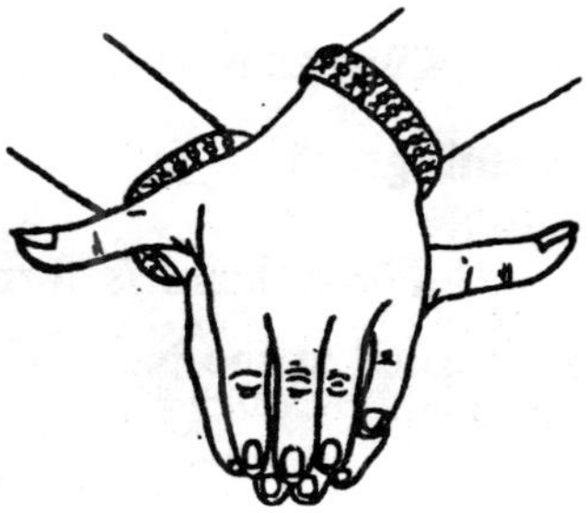

करपृष्ठोपरि न्यस्तो यत्र हस्तस्त्वधोमुखः ।।252।।
किञ्चित्प्रसारिताङ्गुष्ठकनिष्ठो मत्स्यनामकः ।

Transliteration :

Karapṛṣṭhopari nyasto yatra hastastvadhomukhaḥ ||
Kiñcitprasāritāṅguṣṭhakaniṣṭho matsyanāmakaḥ |

Meanings :

When the thumbs and little fingers of the two hands are outstretched, and one hand's palm is placed on the back of the other palm it forms *Matsya* hasta.

विनियोगः (Application)

एतस्य विनियोगस्तु सम्मतो मत्स्यदर्शने ।।253।।

Transliteration :

Etasya viniyogastu sammato matsyadarśane ||

Meanings :

Etasya, viniyogaḥ (tu), matsya-arthe, sammatoḥ, bhavet = it is used is to denote a fish.

कूर्म हस्तः

Kūrma hasta (Tortoise)

कुञ्चिताङ्गुलिश्चक्रे त्यक्ताङ्गुष्ठकनिष्ठकः ।
कूर्महस्तः स विज्ञेयः कूर्मार्थे विनियुज्यते ।।254।।

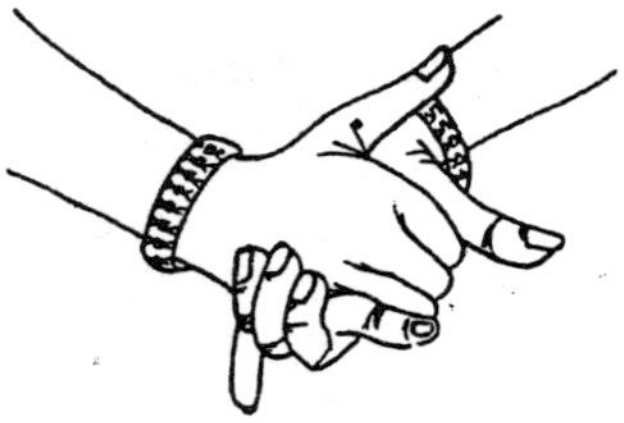

Transliteration :

Kuñcitāṅguliścakre tyaktāṅguṣṭhakaniṣṭhakaḥ |
Kūrmahastaḥ sa vijñeyaḥ Kūrmārthe viniyujyate ||

Meanings :

Kūrma hand is formed when the thumb and little finger in Cakra are stretched and remaining fingers are placed at the back of the other palm. It is used to denote a tortoise.

वराह हस्तः

Varāha hasta (boar)

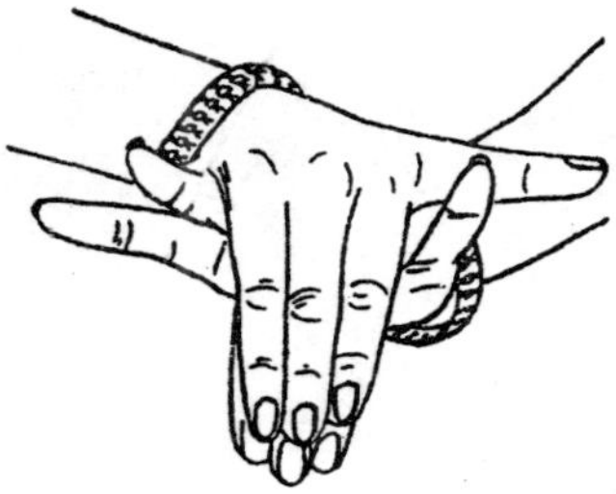

मृगशीर्षे त्वन्यतरे स्वोपर्येकः स्थिते यदि ।
कनिष्ठाङ्गुष्ठयोर्योगाद्वराहकर ईरितः ।।255।।

Transliteration :

Mṛgaśīrṣe tvanyatare svoparyekaḥ sthite yadi |
Kaniṣṭhāṅguṣṭhayoryogādvarāhakara īritaḥ ||

Meanings :

When the two mṛgaśīrṣa hands are placed one upon the other with one hand's thumb joining the other hand's little finger and others outstretched, it forms *Varāha* hasta.

विनियोगः (Application)

एतस्य विनियोगः स्याद्वराहार्थं प्रदर्शने ।

Transliteration :

Etasya viniyogaḥ syādvarāhārthaṃ pradarśane |

Meanings :

Etasya viniyogaḥ, varāha - ārtha pradarśane syāt = it is used in denoting a boar.

गरुड़ हस्तः

Garuḍa hasta (Eagle)

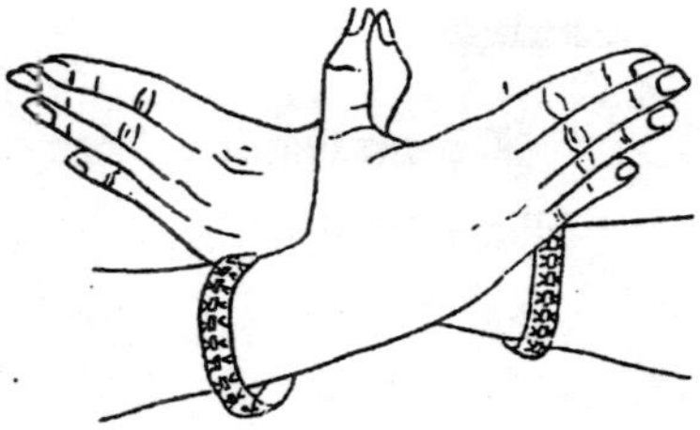

तिर्यकतलस्थितावर्धचन्द्रावङ्गुष्ठयोगतः ।।256।।
गरुडहस्त इत्याहुर् - गरुडार्थे नियुज्यते ।

Transliteration :

Tiryakatalasthitāvardhacandrāvaṅguṣṭhayogataḥ ||
Garuḍahasta ityāhur - garuḍārthe niyujyate |

Meanings :

When the thumbs of two Ardhacandra are interlocked with the hands stretched out on either directions it is called *Garuḍa* hasta. This hasta denotes an eagle.

नागबन्ध हस्तः

Nāgabandha hasta (Entwined Snakes)

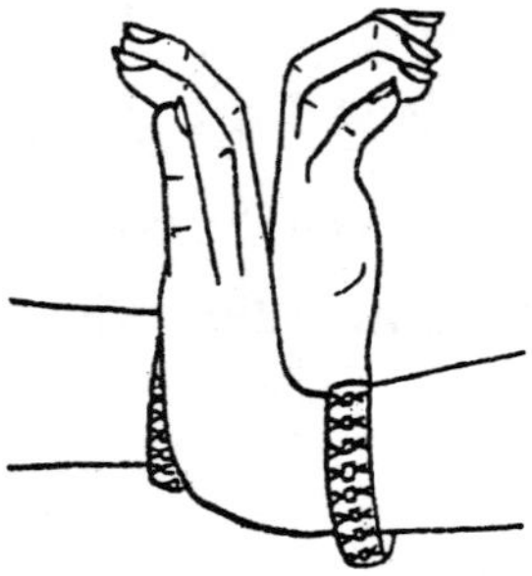

सर्पशीर्षस्वस्तिकञ्च नागबन्ध इतीरितः ।।257।।

Transliteration :

Sarpaśīrṣasvastikañca nāgabandha itīritaḥ ||

Meanings :

Sarapaśirṣa hasta placed across the wrist forms *Nāgabandha.*

विनियोगः (Application)

एतस्य विनियोगस्तु नागबन्धे हि सम्मतः ।

Transliteration :

Etasya viniyogastu nāgabandhe hi sammataḥ |

Meanings :

Etasya, viniyogaḥ (tu), nāgabandhe (hi) sammataḥ = it represents two entwined snakes.

खट्वा हस्तः
Khaṭva hasta (Bed)

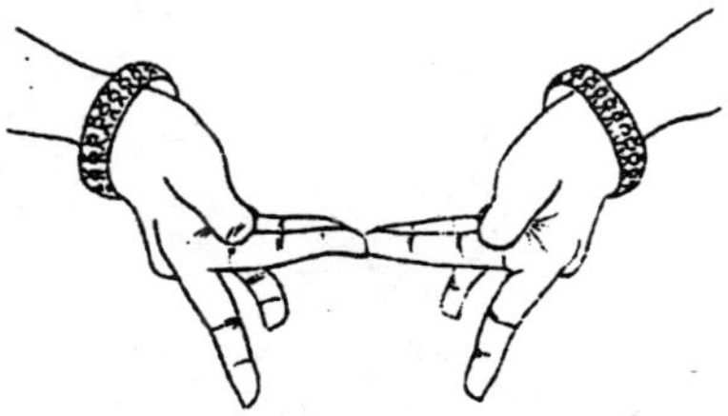

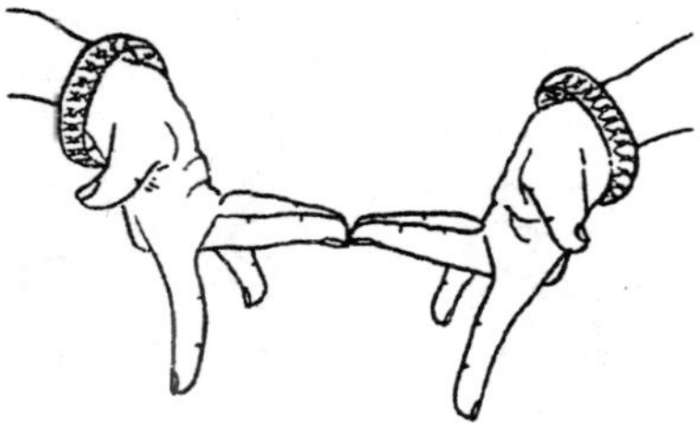

चतुरे चतुरं न्यस्य तर्जन्यङ्गुष्ठमोक्षतः ।।258।।
खट्वाहस्तो भवेदेष खट्वाशिविकयोछ स्मृतः ।

Transliteration :

Cature caturaṃ nyasya tarjanyaṅguṣṭhamokṣataḥ ||
Khaṭvāhasto bhavedeṣa khaṭvāśivikayocha smṛtaḥ |

Meanings :

Khaṭva is represented by two gestures

(1) *Khaṭva* is formed when in catura gesture the index finger and little finger of both hands are stretched out, the thumb is placed at the base of the ring finger, and the middle and ring finger touch one and another.

(2) *Khaṭva* is formed when in catura gesture the index finger, little finger and thumb of both the hands are stretched out, and the middle and ring finger touch one and another.

विनियोगः (Application)

खट्वाशिविकयोः स्मृतः ।।259।।

Transliteration :

Khaṭvāśivikayoḥ smṛtaḥ ||

Meanings :

Khaṭva = bed; śivika = palanquin; smṛtaḥ = thought to denote.

भेरुण्ड हस्तः

Bherunda hasta (A mythical two-headed bird)

मणिबन्धे कपित्थाभ्यां भेरुण्डकर इष्यते।

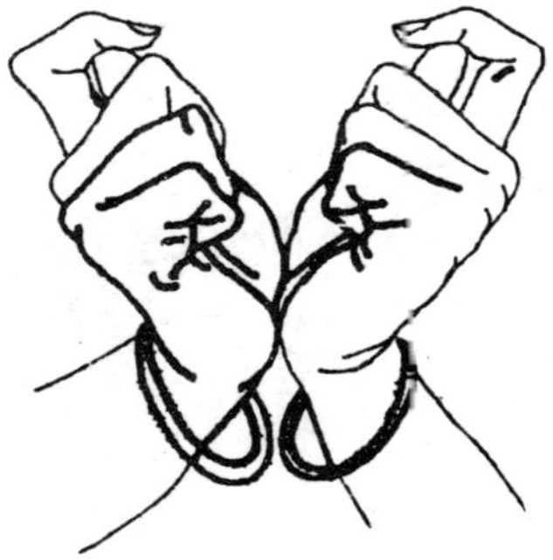

Transliteration :

Maṇibandhe kapitthābhyāṃ bheruṇḍakara iṣyate |

Meanings :

When two kapittha hands are held together at writsts, it forms *Bheruṇḍa* hasta.

विनियोगः (Application)

भेरुण्डे पक्षिदम्पत्योर्भेरुण्डो युज्यते करः ।।260।।

Transliteration :

Bheruṇḍe pakṣidampatyorbheruṇḍo yujyate karaḥ ||

Meanings :

Bheruṇḍe pakṣi-dampatyoḥ, bheruṇḍaḥ karaḥ yujyate = Bheruṇḍa hasta is used to denote a pair of birds or a two-headed bird

अवहित्थ हस्तः

Avahittha hasta (Dissimulation)

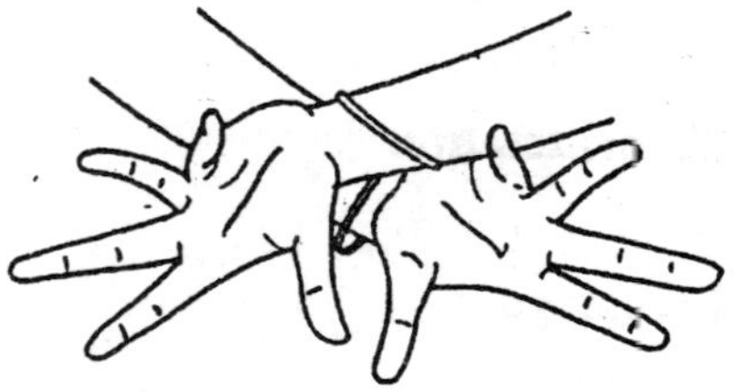

सोलपद्मौ वक्षशिष्टा ववहित्थ करो मतः ।

Transliteration :

Sōlapadmau vakṣaśiṣṭā vavahittha karō mata |

Meanings :

When two alapadma hastas are held across the wrist it is *Avahittha* hasta.

विनियोगः (Application)

शृङ्गार नटने चैव लीलाकन्दुक धारणे ।।261।।
कुचार्थे युज्यतेसोऽयं अवहित्थकराभिदाः ।

Transliteration :

Śṛṅgāra naṭane caiva līlākanduka dhāraṇe ||
Kucārthe yujyateso-ayaṃ avahitthakarābhidāḥ |

Meanings :

Śṛṅgāra naṭane (ca-eva) = erotic dances; līlākanduka - dhāraṇe = holding a ball for play; kuca-arthe = the breasts; yujyate (saḥ, ayam) avahitthakarā - abhidāḥ = in denoting the above, avathittha hasta is used.

गजदन्त हस्तः

Gajadanta hasta (Elephant's tusk)

बाहुमध्यगतौ सर्पशीर्षौ स्वस्तिकतामितौ ।।262।।
यदि स्यात् गजदन्तोयं परमात्मादिदेवता ।

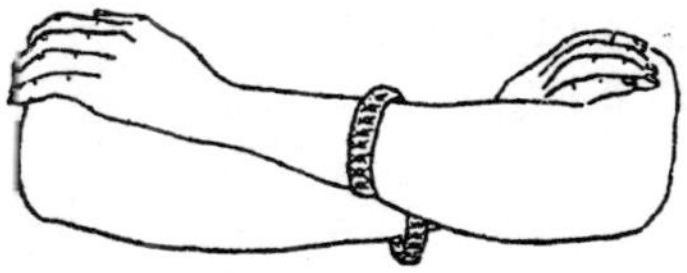

Transliteration :

Bāhumadhyagatau sarpaśīrṣau svastikatāmitau ||
Yadi syāt gajadantoyaṃ paramātmādidevatā |

Meanings :

When Two sarpaśirṣahastas are crossed and their palms reach the middle of the opposite arms, it is Gajandanta (elephant's tusk) hasta.

विनियोगः (Application)

स्तम्भग्रहे शिलोत्पाटे भारग्रहे नियुज्यते ।।263।।

Transliteration :

Stambhagrahe śilotpāṭe bhāragrahe niyujyate ||

Meanings :

Stambhagrahe śilotpāṭe bhāragrahe niyujyate = this is used to denote grasping a pillar, pulling up a stone and lifting anything heavy.

संयामी हस्तः
Saṃyāmi hasta

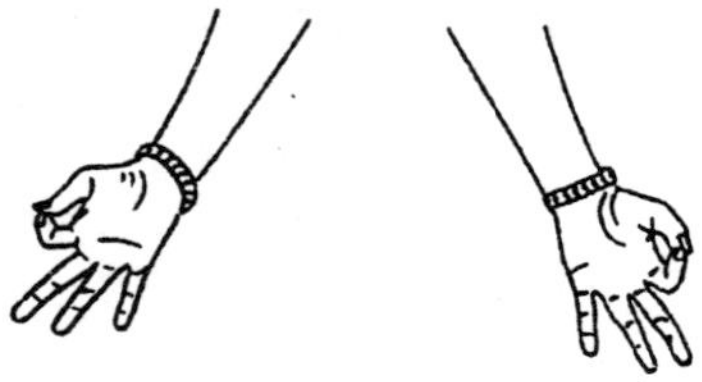

When two hands in hamsa hasta are opened out and stretched below, it is *Samyāmi.*

मुकुल भेद हस्तः
Mukula bheda hasta

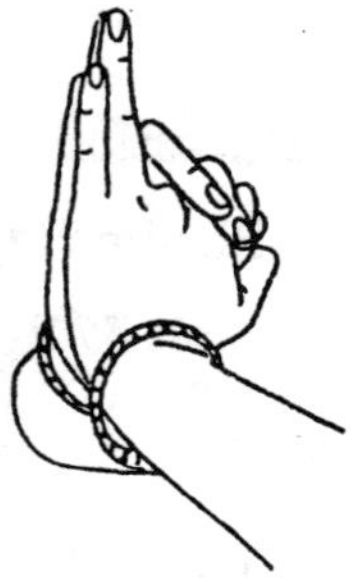

When facing palm to palm, the ring finger and little finger are outstretched upwards and the other fingers are interlaced, it is *Mukula bheda* hasta.

उत्तरबोधि हस्तः

Uttarabodhi hasta (Supreme enlightenment)

When facing palm, the index fingers are outstretched upwards and the other fingers are interlaced, it is *Utharabodhi* hasta.

वज्रमानस हस्तः

Vajra mānas (Strong minded)

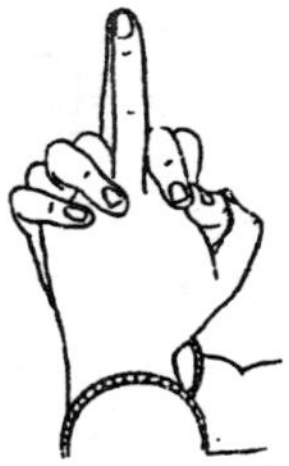

When facing palm to palm, the middle fingers are outstretched upwards and the other fingers are interlaced it is *Vajra manas* hasta.

कवच हस्तः

Kavaca hasta (Shield)

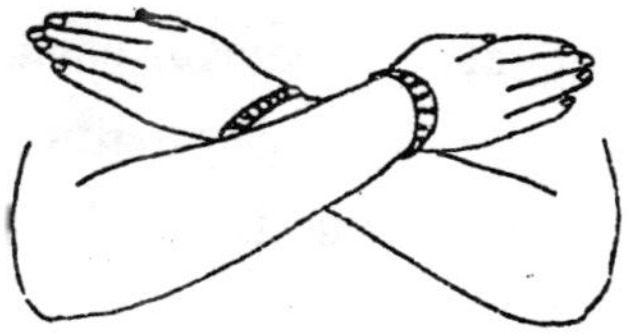

When two palms facing inwards are place across on the biceps of the arm it is *Kavaca* hasta.

हस्त स्वस्तिक हस्तः

Hasta svastika

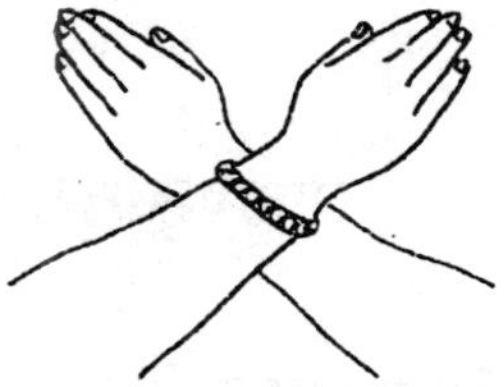

When two palms facing inwards are place across on the shoulders of the arm it is *Hastasvāstikā* hasta.

Chapter 10

देव हस्ताः

Deva hastāḥ

(Abhinayam for Gods and Goddesses)

अथात्र ब्रह्मादि देवानाम् भावनाभिनयक्रमात् ।
मूर्तिभेदेन ये हस्तः तेषाम् लक्षणमुच्यते ।।264।।

Transliteration:

Athātra brahmādi devānām bhāvanābhinayakramāt |
Mūrtibhedena ye hastāḥ teṣām lakṣaṇamucyate ||

Meaning:

Athātra, Brahmādi devānām bhāvana = now, the indication of Brahma and other gods; abhinayakramāt, mūrtibhedena = in the order of abhinaya and according to the different forms; ye hastah, teshām, lakshaṇam-ucyate = whatever hastas are there, their characteristics are now being described.

Now, the qualities of hands that indicate the forms which accord with the character and actions of Brahma and other gods will be explained.

1. ब्रह्म हस्तः

Brahma hastaḥ

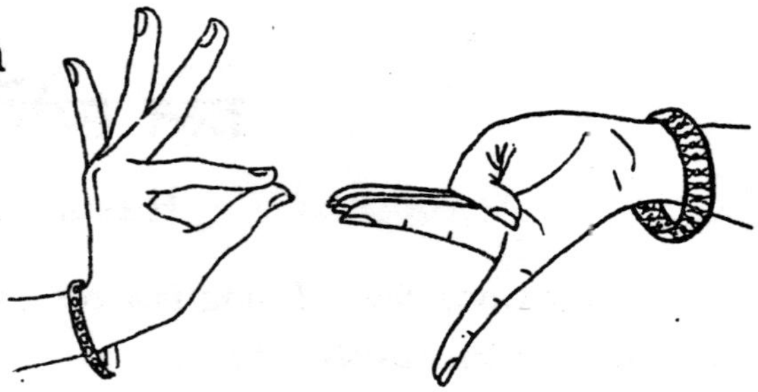

ब्राह्मणश्चतुरो वामे हंसास्या दक्षिणे करः।

Transliteration:

Brāhmaṇa ścaturo vāme haṃsāsyā dakṣiṇe karaḥ |

Meaning:

Caturaḥ karaḥ vāme, hamsāsyaḥ dakshine, Brahmanah karaḥ = if Catura hasta by left hand and Hamsāsya hasta by the right hand are held, then it is Brahma hasta.

If Catura and Hamsāsya hastas are held by left and right hands respectively, it is Brahma hasta.

2. शम्भु हस्तः
Śambhu hastaḥ

शम्भोर्वामे मृगशीर्षः त्रिपताकस्तु दक्षिणे ।।265।।

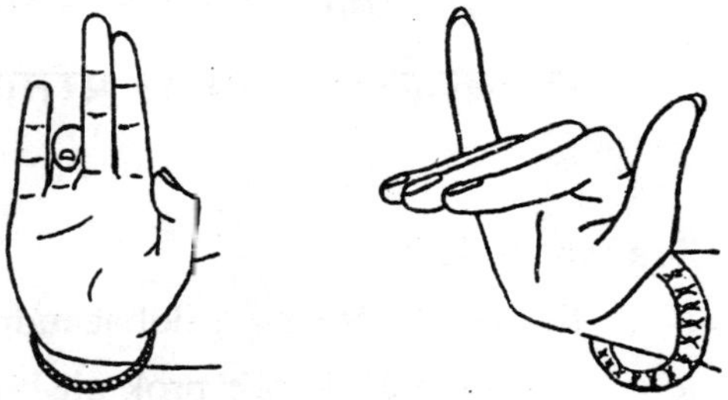

Transliteration:

Śambhorvāme mṛgaśīrṣaḥ tripatākastu dakṣiṇe ||

Meaning:

Vāme mṛgaśīrṣaḥ, dakshiṇe tripatākaḥ (tu), śambhc = if left hand holds Mṛgaśīrṣa hasta and the right hand holds Triptāka hasta, it is Sambhu hasta.

When Mṛgaśīrṣa and Tripatāka hastas are held by the left and right hand respectively, it is Śambhu hasta.

3. विष्णु हस्तः
Viṣṇu hastaḥ

हस्ताभ्याम् त्रिपताकाभ्याम् विष्णुहस्तः प्रकीर्तितः।

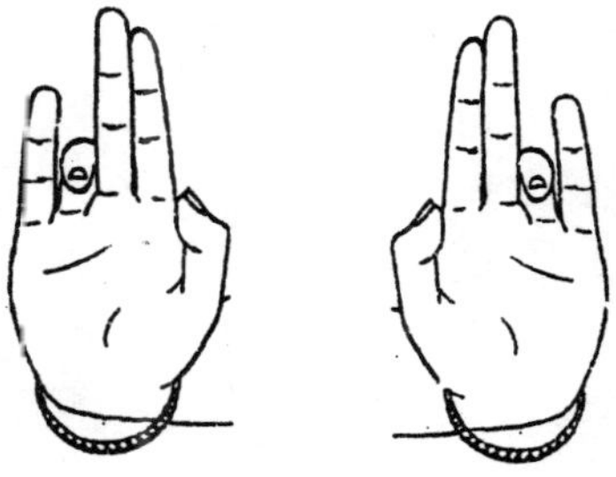

Transliteration:

Hastābhyām tripatākābhyām viṣṇuhastaḥ prakīrtitaḥ|

Meaning:

Tripatākābhyām hastābhyām, Viṣṇu hastāḥ parakīrtitaḥ = two Tripataka hastas denote lord Viṣṇu. Both hands holding Tripatāka hastas denote Lord Vishṇu.

4. सरस्वती हस्तः
Sarasvatī Hastaḥ

सूचीकृते दक्षिणे-अर्द्धचन्द्रे वामकरे तथा ।।266।।
सरस्वत्याः करः प्रोक्तः भरतागमवेदिभिः ।

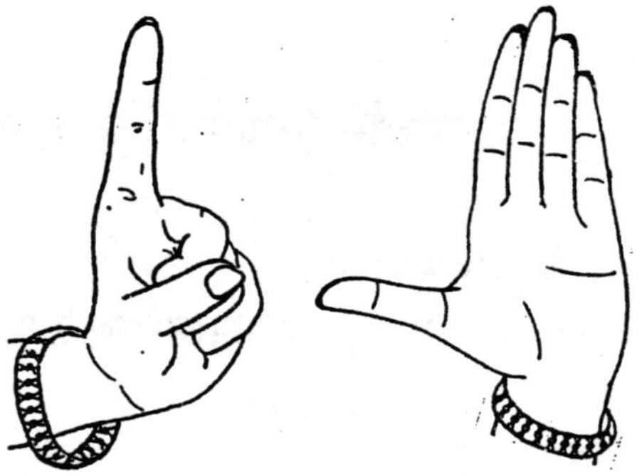

Transliteration:

Sūcīkṛte dakṣiṇe-arddhacandre vāmakare tathā|
Sarasvatyāḥ karaḥ proktaḥ bharatāgamavedibhiḥ ||

Meaning:

Dakṣiṇe, sūcīkṛte, vāmakare, arddhacandre = if right hand holds Sūcīhasta and left hand holds ardhacandra hasta; Sarasvatyāḥ karaḥ, bharatāgama vedibhiḥ, proktaḥ = then it is Saraswati hasta as described by the experts on Nāṭya Śāstra.

When right hand holds Sūcīhasta and left hand holds Arddhacandrhasta, then it is Saraswati hasta.

5. पार्वती हस्तः
Pārvatī hastaḥ

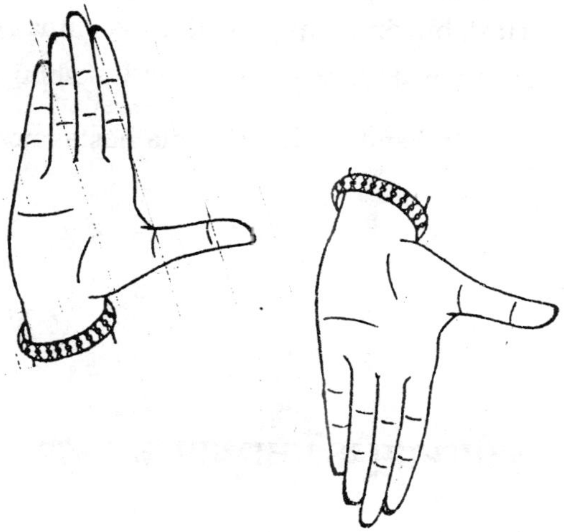

ऊर्ध्वाधः प्रसृतावर्धचन्द्राख्यौ वामदक्षिणौ ।।267।।
अभयो वरदश्चैव पार्वत्यः कर ईरितः ।

Transliteration:

Ūrdhvādhaḥ prasṛtāvardhacandrākhyoa vāmadakṣiṇau ||
Abhayo varadaścaiva pārvatyāḥ kara īritaḥ |

Meaning:

Vāma-dākṣiṇau ardhacandra-akhyou, abhayaḥ - vādhāḥ (ca-eva), ūrdhwa - adhaḥ-prasṛtou = when two Ardhacandra hastas are held by left hand and right hand as Abhaya hasta and Varada hasta, respectively and extended upward and downward, respectively; pārvatyaḥ kara īritaḥ = then it is said to be Pārwati hasta.

When two ardhacandra hastas are held by the left hand and the right hand as Varada hasta and Abhayahasta, respectively and extended downward (left hand) and up wards (right hand) respectively, it is known as Pārwati hasta.

6. लक्ष्मी हस्तः
Lakṣmī hastaḥ

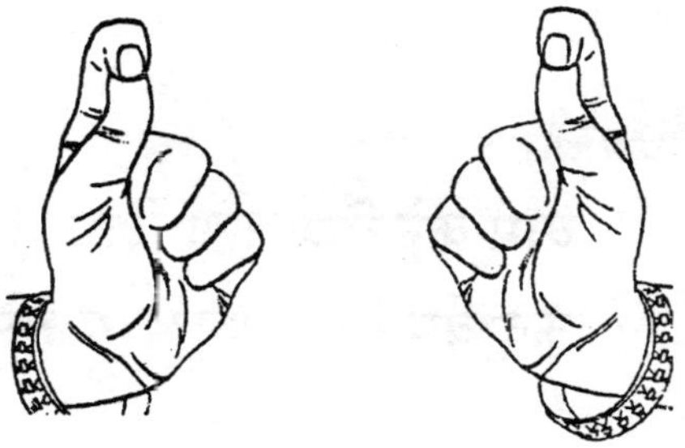

अंसोपकण्ठे हस्ताभ्याम् कपित्थस्तु श्रियः करः ।।268।।

Transliteration:

Aṃsopakaṇṭhe hastābhyām kapitthāstu śriyaḥ karaḥ ||

Meaning:

Hastābhyām, kapitthastu amsa - upakaṇṭhe, śriyaḥ karaḥ = when both hands hold Kapittha hastas near the respective shoulders, then it is Lakshmi hasta.

If both hands hold Kapittha hastas near the respective shoulders, it becomes Lakshmī hasta.

7. विघ्नेश्वर हस्तः

Vighneśvara hastaḥ

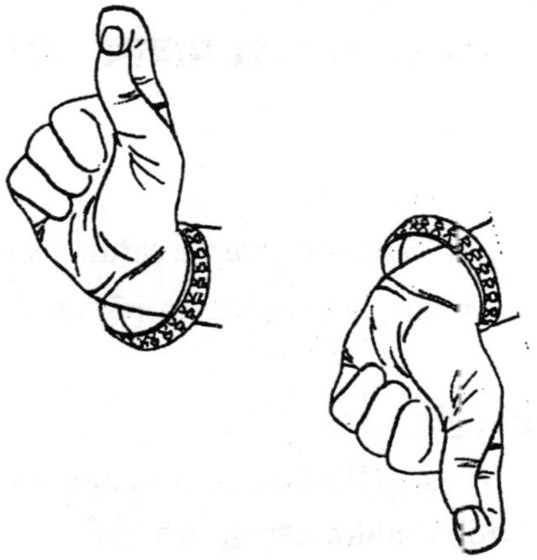

पुरोगभ्याम् कपित्ताभ्याम कराभ्याम विघ्नारातकरः ।

Transliteration:

Purogabhyām kapittābhyāma karābhyāma vighnārātakaraḥ |

Meaning:

Kapittābhyām, karābhyām, purogabhyām = when two Kapittha hastas are held forward; vighnārāt karaḥ = then it is Vighneśvara hastā.

When two Kapittha hastas are held in front or on the chest, then it is Vighneśvara hastā.

8. षण्मुख हस्तः

Ṣaṇmukha hastaḥ

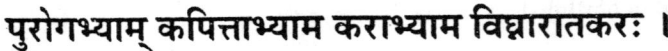

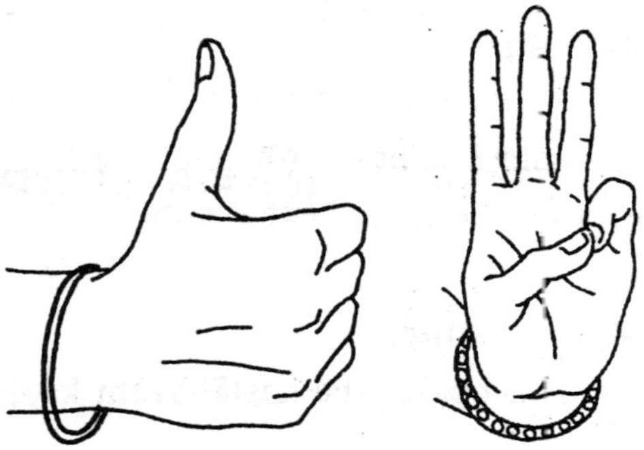

वामे करे त्रिशूलाश्च शिखरो दक्षिणे करे ।।269।।
ऊद्र्ध्वम् गते षण्मुखस्य हस्तः स्यादिति कीर्तितः ।

Transliteration:

Vāme kare triśūlaśca śikharo dakṣiṇe kare ||
Ūrddhvam gate ṣaṇmukhasya hastaḥ syāditi kīrtitaḥ |

Meaning:

Vāme kare triśūlaḥ (ca) dakṣiṇe kare śikharaḥ = if the left hand holds Triśūla hasta and the right hand holds śikhara hasta; ūrddhvam gate = and both the hastas are extended upwards; shanmukhasya hastaḥ, syāt, iti, kīrtitaḥ = then it is said to be Shanmukha hasta.

If Triśūlā hasta in left hand and Śikhara hasta in right hand are extended upwards, then it is to be known as Shanmukha hasta.

9. मन्मथ हस्तः

Manmatha hastaḥ

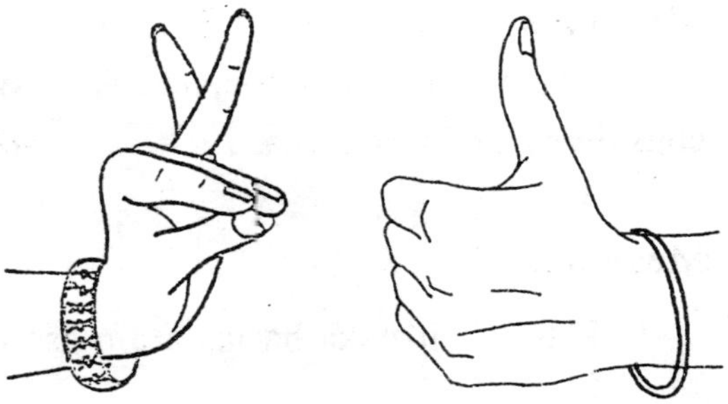

वामे करे तु शिखरो दक्षिणे कटकामुखः ।।270।।
मन्मथस्य करः प्रोक्तो नाट्यशास्त्रार्थ कोविदः ।

Transliteration:

Vāme kare tu śikharo dakṣiṇe kaṭakāmukhaḥ ||
Manmathasya karaḥ prokto nāṭyaśāstrārtha kovidaḥ |

Meaning:

Vāme kare (tu) śikharaḥ dakṣiṇe kaṭakamukhaḥ = if left hand holds Śikhara hasta and right hand holds Kaṭakāmukha hasta; Manmathasya karaḥ nāṭya śāstra - artha - kovidaḥ, proktaḥ = then it is Manmatha hasta as described by the experts on Nāṭya śāstra.

If left and right hands hold Śikhara hasta and Kaṭakamukha hasta, respectively, then it is known as Manmatha hasta.

Chapter 11

दिक्पाल हस्तः

Dikpāla Hastaḥ

इन्द्रहस्तः

Indrahastaḥ

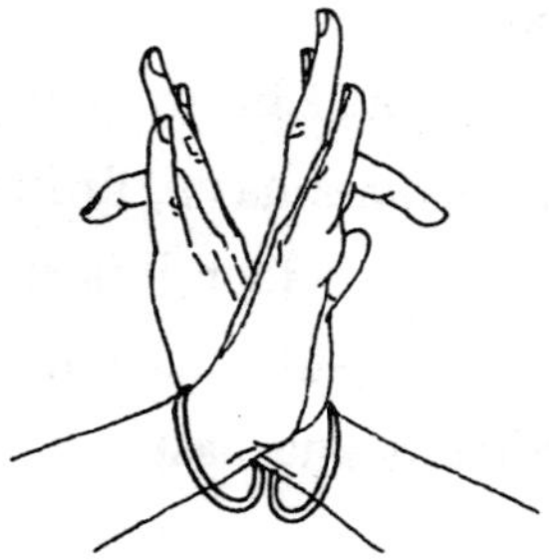

त्रिपताकः स्वस्तिकश्च शक्रहस्तः प्रकीर्तितः ।।271।।

Transliteration:

Tripatākaḥ svastikaśca śakrahastaḥ prakīrtitaḥ ||

Meanings:

Tripatākou, svastikou, cet = if two Tripatāka hastas are crossed; indra hastaḥ prakīrtitaḥ = it is considered as Indra hasta.

Meanings:

If two Tripatāka hastas are crossed, it is considered as Indra hasta.

अग्निहस्तः

Agnihastaḥ

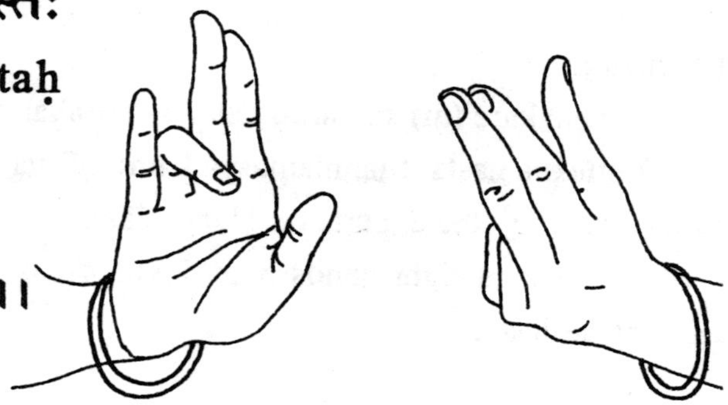

त्रिपताको दक्षिणे तु वामे काङ्गुलहस्तकः ।
अग्निहस्तः स विज्ञेयो नाट्यशास्त्रविशारदैः ।।272।।

Transliteration:

Tripatāko dakṣiṇe tu vāme kāṅgulahastakaḥ |
Agnihastaḥ sa vijñeyo nāṭyaśāstraviśāradaiḥ ||

Meanings:

Tripatākaḥ dakṣiṇe kāṅgula hastakaḥ vāme = if Tripatāka hasta is held by right hand and Kāṅgula hasta by the left hand; nātya śāstra viśāradaiḥ saḥ vijñeyaḥ agni hastaḥ = experts on Nāṭyaśāstra know it as Agni hasta.

If Tripatāka hasta is held by right hand and Kāṅgula hasta by the left hand experts on Nāṭyaśāstra describe it as Agni hasta.

यमहस्तः

Yamahastaḥ

वामे पाशं दक्षिणे तु सूची यमकरः स्मृतः।

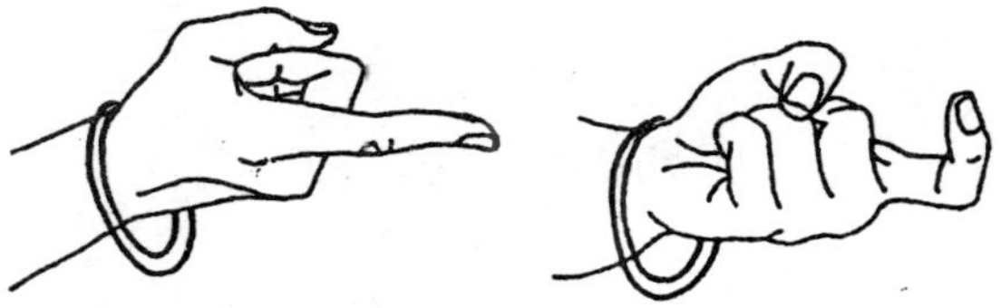

Transliteration:

Vāme pāśaṃ dakṣiṇe tu sūcī yamakaraḥ smṛtaḥ |

Meanings:

Vame pāśaṃ dakṣiṇe tu sūcī = when left hand assumes Pāśahasta and right hand assumes Sūci hasta; yama karaḥ smṛtaḥ=then it is considered as Yama hasta.

When left hand assumes Pāśahasta and right hand assumes Sūcī hasta then it is considered as Yama hasta.

निऋर्रतिहस्तः

Nirrtihastaḥ

खट्वा च शकटश्चैव कीर्तितो निऋर्रतेः करः ।।273।।

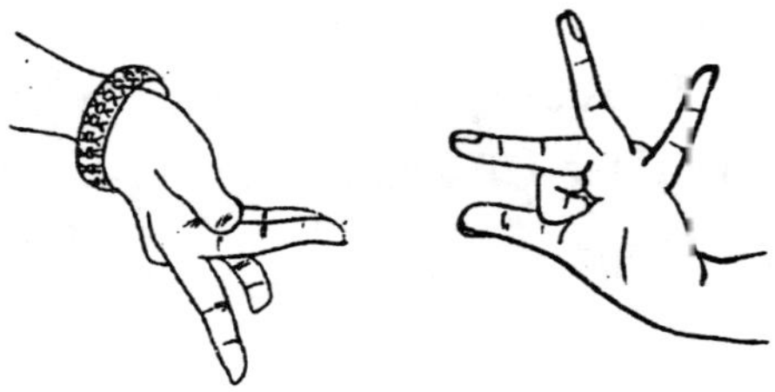

Transliteration:

Khaṭvā ca śakaṭaścaiva kīrtito nirrrateḥ karaḥ ||

Meanings:

Khaṭvā ca śakaṭa ca eva = when one hand holds Khaṭvā hasta and the other śakaṭa hasta ; nirrrateḥ karaḥ, kīrtitaḥ = then it is considered as Nirrti hasta.

When one hand holds Khaṭvā hasta and the other śakaṭa hasta, then it is considered as Nirrti hasta.

वरुण हस्तः

Varuṇa hastaḥ

पताको दक्षिणे वामे शिखरो वरुणः करः ।

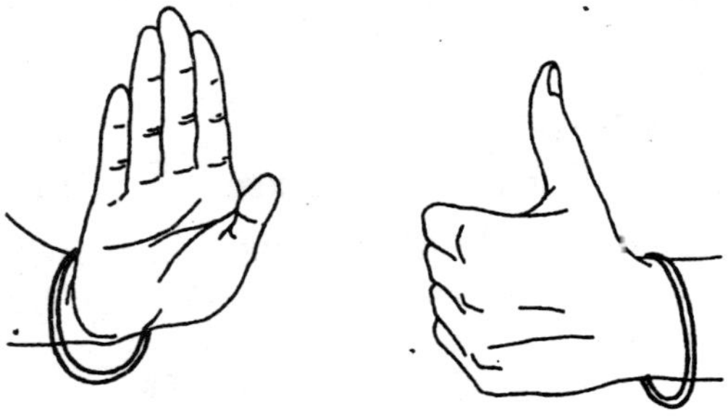

Transliteration:

Patāko dakṣiṇe vāme śikharo varuṇaḥ karaḥ |

Meanings:

Dakshine patākah, vāme śikharah = when right hand assumes patāka hasta and left hand śikhara hasta; varuṇaḥ karaḥ = then it is Varuna hasta.

When right hand assumes patāka hasta and left hand śikhara hasta then it is Varuṇa hasta.

वायु हस्तः

Vāyu hastaḥ

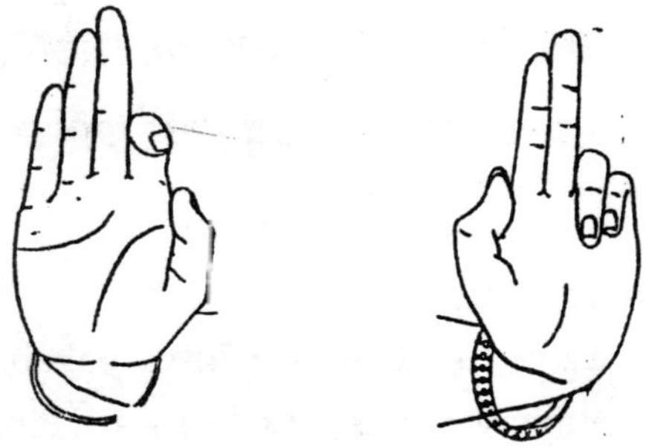

अरालो दक्षिणे हस्ते वामे चार्धपताकिका ।।274।।

धृता चेद्वायुदेवस्य कर इत्यभिधीयते ।

Transliteration:

Arālo dakṣiṇe haste vāme cārdhapatākikā ||

Dhṛtā cedvāyudevasya kara ityabhidhīyate |

Meanings:

Dakṣiṇe haste arālah, vāme ca - ardhapatākikā dhṛtā cet = when right hand holds Arāla hasta and left hand Ardhapatāka hasta; vayudevasya karah, iti-abhidhīyate = then, it is said to be vāyu hasta (god of wind).

When right hand holds Arāla hasta and left hand Ardhapatāka hasta then, it is said to be vāyu hasta (god of wind).

कुबेरहस्तः

Kubera hastaḥ

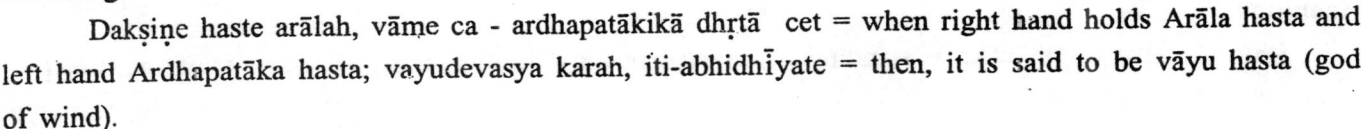

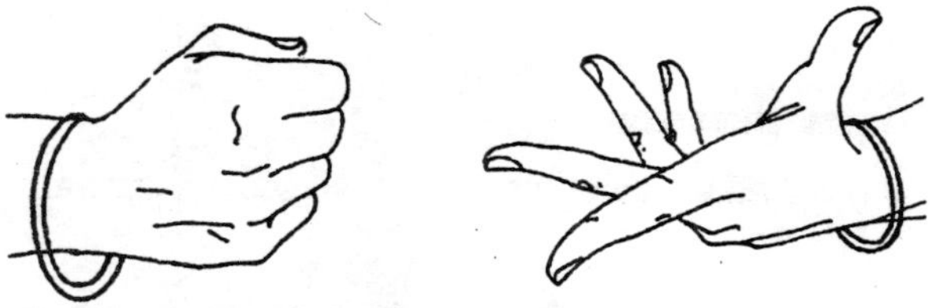

वामे पद्मं दक्षिणे तु गदा यक्षपतेः करः ।।275।।

Transliteration:

Vāme padmaṃ dakṣiṇe tu gadā yakṣapateḥ karaḥ ||

Meanings:

Vāme padmaṃ dakṣiṇe tu gadā = when left hand assumes alapadma hasta and right hand assumes gadā hasta; yakshapateh karaḥ = then, it is Kubera hasta.

When left hand assumes alapadma hasta and right hand assumes gadā hasta then, it is Kubera hasta.

ईशान हस्तः
Īśāna hastaḥ

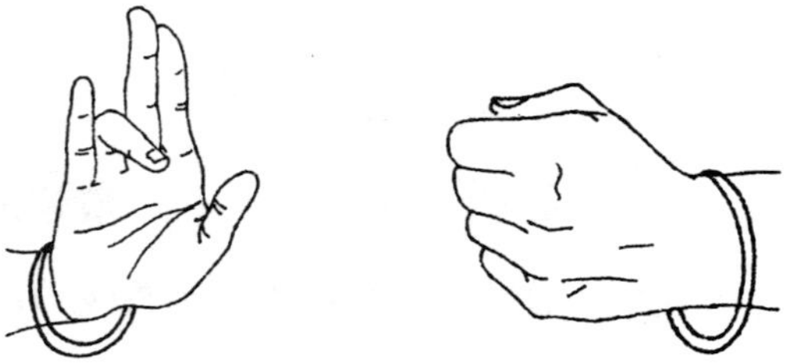

शैवे तु स्थानके स्थित्वा दक्षिणं त्रिपताकिकम् ।
वामश्च मुष्टिस्तिर्यकस्यादीशानस्य प्रदर्शिनी ।।276।।

Transliteration:

Śaive tu sthānake sthitvā dakṣiṇaṃ tripatākikaṃ |
Vāmaśca muṣṭistiryakasyādīśānasya pradarśinī ||

Meanings:

Sthitvā śaive tu sthānake = standing on śaivasthānaka; dakṣiṇaṃ tripatākikaṃ vāma ca, muṣṭiḥ-tiryak=when the right hand holds Tripataka hasta and the left hand holds Muṣṭi hasta obliquely; īśānasya pradarśinī syāt = then it denotes īśāna hasta.

Standing on śaivasthānaka when the right hand holds tripatāka hasta and the left hand holds muṣṭi hasta obliquely then it denotes Īśāna hasta.

Chapter 12

दशावतारहस्ताः

Daśāvatārahastāḥ

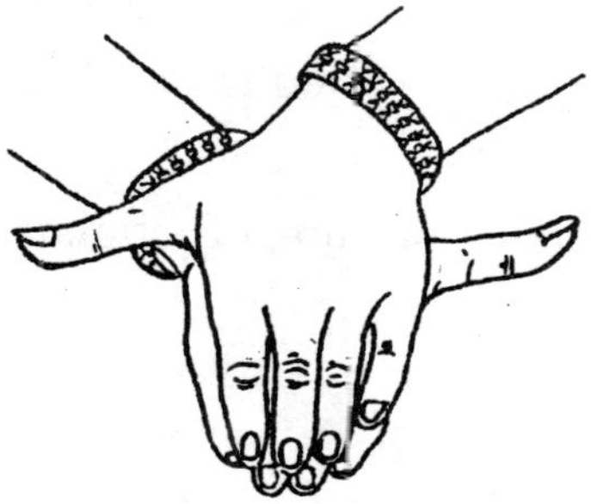

1. मत्स्यावतारहस्तः

Matsya-Avatāra Hastaḥ

मत्स्यहस्तं दर्शयित्वा ततः स्कन्धसमौ करौ ।
धृतौ मत्स्यावतारस्य हस्त इत्यभिधीयते ।।277।।

Transliteration:

Matsyahastaṃ darśayitvā tataḥ skandhasamau karau ¡
Dhṛtau matsyāvatārasya hasta ityabhidhīyate ||

Meaning:

Karau, Matsyahastaṃ darśayitvā tataḥ, skandha-samau dhṛtau = when the hands assuming Matsya hasta, are held at the level of the shoulders; matsyāvatārasya hastaḥ iti abhidhīyate = it is said to be Matsya - avatāra hasta.

When the hands assuming Matsya hasta are held at the level of the shoulders, it is said to be Matsya avatāra hasta (form of fish).

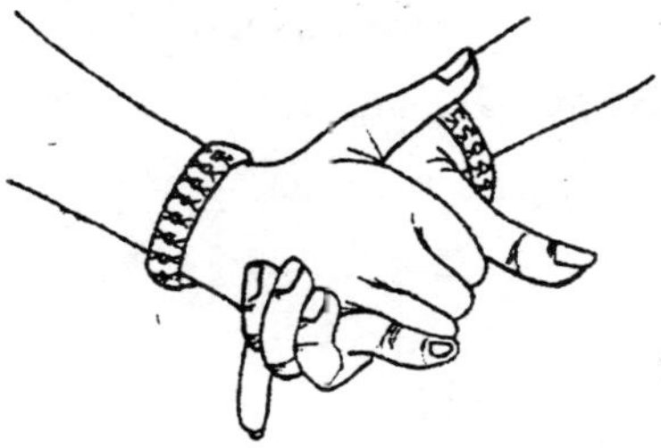

2. कूर्मावतारहस्तः

Kūrma-Avatāra Hastaḥ

कूर्महस्तं दर्शयित्वा ततः स्कन्धसमौ करौ ।
धृतौ कूर्मावतारस्य हस्त इत्यभिधीयते ।।278।।

Transliteration:

Kūrmahastaṃ darśayitvā tataḥ skandhasamau karau |
Dhṛtau kūrmāvatārasya hasta ityabhidhīyate ||

Meaning:

Kūrmahastaṃ darśayitvā = after showing Kūrma hasta; tataḥ skandhasamour karau dhṛtau = if the two hands are held at the level of the shoulders ; kūrmāvatārasya hastaḥ iti abhidhīyate = it is said to be kūrma avatāra hasta.

Holding Kūrma hasta at the level of the shoulders is said to be kūrma avatāra hasta (form of tortoise).

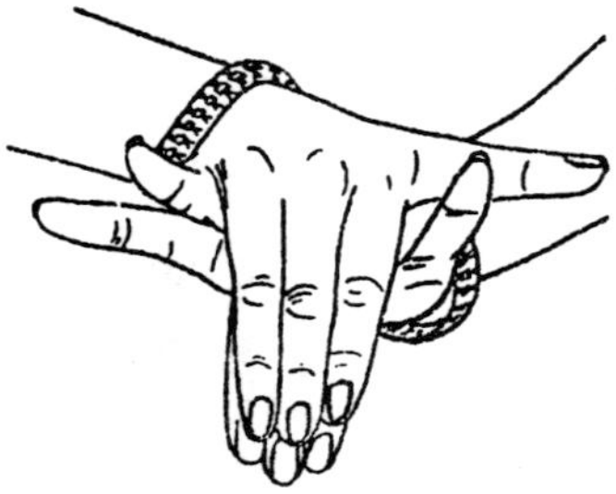

3. वराहवतारहस्तः
Varāha-Avatāra Hastaḥ

दर्शयित्वा वराहं तु कटिपार्श्वसमौ करौ ।
धृतौ वराहवतारस्य देवस्य इत्यभिधीयते ।।279।।

Transliteration:

Darśayitvā varāhaṃ tu kaṭipārśvasamau karau |
Dhṛtau varāhavatārasya devasya ityabhidhīyate ||

Meaning:

Darśayitvā varāhaṃ (tu) = after showing Varāha hasta; kaṭipārśvasamau karau dhṛtau= if the hands are held on the side of the waist; varāha devasya hastaḥ iti abhidhīyate = then it is said to be the hasta of Varāha.

When Varāha hasta is held on the sides of the waist it is said to be Varāha avatāra hasta, (form of wild boar).

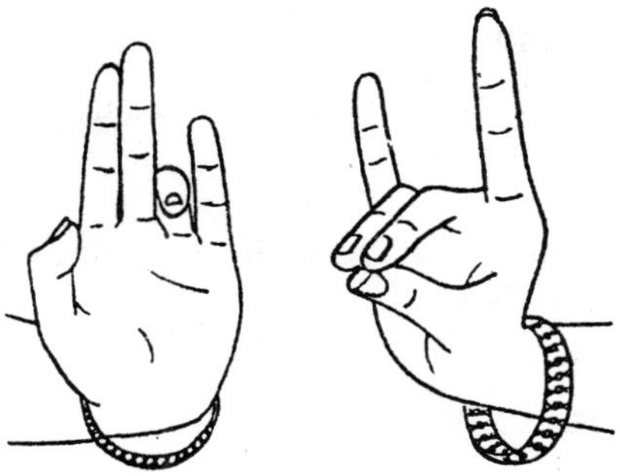

4. नृसिंहावतारहस्तः

Nṛsiṃha-Avatāra Hastaḥ

वामे सिंहमुखं धृत्वा दक्षिणे त्रिपताकिका ।
नरसिंहावतारस्य हस्त इत्युच्यते बुधैः ।।280।।

Transliteration:

Vāme siṃhamukhaṃ dhṛtvā dakṣiṇe tripatākikā |
Narasiṃhāvatārasya hasta ityucyate budhaiḥ ||

Meaning:

Vāme siṃhamukhaṃ dakṣiṇe tripatākikā dhṛtvā = when left and right hand assume simhamukha and tripatāka hasta respectively; Narasiṃha - avatārasya hastaḥ iti abhidhīyate = it is said to be Narasimha - avatāra hasta.

When left assumes simhamukha and right hand tripatāka hasta, it is said to be Narasimha - avatāra hasta (form of half lion and half man).

5. वामनावतारहस्तः

Vāmana-Avatāra Hastaḥ

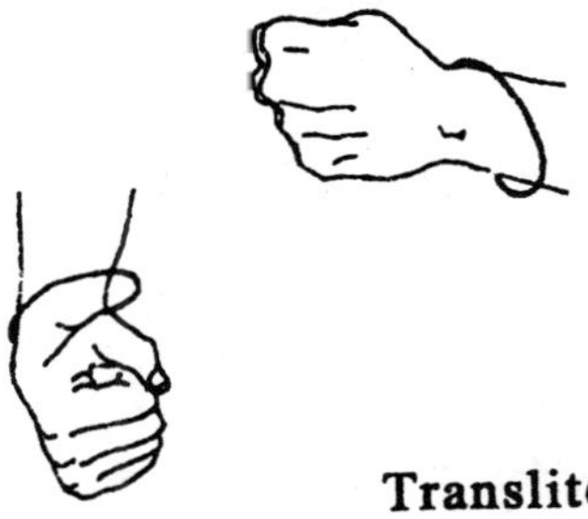

ऊर्ध्वाधो धृतमुष्टिभ्यां सव्याग्याभ्यां यदि स्थितः ।
स वामनावतारस्य हस्त इत्यभिधीयते ।।281।।

Transliteration:

Ūrdhvādho dhṛtamuṣṭibhyāṃ savyāgyābhyāṃ yadi sthitaḥ |
Sa vāmanāvatārasya hasta ityabhidhīyate ||

Meaning:

Savya - gyābhyāṃ dhṛta, muṣṭibhyāṃ = assuming muṣṭi hasta with left and right hand ; ūrdhvād hah, yadi sthitaḥ = if left hand is held upwards and the right hand downwards, sah, Vāmana-avatārasya hastah, iti abhidhīyate = then it is said to be hasta for Vāmana-avatāra.

Assuming Muṣṭi hasta in both left and right hand; if left hand is held upwards and the right hand downwards, then it is said to be hasta for Vamana-avatāra (form of dwarf).

6. परशुरामावतारहस्तः

Paraśurāma-Avatāra Hastaḥ

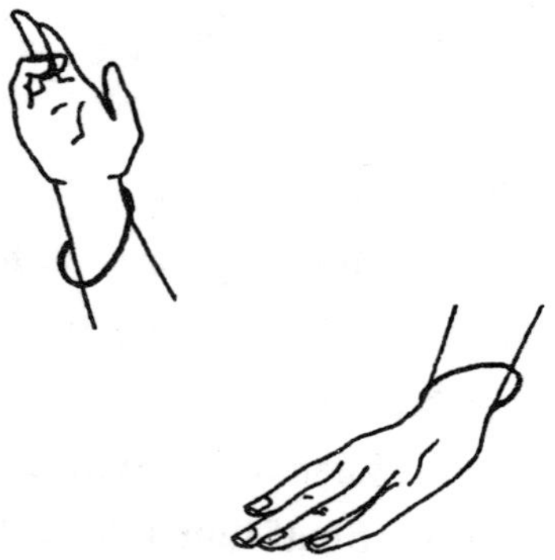

वामं कटितटे व्यस्य दक्षिणेऽर्धपताकिका ।
धृतौ परशुरामस्य हस्त इत्यभिधीयते ।।282।।

Transliteration:

Vāmaṃ kaṭitaṭe vyasya dakṣiṇe'rdhapatākikā |
Dhṛtau Paraśurāmasya hasta ityabhidhīyate ||

Meaning:

Vāmaṃ kaṭi-taṭe vyasya, dakshine'ardhapatākiKā dhṛta = when the left hand is placed on the left side of the waist and the right hand assumes ardhapataka hasta; Paraśurāmasya, hastah, iti-abhidhīyate = then it is said to be Paraśurāma hasta.

When the left hand is placed on the left side of the waist and the right hand assumes ardhapataka hasta; then it is said to be Paraśurāma-Avatāra hasta.

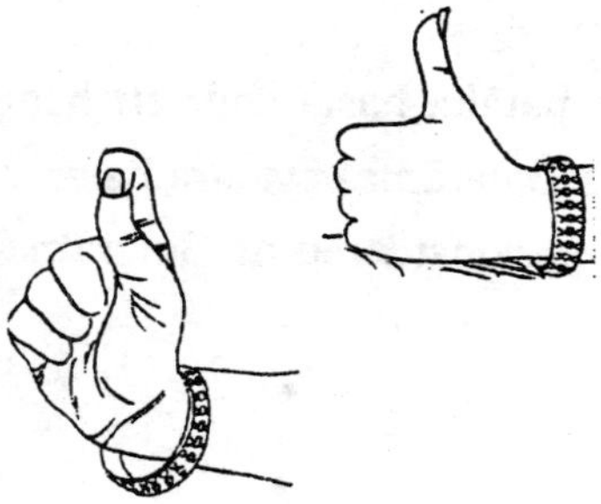

7. रामचन्द्रावतारहस्तः

Rāmacandra-Avatāra Hastaḥ

कपित्थो दक्षिणे हस्ते वामे तु शिखरः करः ।
ऊर्ध्वं धृतौ रामचन्द्रहस्त इत्युच्यते बुधैः ।।283।।

Transliteration:

Kapittho dakṣiṇe haste vāme tu śikharaḥ karaḥ |
Ūrdhvaṃ dhṛtau Rāmacandrahasta ityucyate budhaiḥ ||

Meaning:

Dakṣiṇe haste kapitthah = right hand assumes Kapittha hasta : vame (tu), sikharaḥkaraḥ urdhwaṃ dhṛtau = (while) left hand holds Shikara hasta pointing upwards, Rāmacandra hastah iti, budhaiḥ ucyate = then, it is considered by the scholars as Rāmachandra hastha.

When the right hand assumes kapittha hasta and left hand shikara hasta pointing upwards, it is Rāmacandra hasta.

8. बलरामवतारहस्तः

Balarāma -Avatāra Hastaḥ

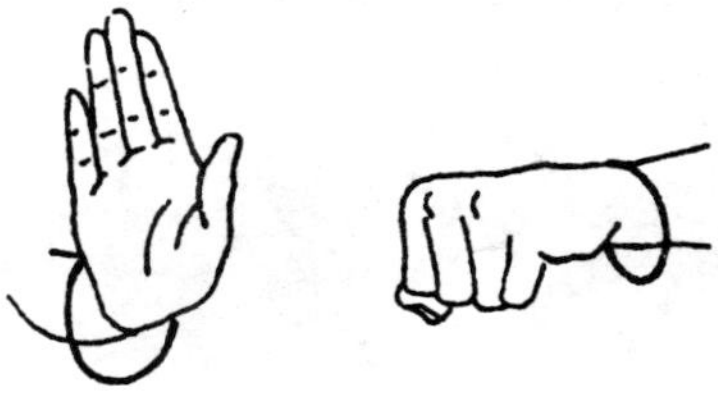

पताको दक्षिणे हस्ते मुष्टिर्वामकरे तथा ।
बलरामवतारस्य हस्त इत्युच्यते बुधैः ।।284।।

Transliteration:

Patāko dakṣiṇe haste muṣṭirvāmakare tathā |
Balarāmavatārasya hasta ityucyate budhaiḥ ||

Meaning:

Dakṣiṇe haste patakah, (tatha) vāmakare muṣṭi= when right hand assumes patāka hasta and left hand muṣṭi hasta; Balarama - avatārasya hasta iti-abhidhīyate = then it is considered as Balarāma- avatāra hasta.

When right hand assumes patāka hasta and left hand muṣṭi hasta; then it is considered as Balarāma-avatāra hasta.

9. कृष्णावतारहस्तः

Kṛṣṇa-Avatāra Hastaḥ

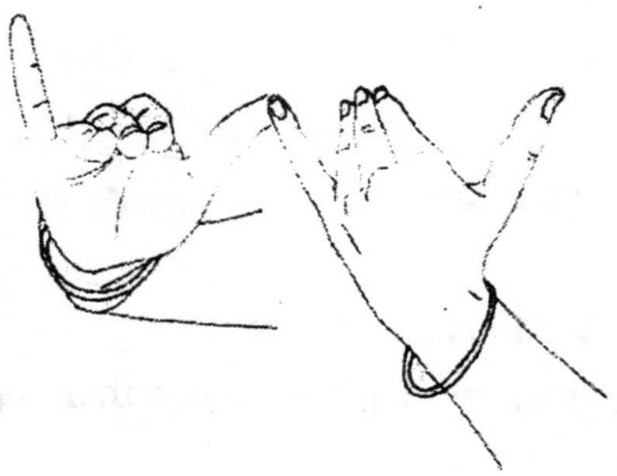

मृगशीर्षे तु हस्ताभ्यामग्योभ्याभिमुखे कृते ।
मास्योपकण्ठे कृष्णस्य हस्त इत्युच्यते बुधैः ।।285।।

Transliteration:

Mṛgaśīrṣe tu hastābhyāmagyobhyābhimukhe kṛte |
Māsyopakaṇṭhe kṛṣṇasya hasta ityucyate budhaiḥ ||

Meaning:

Hastābhyām, mṛgaśīrṣetu = the two hands assume Mrgaśīrṣa hasta; asya - upakaṇṭhe, agyobhya abhimukhe kṛte = facing one another near the face; kṛṣṇsya hastah, iti budhaiḥ, ucyate = this is said to be Kṛṣṇa hasta by the scholars.

When the two hands assume Mrgaśīrṣa hasta facing one another near the face, it is said to be Kṛṣṇa hasta by the scholars.

10. कल्क्यवतारहस्तः
Kalkya-Avatāra Hastaḥ

पताको दक्षिणे वामे त्रिपताकः करो धृतः ।
कल्क्याख्यस्यावतारस्य हस्त इत्यभिधीयते ।।286।।

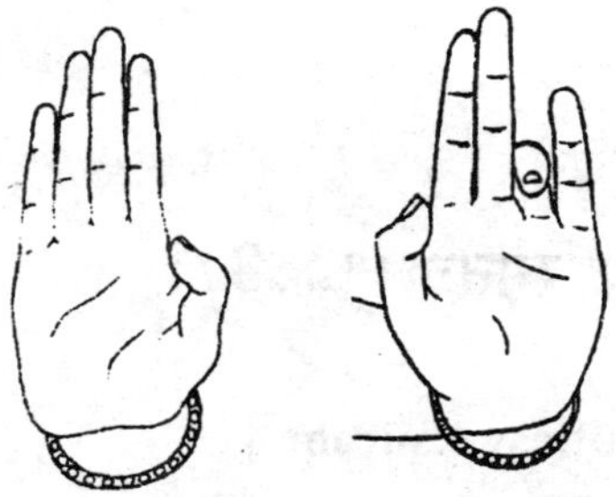

Transliteration:

Patāko dakṣiṇe vāme tripatākaḥ karo dhṛtaḥ |
Kalkyākhyasyāvatārasya hasta ityabhidhīyate ||

Meaning:

Dakṣiṇe patākah, vāme tripatākaḥ karo dhṛtaḥ = if right hand assumes patāka hasta and left hand assumes tripatāka hasta; kalki-akhyasya avatārasya, iti abhidhīyate = it is said to be the hasta for Kalki avatāra

If right hand assumes patāka hasta and left hand assumes tripatāka hasta, it is said to be the hasta for Kalki-avatāra.

11. बुद्ध अवतारहस्तः
Buddha-Avatāra Hastaḥ

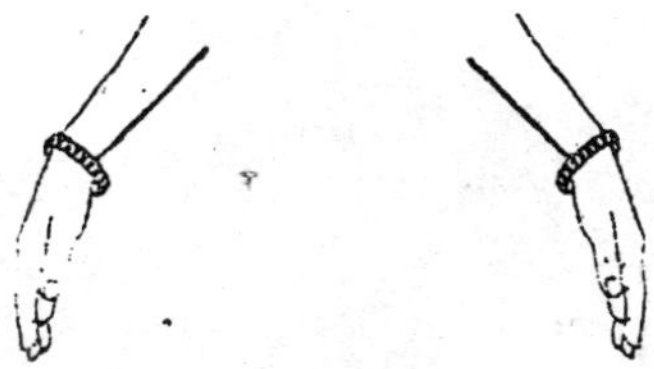

समपादौ यदा स्याताम् डोलाहस्तौ च पार्श्वयोः ।
ततो बुद्ध इति ज्ञेयो नाट्य तत्त्वविशारदैः ।।287।।

Transliteration:

Samapādau yadā syātām ḍolāhastau ca pārśvayoḥ |
Tato buddha iti jñeyo nāṭya tattvaviśāradaiḥ ||

Meaning:

Samapādau yadā syātām ḍolāhastau ca pārśvayoḥ = When standing with feet together and holding dola hasta on the sides; tato buddha iti jñeyo nāṭya tattvaviśāradaiḥ = that hand is understood as Buddha in the philosophical texts.

Standing with feet together while assuming Dola hasta on the sides is said to be Buddha avatāra hasta.

Chapter 13
VARNA HASTA

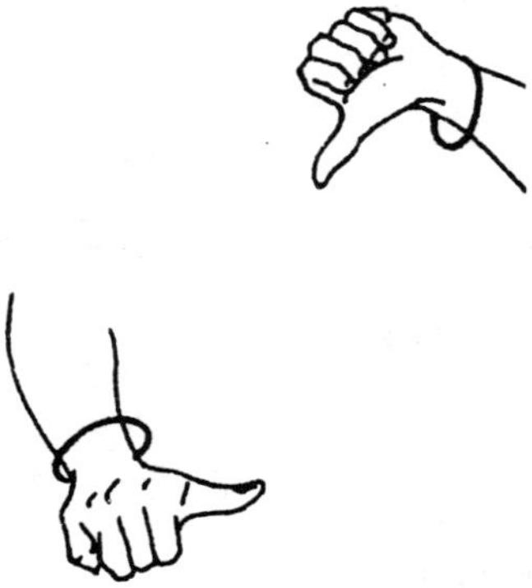

1. ब्राह्मणहस्तः
Brāhmaṇa Hastaḥ

कराभ्यां शिखरं धृत्वा यज्ञसूतस्य सूचने ।
दक्षिणेन कृते तिर्यग् ब्राह्मणानां करः स्मृतः ।।288।।

Transliteration:

Karābhyāṃ śikharaṃ dhṛtvā yajñasūtrasya sūcane |
Dakṣiṇena kṛte tiryag brāhmaṇānāṃ karaḥ smṛtaḥ ||

Meaning:

Karābhyāṃ śikharam dhṛtvā = assuming śikhara hasta with both hands; dakṣiṇena, tiryag, yajñasūtrasya sūcane kṛte = if the right hand obliquely moves to and fro suggesting the holding of sacred thread ; bāhmaṇānāṃ karaḥ smṛtaḥ = then it is considered as Brahmana hasta.

Assuming śikhara hasta with both hands, if the right hand obliquely moves to and fro suggesting the holding of sacred thread, then it is considered as Brāhmana hasta.

2. क्षत्रियहस्तः
Kṣatriya Hastaḥ

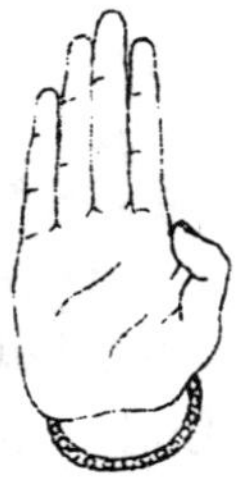

वामेन शिखरं तिर्यग् धृत्वाभ्येन पताकिका ।
धृता यदि क्षत्रियाणां हस्त इत्यभिधीयते ।।289।।

Transliteration:

Vāmena śikharaṃ tiryag dhṛtvābhyena patākikā |
Dhṛtā yadi kṣatriyāṇāṃ hasta ityabhidhīyate ||

Meaning:

Vamena śikharam tiryak dhṛtvā = assuming śikhara hasta obliquely with the left hand; yadi, abhyena patākikā dhṛtā = if patāka hasta is assumed with the right hand; kṣatriyāṇāṃ hastah, iti-abhidhīyate = it is said to be Kṣatriya hasta.

Assuming śikhara hasta obliquely with the left hand, if patāka hasta is assumed with the right hand, it is said to be Kṣatriya hasta.

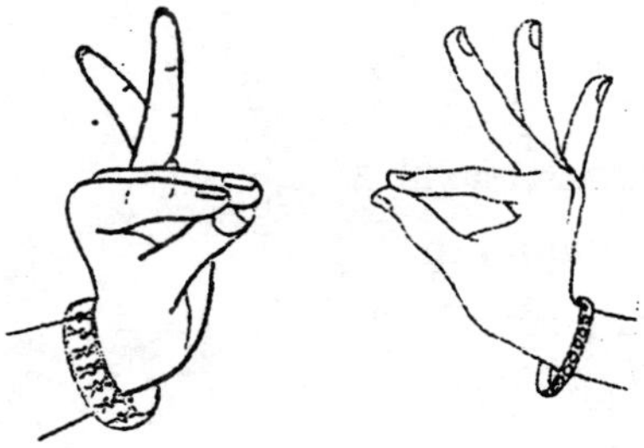

3. वैश्यहस्तः

Vaiśya Hastaḥ

करे वामे तु हंसास्यो दक्षिणे कटकामुखः ।
वैश्यहस्तो-यमाख्यातो मुनिभिर्भरतादिभिः ।।290।।

Transliteration:

Kare vāme tu haṃsāsyo dakṣiṇe kaṭakāmukhaḥ |
Vaiśyahasto-yamākhyāto munibhirbharatādibhiḥ ||

Meaning:

Vāme kare (tu) hamsāsyah, dakṣiṇe kaṭakāmukhaḥ, when left hand assumes hamsāsya hasta and the right hand assumes katakāmukha hasta; ayam, ākhyātah vaiśya hasta munibhih - bharata- adibhiḥ = then it is Vaiśya hasta as considered by Bharatamuni and others.

When left hand assumes hamsāsya hasta and the right hasta assumes katakāmukha hasta, then it is Vaiśya hasta as considered by Bharatamuni and others.

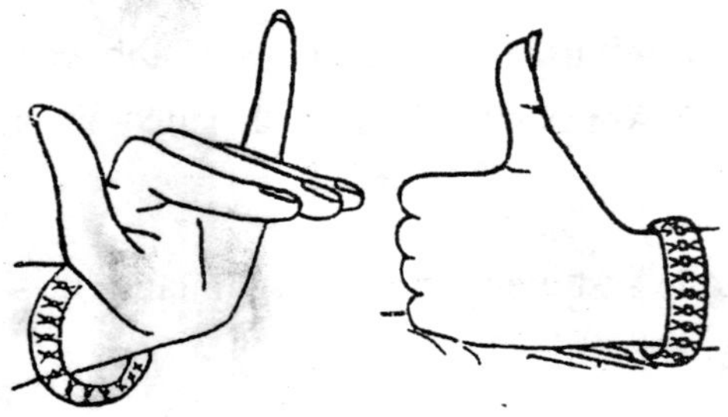

4. शूद्रहस्तः
Śūdrahastaḥ

वामे तु शिखरं धृत्वा दक्षिणे मृगशीर्षकः ।
शूद्रहस्तः स विज्ञेयो मुनिभिर्भरतादिभिः ।।291।।

Transliteration:

Vāme tu śikharaṃ dhṛtvā dakṣiṇe mṛgaśīrṣakaḥ |
Śūdrahastaḥ sa vijñeyo munibhirbharatādibhiḥ ||
Yadaṣṭādaśajātīmāṃ karma tena karāḥ smṛtāḥ |
Tattaddeśajānāmapi evamuhyaṃ budhottamaiḥ ||

Meaning:

Vame (tu) śikharam, dakshine mrgasirshakah, dhṛtvā = When left hand assumes śikhara hasta and right hand Mrgaśīrṣa hasta; sah, śūdra hastah, bharata-adibhih, munibhih, vijñeyah = then it is considered as Śūdra hasta by Bharata and other sages.

When left hand assumes śikhara hasta and right hand mrgaśirsha hasta, then it is considered as Śūdra hasta by Bharata and other sages.

Chapter 14

बान्धवहस्ताः

Bāndhava Hastāḥ (Abhinayam for relatives)

अथैकदासा बान्ध्व्यः तेषाम् लक्षणामुच्यते ।

Transliteration:

Athaikadāsā bāndhvyaḥ teṣāma lakṣaṇāmucyate | ।

There are eleven types of relationships. Their hastas will now be described

1. दम्पतिहस्तः

Dampati Hastaḥ (Wife and Husband)

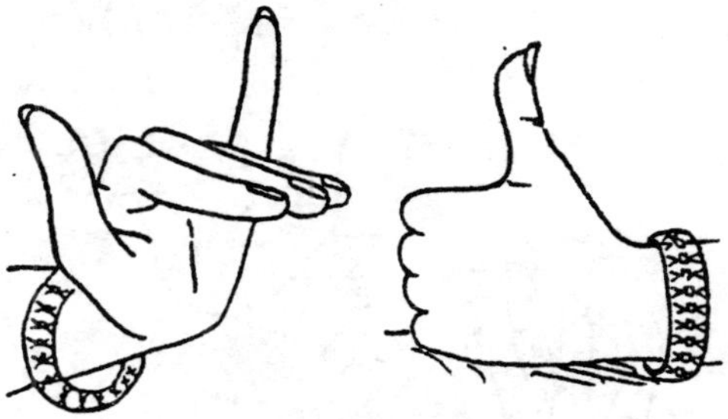

वामे तु शिखरं धृत्वा दक्षिणे मृगशीर्षकः ।।292।।
धृतः स्त्रीपुंसयोर्हस्तः ख्यातो भरतकोविदैः ।

Transliteration:

Vāme tu śikharaṃ dhṛtvā dakṣiṇe mṛgaśīrṣakaḥ ||
Dhṛtaḥ strīpuṃsayorhastaḥ khyāto bharatakovidaiḥ |

Meaning:

Vāme (tu) śikharam dhṛtvā, dakṣiṇe mṛgaśīrṣakaḥ dhṛtaḥ = if left hand assumes śikhara hasta while right hand assumes Mrgaśīrṣa hasta; bharatakovidaiḥ strī - puṃsayoh hastaḥ khyātaḥ = experts on Bharata's śāstra, consider it as Stri-pumsa (wife and husband = Dampati) hasta.

If left hand assumes śikhara hasta and right hand assumes mrgaśirsha hasta, experts on Bharata's śāstra, consider it as Stri-pumsa or Dampati hasta.

2. मातृहस्तः

Mātṛ Hastaḥ (Mother)

वामे हस्तेऽर्धचन्द्रश्च सन्दंशो दक्षिणे करे ।।293।।
आवर्तयित्वा जठरे वामहस्तं ततः परम् ।
स्त्रियाः करो धृतो मातृहस्त इत्युच्यते बुधैः ।।294।।

Transliteration:

Vāme haste-rdhacandraśca sandaṃśo dakṣiṇe kare ||
Āvartayitvā jaṭhare vāmahastaṃ tataḥ paraṃ |
Striyāḥ karo dhṛto mātṛhasta ityucyate budhaiḥ ||

विनियोगः (Application)

जनन्यां च कुमार्यां च मातृहस्तो नियुज्यते ।

Transliteration:

Jananyāṃ ca kumāryāṃ ca mātṛhasto niyujyate |

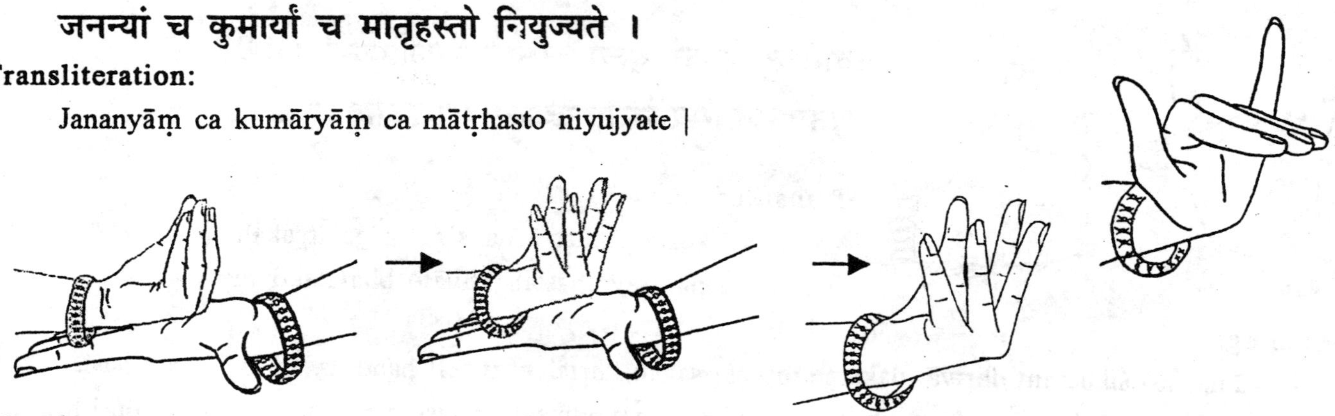

Meaning:

Vāme haste ardhacandraḥ dakṣiṇe kare samdaṃśaḥ = after left and right hand assume ardhacandra and sandaṃśa hastas, respectively, vāma hastaṃ jaṭhare āvartayitvā = the left hand is turned around on the stomach, striyāḥ karaḥ dhṛtaḥ = and assumes Strīhasta; mātṛhastaḥ iti budhaiḥ ucyate = then scholars consider it as Mātṛ (mother's) hasta;

Jananyāṃ (ca), kumāryāṃ (ca), mātṛ hastaḥ niyujyate = Mātṛ hasta denotes both mother and daughter.

After left and right hand assume ardhacandra and sandaṃśa hastas respectively, if the left hand is turned around on the stomach, and assumes Strihasta; then scholars consider it as Mātṛ (mother) hasta. This hasta denotes both mother and daughter.

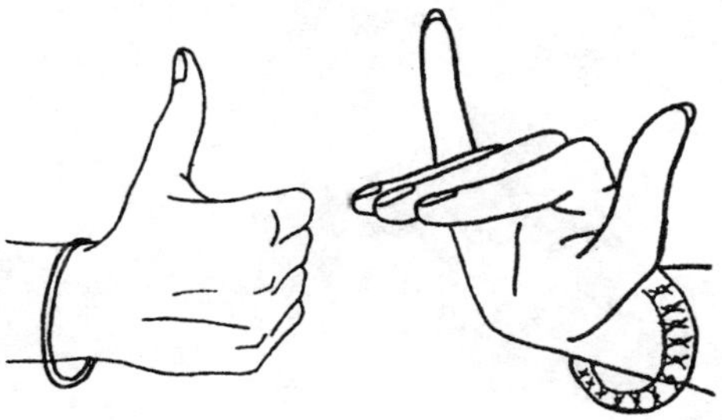

3. पितृहस्तः
Pitṛ Hastaḥ (Father)

एतस्मिन् मातृहस्ते तु शिखरे दक्षिणेन तु ।।295।।
धृते सति पितृहस्त इत्याख्यातो मनीषिभिः ।

Transliteration:

Ētasmin mātṛhaste tu śikhare dakṣiṇe tu ||
Dhṛte sati pitṛhasta ityākhyāto manīṣibhiḥ |

विनियोगः **(Application)**

अयं हस्तस्तु जनके जामातरि च युज्यते ।।296।।

Transliteration:

Ayaṃ hastastu janake jāmātari ca yujyate ||

Meaning:

Ētasmin mātṛhaste (tu), dakṣiṇe (tu) śikharaḥ dhrtaḥ cet = if the right hand of Matṛ hasta assumes śikhara hasta; sati pitṛhasta ityākhyāto manīṣibhiḥ = it is considered as Pitṛ hasta by the experts.

Ayam hastaḥ (tu) janake jāmātari (ca) niyujyate = this hasta denotes both janaka (father) and Jāmāta (son-in-law).

If the right hand of Matṛ hasta assumes śikhara hasta, it is considered as Pitṛ hasta by the experts. This hasta denotes both Janaka (father) and Jāmāta (son-in-law).

4. श्वश्रूहस्तः

Śvaśrūhastaḥ (Mother-in-law).

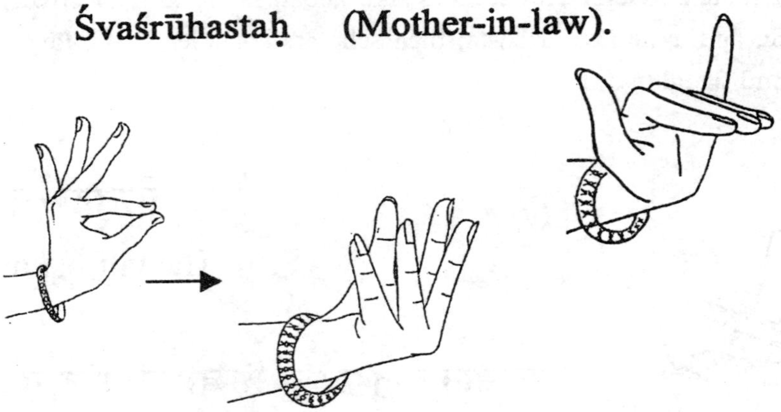

विन्यस्य कण्ठे हंसास्यं सन्दंशं दक्षिणे करे ।
उदरे च परामृश्य वामहस्तं ततः परम् ।।297।।
स्त्रियाः करो धृतः श्वश्रूहस्तस्तस्यां नियुज्यते ।

Transliteration:

Vinyasya kaṇṭhe haṃsāsyaṃ sandaṃśaṃ dakṣiṇe kare |
Udare ca parāmṛśya vāmahastaṃ tataḥ paraṃ ||
Striyāḥ karo dhṛtaḥ śvaśrūhastastasyāṃ niyujyate |

Meaning:

Kaṇṭhe haṃsāsyaṃ dakṣiṇe kare sandaṃśaṃ vinyasya = right hand with haṃsāsya hasta is held near throat at first and then changed to Sandaṃśaṃ hasta ; vāmahastaṃ udare parāmṛśya tataḥ paraṃ striyāḥ karaḥ dhṛtaḥ = left hand, turned around the belly and then as Strihasta; śvaśrūhastaḥ tasyāṃ niyujyate = it becomes Śvaśrūhasta and this hasta denotes Śvaśrū (mother-in-law).

Right hand with haṃsāsya hasta is held near throat at first and then changed to Sandaṃśaṃ hasta. Left hand turned around the belly, is held as Strihasta; then it becomes Śvaśrūhasta and this hasta denotes Śvaśrū.

5. श्वशुरहस्तः

Śvaśurahastaḥ (Father-in-law).

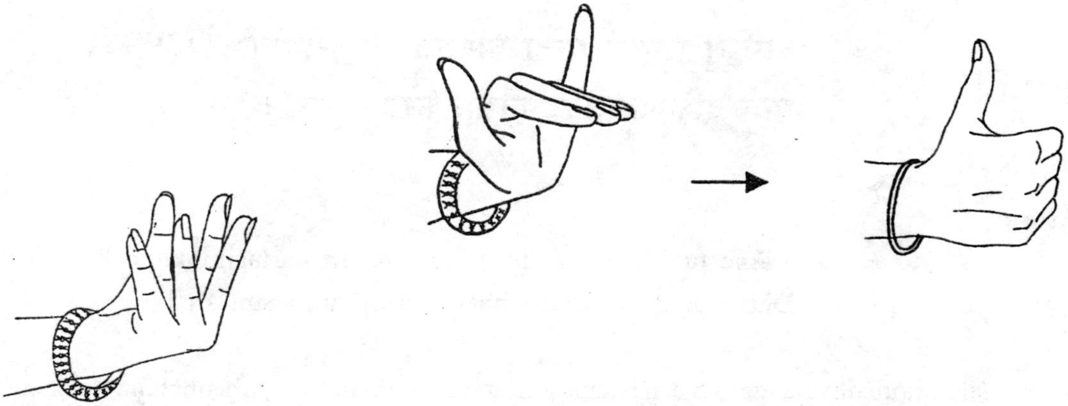

एतस्यान्ते तु हस्तस्य शिखरो दक्षिणे यदि ।।298।।
धृतश्च श्वशुरस्यायं हस्त इत्युच्यते बुधैः ।

Transliteration:

Ētasyānte tu hastasya śikharo dakṣiṇe yadi ||
Dhṛtaśca śvaśurasyāyaṃ hasta ityucyate budhaiḥ |

Meaning:

Etasya hastasya ante (tu), yadi dakṣiṇe śikharaḥ dhṛtaḥ (ca) = at the end of Śvaśru hasta, if the right hand assumes śikhara hasta; ayaṃ śvaśurasya hastaḥ iti budhaiḥ ucyate = it is considered by the scholars as śvaśura hasta.

At the end of Śvaśru hasta, if the right hand assumes śikhara hasta, it is considered by the scholars as Śvaśura hasta.

6. भर्तृभ्रातृहस्तः

Bhartṛbhrātṛ Hastaḥ (Husband's Brother).

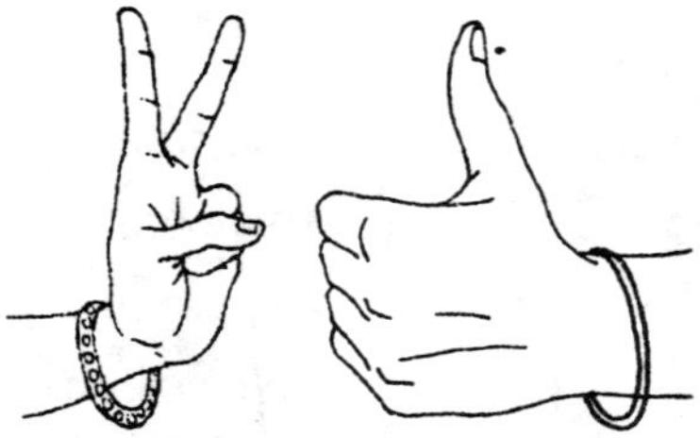

वामे तु शिखरं धृत्वा पार्श्वयोः कर्तरीमुखः ।।299।।
धृतो दक्षिणहस्तेन भर्तृभ्रातृकरः स्मृतः ।

Transliteration:

Vāme tu śikharaṃ dhṛtvā pārśvayoḥ kartarīmukhaḥ ||
Dhṛto dakṣiṇahastena bhartṛbhrātṛkaraḥ smṛtaḥ |

Meaning:

Vāme (tu) śikharaṃ dhṛtvā dakṣiṇa hastena kartarīmukhaḥ pārśvayoḥ dhṛtaḥ = when left hand assumes śikhara hasta and right hand asumes kartarīmukha hasta, and are held on the respective sides; bhartṛ bhrātṛ karaḥ smṛtaḥ = then, it is considered as Bhartṛbhrātṛ hasta.

When left hand assumes śikhara hasta and right hand asumes Kartarīmukha hasta and are held on the respective sides, then, it is considered as husband's brother i.e brother-in-law.

7. ननान्दृहस्तः

Nanāndṛ Hastaḥ (Husband's Sister).

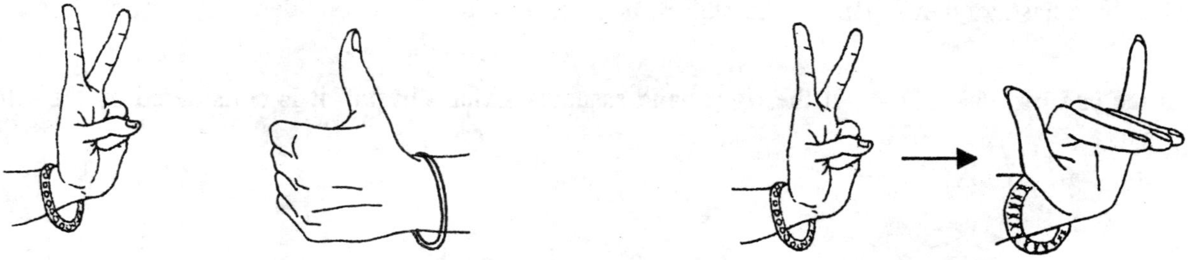

अन्ते त्वेतस्य हस्तस्य स्त्रीहस्तो दक्षिणे करे ।।300।।
धृतो ननान्दृहस्तः स्यादिति नाट्यविदां मतम् ।

Transliteration:

Ante tvetasya hastasya strīhasto dakṣiṇe kare ||
Dhṛto nanāndṛhastaḥ syāditi nāṭyavidāṃ mataṃ |

Meaning:

Bhartṛ-bhrātṛ karasya-ante dakṣiṇe kare strī hastaḥ dhṛtaḥ = if Stri hasta is assumed by the right hand after showing Bhartr-bhratr hasta ; nanāndṛ hastaḥ syāt iti nāṭyavidāṃ mataṃ = experts on Nātya consider it as Nanāndṛ hasta.

If Stri hasta is assumed by the right hand after showing Bhartṛ-bhrātṛ hasta, experts on Nātya consider it as husband's sister.

8. ज्येष्ठकनिष्ठभ्रातृहस्तः

Jyeṣṭhakaniṣṭhabhrātṛ Hastaḥ (Elder and younger brother)

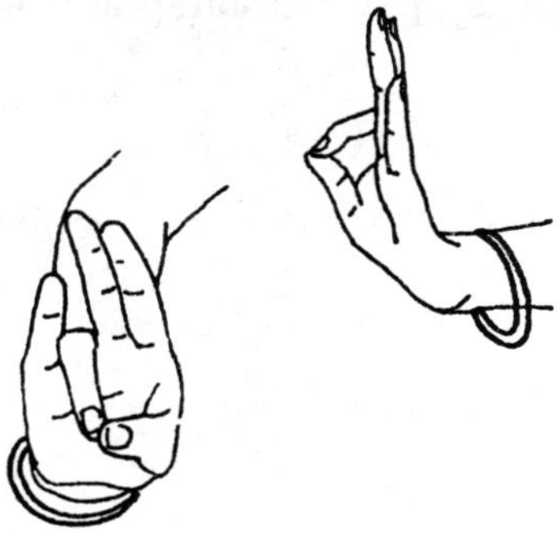

मयूरहस्तः पुरतः पार्श्वभागे च दर्शितः ।।301।।
ज्येष्ठभ्रातुः कनिष्ठस्याप्ययं हस्त इति स्मृतः ।

Transliteration:

Mayūrahastaḥ purataḥ pārśvabhāge ca darśitaḥ ||
Jyeṣṭhabhrātuḥ kaniṣṭhasyāpyayaṃ hasta iti smṛtaḥ |

Meaning:

Mayūrahastaḥ purataḥ pārśvabhāge (ca) darśitaḥ = when mayūra hasta is held in front or on the side, ayam jyeṣṭha bhrātuḥ kaniṣṭhasya - api hastaḥ iti smṛtaḥ = then it is considered as hasta for Jyeṣṭha bhrāta (elder brother) or Kaniṣṭhabhrāta (younger brother).

When mayura hasta is held in front or on the side, then it is considered as gesture for elder brother and younger brother.

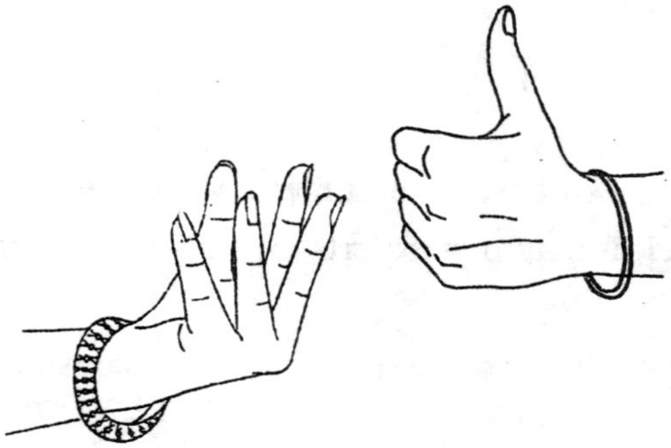

9. पुत्रहस्तः

Putra Hastaḥ (Son)

सन्दंशमुदरे न्यस्य भ्रामयित्वा ततः परम् ।।302।।
धृतो वामेन शिखरं पुत्रहस्तः प्रकीर्तितः ।

Transliteration:

Sandaṃśamudare nyasya bhrāmayitvā tataḥ paraṃ ||
Dhṛto vāmena śikharaṃ putrahastaḥ prakīrtitaḥ |

Meaning:

Udare sandaṃśaṃ ayasya tataḥ paraṃ hrāmayitvā = samdaṃśa hasta held in right hand on the belly and then moved around; āmena śikharaṃ dhṛtva = while left hand assumes śikhara hasta ; putra hastaḥ prakīrtitaḥ = it is considered as Putra hasta.

Samdaṃśa hasta is held in right hand on the belly and then moved around, while left hand assumes śikhara hasta, it is considered as Putra hasta.

10. स्नुषाहस्तः

Snuṣā Hastaḥ (Daughter-in-law)

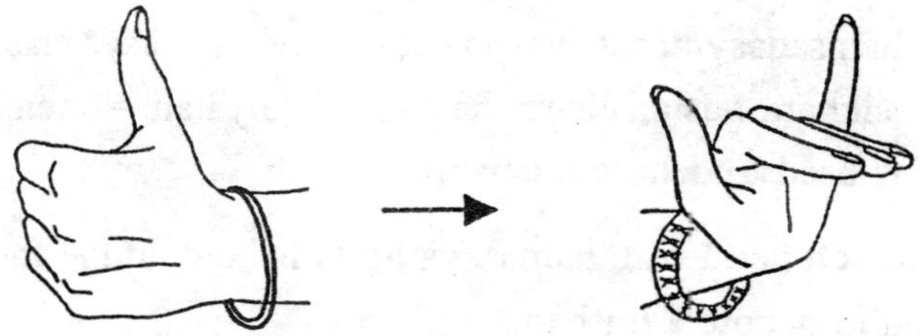

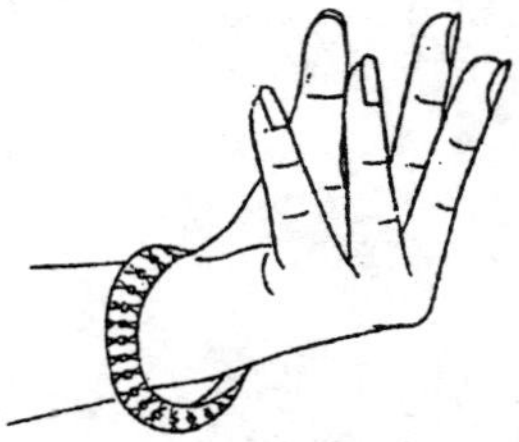

एतदन्ते दक्षिणेन स्त्रोहस्तश्च धृतो यदि ।।303।।
स्नुषाहस्त इति ख्यातो भरतागमकोविदैः ।

Transliteration:

Ētadante dakṣiṇena srohastaśca dhṛto yadi ||
Snuṣāhasta iti khyāto bharatāgamakovidaiḥ ||

Meaning:

Ētat-ante yadi dakṣiṇena strī hastaḥ (ca) dhṛtaḥ = at the end of Putra hasta, if right hand assumes Strihasta; Snuṣā hastah, iti bharata āgamakovidaiḥ khyātaḥ =it is said to denote a daughter-in-law by the experts on Nātyaśastra.

At the end of Putra hasta if right hand assumes Strīhasta; it is said to be Snuṣā hasta by the experts on Nātyaśastra.

11. भर्तृहस्तः

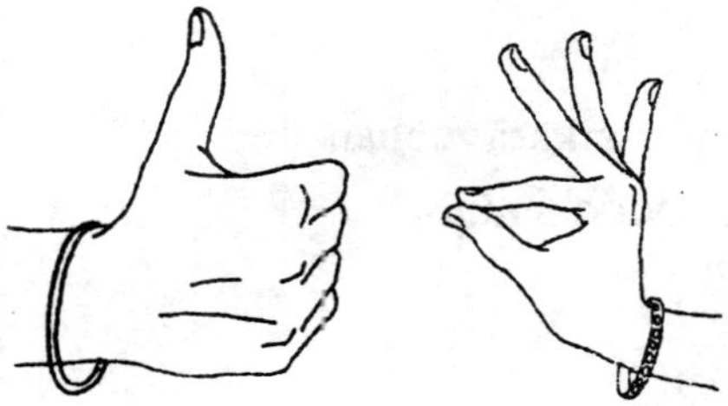

Bhartṛ Hastaḥ (Husband)

विनयस्य कन्ठे हम्सदस्यौ शिखरो दक्षिणे करे ।।304।।
भर्तृ हस्त इति ख्यातः तस्मिनेव नियुष्यते ।

Transliteration:

Vinayasya kaṇṭhe hamsadasyau śikharo dakṣiṇe kare ||
Bhartṛ hasta iti khyātaḥ tasmineva niyuṣyate |

Meaning:

Kaṇṭhe hamsadasyou vinayasya = holding hamsāsya hasta at the throat ; dakṣiṇe kare sikharah = right hand assumes śikhara hasta; bhartr hastah, iti khyatah = then, it is considered as Bhartṛ hasta ; tasmin eva niyujyate = it is used to denote husband.

When the left hand with hamsasya hasta is held at the throat and right hand assumes śikhara hasta,then, it is considered to denote a husband.

12. सपत्नीहस्तः

Sapatnī Hastaḥ (Another wife of husband)

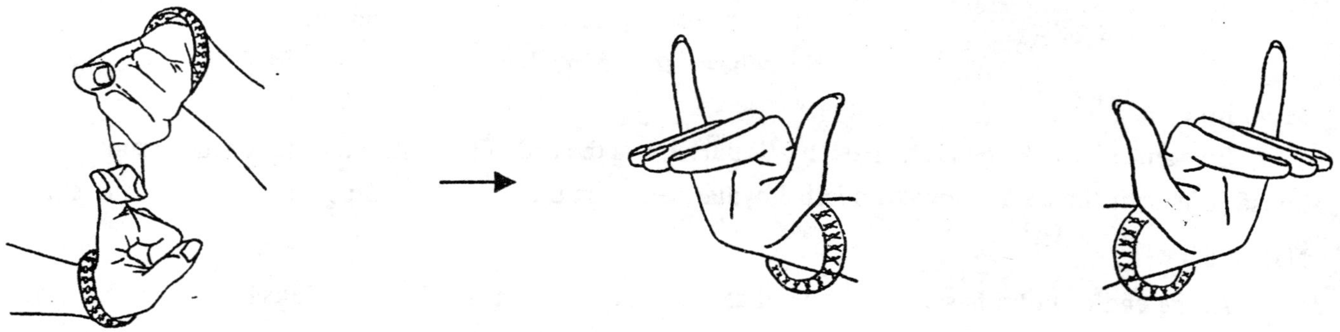

दर्शयित्वा पाशहस्तं कराभ्यां स्त्रीकरावुभौ ।।305।।
धृतौ सप्तनीहस्तः स्यादिति भावविदो विदुः ।

Transliteration:

Darśayitvā pāśahastaṃ karābhyāṃ strīkarāvubhau ||
Dhṛtau saptanīhastaḥ syāditi bhāvavido viduḥ |

Meaning:

Pāśa hastaṃ darśayitvā = after showing pāśa hasta ; ubhou karābhyāṃ strī karou dhṛtau = if both hands assume stri hasta; sapatnīhastaḥ syāt iti bhāvavidaḥ viduḥ = experts on bhāva know it as Sapatni hasta.

After holding pāśa hasta if both hands assume stri hasta experts on bhāva know it as another wife of her husband.

Chapter 15

नवग्रहहस्ताः

Navagrahahastāḥ

1. सूर्यहस्तः

Sūrya (Sun) hastaḥ

अंसोपकण्ठे हस्ताभ्यामलपद्मकपित्थकः ।।306।।
धृतो यदि करो ह्येष दिवाकर करः स्मृतः ।

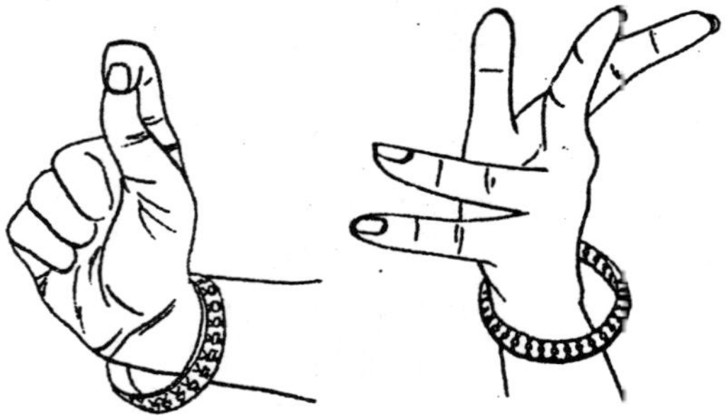

Transliteration:

Aṃsopakaṇṭhe hastābhyāmalapadmakapitthakaḥ ||
Dhṛto yadi karo hyeṣah divākara karaḥ smṛtaḥ |

Meanings :

Yadi, aṃsa-upakaṇṭhe, hastābhyām, alapadma - kapitthakou, dhṛto = if Alapadma and Kapittha hastas are held near the shoulders; eshā karaḥ divākara karaḥ smṛtaḥ = then that hasta is considered to represent Sun.

If Alapadma and Kapittha hastas are held near the shoulders; then that hasta is considered to represent Sun.

2. चन्द्रहस्तः
Candra (Moon) hastaḥ

अलपद्मो वामहस्ते दक्षिणे च पताकिका ।।307।।
निशाकरकरः प्रोक्तो भरतागमदर्शिभिः ।

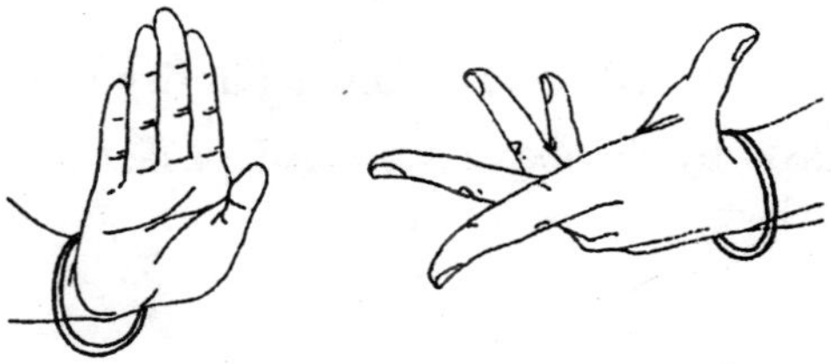

Transliteration:

Alapadmo vāmahaste dakṣiṇe ca patākikā ||
Niśākarakaraḥ prokto bharatāgamadarśibhiḥ |

Meanings :

Alapadma vāmahaste patākikā dakṣiṇe = if Alapadma is assumed by left hand and patāka hasta by right hand; niśākara karaḥ, bharata-āgama darśibhiḥ, proktaḥ = it is said to represent moon by scholars.

If Alapadma is assumed by left hand and patāka hasta by right hand, it is said to represent moon by scholars.

3. कुजहस्तः
Kujahastaḥ / Angāraka (Mars) Hasta

वामे करे तु सूची स्यान्मुष्टिहस्तस्तु दक्षिणे ।।308।।
धृतश्चेत् नाट्यशास्त्रज्ञैः अङ्गारक करः स्मृतः ।

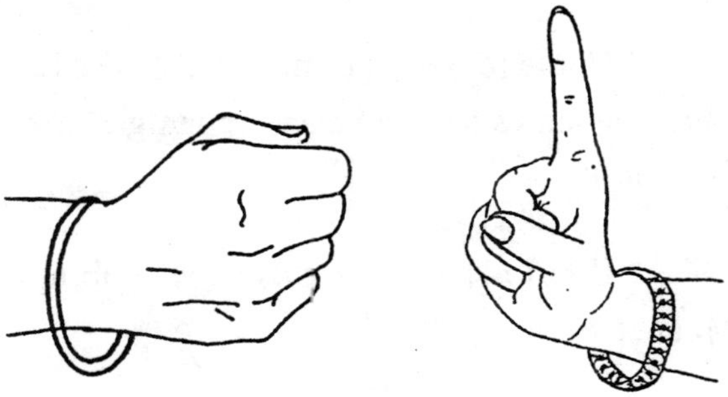

Transliteration:

Vāme kare tu sūcī syāgmuṣṭihastastu dakṣiṇe ||
Dhṛtaścet nāṭyaśāstrajñaiḥ aṅgāraka karaḥ smṛtaḥ |

Meanings :

Vāmakare (tu) sūcī syāt, dakṣiṇe muṣṭi hastaḥ (tu) dhṛtaḥ cet = if left hand assumes sūcī hasta and right hand holds Mushṭi hastaḥ; angāraka karaḥ, nāṭya śāstrajñah smṛtaḥ = then it is considered as Angāraka hasta by the experts on Nāṭyaśāstra.

If left hand assumes sūcī hasta and right hand holds Mushṭi hastaḥ, then it is considered as Angāraka hasta by the experts on Nāṭyaśāstra.

4. बुधहस्तः

Budha (Mercury) Hastaḥ

तिर्यग्वामे च मुष्टिः स्याद्दक्षिणे च पताकिका ।।309।।
बुधग्रहकरः प्रोक्तो भरतागमवेदिभिः ।

Transliteration:

Tiryagvāme camuṣṭiḥ syāddakṣiṇe ca patākikā ||
Budhagrahakaraḥ prokto bharatāgamavedibhiḥ |

Meanings :

Vāme (ca) muṣṭiḥ tiryak, dakṣiṇe (ca) patākikā syāt = if left hand holds muṣṭi hasta obliquely and right hand assumes patāka hasta; budha graha karaḥ, bharat - āgama = it is said to represent the planet Budha.

If left hand holds muṣṭi hasta obliquely and right hand assumes patāka hasta, it is said to represent the planet Budha.

5. गुरुहस्तः

Guru, Brahaspati (Jupiter) Hastaḥ

हस्ताभ्यां शिखरं धृत्वा यज्ञसूत्रस्य दर्शनम् ।।310।।
ऋषिब्राह्मणहस्तोऽयं गुरोश्चापि प्रकीर्तितः ।

Transliteration:

Hastābhyāṃ śikharaṃ dhṛtvā yajñasūtrasya darśanam ||
Ṛṣibrāhmaṇahasto-yaṃ guroścāpi prakīrtitaḥ |

Meanings :

Hastābhyāṃ śikharaṃ dhṛtvā, yajñasūtrasya darśanam = when both hands with śikhara hasta are held as if holding the sacred thread; ayam guroḥ hastaḥ iti prakīrtitaḥ = then, it is considered as Guru hasta; ṛṣi-brāhmaṇa hastaḥ api = this is the hasta for ṛshi as well as brāhmin.

When both hands with śikhara hasta are held as if holding the sacred thread, then, it is considered as Guru hasta, This is the hasta for ṛshi as well as brāhmin.

6. शुक्रहस्तः

Śukra (Venus) Hastaḥ

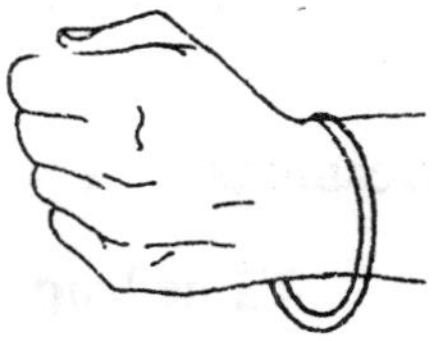

वामोर्ध्वभागे मुष्टिः स्यादधस्ताद्दक्षिणे तथा ।।311।।
शुक्रग्रहकरः प्रोक्तो भरतागमवेदिभिः ।

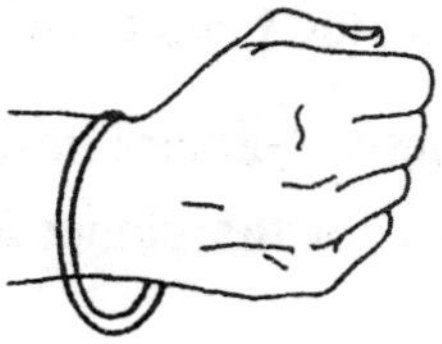

Transliteration:

Vāmordhvabhāge muṣṭiḥ syādadhastāddakṣaiṇe tathā ||
Śukragrahakaraḥ prokto bharatāgamavedibhiḥ |

Meanings :

Vāma-urdhwabhāge, tathā dakshiṇe adhastā muṣṭiḥ syāt = after assuming Mushṭi hasta in both hands, if the left hand is raised and the right hand is lowered; Śukragraha karaḥ proktaḥ, bharata-āgama vedibhiḥ = then experts on Nāṭyaśāstra consider it as hasta for the planet Śukra.

After assuming Mushṭi hasta in both hands, if the left hand is raised and the right hand is lowered then experts on Nāṭyaśāstra consider it as hasta for the planet Śukra.

7. शनिहस्तः

Śani (Saturn) Hastaḥ

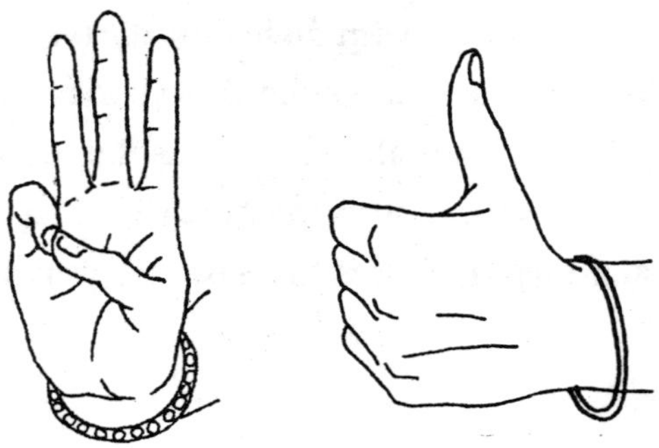

वामे करे तु शिखरस्त्रिशूलो दक्षिणे करे ।।312।।
शनैश्चरकरः प्रोक्तो भरतागमकोविदैः ।

Transliteration:

Vāme kare tu śikharastriśūlo dakṣiṇe kare ||
Śanaiścarakaraḥ prokto bharatāgamakovidaiḥ |

Meanings :

Vāme kare (tu) śikharaḥ, dakṣiṇe kare triśūlaḥ = when left hand assumes Śikhara hasta and right hand Triśūla hasta; śanaiścara karaḥ proktaḥ bharata - āgama vedibhiḥ = then it is considered by the experts on Nāṭyaśāstra as the hasta for the planet Saturn.

When left hand assumes Śikhara hasta and right hand Triśūla hasta, then it is considered by the experts on Nāṭyaśāstra as the hasta for the planet Saturn.

8. राहुहस्तः

Rāhu (Dragon's head) hastaḥ

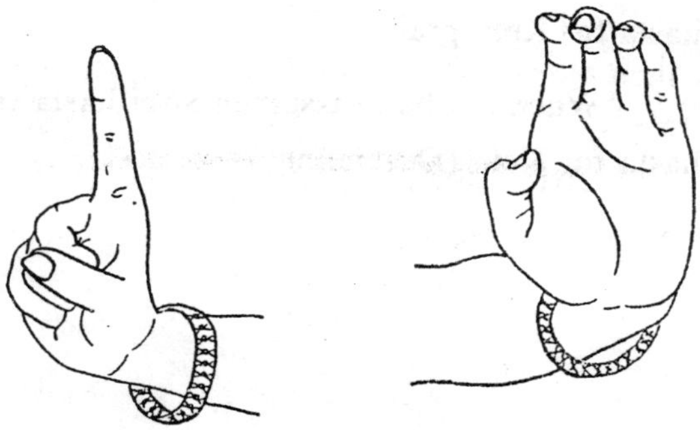

सर्पशीर्षो वामकरे सूची स्याद्दक्षिणे करे ।।313।।
राहुग्रहकरः प्रोक्तो नाट्यविद्याधिपैर्जनैः ।

Transliteration:

Sarpaśīrṣo vāmakare sūcī syāddakṣiṇe kare ||
Rāhugrahakaraḥ prokto nāṭyavidyādhipairjanaiḥ |

Meanings :

Vāmakare sarpaśīrshaḥ dakṣiṇe kare sūcī syāt = when left hand assumes Sarpaśīrshaḥ hasta and right hand sūcī hasta; rāhugraha karaḥ bharata-āgama kovidaiḥ proktaḥ = then it is considered by the experts on Nāṭya as the hasta for Rāhu graha.

When left hand assumes Sarpaśīrshaḥ hasta and right hand sūcī hasta, then it is considered by the experts on Nāṭyaśāstra as the hasta for Rāhu (Ascending lunar node).

केतुहस्तः

Ketu (Dragon's tail) hastaḥ

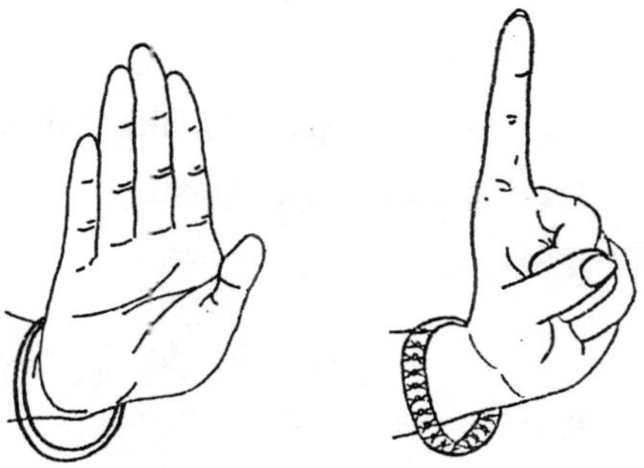

वामे करे तु सूची स्याद्दक्षिणे तु पताकिका ।।314।।
केतुग्रहकरः प्रोक्तो भरतागमदर्शिभिः ।

Transliteration:

Vāme kare tu sūcī syāddakṣiṇe tu patākikā ||
Ketugrahakaraḥ prokto bharatāgamadarśibhiḥ |

Meanings :

Vāme kare (tu) sūcī, dakṣiṇe (tu) patākikā syāt = when left hand assumes Sūcī hasta and right hand Patāka hasta; ketugraha karaḥ proktaḥ, bharata - āgama - darśibhiḥ = then it is considered by Bharata, as the hasta for Ketu graha.

When left hand assumes Sūcī hasta and right hand Patāka hasta, then it is considered by Bharata, as the hasta for Ketu (Desending lunar node).

Chapter 16

राज हस्ताः

Rāja Hastāḥ

(Gesture for kings)

King	-	Gesture
हरिश्चन्द्र Hariścandra	-	Śukatunda
नल Nala	-	Mayūra
पुरुकुत्स Purukutsa	-	Alapadma
पुरूरव Purūrava	-	Muśṭi
सगर Sagara	-	Alapadma held over the head.
दिलीप Dilīpa	-	Patāka
अम्बरीष Ambarisha	-	Kartari
शिबि Śibi	-	Kapittha to be shaken in front.
कार्तवीर्य Kārtavirya	-	Two Patāka hastas with thumbs curved round, held at the shoulders as if denoting divine pose.
रावण Rāvaṇa	-	Two Patāka hastas held in puṃkhita.
धर्मराज Dharmarāja	-	Sūci to be shaken at the shoulder.
अर्जुन Arjuna	-	Tripatāka to be shaken repeatedly in front.
भीम Bhīma	-	Muśti to be shaken in front.

शैव्य Śaibya	-	Sūci with the finger twisted upwards.
नकुल Nakula	-	Kaṭaka
सहदेव Sahadeva	-	Śikhara
नहुष Nahusha	-	Calapatāka
ययाति Yayāti	-	Tāmracūda
भगीरथ Bhagiratha;		
चंद्र ग्रहणम Candra grahanam (=eclipse of moọn)	-	Ardhacandra to be shown as tripatāka.
मांधाता, मारुतवंता Māndhāta; Marutwanta	-	Mukula, Sūci, Mushti and Ardhapatāka- in this order they are twisted upward touching the body.
रघु Raghu	-	Ardhapatāka to be held above on the right side.
दशरथ Daśaratha	-	Alapadma held in both hands.
राम Rāma	-	Śikhara
Other kings with the bow	-	Śikhara
भरत Bharata	-	Śikhara over the right shoulder.
लक्ष्मणा Lakshmana	-	Śikhara over to the left shoulder.
शत्रुघ्न Śatrughna	-	Śikhara over the forehead.
Kings of lunar race	-	Left Śikhara over the left shoulder

These hastas are to be used depending on the context.

Chapter 17

समुद्र हस्ताः

Samudra Hastāḥ

(Abhinayaṃ for the seven seas/oceans)

लवणेक्षु सुरा सर्पिः दधि क्षीर जलार्णवः ।।315।।
एतेषाम् हस्तकलनां विशेषात् प्रतिपाद्यते ।

Transliteration:

Lavaṇekṣu surā sarpiḥ dadhi kṣīra jalārṇavaḥ ||
Ēteśām hastakalanā viśeṣāt pratipādyate |

Meaning:

Lavana - ikshu - surā - sarpih - dadhi-kshira - jala - arnavāh = the seven seas are - lavana, ikshu, sura, sarpi, dadhi, kshira and jala; eteshām hastakalanā viseshāt pratipādyate = the characteristics of their hastas will be proposed now in detail.

There are seven seas - 1. Lavana (salt), 2. Ikshu (sugarcane juice), 3. Sura (intoxicating drink), 4. Sarpi (ghee), 5. Dadhi (curds), 6. Kshira (milk), and 7. Jala (water); the hastas for them will be described, now.

1. लवण समुद्र हस्तः

Lavaṇa Samudra Hastaḥ

मुकुलाख्या-करौ चैव व्यावृत्तौ चापवेष्टितौ ।।316।।
प्रयोज्यो लवणांबोधो धिषणस्य मातांतरे ।

Transliteration:

Mukulākhyā-karau caiva vyāvṛttau cāpaveṣṭitau ||
Prayojyo lavaṇāmbodho dhiṣṇasya mātāntare |

Meaning:

Vyāvṛttau (ca), apaveṣṭitau, mukula-ākhya karau (caiva) = when two Mukula hastas perform the two hasta prānas viz. vyāvṛtta and apaveshtita; lavana-ambhodhau, prayojyau = it is to be used to denote Lavana samudra; dhiṣanasya mata -antare = this is the view of Dhiṣana i.e. Bṛhaspati.

If two Mukula hatas perform vyāvṛtta and apaveshtita hasta prāna, it denotes lavana samudram.

2. इक्षु समुद्र हस्तः
Ikṣu Samudra Hastaḥ

अलपदमः तथाभूत इक्ष्वाब्धौ संप्रयुज्यते ।।317।।

Transliteration:

Alapadamaḥ tathābhūta ikṣvābdhau samprayujyate ||

Meaning:

Alpadmah tathābhūta = if two Alpadma hastas perform the same hasta prānas i.e. vyāvṛtta and apaveshtita ; ikshwabdhou samprayujyate = it is used to denote Ikshu samudram.

When two Alapadma hastas perform vyāvṛtta and apaveṣṭita hasta prāna, it denotes Ikshu Samudram

3. सूरा समुद्र हस्तः
Sūrā Samudra Hastaḥ

संकीर्णाख्या पताकौ च तथैव गुणमासृतौ ।
सूरांबुधौ प्रयोक्तव्यो शुक्रचार्यमातांतरे ।।318।।

Transliteration:

Saṅkīrṇākhyā patākau ca tathaiva guṇāmāsṛtau |
Sūrāmbudhau prayoktavyo śukracāryamātāntare ||

Meaning:

Samkirna ākhya patākou, tathā eva gunam - āsritou = in the same manner if two Samkirnapatāka hastas, perform vyāvṛtta and apaveṣṭita hasta prānas : sura -abdhou prayoktavyau = then it denotes Surā samudram; Sukra-ācārya mata-antare= this is the view of Sukra-ācārya.

When two Samkirnapatāka hastas perform Vyāvṛtta and apaveṣṭita hasta prāna it denotes Surā samudra, this is the view of Sukrācārya.

4. सर्पि समुद्र हस्तः
Sarpi Samudra Hastaḥ

सुरप्रिरब्धेष्टु चातुरो वायुसूनुमातांतरे ।

Transliteration:

Suraprirabdheṣṭu cāturo vāyusūnumātāntare |

Meaning:

Caturah = if two Catura hastas perform vyāvṛtta and apaveṣṭita hasta prānas; sarpih-abdheh (tu) = It denotes Sarpi samudram; vāyūsūnu mata-antare = this is the view of Vāyusūnu i.e. Ānjaneya.

If two Catura hastas perform vyāvṛtta and apaveṣṭita hasta prāna it denotes Sarpi samudram, this is the view of Ānjaneya.

5. दधि समुद्र हस्तः
Dadhi Samudra hastaḥ

त्रिपटाकाभिधौ हस्तौ पूर्ववत् गुणमास्त्रितौ ।।319।।
दध्यर्णवे प्रयोक्तव्यो दत्तिलाचार्या सम्मतौ ।

Transliteration:

Tripaṭākābhidhau hastau pūrvavat guṇamāstritau ||
Dadhyarṇave prayoktavyo dattilācāryā sammatau |

Meaning:

Tripatāka-abhidhou hastou, pūrwavat gunam - āsritou = when two Tripatāka hastas perform the same vyāvṛtta and apaveṣṭita hasta prāna; dadhi-arnave prayoktavyou = it denotes Dadhi samudram; dattila -ācārya sammatou = this is the view of Dattila Acārya.

When two Tripatāka hastas perform vyāvṛtta and apaveṣṭita hasta prāna then it denotes Dadhi samudram, this is the view of Dattilācārya.

6. क्षीर समुद्र हस्तः
Kṣīra Samudra hastaḥ

सर्पशीर्षाव्यौ हस्तौ यथापूर्वा-गुणाश्रयो ।।320।।
क्षीरसागर रूपार्थे नारदाभिमतौ स्मृतौ ।

Transliteration:

Sarpaśīrṣāhavyo hastau yathāpūrvā-guṇāśrayo ||
Kṣīrasāgara rūpārthe nāradābhimatau smṛtau |

Meaning:

Sarpaśīrṣāwayou hastou, yathāpūrwa-gunā-āsrayou= when two Sarpaśīrṣa hastas perform the same vyāvṛtta and apaveṣṭita hasta prānas; kshirasāgara-rūpa-arthe smrtou =it is considered as denoting Kṣīra samudram; nārada-abhimatou = this is the view of Nārada.

When two sarpaśīrṣa hatas perform vyāvṛtta and apaveṣṭita hasta prāna it denotes Kṣhīra samudram, this is the view of Nārada,

7. जल समुद्र हस्तः
Jala Samudra Hastaḥ

पताकगुणसंयुक्तौ पूर्वात् मिलितौ कृतौ ।।321।।
जलार्णवे प्रयोतव्यौ कोहलाचार्य सम्मतौ ।

Transliteration:

Patākaguṇasaṃyuktau pūrvāt militau kṛtau ||
Jalārṇave prayotavyau kohalācārya sammatau |

Meaning:

Patāka - guna-samyuktau, pūrvavat militau kṛtau = if two patāka hatas, perform the same vyāvṛtta and apaveṣṭita hasta prānas; jala-arnave prayoktavyou = it is to be used to denote Jala samudram; kohala-ācārya sammatau = this is the view of Kohala Acārya.

When two Pataka hastas together perform vyāvṛtta an apaveṣṭita hasta prāna it denotes Jala samudram, this is the view of Kohala Acārya. .

Chapter 18

नदी हस्ताः

Nadī hastāḥ (Abhinayam for the rivers)

गंगादीनाम् निर्णयेतु व्यवृत्तश्चापवेष्टितः ।।322।।
नडीनामपि सर्वमासाम् पताकः समुदाहृतः ।
गंगादीनाम् विशेषेण तद्गुणाद्यानुवर्णनात् ।।323।।
हस्तानाम् भेदकलना गुरुणा पूर्वमीरिता ।
तत्स्वारूपम् प्रवक्ष्यामि नाट्याभिनय योगतः ।।324।।

Transliteration :

Gaṅgādīnām nirṇayetu vyāvṛttaścāpaveṣṭitaḥ |
Naḍīnāmapi sarvamāsām patākaḥ samudāhṛtaḥ |
Gaṅgādīnām viśeṣeṇa tadguṇādyānuvarṇanāt |
Hastānām bhedakalanā guruṇā pūrvamīritā ||
Tatsvārūpam pravakṣyāmi nāṭyābhinaya yogataḥ ||

Meaning :

Patāka hasta, performing vyāvṛtta and apaveṣṭita hastaprānas denotes all the rivers like Gaṅga. However, keeping in view the special virtues of rivers like Ganga. Brhaspati had expounded different hatas for them. I shall now describe those hastas which could be used in nātya.

1. Ganga : Tāmracūda hasta denotes Ganga.

When the left and right hand assume Kataka and Patāka hasta, respectively: the pose is Yānasthiti i.e. as if on the move with toes spreadout and bent slightly upward.

Patāka hasta, pointing downward with moving fingers, denote Jāhnavi (i.e. Ganga).

2.	Ākāśa Ganga	:	Right hand as Patāka hasta held upward and shaken obliquely; shoulders to be kept high and the right hand to be brought down on the left side.
3.	Godāvari	:	Patāka hasta held with fingers apart, pointing downwards and shaking.
4.	Kāveri	:	Catura hasta denotes Kāveri. The hand assumes Pataka hasta with its forefinger pointing downwards, stretched forward and then held high in air and shaken. Then the Patāka hasta, with fingers apart and pointing downward has to be shaken.
5.	Tungabhadra	:	Hamsāsya hasta denotes tungabhadra. Right hand assumes Patāka hasta in which the forefinger and the ring finger are joined, the middle finger is held over them, the thumb and the little finger are slightly raised. In this pose, the right hand thumb alone is shaken while the other fingers point towards the face.
6.	Narmada	:	Ardhapataka denotes Narmada. To indicate Narmada- in the pose mentioned in the case of Godāvāri, the two patāka hastas have to move in a circle.
7 :	Reva	:	Patāka hasta has to show winding course

8. Hastas for some other rivers.

sūryaja (yamuna)	-	rekhā hasta
kṛṣṇaveṇī	-	siṃhamukha hasta
sarasvatī	-	patākacatura hasta
vetrāvati	-	sūci hasta hasta
candrabhāgā	-	cālapatāka hasta
sarayū	-	alapadma hasta
bhīmārti	-	arāla hasta
suvarṇamukhī	-	ardhacandra hasta
pāpanāśani	-	śukatuṇḍa hasta
śrāvatī	-	bāṇu hasta

Chapter 19

लोक हस्ताः

Loka Hastāḥ (Abhinayam for the Worlds)

ऊर्ध्वलोकाः

Ūrdhvalokāḥ (Upper worlds)

भूलोकश्च भुवर्लोकः स्वर्गलोकः ततःपरम् ।
जानोलोकः तपोलोकः सत्यलोकभिधः ततः ।।325।।
महर्लोकः च सप्तैते लोकश्चोर्ध्वम् समाश्रितः ।
उद्वेष्टितः पताकस्तु एतेषु विनियुज्यते ।।326।।

Tranliteration:

Bhūlokaśca bhuvarlokaḥ svargalokaḥ tataḥparama |
Jānolokaḥ tapolokaḥ satyalokabhidhaḥ tataḥ ||
Maharlokaḥ ca saptaite lokaścordhvam samāśritaḥ |
Udveṣṭitaḥ patākastu eteṣu viniyujyate ||

Meaning:

Bhūlokaḥ (ca), bhuvarlokaḥ, swargalokaḥ, (tataḥ-param) janolokaḥ, tapolokaḥ, satyaloka (abhidhaḥ), (tataḥ), Maharlokaḥ (ca), = 1. Bhūlokam, 2. Bhuvarlokam, 3. Swargalokam, 4. Janolokam, 5. Tapolokam, 6. Satyalokam and 7. Maharlokam; sapta ete lokāḥ (ca), ūrdhwam samāśritaḥ = these are the seven upper worlds eteṣu udveṣṭitaḥ patākaḥ (tu), viniyujyate = Patāka hasta, performing udveṣṭita hastaprāna, denotes these seven upper worlds.

अधोलोकाः

Adholokāḥ (Lower worlds)

अतलो वितलः चैव सुतलः च तलातलः।
महातल इति ख्यातो रसातल इतीरितः ।।327।।
पातालः चैव सप्तैते हि अधोलोकः प्रकीर्तितः।
अधोलोकेषु युज्येत पताकः चापवेष्टितः ।।328।।

Tranliteration:

Atalo vitalaḥ caiva sutalaḥ ca talātalaḥ |
Mahātala iti khyāto rasātala itītaḥ ||
Pātālaḥ caiva saptāte hyādholokaḥ prakīrtitaḥ |
Adholokeṣu yujyeta patākaḥ cāpaveṣṭitaḥ ||

Meaning:

Atalah, vitalah (caiva), sutalah (ca), talātalah, mahātalah (iti) (iritah), pātālah (caiva) = 1. Atala loka, 2. Vitala loka, 3. Sutala loka, 4. Talātala loka, 5. Mahātala loka, 6. Rasātala loka, and 7. Pātāla loka; sapta ete (hi), adholokāh prakirtitāh, = these are considered as the seven lower worlds; patākah (ca), apaveṣṭitah, adholokeshu, yujyeta = Pataka hasta, performing apaveṣṭhita hasta prāna, is to be used to denote these seven lover worlds.

Upper worlds are seven ; these are to be depicted by Patāka performing udweṣtita hasta prāna.

Lower Worlds are seven : These are to be depicted by Patāka hasta performing apaveṣtita hasta prāna.

Chapter 20

नृत्तहस्ताः

Nṛttahastaḥ

भवन्ति नृत्तहस्तानां गतयः पञ्चधा भुवि ।
ऊर्ध्वा-धरोत्तरा प्राची दक्षिणा चेति विश्रुता ।।329।।
यथा स्यात् पादविन्यास्तथैव करयोरपि ।
वामाङ्गभागे वामस्य दक्षिणे दक्षिणस्य च ।।330।।
कुर्यात् प्रचलनं ह्येतनृत्तसिद्धान्तलक्षणम् ।
यतो हस्तस्ततो दृष्टिर्यतो दृष्टिस्ततो मनः ।।331।।
यतो मनस्ततो भावो यतो भावस्ततो रसः ।

Transliteration:

Bhavanti nṛttahastānāṃ gatayaḥ pañcadhā bhuvi |
Ūrdhvā-dharottarā prācī dakṣiṇā ceti viśrutā ||
Yathā syāt pādavinyāstathaiva karayorapi |
Vāmāṅgabhāge vāmasya dakṣiṇe dakṣiṇasya ca ||
Kuryāt pracalanaṃ hyetanṛttasiddhāntalakṣaṇam |
Yato hastastato dṛṣṭiryato dṛṣṭistato manaḥ ||
Yato manastato bhāvo yato bhāvastato rasaḥ |

Meanings:

In the world, the movements of Nṛttahastas are of five types : 1. ūrdhwa = upwards; 2. adhara = downwards; 3. uttara = on the left; 4. prāçi = in the front, 5. dakshiṇa = on the right.

The movements of the hastas folow the movements of the feet. Generally, the movements of the left hand and foot are to be on the left side and the movements of the right hand and foot are to be on the right side - this is the rule in nṛtta.

Wherever the hand moves, the glance should follow; where the glance is, the mind should follow; where the mind is fixed, there the bhāva arises; when the bhāva is expressed, there is rasa.

पताकास्वस्तिकाख्यश्च डोलाहस्तस्तथाञ्जलिः ।।332।।
कटकावर्धनश्चैव शकटः पाशकीलकौ ।
कपित्थ शिखरः कूर्मो हंसास्य-श्चालपद्मकः ।।333।।
त्रयोदशैते हस्तास्युः नृत्तस्या-प्युपयोगिनः ।

Transliteration:

Patākāsvastikākhyaśca ḍolāhastastathāñjaliḥ ||
Kaṭakāvardhanaścaiva śakaṭaḥ pāśakīlakau |
Kapittha śikharaḥ kūrmo haṃsasya-ścālapadmakaḥ ||
Trayodaśaite hastāyyuḥ nṛttasyā-pyupayoginaḥ |

Meanings:

Patākā,svastika, ca ḍolāhasta,tath āñjaliḥ= the hand gestures patākā,svastika, and ḍolāhasta,like that āñjaliḥ; kaṭakāvardhana ca eva śakaṭaḥ, pāśa, kīlakau= kaṭakāvardhana and also the mudras śakaṭaḥ, pāśa, kīlakau (are the Nṛtta hastas).

1. Patāka hasta, 2. Svastika hasta, 3. Ḍolā hasta, 4. Anjali hasta, 5. Katakāvardhana hasta, 6. Śakata hasta, 7. Pāśa hasta, 8. kilaka hasta, 9. Kapittha hasta, 10. Śikhara hasta, 11. Kūrma hasta, 12. Hamsāsya hasta, and 13. Alapadma hasta- these are the thirteen Nṛtta hastas.

Chapter 21

पादभेदाः

Pādabhedāḥ

वक्ष्यते पादभेदानां लक्षणं पूर्वसम्मतम् ।।334।।
मण्डलोत्प्लवने चैव भ्रमरी पादचारिका ।
चतुर्धा पादभेदाः स्युस्तेषां लक्षणमुच्यते ।।335।।

Transliteration:

Vakṣyate pādabhedānāṃ lakṣaṇaṃ pūrvasammatam ||
Maṇḍalotplavane caiva bhramarī pādacārikā |
Caturdhā pādabhedāḥ syuḥ teṣāṃ lakṣaṇamucyate ||

Meaning:

Vakṣyate pādabhedānāṃ lakṣaṇaṃ pūrvasammatam= The various movements of the feet as accepted by ancient scholars are described; Maṇḍalotplavane ca eva bhramarī pādacārikā=Maṇḍala, utplavna, 2. bhramaris and 4. Pāda cārika; caturdhā pādabhedāḥ syuḥ teṣāṃ lakṣaṇam ucyate= the four types of movements of the feet and their characterstics will be described.

The various movements of the feet, as accepted by the ancient scholars, are : 1. Maṇḍalas, 2. Utplavanas, 2. Bhramaris and 4. Pādacārikas - these are the four types of movement of the feet.

Chapter 22

मण्डलभेदाः

Maṇḍalabhedāḥ

स्थानकं चायतालीढं प्रेङ्खणप्रेरितानि च ।
प्रत्यालीढं स्वस्तिष्कं च मोटितं समसूचिका ।।336।।
पार्श्वसूचिति च दश मण्डलानीरितानीह ।

Transliteration:

Sthānakaṃ cāyatālīḍhaṃ preṅkhaṇapreritāni ca |
Pratyālīḍhaṃ svastiṣkaṃ ca mōṭitaṃ samasūcikā ||
Pārśvasūciti ca daśa maṇḍalānīritānīha |

Meaning:

Sthānakaṃ, ca āyatam, ālīḍhaṃ, preṅkhaṇa, preritāni, ca= Sthānakam, āyatam, ālīḍham, preṅkhaṇa, preritāni, and;pratyālīḍhaṃ svastiṣkaṃ ca mōṭitaṃ, samasūcikā= pratyālīḍhaṃ, svastiṣkaṃ and mōṭitaṃ, samasūcikā;pārśvasūci iti ca daśa maṇḍalā nīritānīha= these are the ten maṇḍalās descibed here.

1. Sthānaka maṇḍalam, 2. Āyata maṇḍalam, 3. Alīḍha maṇḍalam. 4. Prekhaṇa maṇḍalam, 5. prerita maṇḍalam, 6. Pratyālīḍha maṇḍalam, 7. Svastika maṇḍalam, 8. Mōtita maṇḍalam, 9. Saṃasūci maṇḍalam and 10. Pārśvasūci maṇḍalam - these are the ten Maṇḍalas described here.

1. स्थानकमण्डलम्

Sthānakamaṇḍalaṃ

कटिं स्पृष्ट्वाऽर्धचन्द्राख्यपाणिभ्या समपादतः ।।337।।
समरेखतया तिष्ठेत् तत् स्यात् स्थानकमण्डलम् ।

Tansliteration:

Kaṭiṃ spṛṣṭvā-rdhacandrākhyapāṇibhyā samapādataḥ ||
Samarekhatayā tiṣṭhet tat syāt sthānakamaṇḍalam |

Meaning:

Ardhacandra pāṇibhyām, kaṭiṃ spṛṣṭvā = two ardhacandra hastas are to be placed on either side of the waist; samapādataḥ, samarekhatayā tiṣṭhet = and to stand in Samapāda with the body held upright; tat syāt sthānaka maṇḍalam = then it is Sthānaka maṇḍalam.

Standing on samapāda, keeping the body straight and placing the two Ardhacandra hastas on either side of the waist, is sthānaka maṇḍala.

2. आयतमण्डलम्

Āyatamaṇḍalaṃ

वितस्त्यन्तरितौ पादौ कृत्वा तु चतुरस्रकौ ।।338।।
तिर्यक् कुञ्चितजानुभ्यां स्थितिरायतमण्डलम् ।

Transliteration:

Vitastyantaritau pādau kṛtvā tu caturasrakau ||
Tiryak kuncitajānubhyāṃ sthitirāyatamaṇḍalam |

Meaning:

Vitasti - antaritau pādau kṛtvā (tu) = keeping a distance of avitasti between the two feet; caturasrakau = standing in Caturasra posture; tiryak kuncita jānubhyāṃ = bending the knees slightly and obliquely; sthiti āyatamaṇḍalām = this posture is Āyata maṇḍalam.

Standing in Caturasra, bending the knees slightly and obliquely and keeping a distance of a vitasti between the two feet is called Āyata maṇḍalam.

3. आलीढमण्डलम्

Ālīḍhamaṇḍalaṃ

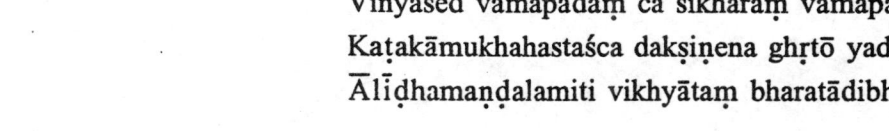

दक्षिणाङ्घ्रेश्च पुरतः वितस्तित्रितयाण्तरम् ।।339।।
विन्यसेद् वामपादं च शिखरं वामपाणिना ।
कटकामुखहस्तश्च दक्षिणेन घृतो यदि ।।340।।
आलीढमण्डलमिति विख्यातं भरतादिभिः ।

Transliteration:

Dakṣiṇāṅghreśca purataḥ vitastitritayāntaram ||
Vinyased vāmapādaṃ ca śikharaṃ vāmapāṇinā |
Kaṭakāmukhahastaśca dakṣiṇena ghṛtō yadi ||
Ālīḍhamaṇḍalamiti vikhyātaṃ bharatādibhiḥ |

Meaning:

Vāmapādaṃ ca dakṣiṇa - aṅghreh ca, purataḥ vitasti-tritaya - antaram vinyaset = left foot is to be placed at a distance of three vitastis (cubit and a half) away in front from the right foot; vāma pāṇinā śikharaṃ, dakṣiṇena kaṭakāmukha hasta, (ca) dhṛtaḥ yadi = if left hand assumes śikhara hasta and right hand assumes kaṭakāmukha hasta; ālīḍha maṇḍalam iti bhārata - ādibhiḥ vikhyātaṃ bharatādībhiḥ= it is considered Ālīḍha maṇḍalam by Bharata and others.

When in front of the right foot, left foot is placed at a distance of 3 vistastis away, left hand and right hand assume Śikhara hasta and Katakāmukha hasta, respectively, then it is considered Ālīḍha maṇḍalam.

4. प्रत्यालीढमण्डलम्

Pratyālīḍhamaṇḍalaṃ

आलीढस्य विपर्यासात् प्रत्यालीढाख्यमण्डलम् ।।341।।

Transliteration:

Ālīḍhasya viparyāsāt pratyālīḍhākhyamaṇḍalam ||

Meaning:

Ālīḍhasya viparyāsāt = if the position in the ālīḍha maṇḍalam is reversed; pratyalīḍha - ākhya maṇḍalam = then it becomes Pratyālīḍha maṇḍalam.

If the position in the Ālīḍha maṇḍalam is reversed, it becomes Pratyālīḍha maṇḍalam. Altering the feet of ālīḍha is pratyālīḍha.

5. प्रेङ्खणमण्डलम्
Preṅkhaṇamaṇḍalam

प्रस्तृत्यैकपदं पार्श्वे पार्ष्णिदेशस्य पादतः।
स्थित्वाऽन्ते कूर्महस्तेन स्थितिः प्रेङ्खणमण्डलम् ।।342।।

Transliteration:
Prastṛtyaikapadaṃ pārśve pārṣṇideśasya pādataḥ |
Sthitvā-nte kūrmahastena sthitiḥ preṅkhaṇamaṇḍalam ||

Meaning:

Ēkapādam pādataḥ pārṣṇideśasya pārśve, prastṛtyai, sthitwā = keeping one foot by the side of the heel of the other foot; ante kūrma hastena sthitiḥ preṅkhaṇa maṇḍalam = and holding Kūrma hasta, is Preṅkhaṇa maṇḍalam.

When one foot is placed by the side of the heel of the other foot and kūrmahasta is assumed, then it is Preṅkhaṇa maṇḍalam.

6. प्रेरित मण्डलम्
Prerita maṇḍalaṃ

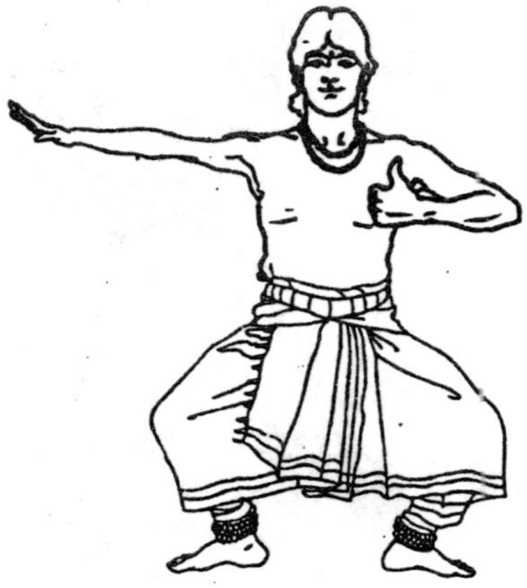

सम्ताड्यैकं पदं पार्श्वे वितस्तित्रितयान्तरम् ।
तिर्यक् कुञ्चितजानुभ्यां स्थित्वाऽथ शिखरं करम् ।।343।।
विधाय वक्ष्यस्यन्येन प्रसृता च पताकिका ।
प्रदर्शयेदिदं तज् ज्ञाः प्रेरितं मण्डलं जगुः ।।344।।

Transliteration:

Samtāḍyaikaṃ padaṃ pārśve vitastitritayāntaram |
Tiryak kunitajānubhyāṃ sthitvā'tha śikharaṃ karam ||
Vidhāya vakṣyasyanyena prasṛtā ca patākikā |
Pradarśayedidaṃ taj jñāḥ preritaṃ maṇḍalaṃ jaguḥ ||

Meaning:

Ēkaṃ padam, pārśve, vitasti- tritayā - anantaram, samtāḍya = one foot strikes the ground on the side of the other foot at a distance of 3 vitastis (27 inches); tiryak kuñcita jānubhyāṃ sthitvā- = to stand with the knees (slightly) bent obliquely; (atha) śikharaṃ karam vakṣyasi vidhāya, anyena patākikā prasṛtā (ca), pradarśayet = while one hand assumes śikhara hasta on the chest, the other hand is to be extended as patāka hasta; idaṃ preritaṃ maṇḍalaṃ tajjñāḥ jaguḥ = knowledgeable persons say that this is Preritaṃ maṇḍalaṃ.

To strike the ground with one foot on the side of the other foot at a distance of three vitastis, and to stand with the knees bent, holding śikhara hasta on the chest with one hand and extending the other hand as Patāka hasta, this posture is called Prerita maṇḍalaṃ.

7. स्वस्तिक मण्डलम्

Svastika maṇḍalaṃ

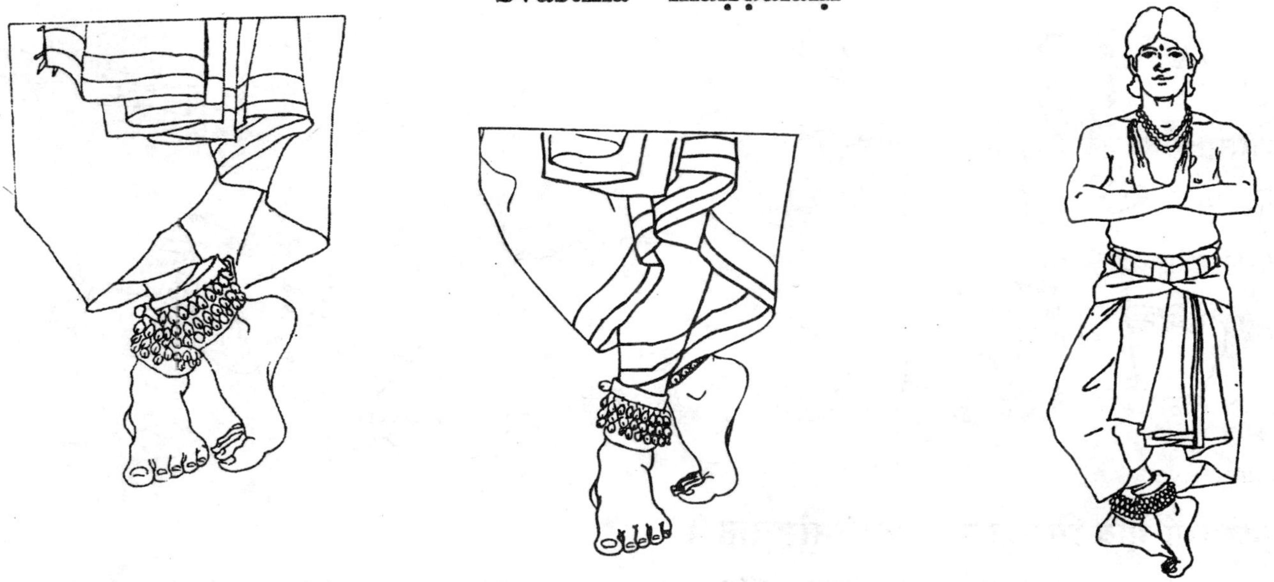

दक्षिणोत्तरतः कुर्यात् पादे पादं करे करम् ।
व्यात्यासेन तदा प्रोक्तं स्वस्तिकं नाम मण्डलम् ।।345।।

Transliteration:

Dakṣiṇōttarataḥ kuryāt pāde pādaṃ kare karam |
Vyātyāsena tadā prōktam svastikaṃ nāma maṇḍalam ||

Meaning:

Dakṣina - uttarataḥ pāde pādaṃ kare karam, vyātyāsena kuryāt = placing right foot over the other and right hand over the other i.e., keeping the feet and hands in svastika (-crossed); tadā prōktam svastikaṃ nāma maṇḍalam = then it is known as Svastika maṇḍalam.

Standing with the right foot placed across the left foot and the right hand placed across the left hand is known as Svastika maṇḍalam.

8. मोटितमण्डलम्

Mōṭitamaṇḍalaṃ

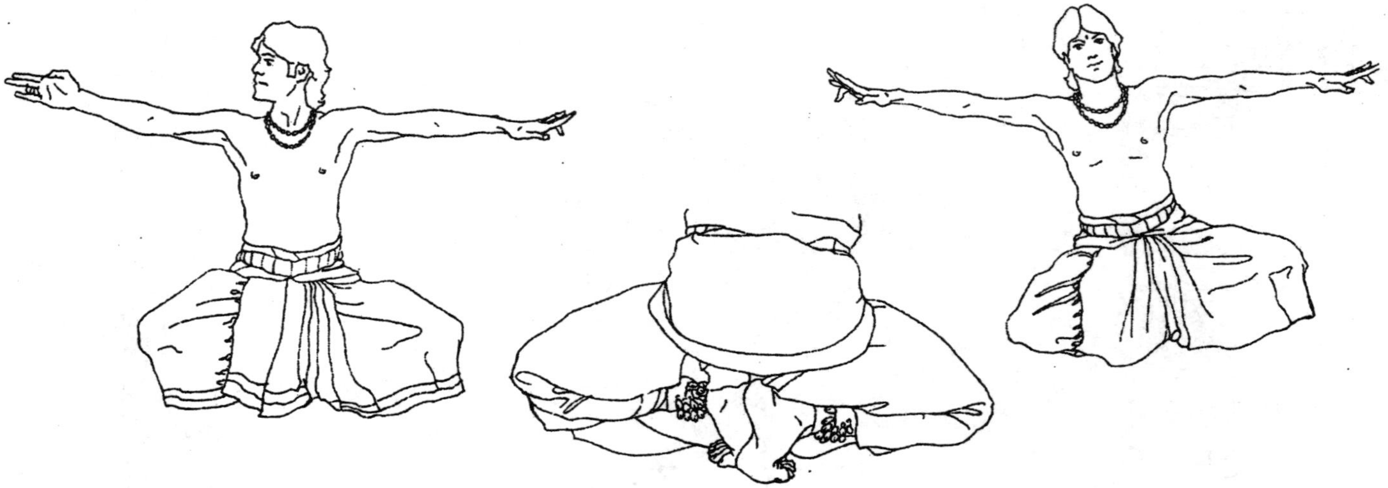

प्रपदाभ्यां भुवि स्थित्वा जानुयुग्मेन संस्पृशेत् ।
क्रमाद् भूतलमेकैकं त्रिपताककरद्वयम् ।।346।।
कृत्वा तन्मोटितं नाम मण्डलं कथितं बुधैः ।

Transliteration:

Prapadābhyāṃ bhuvi sthitvā jānuyugmena saṃspṛśet |
Kramād bhūtalamekaikaṃ tripatākakaradvayam ||
Kṛtvā tanmōṭitaṃ nāma maṇḍalaṃ kathitaṃ budhaiḥ |

Meaning:

Prapadābhyāṃ bhuvi sthitvā = standing on the ground with foreparts of the feet i.e. toes; tripatāka karadvayam kṛtvā = and assuming Tripatāka hastas with both hands; jānuyugmena eka-ekam-kramāt, bhūtalam saṃspṛśet = to touch the ground with the knees, alternately; tat mōṭita maṇḍalaṃ budhaiḥ kathitaṃ = that is considered by the the scholars as Mōṭita maṇḍalaṃ.

When the body is rested on the heels of the feet in full sitting position (muzhumandi) and with a small jump one leg is slid backwards to rest the knee on the ground, it is moṭita.

Standing on the toes and assuming Tripatāka hastas with both hands, if the ground is touched by the knees alternately, then it is considered as Mōṭita maṇḍalaṃ.

9. समसूचीमण्डलम्

Samasūcīmaṇḍalaṃ

पादाग्राभ्यां च जानुभ्यां भूतलं संस्पृशेद्यदि ।।347।।
मण्डलं समसूचीति कथितं पूर्वसूरिभिः ।

Transliteration:

Pādāgrābhyāṃ ca jānubhyāṃ bhūtalaṃ saṃspṛśedyadi ||
Maṇḍalaṃ samasūcīti kathitaṃ pūrvasūribhiḥ |

Meaning:

Yadi pādāgrābhyāṃ ca jānubhyāṃ bhūtalaṃ, saṃspṛśedayadi= if the ground is touched by the fore parts of the feet i.e. toes as well as the knees; samasūcī maṇḍalaṃ iti, pūrvasūribhiḥ kathitaṃ = then the ancient scholars considered it as samasūci maṇḍalaṃ.

If the ground is touched by the toes as well as the knees, then it is samasūci maṇḍalaṃ.

10. पार्श्वसूचीमण्डलम्

Pārśvasūcīmaṇḍalaṃ

स्थित्वा पादाग्रयुग्मेण जानुनैकेन पार्श्वतः ।।348।।
संस्पृशेद् भूतलं पार्श्वसूचीमण्डलमीरितम् ।

Transliteration:

sthitvā pādāgrayugmeṇa jānunaikena pārśvataḥ ||
saṃspṛśed bhūtalaṃ pārśvasūcīmaṇḍalamīritam |

Meaning:

Pādāgra - yugmeṇa sthitvā = standing on the fore parts of the two feet; ekena jānuna pārśwataḥ bhūtalaṃ saṃspṛśet = the ground is to be touched by one knee on one side; pārśvasūcīmaṇḍalam, iti, īritam = then, it is said to be Pārśvasūcī maṇḍalam.

Standing (or sitting) on the toes, if the ground is touched by one knee on one side, it is considered as Pārśvasūcīmaṇḍalam.

Chapter 23

स्थानकभेदाः

Sthānakabhedāḥ

पादविम्यासभेदेन स्थानकं षड्विधं भवेत् ।।349।।
समपादं चैकपादं नागबन्धस्ततः परम् ।
ऐन्द्रं च गारुडं चैव ब्रह्मस्थानमिति क्रमात् ।।350।।

Transliteration:

Pādavimyāsabhedena sthānakaṃ ṣaḍvidhaṃ bhavet ||
Samapādaṃ caekapādaṃ nāgabandhastataḥ param |
Aindraṃ ca gāruḍaṃ caiva brahmasthānamiti kramāt ||

Meaning:

Pādavimyāsa bhedena, sthānakaṃ, kramāt, ṣaḍvidhaṃ bhavet = with variations in placing of the feet, Sthānakas are of six types; samapādaṃ ca, ekapādaṃ nāgabandḥa, tataḥ param, aindraṃ ca, gāruḍaṃ ca-eva brahmasthānam, iti kramāt = the following is the order of the six sthānakas - samapādaṃ. ekapādam, nāgabandḥa, aindraṃ, gāruḍaṃ and Brahma.

By the variation in the movements of the feet, the sthānaka positions are of six types: 1. Samapāda sthānakam, 2. Ēkapāda sthānakam, 3. Nāgabandha sthānakam, 4. Aindra sthānakam, and 5. Gāruḍa sthānakam, 6. Brahma sthānakam,

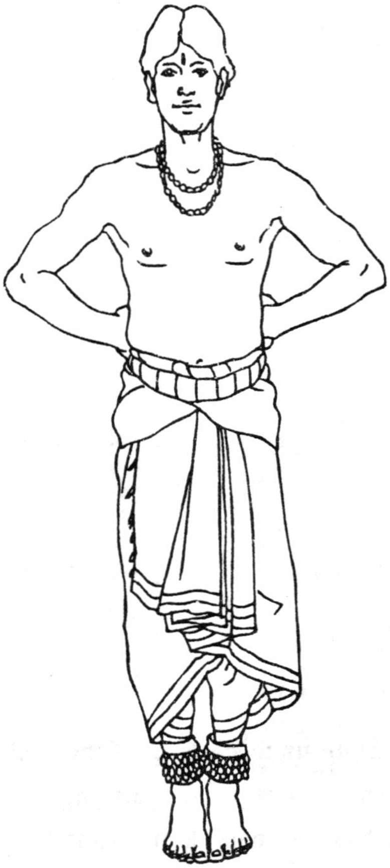

1. समपादस्थानकम्

Samapādasthānakam

स्थितिः समाभ्यां पादाभ्यां समपादमिति स्मृतम् ।

Transliteration:

Sthitiḥ samābhyāṃ pādābhyāṃ samapādamiti smṛtam |

Meaning:

samābhyāṃ pādābhyāṃ sthitiḥ, samapādam iti smṛtam = standing with feet in Sama position is called Samapāda sthānakam.

Standing with feet in Sama position is considered as Samapāda sthānakam.

विनियोगः (application)

पुष्पाञ्जलौ देवरूपे समपादं नियुज्यते ।।351।।

Transliteration:

Puṣpāñjalau devarūpe samapādaṃ niyujyate |

Meaning:

Puṣpāñjalau devarūpe samapādaṃ niyujyate = Samapāda sthānakam is used to depict the offering of Puṣpāñjali and assuming the role of gods.

This sthānaka is used in depicting the offering of Puṣpāñjali (offering of flowers)and assuming the roles of gods.

2. एकपादस्थानकम्
Ekapādasthānakam

जान्वाश्रित्य पदैकेन स्थितिः स्यादेकपादकम् ।

Transliteration:

Jānvāśritya padaikena sthitiḥ syādekapādakam |

Meaning:

Jānu-āśritya, pada-ekena sthitiḥ, ekapādakam syāt = in relation to the knee, standing on one foot is Ēkapāda sthānakam.

Standing on one leg and placing the other leg on the knee of the first leg obliquely, is considered as Ēkapāda sthānakam.

विनियोगः (application)

एकपादं त्विदं स्थानं निश्चले तपसि स्थितम् ।।352।।

Transliteration:

Ēkapādaṃ tvidaṃ sthānaṃ niścale tapasi sthitam ||

Meaning:

Idam tu, Ēkapāda sthānam, niścale, tapasi sthitam = this Ēkapāda sthānakam is used to denote motionlessness and practice of penance.

This sthānakam depicts motionlessness and penance.

3. नागबन्धस्थानकम्

Nāgabandha sthānakam

पादं पादेन संवेष्ट्य तथा पाणिं च पाणिना।
स्थितिः स्यान्नागबन्धाख्या नागबन्धे प्रयुज्यते ।।353।।

Transliteration:

Pādaṃ pādena saṃveṣṭya tathā pāṇiṃ ca pāṇinā |
Sthitiḥ syānnāgabandhākhyā nāgabandhe prayujyate ||

Meaning:

Pādena Pādaṃ, tathā pāṇiṃ ca saṃveṣṭya sthitiḥ = standing with one leg interwined over the other leg, and one hand crossed over the other hand; nāgabandh-ākhya = then it is Nāgabandha sthānakam; sthitiḥ syānāgabandhe prayujyate. = this is used to denote Nāgabandham.

The standing posture in which the two legs are intertwined and the two hands are likewise crossed, is called Nāgabandha sthānakam.This sthānakam is used to depict Nāgabandham.

4. ऐन्द्रकस्थानकम्
Aindrakasthānakam

पादमेकं समाकुञ्च्य स्थित्वाऽन्यपदजानुनी ।
उत्तानिते करं न्यस्य स्थितिरैन्द्रमितिरितम् ।।354।।

Transliteration:

Pādamekaṃ samākuñcya sthitvā'nyapadajānunī |
Uttānite karaṃ nyasya sthitiraindramitīritam ||

Meaning:

Ēkaṃ pādam samākuñcya sthitvā = standing with one leg bent; ayapada-jānunī uttānite = and raising the other knee; karam nyasya sthitiḥ = hands held downwards; aindram - iti iritam = then it is considered as Aindra sthānakam.

Standing with one leg bent, raising the knee of other leg and holding the hands downwards is known as Aindra sthānakam.

विनियोगः (application)

वासवे राजभावे च स्थानमैन्द्रं नियुज्यते ।

Transliteration:

Vāsave rājabhāve ca sthānamaindraṃ niyujyate |

Meaning:

Vāsave, rājabhāve, niyujyate = this Aindra sthānakam is used to denote Indra and a king.
This sthānakam depicts Indra and a king.

5. गरुडस्थानकम्

Garuḍasthānakam

आलीढमण्डले पश्चाद्य जानुतलं भुवि ।
संस्थाप्य पाणियुग्मेन वहन् विरलमण्डलम् ।।355।।
स्थितिस्तु गरुडस्थानं गरुडे विनियुज्यते ।

Transliteration:

Ālīḍhamaṇḍale paścādya jānutalaṃ bhuvi |
Saṃsthāpya pāṇiyugmena vahan viralamaṇḍalam ||
Sthitistu garuḍasthānaṃ garuḍe viniyujyate |

Meaning:

Atha, ālīḍha maṇḍale, paścat, jānutalaṃ bhuvi saṃsthāpya = at first standing with Ālīḍha mandala, then one knee is placed on the ground; pāṇiyugmena, vahan virala maṇḍalam. = and the two hands are held forming a circle; sthitiḥ garuḍa sthānaṃ = this posture is known as garuḍa sthānakam; garuḍe viniyujyate = this Garuḍa sthāna is used to denote Garuḍa.

Standing at first in ālīḍha maṇḍalam, then with one knee placed on the ground and the two hands forming a circle is known as Garuda sthānakam. This sthānakam.depicts the bird Garuḍa.

6. ब्रह्मस्थानकम्

Brahmasthānakam

जानुपरि पदं व्यस्य पदस्योपरि जानु च ।।356।।
स्थितं यदि भवेद् ब्राह्मं जपादिषु नियुज्यते ।

Transliteration:

Jānupari padaṃ vyasya padasyopari jānu ca ||
Sthitaṃ yadi bhaved brāhmaṃ japādiṣu niyujyate |

Meaning:

Jānu-pari padaṃ, padasya-upari jānu ca, nyasya = keeping one leg on the knee of the second leg, and the second leg on the knee of the first leg; yadi sthitam bhavet brahmam = if one sits in this posture it is Brahma sthānakam; japādiṣu niyujyate = this sthānakam denotes japam (repeated chanting of mantras).

If one sits keeping one leg on the knee of the second leg and the second leg on the knee of the first leg, it is Brahma sthānakam.This sthānakam depicts meditation etc.

Chapter 24

उत्प्लवनभेदाः

Utplavana Bhedāḥ

अथोत्प्लवनभेदानां लक्षणं परिकथ्यते ।।357।।
अलगं कर्तरी वाऽश्वोऽत्प्लवनं मोटितं तथा ।
कृपालगमिति ख्यातं पञ्चधोत्प्लवनं बुधैः ।।358।।

Transliteration:

Athotplavanabhedānāṃ lakṣaṇaṃ parikathyate ||
Alagaṃ kartarī vā'śvo'tplavanaṃ moṭitaṃ tathā |
Kṛpālagamiti khyātaṃ pañcadhotplavanaṃ budhaiḥ ||

Meaning:

Athotplavanabhedānāṃ lakṣaṇaṃ parikathyate = the characteristics of Utplavana bhedās are described; Alagaṃ kartarī vā-śvo-tplavanaṃ moṭitaṃ tathā = alagam, kartari, aśwa utplavanam, moṭitam and; Kṛpālagamiti khyātaṃ pañcadhotplavanaṃ budhaiḥ = Kṛpālaga utplavanam - thus utplavanam bhedas are five as considered by the scholars.

The characteristics of Utplavana bhedās as considered by the scholars are : 1. Alaga utplavanam. 2. Kartari utplavanam, 3. Aśva utplavanam, 4. Moṭita utplavanam, and 5. Kṛpālaga utplavanam.

1. अलगोत्प्लवनम्

Alagotplavanaṃ

उत्प्लुत्य पार्श्वयुगलं कटिदेशे तु विन्यसेत्।
बध्वा कराभ्यां शिखरै अलगोत्प्लवनं भवेत् ।।359।।

Transliteration:

Utplutya pārśvayugalaṃ kaṭideśe tu vinyaset |
Badhvā karābhyāṃ śikharai alagotplavanaṃ bhavet ||

Meaning:

Utplutya = after taking a leap; karabhyam, sikharou badhva, = assuming Sikhara hastas with both hands; katidese tu, parswayugalam vinyaset = they have to be placed on both the sides of the waist; alaga-ut-plavanam bhavet = then it is Alaga-utplavanam.

After taking a leap, the two hands holding Śikhara hasta have to be placed on the two sides of the waist, then it is Alagotplavanaṃ.

2. उत्प्लवनकर्तरी

Utplavanakartarī

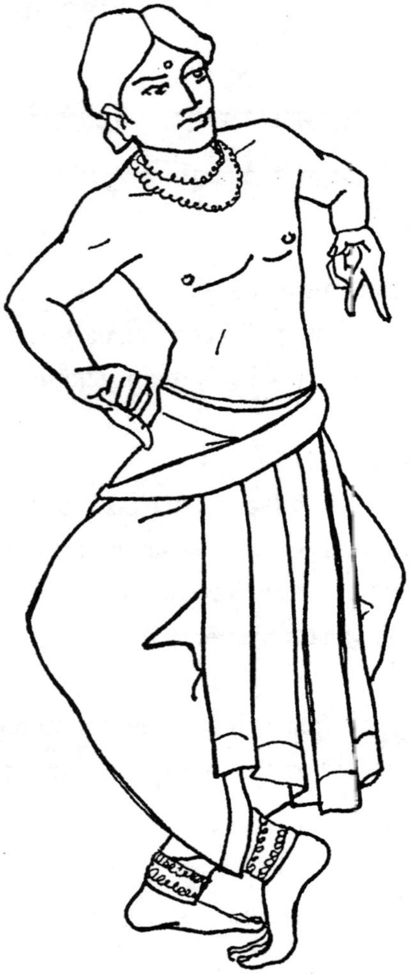

उत्प्लत्य प्रपदैः सव्यपादस्यैकस्य पृष्ठतः ।
कर्तरी विन्यसेदेषा स्यादुत्प्लवनकर्तरी ।।360।।
अधोमुखं च शिखरं कटौ हस्तं न्यसदिह ।

Transliteration:

Utplatya prapadaiḥ savyapādasyaikasya pṛṣṭhataḥ |
Kartarī vinyasedeṣā syādutplavanakartarī |
Adhomukhaṃ ca śikharaṃ kaṭau hastaṃ nyasadiha |

Meaning:

Prapadaiḥ utplatya = after taking a leap standing on the fore-part of the leg i.e. toes; savya pādasya pṛṣṭhataḥ, ekāsyā kartarī vinyaset = at the back of the left leg, one hand (i.e. left hand) with Kartari hasta has to be placed; iha, Śikhara hasta ca kaṭe vinyaset = the other (i.e. right) hand is to be placed on the waist as Śikhara hasta pointing downwards; eshā syāt utplavana kartarī = this posture is Utplavana Kartari or Kartari Utplavanam.

After taking a leap standing on the toes, one foot behind the other, left hand as Kartari hasta is to be placed behind, and the right hand holding Śikhara hasta has to be placed on the right side of the waist pointing downwards. This posture is Kartari Utplavanam or Utplavanam Kartari.

3. अश्वोत्प्लवनम्

Aśvotplavanaṃ

पुरः पादं समुत्प्लुत्य पश्चात्पादं नियोजयेत् ।।361।।
द्वौ करौ तु त्रिपताख्यौ कृत्वा-श्वोत्प्लवनं भवेत्।

Transliteration:

Puraḥ pādaṃ samutplutya paścātpādaṃ niyojayet ||
Dvau karau tu tripatākhyau kṛtvā-śvotplavanaṃ bhavet |

Meaning:

Tripatāka - ākhya katau tu kṛtvā = assuming Tripatāka hasta with both hands; puraḥ pādaṃ samutplutya, paścāt pādaṃ niyojayet = to take a leap to the front with one leg and next, to place the second leg along the first leg; aśwa - utplavanam bhavet = then it is Asva-utplavanam.

Assuming Tripatāka hasta with both hands, a leap to the front has to be taken with one leg and then the second leg has to be placed along the first leg - this is known as Aśvotplavanam.

4. मोटितोत्प्लवनम्

Moṭitotplavanaṃ

पर्यायपार्श्वोत्प्लवनं कर्तरीव तु मोटिता ।।362।।
त्रिपताके च करयोः कृत्वा शश्वत्प्रकाशनात्।

Transliteration:

Paryāyapārśvotplavanaṃ kartarīva tu moṭitā ||
Tripatāke ca karayoḥ kṛtvā śaśvatprakāśanāt |

Meaning:

Karayoḥ tripatāke ca kṛtvā = assuming Tripapatāka hastas with both hands; śaśvat prakāśanāt = showing repeatedly; kartarī-iva paryāya-pārśva-utplavanaṃ = like in Utplavana Kartari, leaps have to be taken on the two sides, alternately; moṭitā = then, it is Motita-utplavanam.

Meaning:

Assuming Tripatāka hasta with both hands, if leaps are made as was done in Kartari on both sides, alternately, it is considered as Motita-utplavanam.

5. कृपालगोत्प्लवनम्

Kṛpālagotplavanam

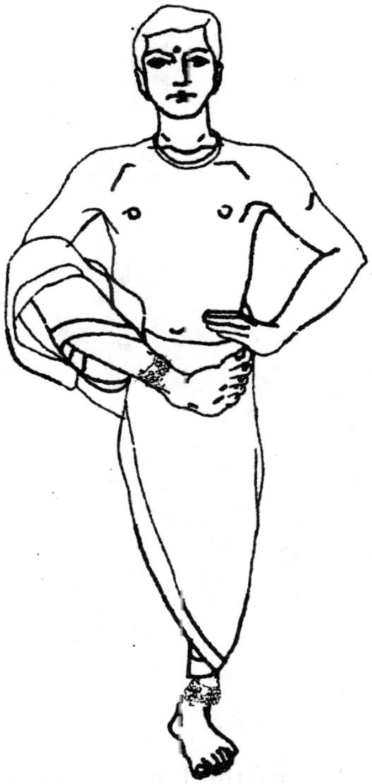

पार्ष्णिमेकै कपादस्य कटौ पर्यायतो म्यसेत् ।।363।।
अर्धचन्द्रकलामध्ये म्यस्तमम्यत् कृपालगम्।

Transliteration:

Pārṣṇimekai kapādasya kaṭau paryāyato myaset ||
Ardhacandrakalāmadhye myastamamyat kṛpālagam |

Meaning:

Ēkaika pādasya, pārṣṇim, paryāyataḥ, kate nyaset = placing the two heels on the waist, alternately; madhye, ardhacandrakalām hastam = and keeping ardhacandra-kalā hasta in between; etat kṛpālagam = then, it is Kṛpālaga utplavanam.

Raising the heels to the hips alternately, holding ardhacandrakala hasta is Kṛpālagotplavanam.

Chapter 25

भ्रमरीलक्षणम्

Bhramarīlakṣaṇaṃ

भ्रमर्या लक्षणाम्यत्र वक्ष्ये लक्षणभेदतः ।।364।।
उत्प्लुतभ्रमरी चक्रभ्रमरी गरुडाभिधा ।
तथैकपादभ्रमरी कुञ्चितभ्रमरी तथा ।।365।।
आकाशभ्रमरी चैव तथाङ्गभ्रमरीति च ।
भ्रमर्यः सप्त विज्ञेया नाट्याशास्त्रविशारदैः ।।366।।

Transliteration:

Bhramaryā lakṣaṇāmyatra vakṣye lakṣaṇabhedataḥ ||
Utplutabhramarī cakrabhramarī garuḍābhidhā |
Tathaekapādabhramarī kuñcitabhramarī tathā ||
Ākāśabhramarī caiva tathāṅgabhramarīti ca |
Bhramaryaḥ sapta vijñeyā nāṭyāśāstraviśāradaiḥ ||

Meaning:

Bhramaryā lakṣaṇām atra vakṣye lakṣaṇabhedataḥ = the various characteristics of the bhramaris are; utplutabhramarī, cakrabhramarī, garuḍābhidhā, tatha ekapādabhramarī, kuñcitabhramarī tathā ākāśabhramarī ca eva tatha aṅgabhramarīti ca = utpluta bhramari, cakra bhramari, garuḍa bhramari, ekapāda bhramari, kuñcita bhramari, ākāśa bhramari, and aṅga bhramari; bhramaryaḥ sapta vijñeyā nāṭyāśāstra viśāradaiḥ = these are the seven variations of bhramari considered by the experts on Nāṭyāśāstra.

I shall now describe the various characteristics of bhramari as considered by the experts on Nāṭyāśāstra : 1. Utpluta bhramari, 2. Cakra bhramari, 3. Garuḍa bhramari, 4. Ēkapāda bhramari, 5. Kuñcita bhramari, 6. Ākāśa bhramari, 7. Aṅga bhramari.

1. उत्प्लुतभ्रमरी
Utplutabhramarī

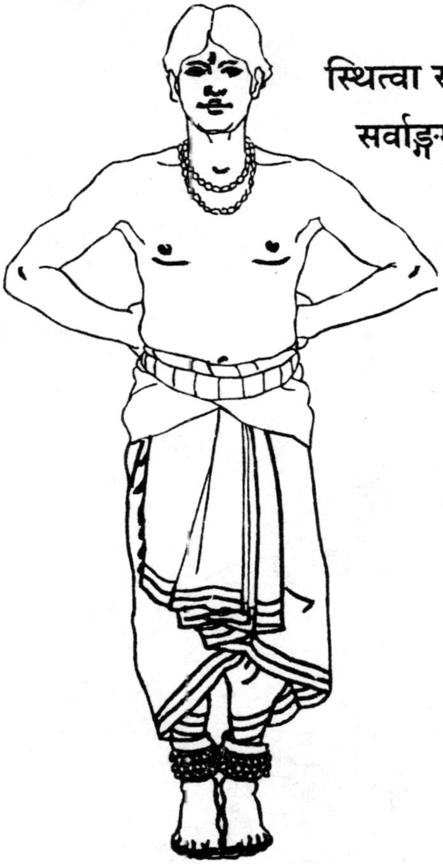

स्थित्वा समाभ्यां पादाभ्यामुत्प्लुत्य भ्रामयेद्यदि ।
सर्वाङ्गमन्तराले स्यादुप्लुत्तभ्रमरी त्वसौ ।।367।।

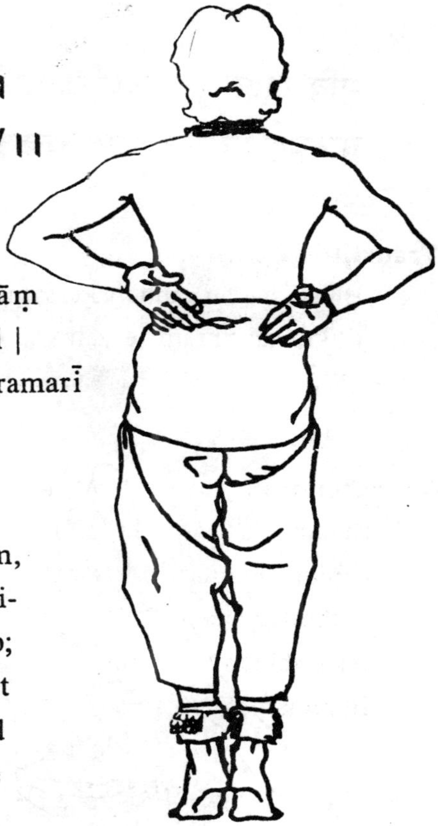

Transliteration:
Sthitvā samābhyāṃ pādābhyāmutplutya bhrāmayedyadi | Sarvāṅgamantarāle syādupluttabhramarī tvasau ||

Meaning:
Samābhyām pādābhyām, sthitvā = standing in Samapādā position; utplutya, = and making a jump; yadi antarāle sarvāṅgam bhrāmayet = if the entire body is turned around in the air (without touching the ground); asou, utpluta bhramari tu, syāt = then it is Utpluta bhramari.

Standing in samapādā position and turning around with a jump (without touching the ground) then it is Utpluta bhramari.

2. चक्रभ्रमरी
Cakrabhramarī

भुवि पादौ मुहुः कर्षंस्त्रिपताकौ करौ वहन् ।
चक्रवद् भ्रमते यत्र सा चक्रभ्रमरी भवेत् ।।368।।

Transliteration:

Bhuvi pādau muhuḥ karṣaṃstripatākau karau vahan |
Cakravad bhramate yatra sā cakrabhramarī bhavet ||

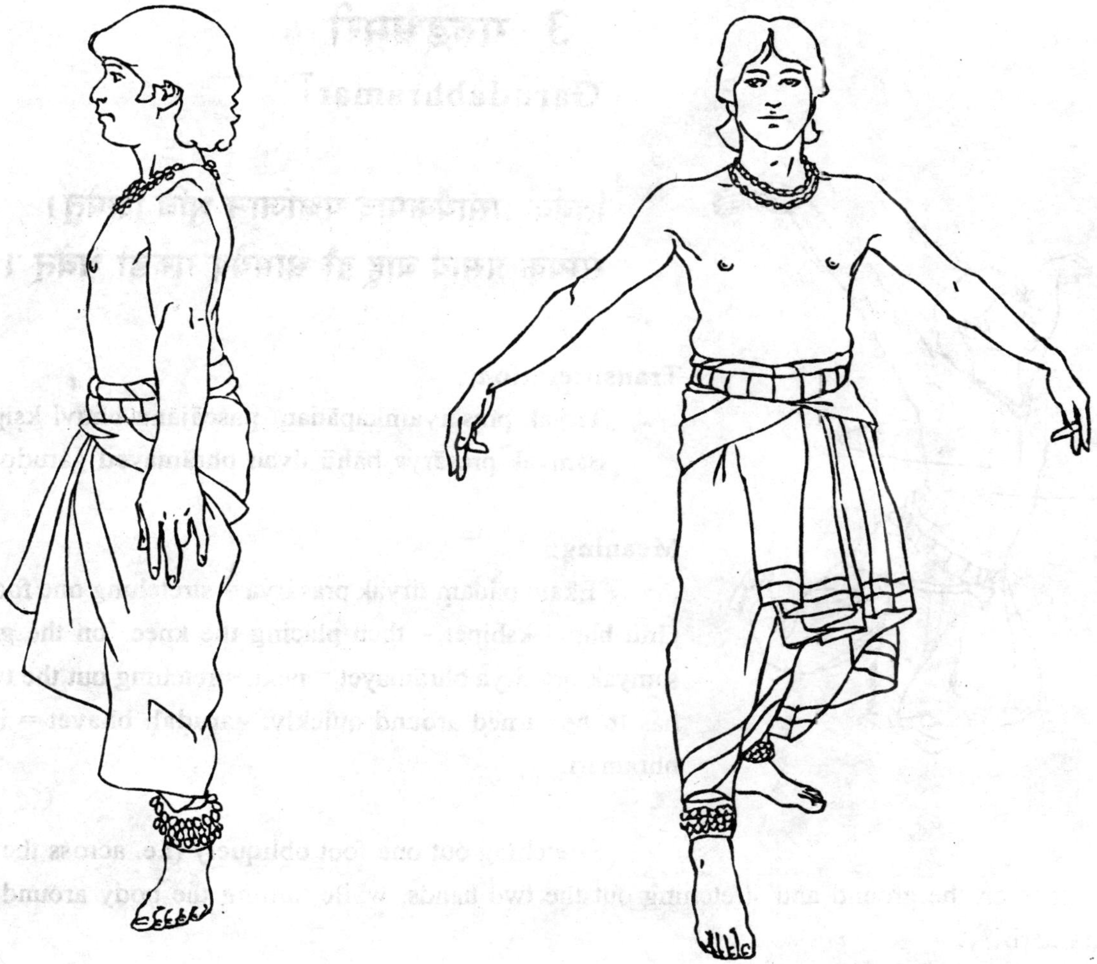

Meaning:

Pādau, muhuḥ bhuvi, karṣaṃ = striking the ground with the feet repeatedly; tripatākau vahan = holding Tripatāka hasta with both hands; yatra cakravat bhramate = when one turns around in a circle; sā cakra bhramarī bhavet =that is Cakra bhramarī.

Holding Tripatāka hasta in both hands and striking the ground with feet repeatedly, if one turns around in a circle, it is considered as cakra bhramari.

3. गरुडभ्रमरी

Garuḍabhramarī

तिर्यक् प्रसार्यैकपादं पश्चाजानु भुवि क्षिपेत्।
सम्यक् प्रसार्य बाहू द्वौ भ्रामयेद् गरुडो भवेत् ।।369।।

Transliteration:

Tiryak prasāryaiṅkapādaṃ paścājānu bhuvi kṣipet |
Samyak prasārya bāhū dvau bhrāmayed garuḍo bhavet ||

Meaning:

Ēkam pādaṃ tiryak prasārya = stretching one foot obliquely; paścāt jānu bhuvi kshipet = then placing the knee on the ground; dwou bāhu samyak prasārya bhrāmayet = next, stretching out the two hands, the body has to be turned around quickly; garuḍaḥ bhavet = it becomes Garuḍa bhramari.

Stretching out one foot obliquely (i.e. across the other leg), placing the knee on the ground and stretching out the two hands, while turning the body around quickly is Garuḍa bhramari.

4. एकपादभ्रमरी
Ēkapādabhramarī

भ्रामयेदेकमेकेन पादं पादेन सत्वरम्।
सा त्वेकपादभ्रमरी भवेदिति विनिश्चिता ।।370।।

Transliteration:

Bhrāmayedekamekena pādaṃ pādena satvaram |
Sā tvekapādabhramarī bhavediti viniścitā |

Meaning:

Ēkapādaṃ, ekena pādena, satvarama bhrāmayet = moving round quickly and alternately on one foot; sā tu ekapāda bhramarī bhavet, iti, viniścitā = is considered as Ēkapāda bhramari.

If one turns around quickly on one foot, it is considered as Ēkapāda bhramari.

5. कुञ्चितभ्रमरी
Kuñcitabhramarī

निकुं चा जानुभ्रमणं कुञ्चितभ्रमरी भवेत्।

Transliteration:

nikun cā jānubhramaṇaṃ kuñcitabhramarī bhavet |

Meaning:

Jānu nikuncya bhramaṇaṃ = bending the knees if one turns around; kuñcita bhramarī bhavet = it becomes Kuñcita bhramari.

Turning around while bending the knees is considered as kuñcita bhramari.

6. आकाशभ्रमरी

Ākāśabhramarī

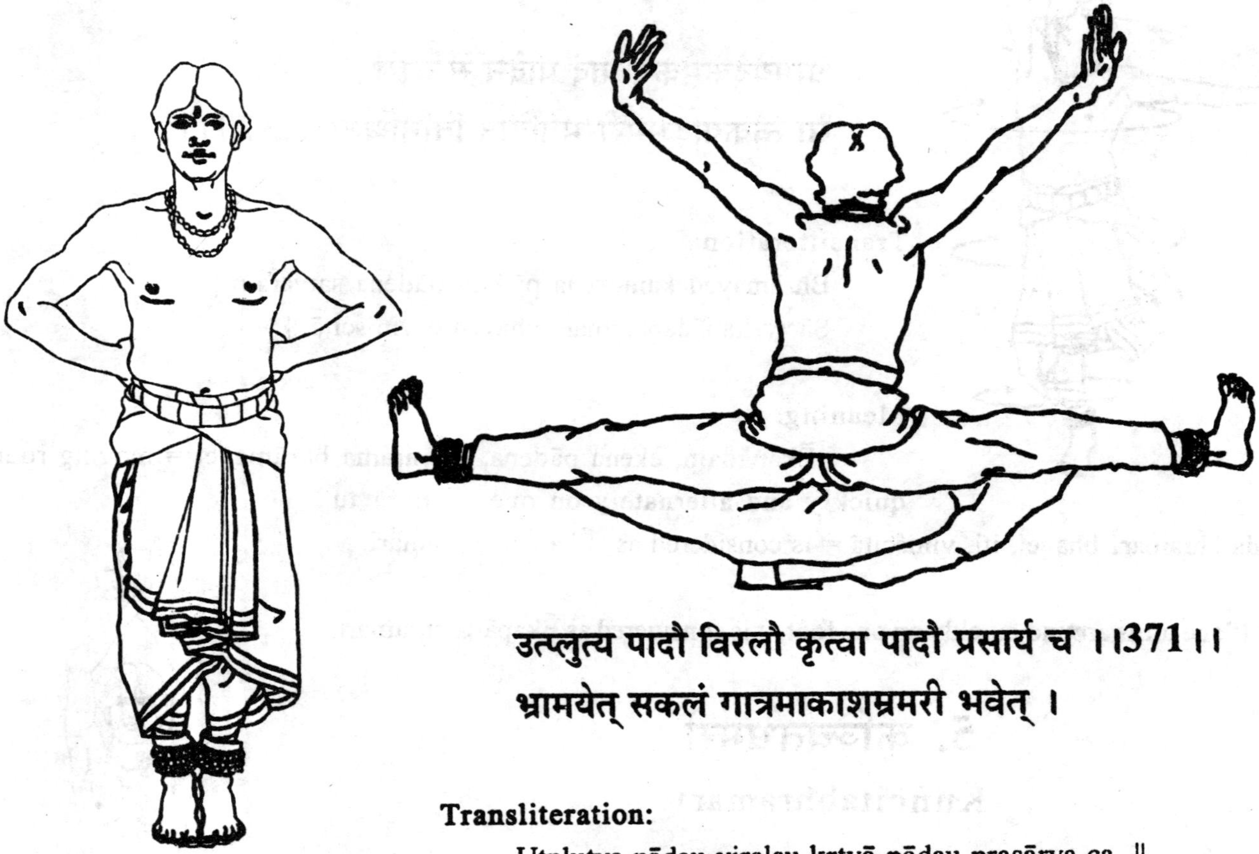

उत्प्लुत्य पादौ विरलौ कृत्वा पादौ प्रसार्य च ।।371।।
भ्रामयेत् सकलं गात्रमाकाशभ्रमरी भवेत् ।

Transliteration:

Utplutya pādau viralau kṛtvā pādau prasārya ca ||
Bhrāmayet sakalaṃ gātramākāśamramarī bhavet |

Meaning:

Utplutya = making a jump; pādau viralau kṛtvā, pādau prasārya (ca) = (at the same time) keeping the feet apart and stretching them; sakalam gātram bhrāmayet = if the entire body is turned round; ākāśa bhramarī bhavet = it becomes Ākāśa bhramari.

Jumping with the two feet stretched apart while turning around the body is Ākāśa bhramari.

7. अङ्गभ्रमरी
Aṅgabhramarī

वितस्त्यन्तरितौ पादौ कृत्वाङ्गभ्रमणं तथा ।।372।।
तिष्ठ यदि भवेदङ्गभ्रमरी भरतोदिता ।

Transliteration:

Vitastyantaritau pādau kṛtvāṅgabhramaṇaṃ tathā ||
Tiṣṭha yadi bhavedaṅgabhramarī bharatoditā |

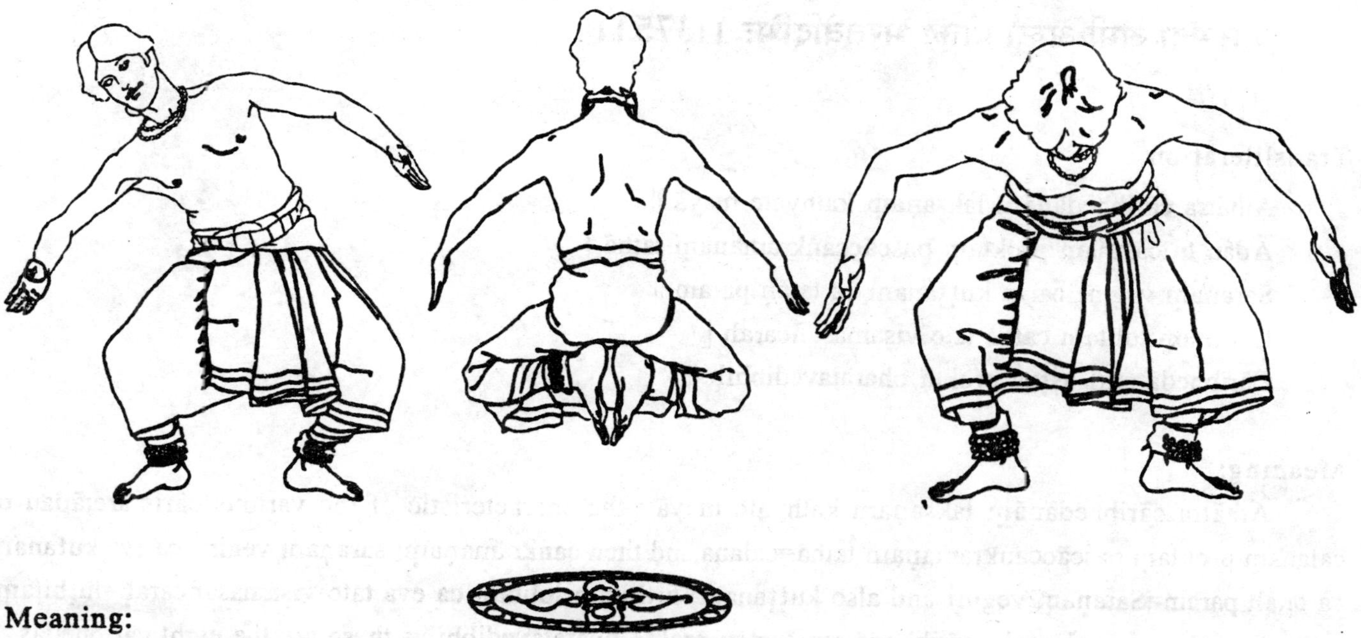

Meaning:

Pādau vitasti-antaritou kṛtvā, tathā, aṅgabhramaṇaṃ = keeping the two feet aprt at a distance of one vitasti (i.e. half cubit), the body is turned around; tiṣṭhet yadi = and then stopped; bharata-udita, aṅga-bhramari bhavet = then it becomes Aṅga bhramari, described by Bharata.

While keeping the two feet apart at a distance of one vitasti, if the body is turned around, it becomes Aṅga bhramari.

Chapter 26

चारिभेदाः

Cāribhedāḥ

अथात्र चारिभेदानां लक्षणं कथ्यते मया ।।373।।
आदौ तु चलनं प्रोक्तं पश्चाच्चंक्रमणं तथा ।
संरणं वेगिनी चैव कुट्टनं च ततः परम् ।।374।।
लुठितं लोलितं चैव ततो विषमसञ्चरः ।
चारिभेदा अमी अष्टौ प्रोक्ता भरतवेदिभिः ।।375।।

Transliteration

Athātra cāribhedānāṃ lakṣaṇaṃ kathyate mayā ||
Ādau tu calanaṃ proktaṃ paścāccaṅkramaṇaṃ tathā |
Saraṇaṃ veginī caiva kuṭṭanaṃ ca tataḥ param ||
Luṭhitaṃ lolitaṃ caiva tato viṣamasañcaraḥ |
Cāribhedā amī aṣṭau proktā bharatavedibhiḥ ||

Meaning:

Athātra cāribhedānāṃ lakṣaṇaṃ kathyate mayā =the characteristic of the various cāris are;ādau tu calanaṃ proktaṃ paścāccaṅkramaṇaṃ tathā=calana,and then caṅkramaṇaṃ; saraṇaṃ veginī ca eva kuṭanaṃ ca tataḥ param=Saraṇaṃ veginī and also kuṭṭanaṃ; luṭhitaṃ lolitaṃ ca eva tato viṣamasañcaraḥ=luṭhitaṃ, lolitaṃ and viṣamasañcaraḥ; cāribhedā amī aṣṭau proktā bharatavedibhiḥ= these are the eight cāribhedās.

The variations of Cāri are eight in numbers : (1) Calana cāri, (2) Caṅkramaṇa cāri, (3) Saraṇam cāri, (4) Veginī cāri, (5) Kuṭṭana cāri, (6) Luṭhita cāri, (7) Lolita cāri, (8) Viṣama sancara cāri.

(1)

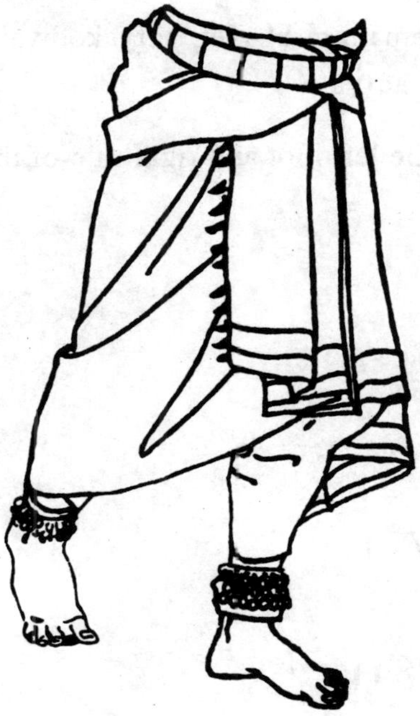

चलनचारि

Calanacāri

स्वस्थामात् स्वस्य पादस्य चलनाञ्चलनं भवेत् ।

Transliteration

Svasthāmāt svasya pādasya calanāñcalanaṃ bhavet |

Meaning:

Svasya pādasya Svasthāmāt calanāt = when the foot is moved from its original place; calanaṃ bhavet = it is known as Calana cāri.

If a foot is moved from its original place, then it is known as Calana cāri.-

(2)

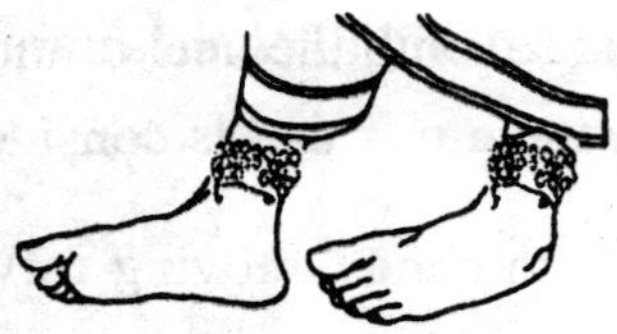

चंक्रमण चारि

Caṅkramaṇa cāri

पादयोर्बाह्यापार्श्वाभ्यामुत्क्षिप्योत्क्षिप्य यत्नतः ।।376।।
गतिभवेञ्चं क्रमणं वर्णितं नाट्यकोदिवैः ।

Transliteration

Pādayorbāhmāpārśvābhyāmutkṣipyotkṣipya yatnataḥ ||
Gatibhaveñcaṃ kramaṇaṃ varṇitaṃ nāṭyakovidaiḥ |

Meaning:

Yatnataḥ, utkṣipya-utkṣipya = with effort, raising up and raising up (the feet alternately); Pādaycḥ bāhya pārśvābhyām gatiḥ = going forward on the outer sides of feet; caṅkramaṇaṃ bhavet, nāṭyakodivaiḥ varṇitaṃ = then it becomes Caṅkramaṇa cāri, as described by the experts on nāṭya.

Moving forward (jumping) with the outer sides of the feet (left side of the left foot and right side of the right foot) alternately, is Caṅkramaṇa cāri.

3. सरणम् चारि

Saraṇam cāri

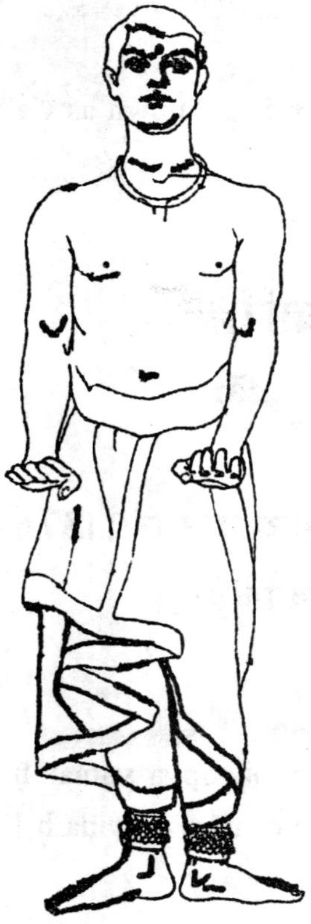

चलनं तु जलूकावदेकेनान्यस्य पार्षिना ।।377।।
तिर्यगाकर्षयेदु भूमिं कराभ्यां तु पताकिके।
धृत्वा च गमनं यत्तु सरणं तदुदीरितम् ।।378।।

Transliteration

Calanaṃ tu jalūkāvadekenānyasya pārṣinā ||
Tiryagākarṣayedu bhūmiṃ karābhyāṃ tu patākike |
Dhṛtvā ca gamanaṃ yattu saraṇaṃ tadudīritam ||

Meaning:

Karābhyāṃ (tu), patākike dhṛtvā (ca) = assuming patāka hasta with both hands; ekenpārṣinā anyasya tiryak ākarṣayet bhūminam yattu jalūkāvat gamanaṃ = dragging (joining) the heel of one foot with the heel of the other foot - moving on the earth like a leech; tat udīritam saraṇaṃ = that is considered as Saraṇaṃ cāri.

Assuming patāka hasta with both hands, moving forward while dragging the heel of one foot with the heel of the other foot like a leech, is considered as Saraṇam cāri.

4. वेगिनी चारि

Veginī cāri

पार्ष्णिनां वा पदाग्रेण द्रतं गत्या तु चालनम् ।
कराभ्यां चालपद्मे च त्रिपताके यथाक्रमम् ।।379।।
धृत्वा नटेद् यदि भवेद् वेगवत्त्वेन वेगिनी ।

Transliteration

Pārṣṇināṃ vā padāgreṇa drataṃ gatyā tu cālanam |
Karābhyāṃ cālapadme ca tripatāke yathākramam ||
Dhṛtvā naṭed yadi bhaved vegavattvena veginī |

Meaning:

Pārṣṇinā, vā padāgreṇa, druta gatyā tu cālanam = moving forward on the heels or the toes karābhyāṃ (ca), yathā kramam, alapadme (ca), tripatāke dhṛtvā = assuming Alapadma hasta with one hand and Tripatāka hasta with the other hand (Alapadma and Tripatāka alternately-Ghosh) naṭet yadi, vegavattvena veginī bhavet = if the above action is performed, then, due to quick movement, it is called Veginī cāri.

Assuming Alapadma and Trapatāka hasta and moving forward quickly on the heels or the toes, is considered as Veginī cāri.

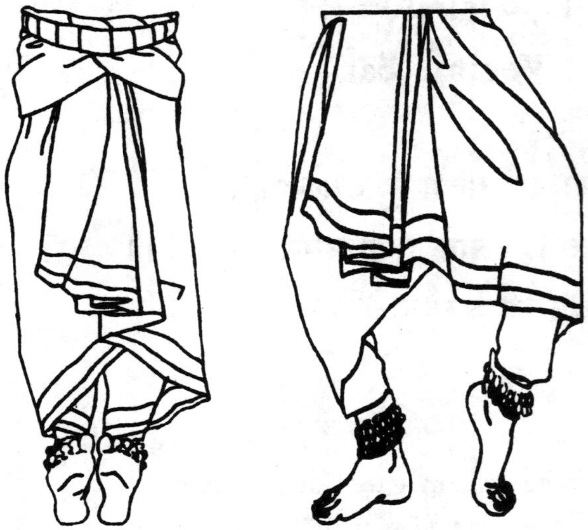

5. कुट्टनम् चारि

Kuṭṭanam cāri

पार्ष्णिना वा पदाग्रेण समस्तेन तलेन वा ।।380।।
यत्ताडनं भूतलस्य कुट्टनं तदुदीरितम् ।

Transliteration

Pārṣṇinā vā padāgreṇa samastena talena vā ||
Yattāḍanaṃ bhūtalasya kuṭṭanaṃ tadudīritam |

Meaning:

Yat, tāḍanaṃ bhūtalasya pārṣṇinā vā padāgreṇa, vā samastena talena = striking the ground with the heel or the forepart or the entire sole of the foot; tat kuṭṭanaṃ, udīritam = that is considered as Kuṭṭanam cāri.

Striking the ground with the heel or the forepart or the entire sole of the foot is considered as Kuṭṭanam cāri.

6. लुठितम् चारि

Luṭhitam cāri

स्वस्तिकस्थितिपादाग्रे कुट्टनाल्लुठितं भवेत् ।।381।।

Transliteration

Svastikasthitipādāgre kuṭṭanālluṭhitaṃ bhavet ||

Meaning:

Svastika sthiti = in the Swastika position of the feet; pādāgrena kuṭṭanāt = foreparts of the feet strike the ground; luṭhitaṃ bhavet = it becomes Luṭhitam cāri.

If in the svastika position of the feet the ground is struck by the forepart of a foot, it is considered as Luṭhita cāri.

7. लोलितम् चारि

Lolitam cāri

पूर्ववत् कुट्टनं कृत्वा मन्दं मन्दमतः परम् ।
अस्पृष्टभूमेः पादस्य चालनं लोलितं भवेत् ।।382।।

Transliteration

Pūrvavat kuṭṭanaṃ kṛtvā mandaṃ mandamataḥ param |
Aspṛṣṭabhūmeḥ pādasya cālanaṃ lolitaṃ bhavet ||

Meaning:

Pūrvavat kuṭṭanaṃ kṛtvā = as described earlier, kuṭṭanaṃ has to be done at first; ataḥ param aspṭuṣṭa-bhūmeḥ mandaṃ mandam, pādasya cālanaṃ = next, without touching the ground, the feet is to be moved forward slowly; lolitaṃ bhavet = then it becomes Lolita cāri.

After striking the ground (as was done earlier), if the feet, without touching the ground are moved forward slowly, then it is Lolita cāri.

8. विषमसञ्चरः चारि

Viṣamasañcaraḥ cāri

वेष्टयित्वा दक्षिणेन वामं वामेन दक्षिणम्।
क्रमेण पादं विन्यस्य भवेद् विषमसञ्चरः
।।383।।

Transliteration

Veṣṭayitvā dakṣiṇena vāmaṃ vāmena dakṣiṇam |
Krameṇa pādaṃ vinyasya bhaved viṣaṇasañcaraḥ ||

Meaning:

Veṣṭayitvā dakṣiṇena vāmaṃ vāmena dakṣiṇam, krameṇa pādaṃ vinyasya = when the left foot is encircled by the right foot and the right food is encircled by the left foot, alternately; vishama-sañcaraḥ bhavet = it is Viṣamasañcaraḥ cāri.

When the left foot is encircled by (placed on the right side of) the right foot and likewise the right foot is encircled by the left foot alternately, and moving forward in this manner is Viṣamasañcaraḥ cāri.

Chapter 27

गति भेदाः

Gati Bhedāḥ

अथात्र गतिभेदानां लक्षणं वक्ष्यते क्रमात्।
हंसी मयूरी च मृगी गजलीला तुरङ्गिणी ।।384।।
सिंही भुजङ्गी मण्डूकी गतिर्वीरा च मानवी।
दशैता गतयो ज्ञेया नाट्यशास्त्रविशारदैः ।।385।।

Transliteration:

Athātra gatibhedānāṃ lakṣaṇaṃ vakṣyate kramāt |
Haṃsī mayūrī ca mṛgī gajalīlā turaṅgiṇī ||
Siṃhī bhujaṅgī maṇḍūkī gatirvīrā ca mānavī |
Daśautā gatayo jñeyā nāṭyaśāstraviśāradaiḥ ||

Meaning:

Athātra gatibhedānāṃ lakṣaṇaṃ vakṣyate kramāt= the characteristics of gati-bhedas are described as, Haṃsī (swan), Mayūrī (peahen) ca (and) Mṛgī (deer), Gajalīlā (sway of an elephant), Turaṅgiṇī (mare), Siṃhī (lioness), Bhujaṅgī (serpent), Maṇḍūkī (frog), Vīrā (herioc), Mānavī (Spirited woman) 1. haṃsī gati, 2. mayūrī gati, 3. mṛgī gati, 4. Gajalīlā gati, 5. turaṅgiṇī, gati, 6. siṃhī, gati, 7. bhujaṅgī gati, 8. maṇḍūkī gati, 9. vīrā gati and 10. mānavī gati; daśautā gatayo jñeyā nāṭyaśāstraviśāradaiḥ=these are the ten gatis, identified by the experts on Nāṭyaśāstra.

The ten characteristics of gati-bhedas identified by the experts on Nāṭyaśāstra are: 1. Haṃsī gati, and 2. Mayūrī gati, 3. Mṛgī gati, 4. Gajalīlā gati, 5. Turaṅgiṇī gati, 6. Simhi gati, 7. Bhujaṅgī gati, 8. Maṇḍūkī gati, 9. Vīrā gati and 10. Mānavī gati.

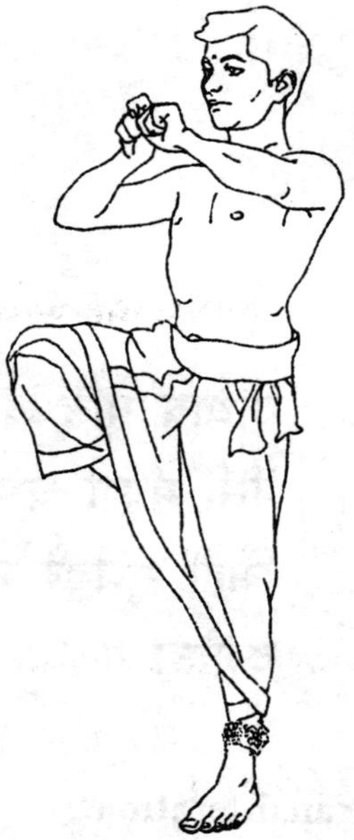

हंसीगतिः

Haṃsīgatiḥ (Female swan)

परिवर्त्य तनुं पार्श्वं वितस्त्यन्तरितं शनैः।
एकैकं तत् पदं न्यस्य कपित्थं करयोर्वहन् ।।386।।
हंसवद्गमनं यत्तु सा हंसी गतिरीरिता ।

Transliteration:

Parivartya tanuṃ pārśvaṃ vitastyantaritaṃ śanaiḥ |
Ēkaikaṃ tat padaṃ nyasya kapitthaṃ karayorvahan ||
Haṃsavadgamanaṃ yattu sā haṃsī gatirīritā |

Meaning:

Tanuṃ pārśvaṃ parivartya = turning the body on bothsides, alternately; vitasti - antaritaṃ tat, eka-eka padaṃ śanaiḥ nyasya = slowly placing one foot from the other at a distance of one vitasti; kapitthaṃ karayoḥ vahan = assuming Kapittha hastas with both hands; haṃsavat gamanaṃ yattu, sā hamsī gatih, īritā = proceeding forward like a haṃsa, is known as haṃsī gati.

Assuming Kapittha hastas with both hands, turning the body on both sides alternately, placing one foot at a distance of one vitasti from the other foot and proceeding forward like a haṃsa is considered as haṃsī gati.

मयूरी गतिः

Mayūrī gatiḥ (Peahen)

प्रपदाभ्यां भूवि स्थित्वा कपित्थं करयीर्वहन् ।।387।।
एकैकजानुचलनात्मयूरी गतिरीरिता।

Transliteration:

Prapadābhyāṃ bhūvi sthitvā kapitthaṃ karayīrvahan ||
Ēkaikajānucalanātmayūrī gatirīritā |

Meaning:

Bhūvi prapadābhyāṃ sthitvā = standing on the ground on the foreparts of the feet; karayoḥ kapitthaṃ vahan = assuming Kapittha hastas with both hands; eka-eka jānucalanāt = moving the knees alternately; mayūrī gatiḥ īritā = this movement is considered as mayūrī gati.

Standing on the ground on the foreparts of the feet, assuming Kapittha hastas with both hands, and moving the knees forward, alternately is considered as mayūrī gati.

मृगीगतिः

Mṛgīgatiḥ (Deer)

मृगवद् गमनं वेगात् त्रिपताककरौ वहन् ।।388।।
पुरतः पार्श्वयोश्चैव यानं मृगगतिर्भवेत् ।

Transliteration:

Mṛgavad gamanaṃ vegāt tripatākakarau vahan ||
Purataḥ pārśvayoścaiva yānaṃ mṛgargāyarbhavet |

Meaning:

Tripatāka karou vahan = assuming Tripataka hastas with both hands; purataḥ pārśvayoḥ (ca-eva) yānaṃ = turing the body towards front and sideways; mṛgavat vegat gamanaṃ = moving forward quickly like a deer; mṛga gatiḥ bhavet = it becomes Mṛgi gati.

Assuming Tripataka hastas with both hands, turning the body towards front and sideways and moving forward quickly is considered Mṛgi gati.

गजलीला गतिः

Gajalīlā gatiḥ (playful gait of an elephant)

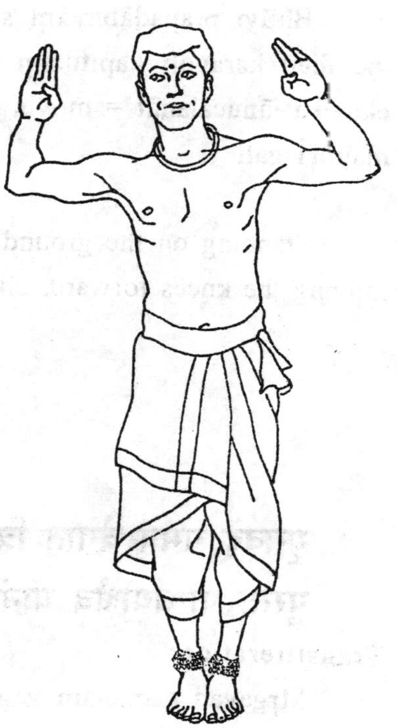

पार्श्वयोस्तु पताकाभ्यां कराभ्यां विचरंस्ततः ।।389।।
समपादगतिर्मन्दं गजलीलेति विश्रुता ।

Transliteration:

Pārśvayostu patākābhyāṃ karābhyāṃ vicaraṃstataḥ ||
Samapādagatirmandaṃ gajalīleti viśrutā |

Meaning:

Pārśvayoḥ patākābhyāṃ = assuming patāka hasta with both hands and holding them on the respective sides; tataḥ mandaṃ vicaraṃ samapāda gatiḥ = then moving forward slowly with Samapada ; gajalīla iti viśrutā = is known as Gajalila gati

Moving forward slowly in Samapada holding patāka hasta on both sides is considered as Gajalila gati.

तुरङ्गिणीगतिः

Turaṅgiṇīgatiḥ (mare)

उत्क्षिप्य दक्षिणं पादमुल्लङ्घ्य च मुहुर्मुहुः ।।390।।
वामेण शिखरं धृत्वा दक्षिणेन पताकिकाम् ।
तुरङ्गिणी गतिः प्रोक्ता नृत्तशास्त्रविशारदैः ।।391।।

Transliteration:

Utkṣipya dakṣiṇaṃ pādamullaṅghya ca muhurmuhuḥ ||
Vāmeṇa śikharaṃ dhṛtvā dakṣiṇena patākikām |
Turaṅgiṇī gatiḥ proktā nṛttaśāstraviśāradaiḥ ||

Meaning:

Dakṣiṇaṃ pādam utkṣipya = raising the right foot; jumping ca muhuḥ-muhuḥ =and jumping repeatedly; vāmeṇa śikharaṃ dakṣiṇena patākikāṃ dhṛtvā = assuming Sikhara hasta with left hand and patāka hasta with right hand; turaṅgiṇī gatiḥ nṛtta-śāstra viśāradaiḥ proktā = then it is considered by the experts on the science of nṛtta as Turangiṇī gati.

Raising the right foot and jumping forward repeatedly, assuming Sikhara hasta with left hand and patāka hasta with right hand, is considerd as Turangiṇī gati.

सिंहीगतिः
Siṃhīgatiḥ (lioness)

पादाग्राभ्यां भुवि स्थित्वा पुर उत्प्लुत्य वेगतः ।
कराभ्यां शिखरं धृत्वा यानं सिंहगतिभवेत् ।।392।।

Transliteration:

Pādāgrābhyāṃ bhuvi sthitvā pura utplutya vegataḥ |
Karābhyāṃ śikharaṃ dhṛtvā yānaṃ siṃhagatibhavet ||

Meaning:

Pāda-agrābhyāṃ bhuvi sthitvā = standing on the ground on the fore-parts of the feet; karābhyāṃ śikharaṃ dhṛtvā= assuming Sikhara hastas with both hands; puraḥ, vegataḥ, utplutya, yānam=moving forward quickly with jumps; siṃha gatiḥ bhavet = it becomes siṃha gati.

Assuming Sikhara hastas with both hands, and standing on the foreparts of the feet, moving to the front quickly with jumps is considered as Siṃhi gati.

भुजङ्गीगतिः
Bhujaṅgīgatiḥ (female serpent)

त्रिपताककरौ धृत्वा पार्श्वयोरुभयोरपि ।
पूर्ववद्गमनं यत्तु सा भुजङ्गी गतिर्भवेत् ।।393।।

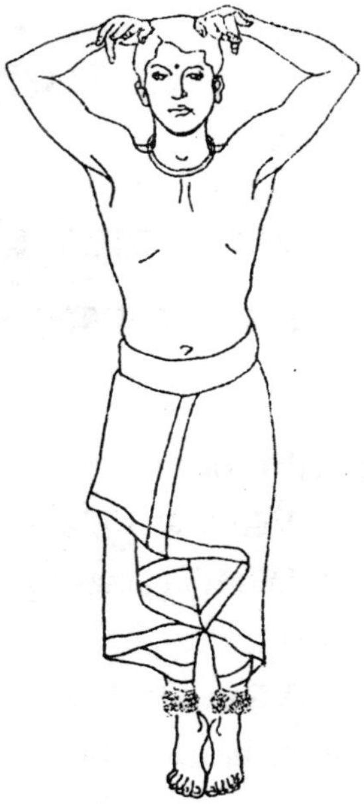

Transliteration:

Tripatākakarau dhṛtvā pārśvayorubhayorapi |
Pūrvavadgamanaṃ yattu sā bhujaṅgī gatirbhavet ||

Meaning:

Ubhayoḥ pārśvayoḥ api tripatāka karou dhṛtvā=holding tripatāka hasta on both sides; yattu pūrvavat gamanaṃ sā bhujaṅgī gatiḥ bhavet= and proceeding forward as in the case of Simhi gati, it becomes Bhujangi (female serpent) gati.

Holding Tripataka hastas with both hands on both sides, if the Simhi gati is repeated, it is considerd as bhujaṅgī gati.

मण्डूकीगतिः

Maṇḍūkīgatiḥ (female frog)

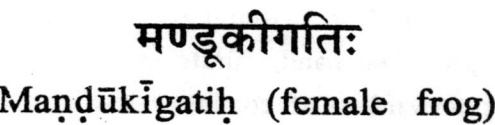

कराभ्यां शिखरं धृत्वा किञ्चित् सिंहीसमा गतिः।
मण्डूकी गतिरित्येषा प्रसिद्धा भरतागमे ।।394।।

Transliteration:

Karābhyāṃ śikharaṃ dhṛtvā kiñcit siṃhīsamā gatiḥ |
Maṇḍūkī gatirityeṣā prasiddhā bharatāgame ||

Meaning:

Karābhyāṃ śikharaṃ dhṛtvā = holding śikhara hasta with both hands; kiñcit siṃhīsamā gatiḥ = repeating the siṃha gati to some measure; eṣā maṇḍūkī gatiḥ iti bharata-āgame prasiddhā = this is popular as maṇḍūkī gati according to Bharata.

Holding śikhara hasta with both hands, and proceeding forward almost like a lioness is considered as Maṇḍūkī gati.

वीरागतिः

Vīrāgatiḥ (heroic gait)

वामे तु शिखरं धृत्वा दक्षिणेन पताकिका ।
दूरादागमनं यत्तु वीरा गतिरीरिता ।।395।।

Transliteration:

Vāme tu śikharaṃ dhṛtvā dakṣiṇena patākikā |
Dūrādāgamanaṃ yattu vīrā gatirīritā ||

Vāme (tu) śikharaṃ dakṣiṇena patākikā dhṛtvā = **assuming** Sikhara hasta with left hand and Pataka hasta with right hand; dūrāt-āgamanaṃ yattu vīra gatiḥ udīritā = moving forward as if coming from a distance, it is considered as vīrā gati.

Holding śikhara hasta with left hand and patāka hasta with right hand, proceeding forward as if coming from a distance, is considered as vīrā gati.

मानवीगतिः

Mānavīgatiḥ (Gait of a spirited woman)

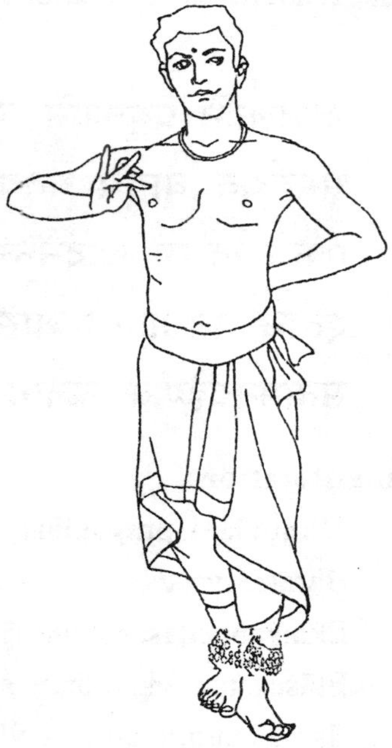

मण्डलाकारवद् भ्रान्त्या समागत्य मुहुर्मुहुः ।
वामं करं न्यस्य कटौ दक्षिणे कटकामुखण् ।।396।।
मानवी गतिरित्येषा प्रसिद्धा पूर्वसूरिभिः ।

Transliteration:

Maṇḍalākāravat bhrāntyā samāgatya muhurmuhuḥ |
Vāmaṃ karaṃ nyasya kaṭau dakṣiṇe kaṭakāmukhaṇ ||
Mānavī gatirityeṣā prasiddhā pūrvasūribhiḥ |

Meaning:

Maṇḍala - ākāravat muhuḥ-muhuḥ bhrāntyā samāgatya = moving in circles repeatedly and coming forward repreadly; kaṭau vāmaṃ karaṃ vyasya dakṣiṇe kaṭakāmukhaṇ = holding left hand on the waist and assuming kaṭakāmukha hasta with right hand; eṣā mānavī gatiḥ iti pūrva sūribhiḥ prasiddhā = this is popularly known as Mānavī gati, according to ancient scholars.

Holding left hand on the waist and assuming Katakāmukha hasta with right hand and moving in circles and coming forward is considered as Mānavī gati.

The relation to one another between Mandalas, Sthanakas, Utplavanas, Bhramaris, Caris and Gatis

मण्डलानि प्रयुक्तानि तथैवोत्प्लवनानि च ।।397।।
भ्रमर्यश्चैव चार्यश्च गतयश्च परस्परम् ।
एकैकभेदसम्बन्धादनन्तानि भवन्ति हि ।।398।।
एताश्च नर्तनविधौ शास्त्रतः सम्प्रदायतः ।
सतामनुग्रहेणैव विज्ञेया नान्यथा भुवि ।।399।।

Transliteration:

Maṇḍalāni prayuktāni tathaivotplavanāni ca ||
Bhramaryaścaiva cāryaśca gatayaśca parasparam |
Ekaikabhedasambandhādanantāni bhavanti hi ||
Etāśca nartanavidhau śāstrataḥ sampradāyataḥ |
Satāmanugraheṇaiva vijñeyā nānyathā bhuvi ||

Meaning:

Maṇḍalāni tathā-eva, utplavanāni ca, bhramaryaḥ ca-eva, cāryaḥ ca, gatayaḥ ca parasparam sambandhāt prayuktāni = Mandalas, Utplavanas, Bhramaris, Caris and Gatis - when these are employed in relation to one another; eka-eka bheda sambandhāt anantāni bhavanti hi= with permutations and combinations there will be innumerable varieties; etāḥ ca nartana vidhou = all these, in the practice of dance; śāstrataḥ sampradāyataḥ satām anugraheṇa eva, vijñeyā =have to be learnt from the śāstra (study of treatises), sampradāya (knowledge of tradition) and the teachings of the learned gurus; anyathā na = not otherwise.

Mandalas, Utplavanas, Bhramaris, Caris and Gatis-when all these are employed with various - combinations, there will be innumerable varieties. All such varieties are to be learnt by studying the śāstrās, by closely observing the tradition and through effective training undergone with a competent and affectionate guru; in no other way can this be achieved. All these in the practice of dance have to be learnt from the śāstra (study of treatises), sampradāya (knowledge of tradition) and the teachings of the learned gurus.There is no other way of learning.

Chapter 28

वृक्ष हस्तः

Vṛkṣa hastaḥ

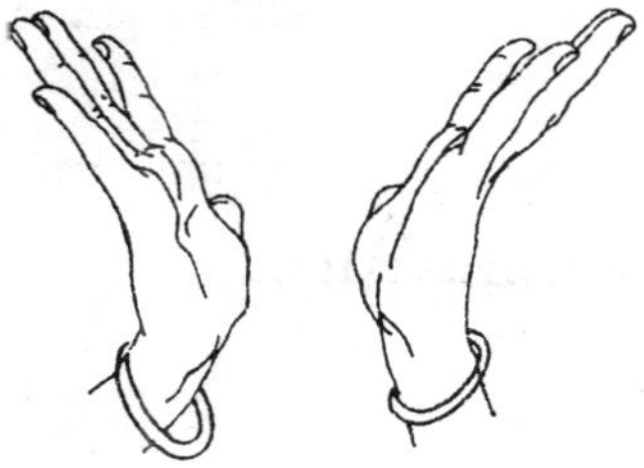

1. अश्वत्थः

Aśvatthaḥ (Pipal tree)

अलपद्मौ रेचितौ चेत् अश्वत्थे संप्रयुज्यते ।

Transliteration:

Alapadamau recitau cet aśvatthe samprayujyate |

Meaning:

When two Alapadma hastas perform recita hasta prānā it denotes Aśvattha vṛkṣa. (Refer page 74).

2. कदलै

Kadalai (Plantain tree)

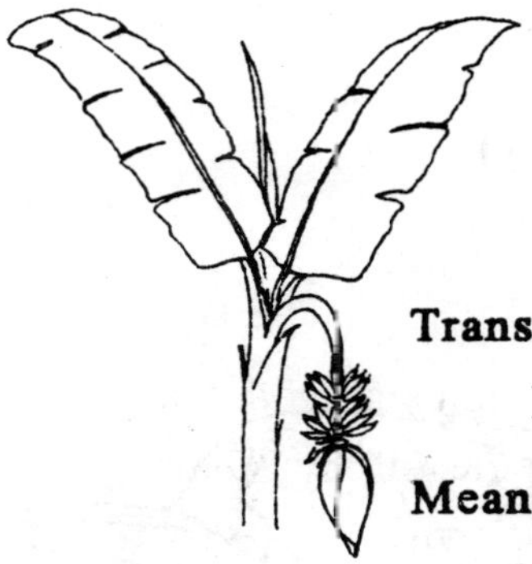

कदल्याम् स्लिष्टमुकुलौ रेचितोद्वेस्थितौ भवेत् ।।400।।

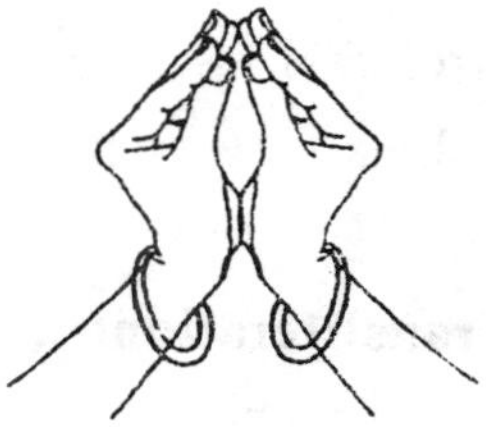

Transliteration:

Kadalyām sliṣṭamukulau recitodvesthitau bhavet ||

Meaning:

If two Mukula hastas joined at the fingers perform recita and udweṣṭita hasta prānās then it denotes Kadali vṛkṣa. (Refer page 74 and 76).

3-4. नारंग व लिकुच

Nāraṅga (Orange tree) and Likuca (A species of lime tree)

नारंगे पद्मकोश स्यात् भ्रमरौ लिकुचे भवेत् ।

Transliteration:

Nāraṅge padmakośa syāt bhramārau likuce bhavet |

=
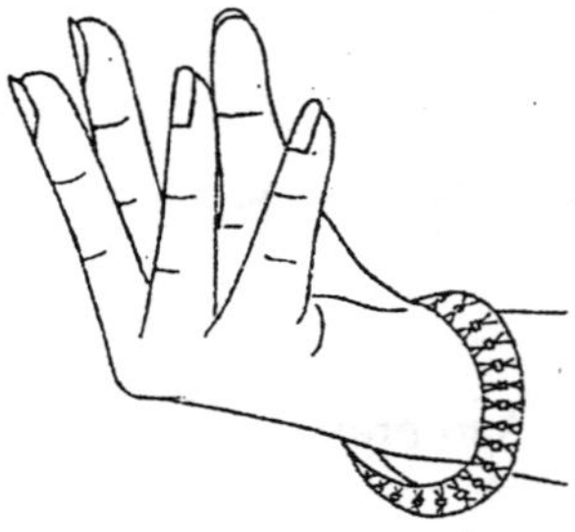

=

Meaning:

Padma kosa hasta denotes Naranga vṛkṣa and Bhramara hasta denotes Likuca vṛkṣa.

5-6. पनस व बिल्वा

Panasa (Jack tree) and Bilvā (Beel tree)

पनसे चतुरः प्रोक्तो बिल्वार्थे चतुरो भवेत् ।।401।।

Transliteration:

Panase caturaḥ prokto bilvārthe caturo bhavet ||

=
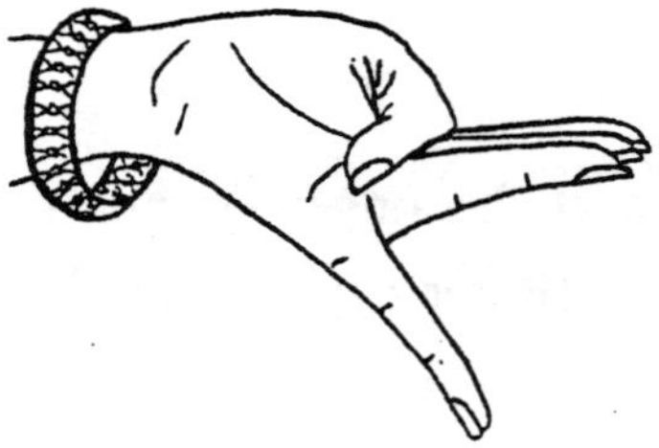

=
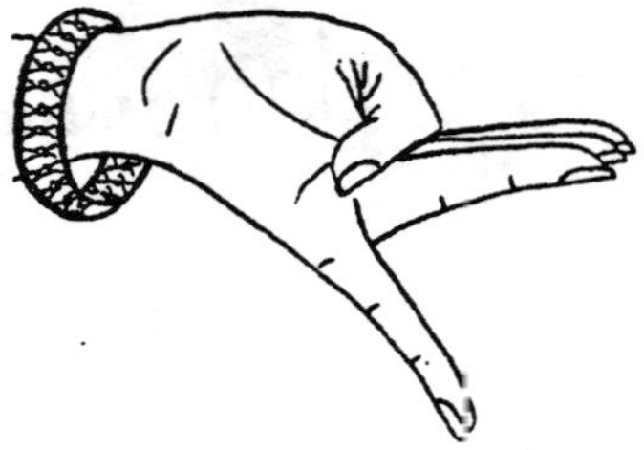

Meaning:

Catura hasta denotes Panasa vṛkṣa as well as Bilva vṛkṣa.

7. पुन्नाग

Punnāga (Oil nut tree)

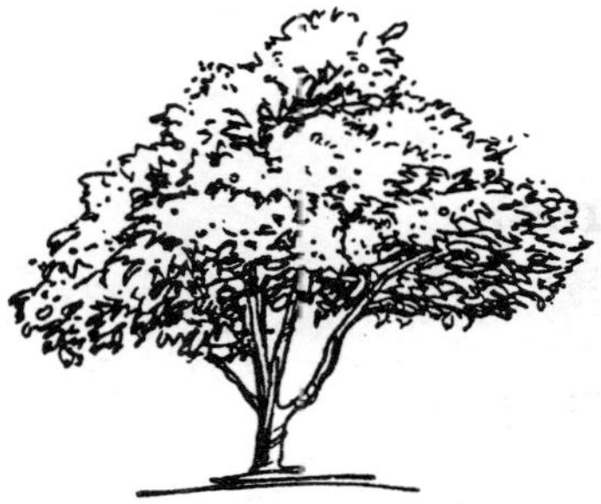

पताक-चतुरौ प्रोक्तो पुन्नागतरु निर्णये ।

Transliteration:

Patāka-caturau prokto punnāgataru nirṇaye ||

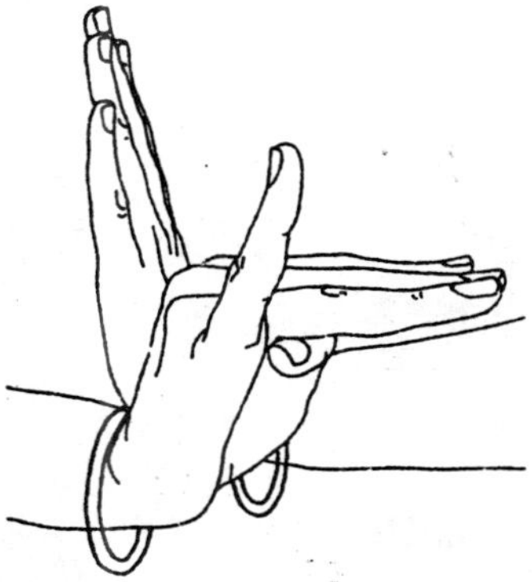

Meaning:

Patākacatura hasta denotes Punnāga vṛkṣa .

8-9. मंदार वकुल

Mandāra (Coral tree) Vakula (Spanish cherry)

मंदारे खण्ड चतुरः संदंशो वकुले भवेत् ।।402।।

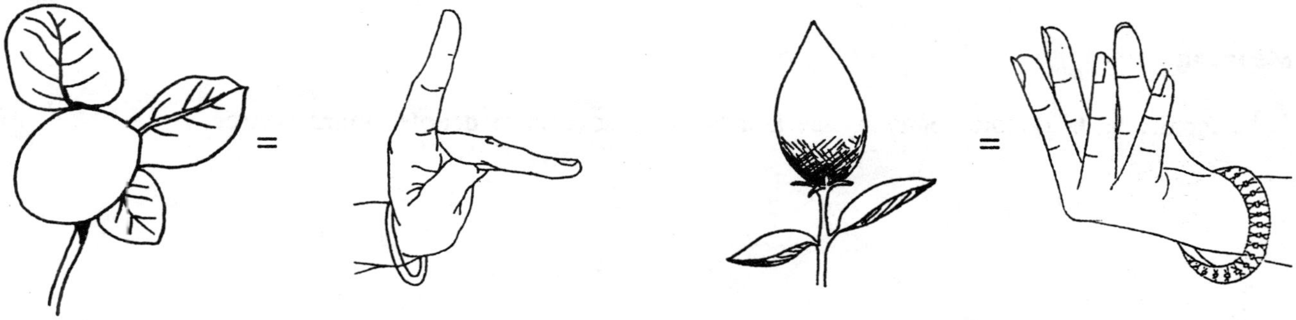

Transliteration:

Mandāre khaṇḍa caturaḥ sandaṃśo vakule bhavet ||

Meaning:

Khaṇḍacatura hasta denotes Mandāra and Saṃdaṃśa hasta denotes Vakula vṛkṣa.

10-11. वट अर्जुनः

Vaṭa (Banyan tree) Arjunaḥ (Kumbuk tree)

पताको वट वृक्षे स्यात् अर्जुने सिम्हवक्त्रकः ।

Transliteration:

Patāko vaṭa vṛkṣe syāt arjune simhavaktrakaḥ |

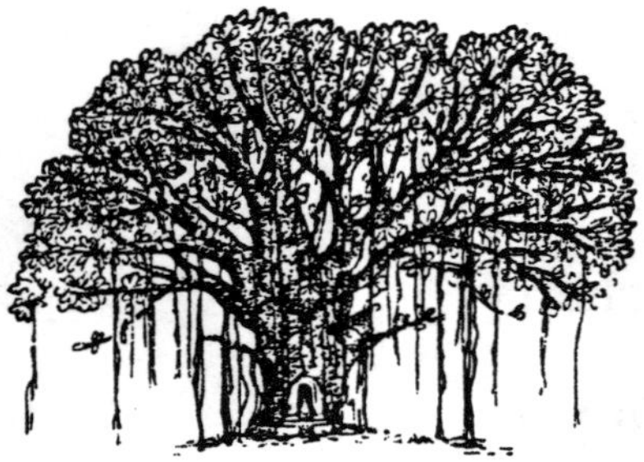
=

=

Meaning:

Patāka hasta denotes banyan tree and Simhamukha hasta denotes kumbuk tree.

12-13 पाटलि हिंताल

Pāṭali (Trumpet flower plant) Hiṇṭalā (Marshy date tree)

पाटल्याम् शुकतुन्डः स्यात् हिंताले कर्तरीमुखः ।।403।।

Transliteration:

Pāṭalyām śukaṭuṇḍaḥ syāt hiṇṭāle kartarīmukhaḥ ||

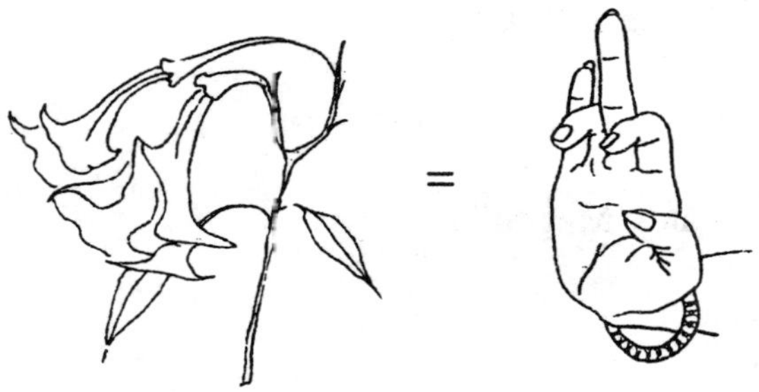

=

=

Meaning:

Śukatuṇḍa hasta denotes trumpet flower plant while Kartarīmukha hasta denotes marshy date tree.

14. फूग

Phūga (Areca nut tree)

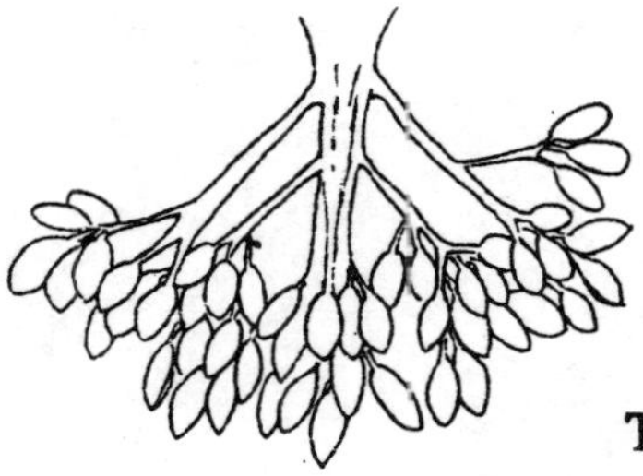

पद्मकोशौ स्वस्तिकौ स्तः फुगवृक्षनिरूपणे ।

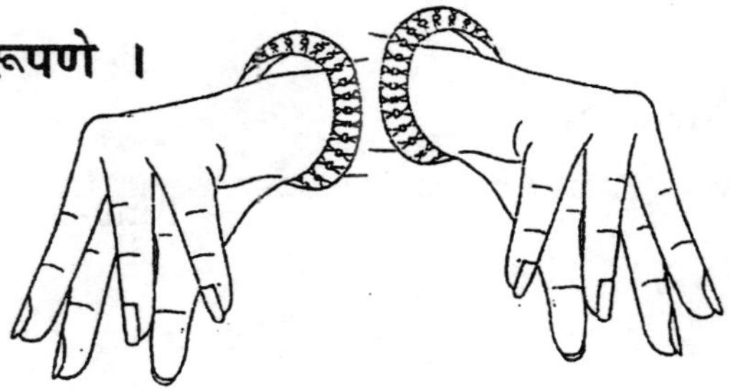

Transliteration:

Padmakośau svastikau staḥ phūgavṛkṣanirūpaṇe |

Meaning:

Padmakośa hastas in svastika position denotes Phūga vṛkṣa.

15. चम्पक

Campaka (Magnolia)

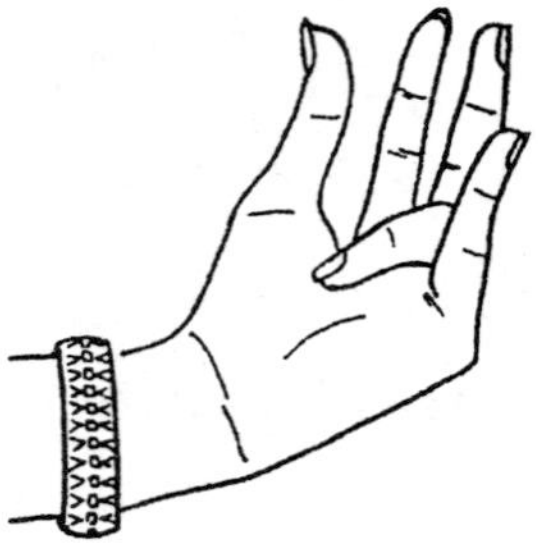

चम्पके पूर्वशास्त्रज्ञै अधोलाङ्गुल मिष्यते ।।404।।

Transliteration:

Campake puravaśāstrajñai adholāṅgūla miṣyate ||

Meaning:

Kāngula hasta held downwards indicates Magnolia.

16. खदिर

Khadira (Kutch Tree)

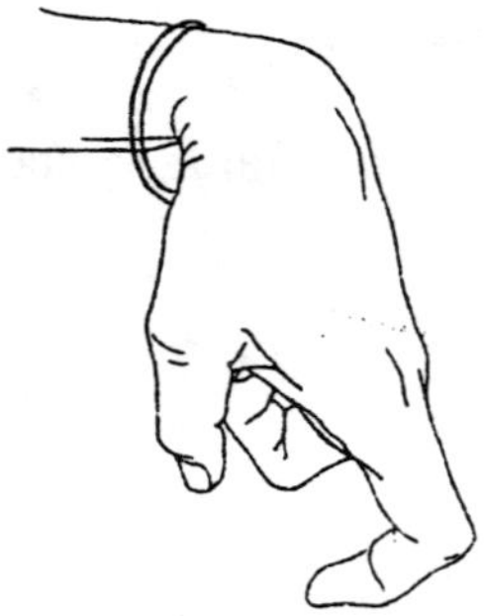

अधोनतः ताम्रचूडः करः खदिर वर्णने ।

Transliteration:

Adhonataḥ tāmracūḍāḥ karaḥ khadira varṇane |

Meaning:

Tāmracūḍa hasta bent downwards denotes Khadira vṛkṣa.

17. शमी

Śamī (White Kutch)

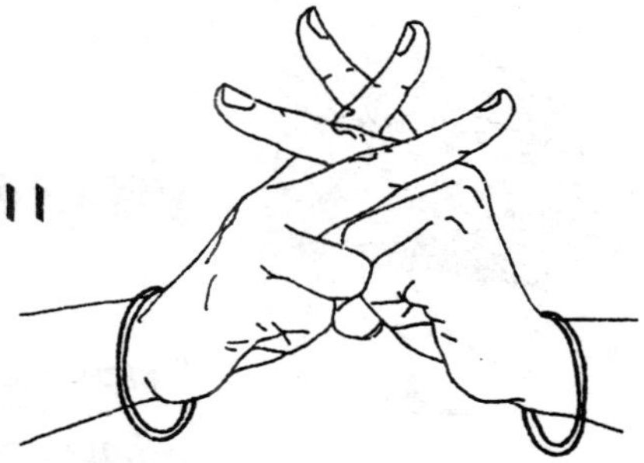

शमी वृक्षे समाख्यातः करो यः श्लिष्टकर्तरी ।।405।।

Transliteration:

Śamī vṛkṣe samākhyātaḥ karo yaḥ śliṣṭakartarī ||

Meaning:

Two Kartarihastas interlocked indicate śamī vṛkṣa.

18. अशोकः

Aśokaḥ (Ashoka tree)

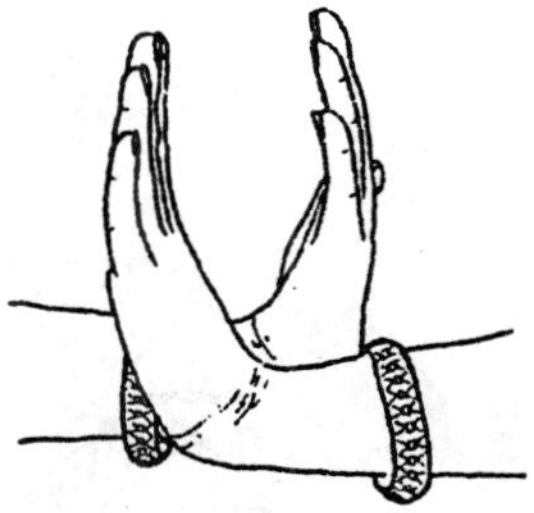

पताकौ मणिबंधस्थौ सम्यक् तिर्यक् कृतौ यदि ।
पताकस्वस्तिको हस्तः कथितो भरतादिभिः ।।406।।
पताकस्वस्तिको हस्तः अशोकाभिनये स्मृतः ।

Transliteration:

Patākau maṇibandhasthau samyak tiryak kṛtau yadi |
Patākasvastiko hastaḥ kathito bharatādibhiḥ ||
Patākasvastiko hastaḥ aśokābhinaye smṛtaḥ |

Meaning:

If two Patāka hastas are in svastika position at the wrists it is considered as Patākasvastika hasta by Bharata and others. This hasta denotes Aśoka vṛkṣa.

19. सिंदुवार

Siṅduvāra (Oak tree)

सिंदुवार तरौ योज्यः करः श्लिष्टमयूरकः ।।407।।

Transliteration:

Siṅduvāra tarau yojyaḥ karaḥ śliṣṭamayūrakaḥ ||

Meaning:

Two Mayūra hastas joined together denote Siṅduvāra vṛkṣa.

20. अमलका

Amalakā (Indian Gooseberry)

तर्जनीमध्यमा हस्ततले सम्मिश्रिते यदि ।
इतरे प्रशृतः सो-अयम् करः सम्यमनामकः ।।408।।
सम्यमाभिधा हस्तो-अयम् भवेत् अमलके द्रुमे ।

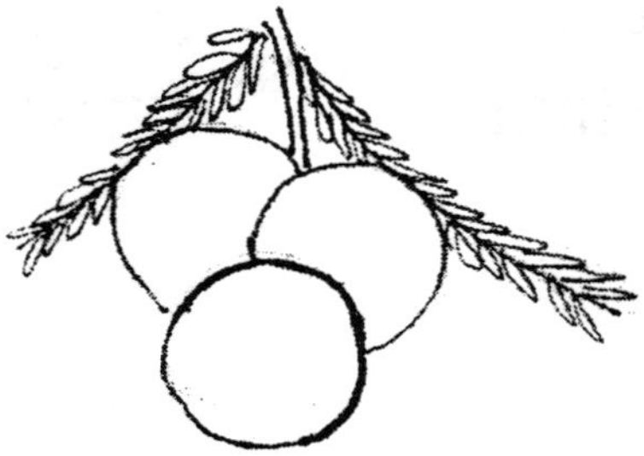

Transliteration:

Tarjanīmadhyamā hastatale sammiśrite yadi |
Itare prasṛtaḥ so-ayam karaḥ samyamanāmakaḥ ||
Samyamābhidhā hasto-ayam bhavet amalake drume |

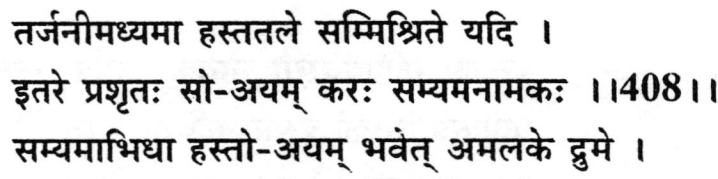

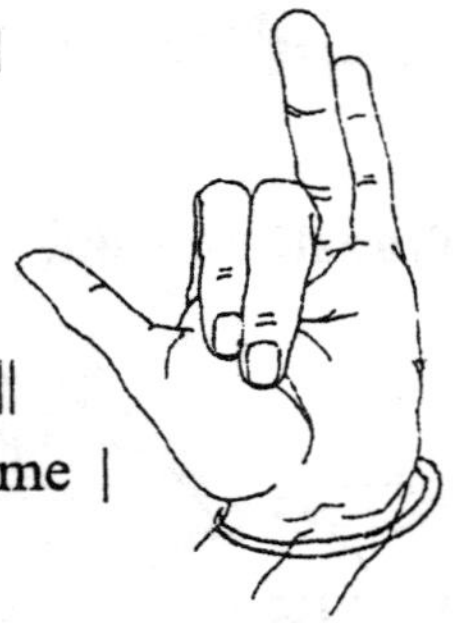

Meaning:

If the fore finger and the middle finger are joined in the palm and the other fingers are extended then it is known as Samyama hasta. This hasta denotes Amalaka vṛkṣa.

21. कुरवक

Kuravaka (A kind of amaranth)

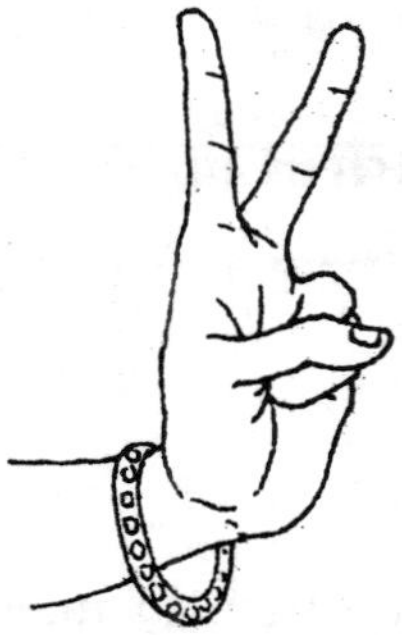
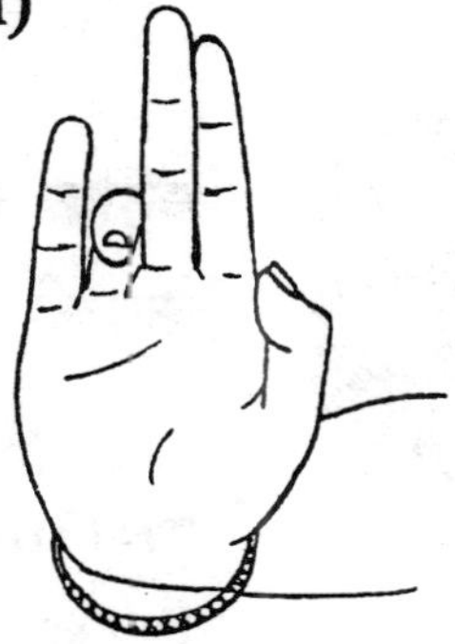

कर्तरी त्रिपताकौ च ज्ञेयौ कुरवक द्रुमे ।।409।।

Transliteration:

Kartarī tripatākau ca jñeyau kuravaka drume ||

Meaning:

Both kartarī and Tripatāka hastas denote Kuravaka vṛkṣa.

22. कपित्थ

Kapittha (Woodapple tree)

अलपद्मौ स्वस्तिकौ चेत् कपित्थार्थे नियुज्यते ।

Transliteration:

Alapadmau svastikau cet kapitthārthe niyujyate |

Meaning:

Two Alapadma hastas in svastika position denotes Kapittha vṛkṣa.

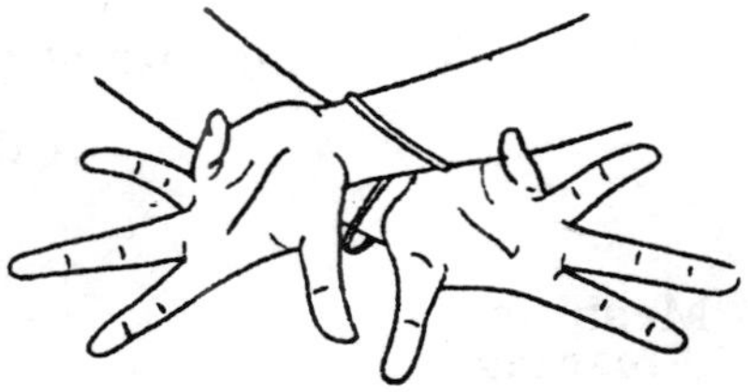

23. केतकी

Ketakī (Screw-pine tree)

पताक चतुराभिख्यौ स्वस्तिकौ मणिबन्धयोः ।।410।।
केतकी वृक्षभेदे-अपि युज्येते देवमन्त्रिणि ।

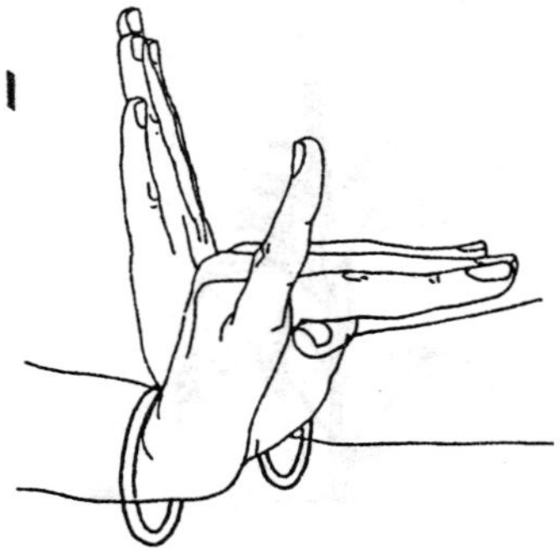

Transliteration:

Patāka caturābhikhyau svastikau maṇibandhayoḥ ||
Ketakī vṛkṣabhede-api yujyete devamantriṇi |

Meaning:

Patāka and Catura hasta crossed at the wrists denotes Ketaki vṛkṣa and devamantri i.e. Bṛhaspati.

24. शिंशपा

Śiṃśapā (Shisham, rosewood)

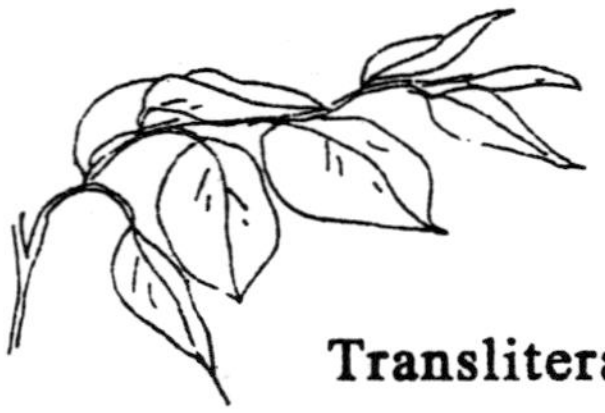

अर्धचन्द्रौ स्वस्तिकौ चेत् प्रयोज्यौ शिम्शपातरे ।।411।।

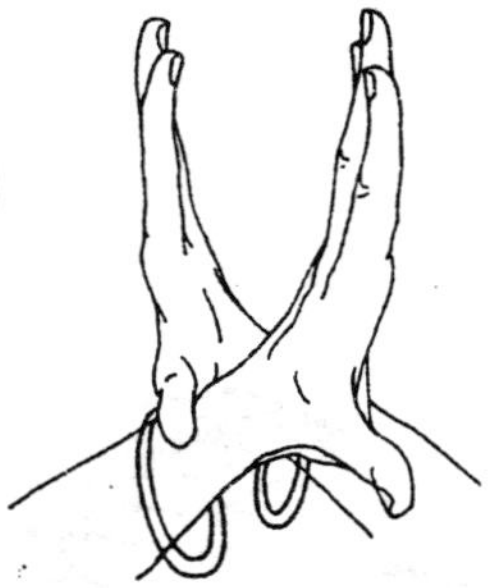

Transliteration:

Ardhacandrau svastikau cet prayojyau śimśapātare ||

Meaning:

Two Ardhacandra hastas in svastika position, denote Simśapā vṛkṣa.

25-26 निम्ब साल

Nimba (Margosa) Sāla (sal)

=
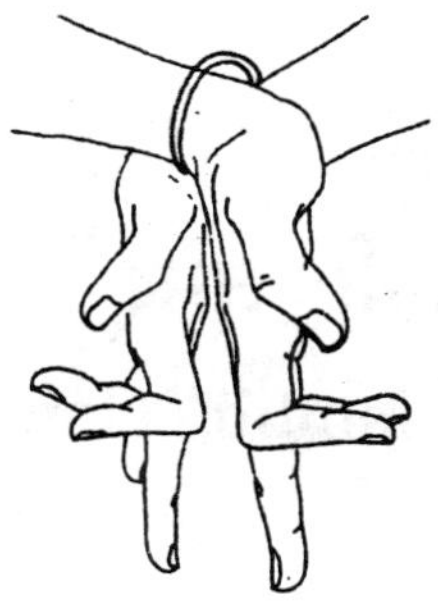

=
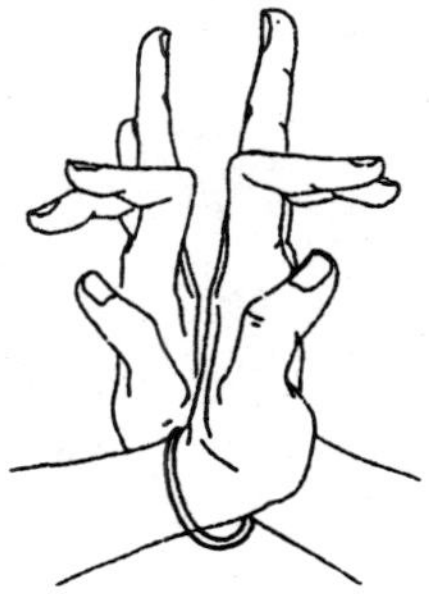

शुकतुन्डौ स्वस्तिकौ चेत् निम्बे साले निरूपितौ ।

Transliteration:

Śukatuṇḍau svastikau cet nimbe sāle nirūpitau |

Meaning:

Two śukatuṇḍa hastas in Svastika position denote Nimba and Sāla vṛkṣas.

27. पारिजात

Pārijāta (Night flowering jasmine)

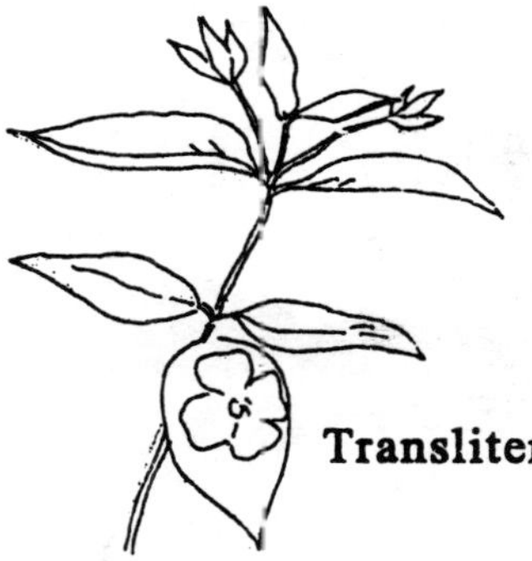

वामे पताकको हस्तः तत्र सव्ये पताकिकः ।।412।।
उद्वेष्टितकृतो हस्तः त्रिज्ञः परिकीर्तितः ।
त्रिज्ञानः पारिजातस्य क्रोडे यदि धृतः करः ।।413।।

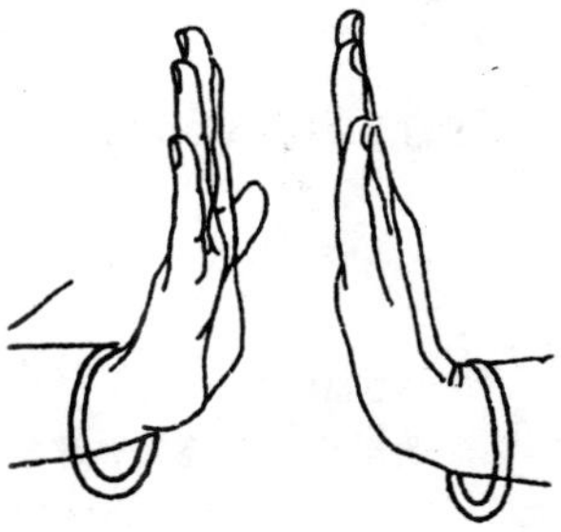

Transliteration:

Vāme patākako hastaḥ tatra savye patākikaḥ ||
Udveṣṭitakṛto hastaḥ trijñaḥ parikīrtitaḥ |
Trijñānaḥ pārijātasya kroḍe yadi dhṛtaḥ karaḥ ||

Meaning:

If two Patāka hastas in both left and right hands perform udweṣtita hasta prānā, then it is considered as Trijñānaḥ hasta. This hasta held before the chest denotes Pārijāta vṛkṣa.

28-29. तिंत्रिणी जम्बू

Tintriṇī (Tamarind tree) Jambū (Jamun tree)

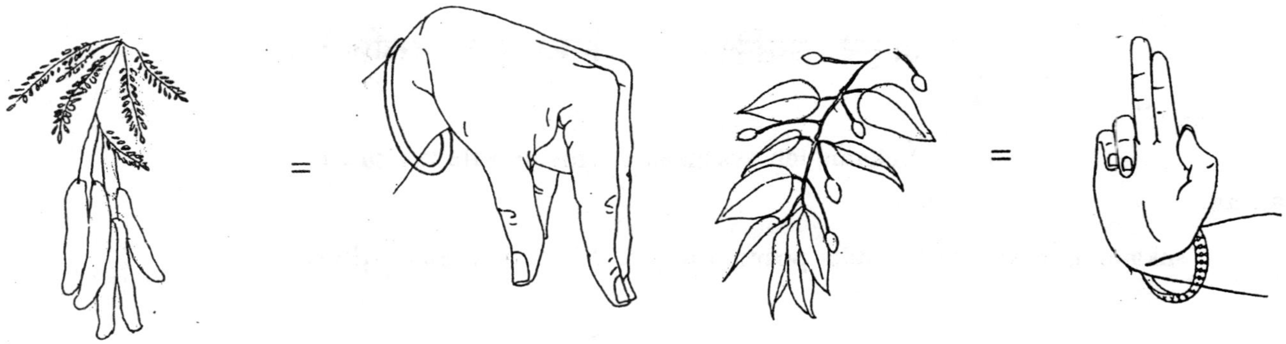

तिंत्रिण्यामपि काङ्गुलो जम्ब्वामर्ध-पताककः ।

Transliteration:

Tintriṇyāmapi kāṅgūlo jambvāmardha-patākakaḥ |

Meaning:

Kāṅgūla hasta denotes Tamarind tree and Ardhapatāka denotes Jamun tree.

30-31. पालाश रसाल

Pālāśa (Flame of the forest tree) Rasāla (Mango tree)

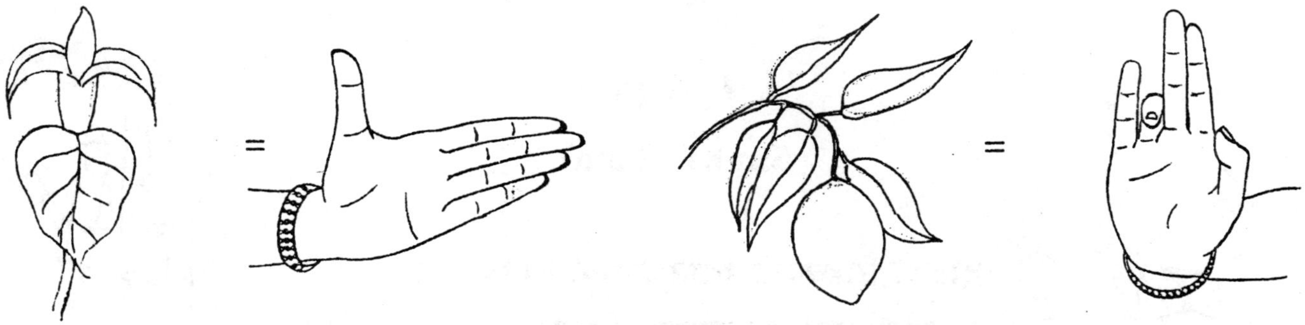

पालाशे चार्ध-चन्द्रश्च रसाले त्रिपताकिकः ।।414।।

Transliteration:

Pālāse cārdha-candraśca rasāle tripatākikaḥ ||

Meaning:

Ardhacandra hasta denotes flame of the forest tree and tripatāka hasta denotes mango tree.

Chapter 29

मृग हस्ताः

Mṛga Hastāḥ

1. सिंह

Siṃha (Lion)

दक्षिणे सिंहवक्त्रः स्यात् तत्पृष्ठे वामहस्ततः ।
पताकहस्तमाश्रित्य चलत्-प्रविरलांगुलिम् ।।415।।
स्लिष्ठसिंहमुखः सोऽयम् सिंहार्थे विनियुज्यते ।

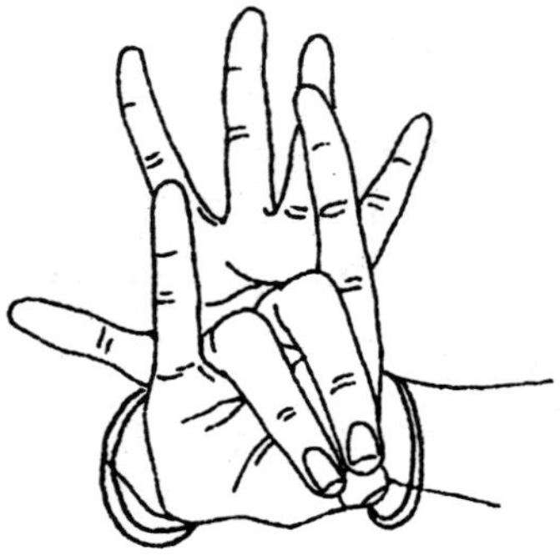

Transliteration:

Dakṣiṇe siṃhāvaktraḥ syāt tatpṛṣṭhe vāmahastataḥ |
Patākahastamāsritya calat-praviralāṅgulim ||
Sliṣṭhasiṃhamukhaḥ so 'ayam siṃhārthe viniyujyate |

Meaning:

Dakṣiṇe siṃhāvaktraḥ syāt tatpṛṣṭhe vāmahastataḥ = Right hand assuming simhamukha hasta, left hand assuming Patāka hasta is placed on the back of the right hand; Patākahastamāsritya calat-praviralāṅgulim = Fingers of the Patāka hasta being apart and wavy; Sliṣṭhasiṃhamukhaḥ so 'ayam siṃhārthe viniyujyate = This is Simhamukha hasta and denotes the lion.

Right hand assuming simhamukha hasta, left hand assuming Patāka hasta is placed on the back of the right hand; the fingers of the Patāka hasta being apart and wavy. This is Simhamukha hasta and denotes the lion.

2. व्याघ्र

Vyāghra (Tiger)

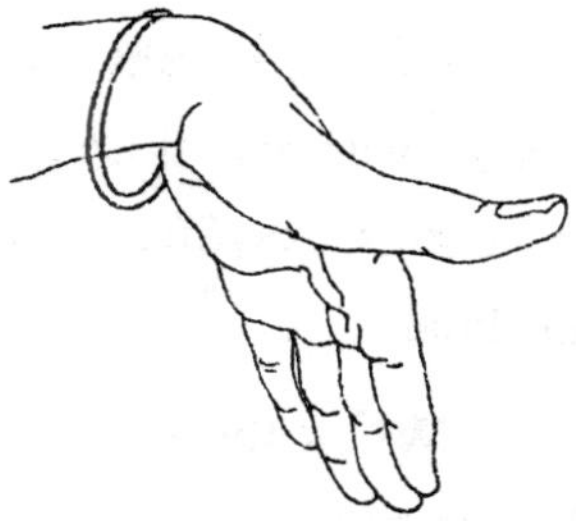

अर्धचंद्रो-अधोमुखः चेत् व्याघ्रार्थे संप्रयुज्यते। ।416। ।

Transliteration:

Ardhacandro-adhomukhaḥ cet vyāghrārthe samprayujyate ||

Meaning:

Ardhacandro-adhomukhaḥ cet vyāghrārthe samprayujyate = Ardhacandra hasta facing downwards, denotes tiger .

Ardhacandra hasta facing downwards, denotes tiger .

3. सूकर

Sūkara (Boar)

पूर्वोक्त मत्स्य हस्ते तु दक्षिणः कुंचितः चलः ।
अस्यांगुल्यः प्रविरलाः पंचसंख्या यथाक्रमम ।।417।।
युज्यते स्तब्धरोमार्थे संकीर्णमकरः करः ।

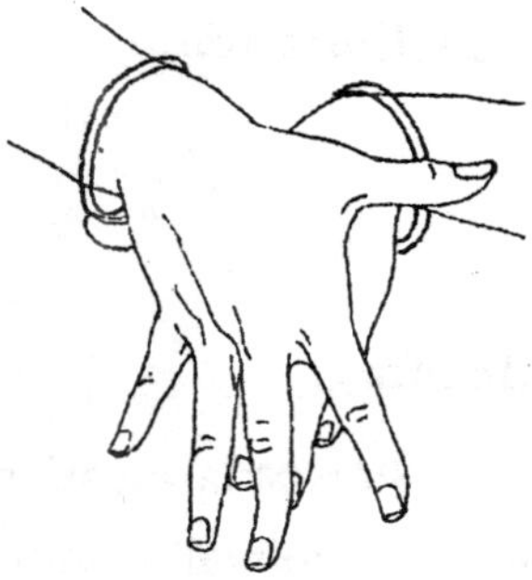

Transliteration:

Pūrvokta matsya haste tu dakṣiṇaḥ kuñcitaḥ calaḥ |
Asyāṅgulyaḥ pravīralāḥ pañcasaṅkhyā yathākramama ||
Yujyate stabdharomārthe saṅkīrṇamakaraḥ karaḥ |

Meaning:

Pūrvokta matsya haste tu dakṣiṇaḥ kuñcitaḥ calaḥ = When the right hand as Matsya hasta is held downwards and shaken; Yujyate stabdharomārthe saṅkīrṇamakaraḥ karaḥ = with the five fingers held apart as bristles; Asyāṅgulyaḥ pravīralāḥ pañcasaṅkhyā yathākramama = it is Saṅkīrṇamakara hasta and denotes the boar.

When the right hand as Matsya hasta, is held downwards with the five fingers apart, and shaken to denote bristles. it is Saṅkīrṇamakara hasta and denotes the boar.

4. कपि

Kapi (Monkey)

पूर्वोक्त मुष्टि हस्तस्तु मध्यमांगुष्ठ योगतः ।।418।।
नाम्ना-अधोमुष्टि मुकुलः कपेरार्थे निरूप्यते ।

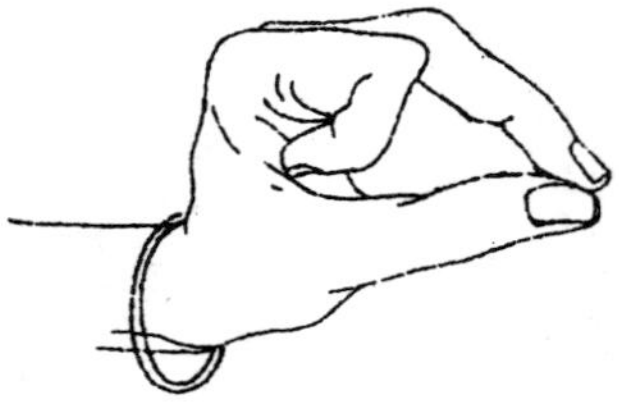

Transliteration:

Pūrvokta muṣṭi hastastu madhyamāṅguṣṭha yogataḥ ||
Nāmnā-adhomuṣṭi mukulaḥ kaperārthe nirūpyate |

Meaning:

Pūrvokta muṣṭi hastastu madhyamāṅguṣṭha yogataḥ = If the middle finger and the thumb of Muṣṭi hasta are joined; Nāmnā-adhomuṣṭi mukulaḥ kaperārthe nirūpyate = then it is Adhomuṣṭi mukula hasta and it denotes the monkey.

If the middle finger and the thumb of Muṣṭi hasta are joined, then it is Adhomuṣṭi mukula hasta and it denotes the monkey.

5. भल्लूक

Bhallūka (Bear)

वामहस्ते प कोशो-अधोमुखत्वा-मुपाश्रितः ।।419।।
दक्षिणे तु पताकाख्यस्तस्य पृष्ठतलाश्रितः ।
भल्लूकार्थे प्रयोज्यः स्यात् प कोशः पताककः ।।420।।

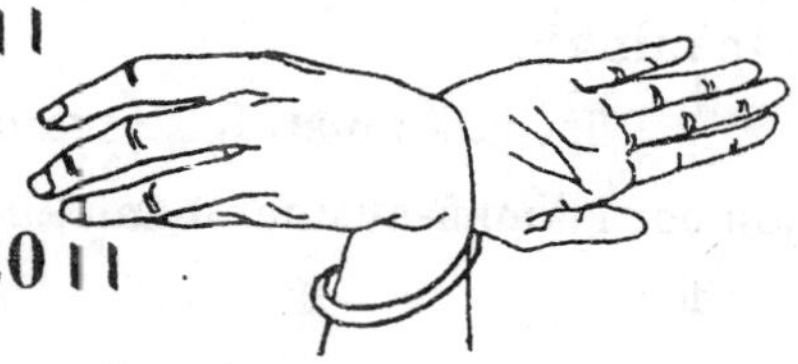

Transliteration:

Vāmahaste padmakośo-adhomukhatvā-mupāśritaḥ ||
Dakṣiṇe tu patākākhyastasya pṛṣṭhatalāśritaḥ |
Bhallūkārthe prayojyaḥ syāt padmakośaḥ patākakaḥ ||

Meaning:

Vāmahaste padmakośo-adhomukhatvā-mupāśritaḥ = When the left hand, as Padmakośa hasta, faces downwards; Dakṣiṇe tu patākākhyastasya pṛṣṭhatalāśritaḥ = and right hand, as patāka hasta, is placed on the back of the left hand; Bhallūkārthe prayojyaḥ syāt padmakośaḥ patākakaḥ = it indicates the bear.

When the left hand, as Padmakośa hasta, faces downwards and right hand, as patāka hasta, is placed on the back of the left hand it indicates the bear.

6. मार्जार

Mārjāra (Cat)

पूर्वोक्त मुष्टि हस्तस्यानामिकांगुष्ठ योगतः ।
नाम्ना-अयमर्धमुकुलो मार्जारे संप्रयुज्यते ॥421।।

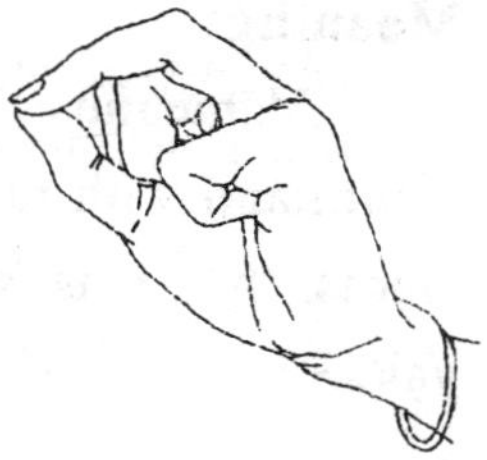

Transliteration:

Pūrvokta muṣṭi hastasyānāmikāṅguṣṭha yogataḥ ||
Nāmnā-ayamardhamukulo mārjāre samprayujyate.

Meaning:

Pūrvokta muṣṭi hastasyānāmikāṅguṣṭha yogataḥ = In muṣṭi hasta, if the thumb and the ring finger are joined; Nāmnā-ayamardhamukulo mārjāre samprayujyate = it is Ardhamukula hasta and it denotes the cat.

In muṣṭi hasta, if the thumb and the ring finger are joined, it is ardhamukula hasta and it denotes the cat.

7. चमरी
Camarī (Yak)

वामे मुष्टिः दक्षिणे वा मणिबंधेन मिश्रिता ।
मुद्रिका-अधोमुख मुष्टिमुद्रा हस्तो-अयमीरितः ॥422॥
मुष्टिमुद्राकर स्चापि चमर्याम संप्रयुज्यते ।

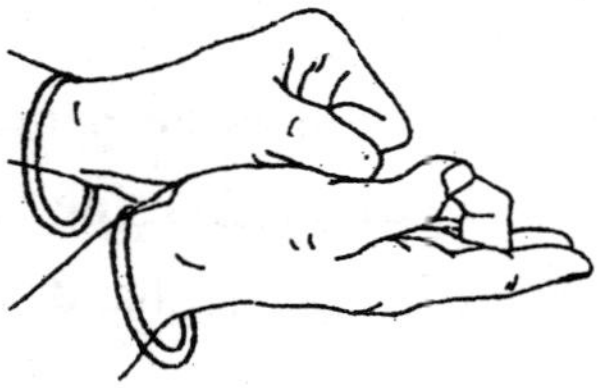

Transliteration:

Vāme muṣṭiḥ dakṣiṇe vā maṇibandhena miśritā |
Mudrikā-adhomukha muṣṭimudrā hasto-ayamīritaḥ ||
Muṣṭimudrākara scāpi camaryāma samprayujyate |

Meaning:

Vāme muṣṭiḥ dakṣiṇe vā maṇibandhena miśritā = When left hand with muṣṭi hasta joins the wrist of the right hand with mudrā hasta, Mudrikā-adhomukha muṣṭimudrā hasto-ayamīritaḥ = and held facing down wards, then it is Muṣṭimudrā hasta; Muṣṭimudrākara scāpi camaryāma samprayujyate = and it denotes the yak.

When left hand with muṣṭi hasta joins the wrist of the right hand with mudrā hasta, and held facing down wards, then it is Muṣṭimudrā hasta and it denotes the yak.

8. गोधा

Godhā (Iguana)

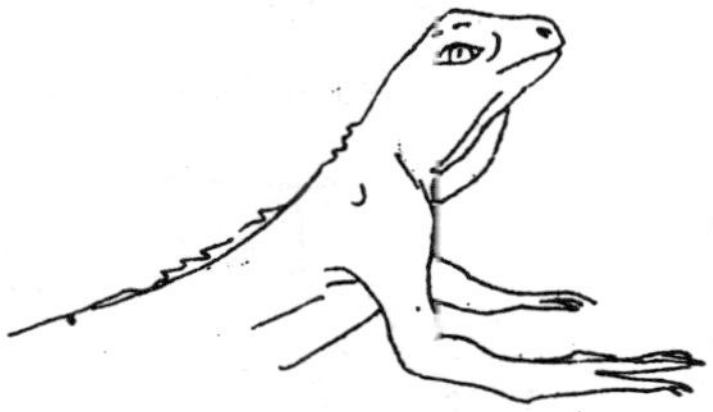

ऊर्ध्वौ कनिष्ठिकांगुष्ठौ पताके किंचिदीरितौ ॥423॥
नाम्ना तालपताकोऽयम् गोधायाम् पुंजितो भवेत् ।

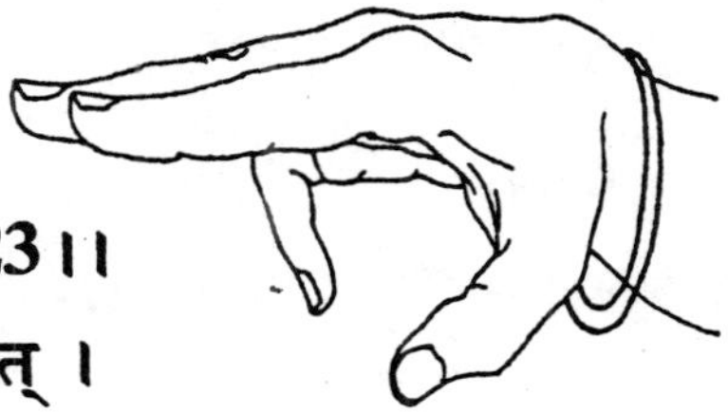

Transliteration:

Ūrdhvau kaniṣṭhikāṅguṣṭhau patāke kiñcidīritau ||
Nāmnā tālapatāko-ayam godhāyām pūjito bhavet |

Meaning:

Ūrdhvau kaniṣṭhikāṅguṣṭhau patāke kiñcidīritau = If the thumb and the little finger of Patāka hasta are slightly raised, Nāmnā tālapatāko-ayam godhāyām pūjito bhavet = it is Tālpatāka hasta and when bent, it denotes godha.

If the thumb and the little finger of Patāka hasta are slightly raised, it is Tālpatāka hasta and when bent, it denotes godha.

9. शल्य

Śalya (Porcupine)

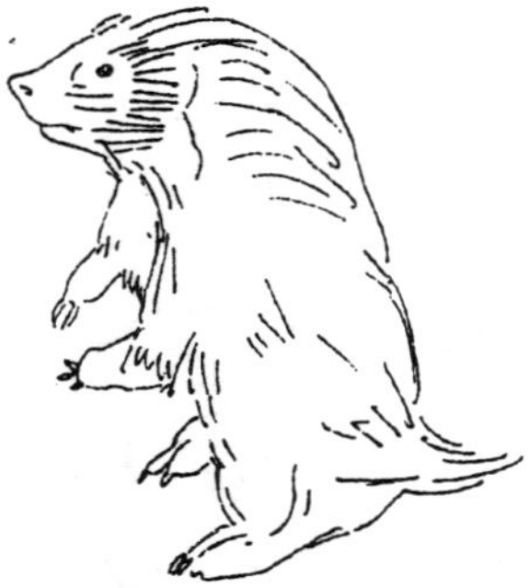

पूर्वोक्त मृगशीर्षस्य तर्जन्यूर्ध्व प्रसारिता ।।424।।
नाम्ना चंद्रमृगो हस्तः शल्यार्थे संप्रयुज्यते ।

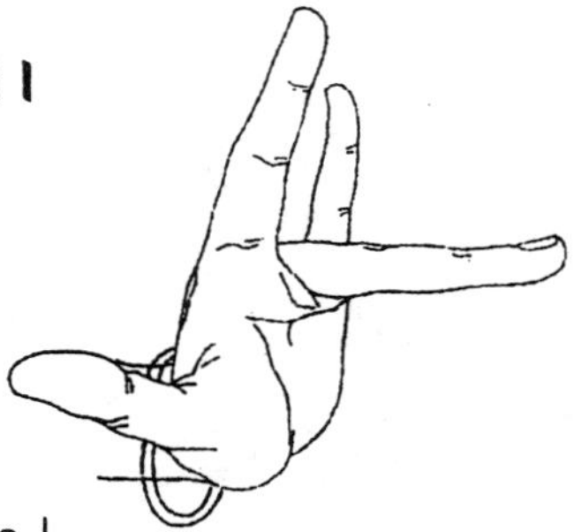

Transliteration:

Pūrvokta mṛgaśīrṣasya tarjanayūrdhva prasāritā ||
Nāmnā candramṛgo hastaḥ śalyārthe samprayujyate |

Meaning:

Pūrvokta mṛgaśīrṣasya tarjanayūrdhva prasāritā = If the forefinger of Mṛgaśīrṣa hasta is raised, Nāmnā candramṛgo hastaḥ śalyārthe samprayujyate = then it is Candramṛga hasta and denotes the porcupine deer.

If the forefinger of Mṛgaśīrṣa hasta is raised, then it is Candramṛga hasta and denotes the porcupine deer.

10. कुर

Kuraṅga (Antelope)

कुरंगे च प्रयोक्तव्यो मृगशीर्षकनामकः।।425।।

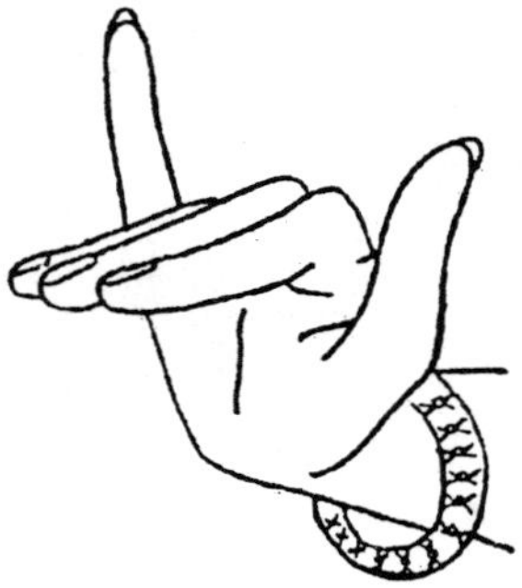

Transliteration:

Kuraṅge ca prayoktavyo mṛgaśīrṣakanāmakaḥ ||

Meaning:

Kuraṅge ca prayoktavyo mṛgaśīrṣakanāmakaḥ = Mṛgaśīrṣa hasta denotes the antelope.
Mṛgaśīrṣa hasta denotes the antelope.

11. कृष्णसार

Kṛṣṇasāra (Black Antelope)

पूर्वोक्त मुष्टि हस्ते तु कनिष्ठांगुष्ठ सारनात् ।
नाम्ना मुष्टिमृगोहस्तः कृष्णसारे प्रयुज्यते ॥426॥

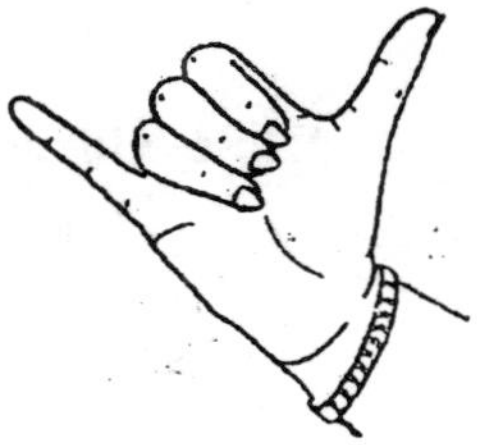

Transliteration:

Pūrvokta muṣṭi haste tu kaniṣṭhāṅguṣṭha sāranāt |
Nāmnā muṣṭimṛgohastaḥ kṛṣṇasāre prayujyate ||

Meaning:

Pūrvokta muṣṭi haste tu kaniṣṭhāṅguṣṭha sāranāt = If the little finger and the thumb of muṣṭi hasta are extended; Nāmnā muṣṭimṛgohastaḥ kṛṣṇasāre prayujyate = it is Muṣṭimṛgahasta and it denotes the black antelope.

If the little finger and the thumb of muṣṭi hasta are extended, it is Muṣṭimṛgahasta and it denotes the black antelope.

12. गोकर्ण

*Gokarṇa (Ears of a cow)

धेनुकर्णे नागबन्धौ रेचितौ यदि योजितौ ।

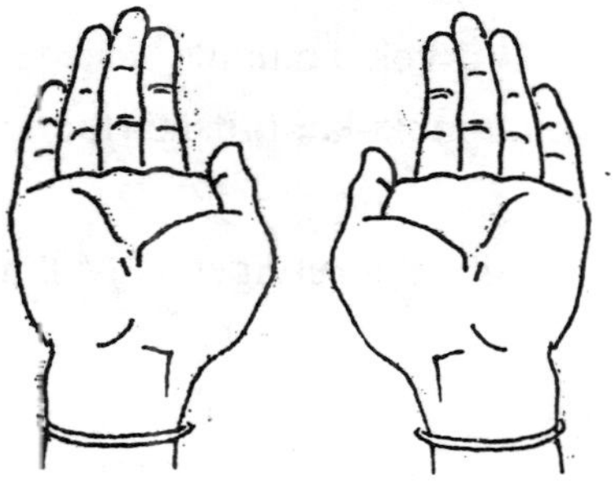

Transliteration:

Dhenukarṇe nāgabandhau recitau yadi yojitau |

Meaning:

Dhenukarṇe nāgabandhau recitau yadi yojitau = nāgabandha hasta when directed upwards, denotes gokarṇa.

Nagabandha hasta, when directed upwards, denotes gokarṇa.

*Note: Gokarna also means a mule, Antelope deer and the span from the tip ofthe thumb to that of the ring finger. (M. Monier-Williams)

13. मूषिक
Mūṣika (Rat)

पूर्वोक्त मुकुले हस्ते तर्जनी संप्रसारिता ।।427।।
नाम्नायाम् खंड-मुकुलो मूषिकार्थे नियुज्यते ।

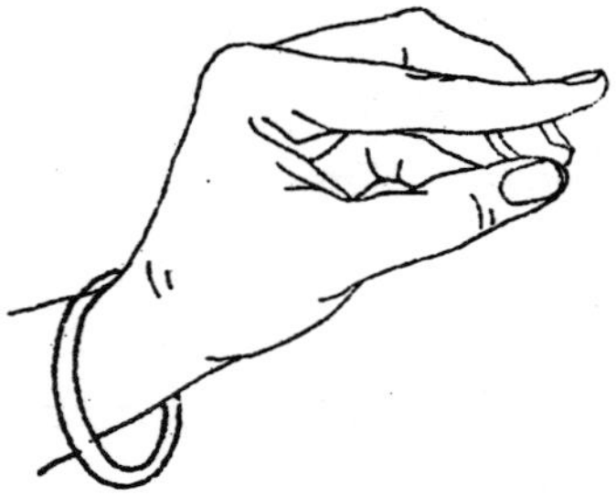

Transliteration:

Pūrvokta mukule haste tarjanī samprasāritā ||
Nāmnāyām khaṇḍa-mukulo mūṣikārthe niyujyate |

Meaning:

Pūrvokta mukule haste tarjanī samprasāritā If the forefinger of Mukula hasta is fully extended; nāmnāyām khaṇḍa-mukulau mūṣikārthe niyujyate = it is khaṇḍamukulau hasta and it denotes the rat.

If the forefinger of Mukula hasta is fully extended, it is khaṇḍamukulau hasta and it denotes the rat.

14. गिरिक

Girika (Mouse)

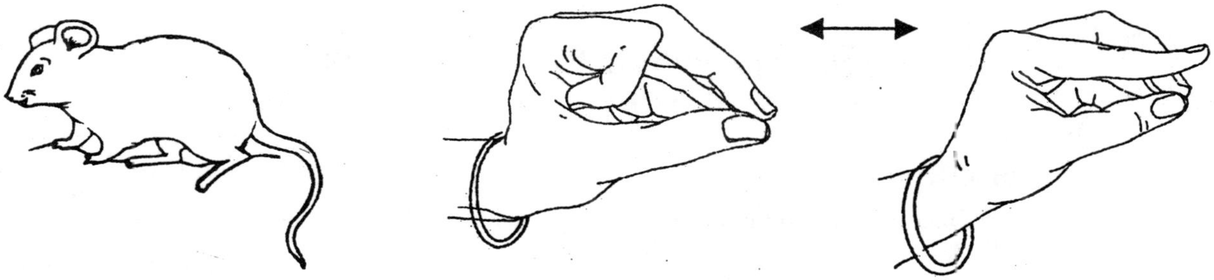

पूर्वोक्त मुकुले भूयस्तर्जनी कुंचिता यदि ।।428।।
तिर्यक् प्रसारितः खड्गमुकुलो गिरिकार्थे ।

Transliteration:

Pūrvokta mukule bhūyastarjanī kuñcitā yadi ||
Tiryak prasāritaḥ khaḍgamukulo girikārthe |

Meaning:

Pūrvokta mukule bhūyastarjanī kuñcitā yadi = If the forefinger of Mukula hasta is bent fully and stretched obliquely or moved to and fro, Tiryak prasāritaḥ khaḍagamukulau girikārthe = it is Khaḍagamukula hasta and it denotes girika.

If the forefinger of Mukula hasta is bent fully and stretched obliquely or moved to and fro, it is Khaḍgamukula hasta and it denotes girika.

15. शश

Śaśa (Hare)

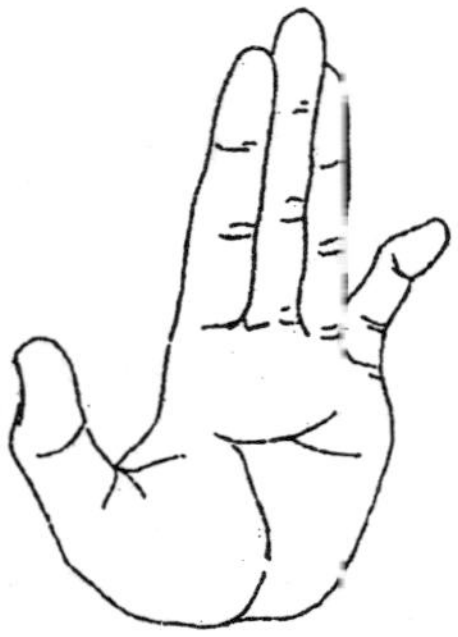

हस्तः तालपताख्यः शशके त्रियगाश्रयः ।।429।।

Transliteration:

Hastāḥ tālapātākhyaḥ śaśake triyagāṣrayaḥ ||

Meaning:

Hastāḥ tālapātākhyaḥ śaśake triyagāṣrayaḥ = Tālapatāka hasta, moved obliquely, denotes the hare.

Tālapatāka hasta, moved obliquely, denotes the hare.

16. वृष्चिक

Vṛṣcika (Scorpion)

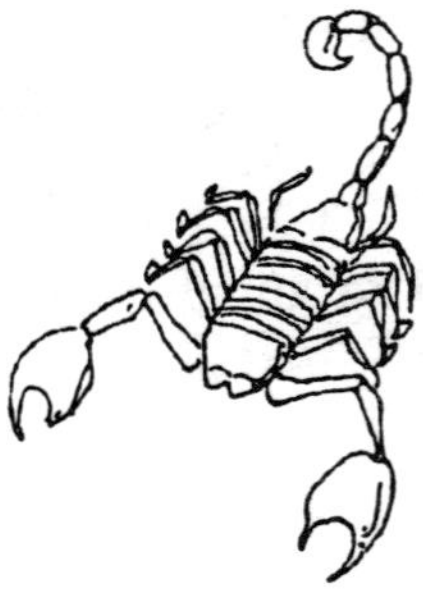

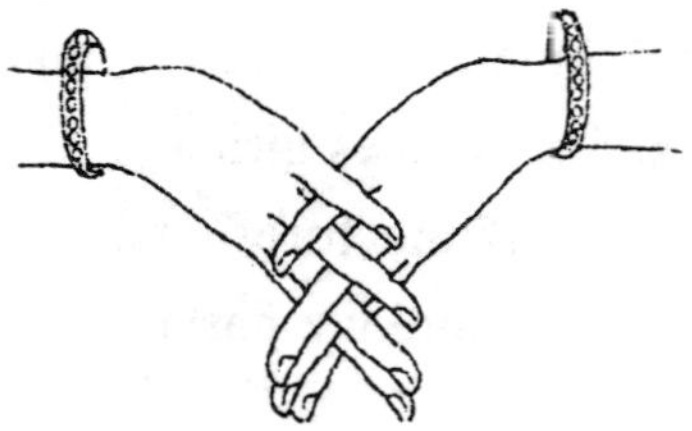

अधोमुखो रेचितः चेत् कर्कटौ वृ के भवेत् ।

Transliteration:

Adhomukho recitaḥ cet karkaṭau vṛścike bhavet |

Meaning:

Adhomukho recitaḥ cet karkaṭau vṛścike bhavet = Karkaṭa hasta directed downwards denotes the scorpion.

Karkaṭa hasta directed downwards denotes the scorpion.

17. शुनक

Śunaka (Dog)

पताकाभिध हस्ते तु कुंचिता चेत् कनिष्ठिका ।।430।।
नाम्ना मध्यपताको-अयम् शूनकार्थे प्रयुज्यते ।

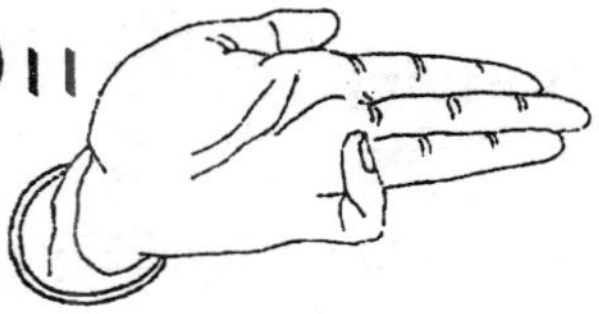

Transliteration:

Patākābhidha haste tu kuñcitā cet kaniṣṭhikā |
Nāmnā madhyapatāko-ayam śunakārthe prayujyate ||

Meaning:

Patākābhidha haste tu kuñcitā cet kaniṣṭhikā = If the little finger of Pātaka hasta is bent, it is Madhya patāka hasta; Nāmnā madhyapatāko-ayam śunakārthe prayujyate = it denotes the dog.

If the little finger of Pātaka hasta is bent, it is Madhyapatāka hasta; it denotes the dog.

18. उष्ट्र

Uṣṭra (Camel)

पूर्वोदितांजलि करे चा ष्ठौ कुंचितौ युतौ ।।431
प्रसारितावुदर्ध्वभागे चलितौ चाप्यधोमुखौ ।
नाम्ना खडाञ्जलि-रयमुष्ट्रार्थे संप्रयुज्यते।।432।।

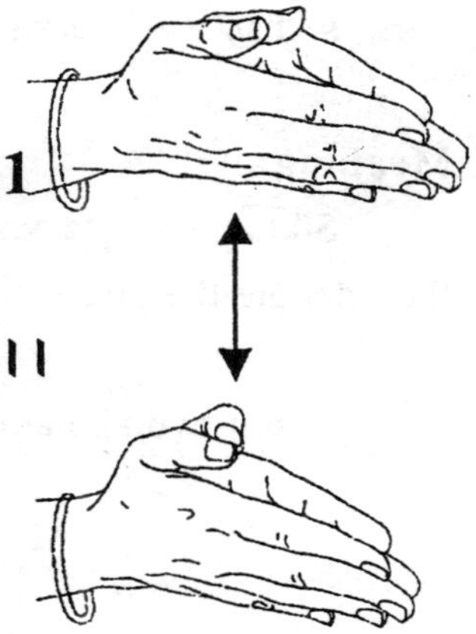

Transliteration:

Pūrvoditāñjali kare cānguṣṭhau kuñcitau yutau ||
Prasāritāvurdhvabhāge calitau cāpyadhomukhau |
Nāmnā khaḍañjali-rayamuṣṭrārthe samprayujyate ||

Meaning:

Pūrvoditāñjali karc cānguṣṭhau kuñcitau yutau = If the thumbs of Anjali hasta arc bent; Prasāritāvurdhvabhāge calitau cāpyadhomukhau = it is Khaḍañjali hasta; Nāmnā khanḍañjali-rāyamuṣṭrārthe samprayujyate = it is Khaḍañjali hasta; it denotes the camel.

If the thumbs of Anjali hasta are bent, and moved up and down, it is Khaḍañjali hasta; it denotes the camel.

19. अज

Aja (Goat)

शिखरौ श्लिष्ट वदनौ मेषार्थे संप्रयुज्यते ।

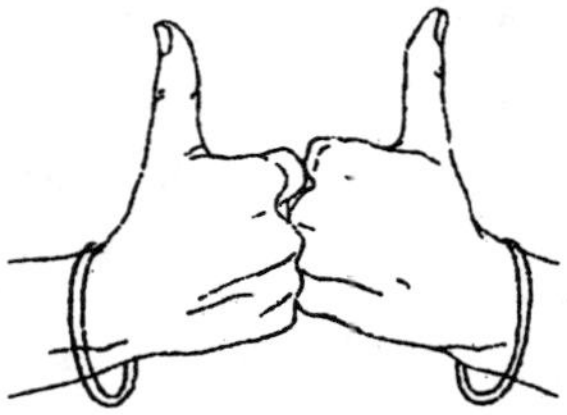

Transliteration:

śikharau śliṣṭa vadanau meṣārthe samprayujyate |

Meaning:

Śikharau śliṣṭa vadanau meṣārthe samprayujyate = When two śikharau hastas are joined face to face, they denoie the goat.

When two śikharau hastas are joined face to face, they denote the goat.

20. गार्दभ

Gārdabha (Ass)

पूर्वाखंडाञ्जलौ मिश्रे कुंचिते तर्जनीद्वये ।।433।।
भिन्नांजलिरयम् नाम्ना गार्दभार्थे नियुज्यते ।

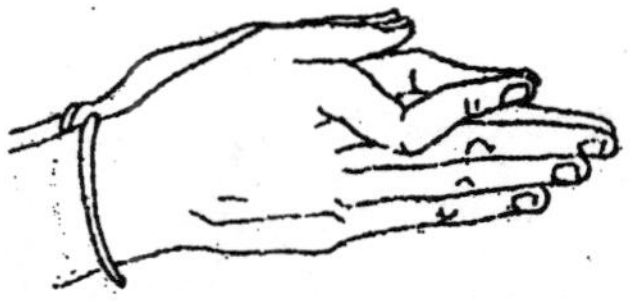

Transliteration:

Pūrvākhaṇḍāñjalau miśre kuñcite tarjanīdvaye.
Bhinnāñjalirayam nāmnā gārdabhārthe niyujyate.

Meaning:

Pūrvākhaṇḍāñjalau miśre kuñcite tarjanīdvaye = If the two forefingers of Khanḍañjali hasta touch each other and are bent; Bhinnāñjali-rayama nāmnā gārdabhārthe niyujyate = it is bhinnājali hasta; it denotes the ass.

If the two forefingers of Khaḍañjali hasta touch each other and are bent, it is bhinnājali hasta; it denotes the ass.

21. वृषभ

Vṛṣabha (Bull)

मध्यमानामिके किंचित् कुंचिते तलमाश्रिते ।।434।।
अंगुष्ठेनोपरियुते शेषे द्वे च प्रसारिते ।
तलसिंह करः सोऽयम्-ऋषभार्थे नियुज्यते ।।435।।

Transliteration:

Madhyamānāmike kiñcita kuñcite talamāśrite ||
Anguṣṭhenopariyute śeṣe dve ca prasārite |
Talasiṃha karaḥ so'ayama-ṛṣabhārthe niyujyate ||

Meaning:

Madhyamānāmike kiñcita kuñcite talamāśrite = If the middle finger and the ring finger are bent into the palm slightly; Anguṣṭhenopariyute śeṣe dve ca prasārite = the thumb is placed over them and the other two fingers are extended; Talasiṃha karaḥ so-ayama-ṛṣabhārthe niyujyate = it is Talasimha hasta; it denotes the bull.

If the middle finger and the ring finger are bent into the palm slightly, the thumb is placed over them and the other two fingers are extended, it is Talasimha hasta; it denotes the bull.

22. धेनु

Dhenu (Cow)

मध्यमा वक्रिता यत्र शेषाः सर्वे प्रसारितः ।
धेनौ योज्यौ यंत्र भेदे भवेत् संकीर्णमुद्राकः ।।436।।

Transliteration:

Madhyamā vakritā yatra śeṣāḥ sarve prāsāritāḥ |
Dhenau yujyau yantra bhede bhavet samkīrṇamudrākaḥ ||

Meaning:

Madhyamā vakritā yatra śeṣāḥ sarve prāsāritāḥ = If the middle finger is bent and all the rest are extended; Dhenau yujyau yantra bhede bhavet samkīrṇamudrākaḥ = it is Samkīrṇāmudrā hasta; it denotes the cow as well as 'yantra bheda'.

If the middle finger is bent and all the rest are extended, it is Samkīrṇāmudra hasta; it denotes the cow as well as 'yantra bheda'.

Chapter 30

पक्षी हस्त

Pakṣī hasta

(Abhinayam for the Birds)

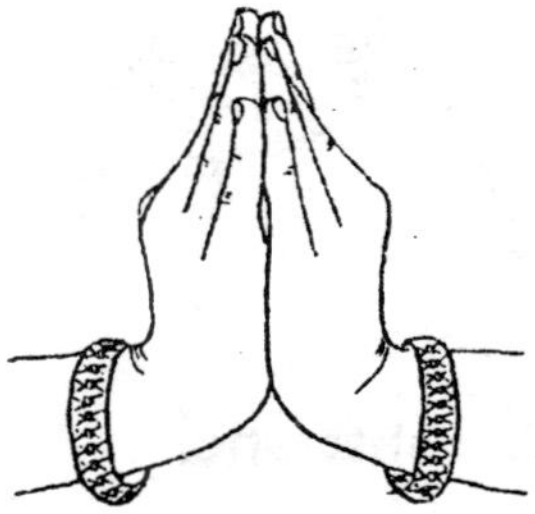

1. पारावत

Pārāvata (Dove)

पारावते कपोताख्य करः स्यात् पुंखिताकृतिः ।

Transliteration:

Pārāvate kapotākhya karaḥ syāt puṃkhitākṛtiḥ |

Meaning:

Pārāvate kapotākhya karaḥ syāt puṃkhitākṛtiḥ = Kapota hasta performing puṃkhita hasta prāṇa denotes dove.

Kapota hasta performing puṃkhita hasta prāṇa denotes dove.

2. कपोत

Kapota (Pigeon)

कपोतः तिर्यगाकारः कपोते विनियुज्यते ।।437।।

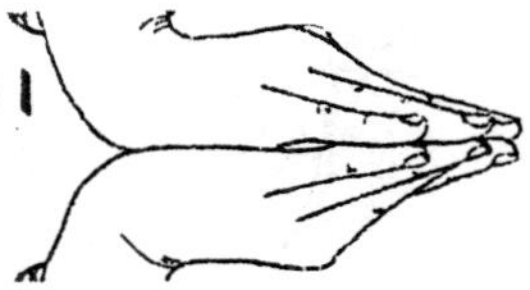

Transliteration:

Kapotaḥ tiryagākāraḥ kapote viniyujyate ||

Meaning:

Kapotaḥ tiryagākāraḥ kapote viniyujyate = Kapota hasta moved obliquely denotes the pigeon.

Kapota hasta moved obliquely denotes the pigeon.

3. शशादन

Śaśādana (Hawk)

ब्रहमोक्त शुकतुंडः स्यात् शशादन निरूपणे ।

Transliteration:

Brahamoktā śukatuṇḍaḥ syāt śaśādana nirūpaṇe |

Meaning:

Brahamoktā śukatuṇḍaḥ syāt śaśādana nirūpaṇe = In denoting the hawk, Brahmoktā śukatuṇḍa hasta is to be used.

In denoting the hawk, Brahmoktā śukatuṇḍa hasta is to be used.

4. उलूक

Ulūka (Owl)

गजदन्तौ श्लिष्टमुखौ संकीर्णगजदंतकः ।।438।।
संकीर्ण गजदंतोऽयमुलूकार्थे नियुज्यते ।

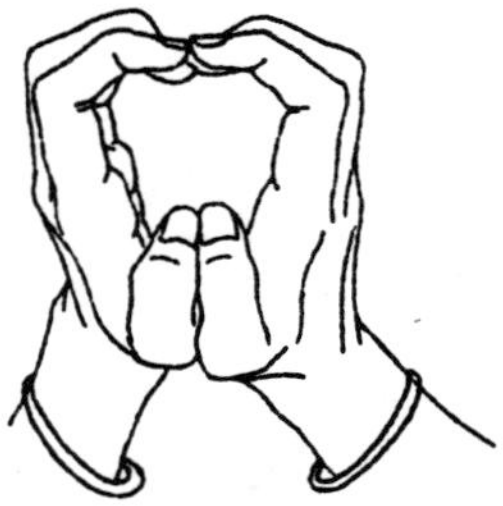

Transliteration:

Gajadantau śliṣṭamukhau saṅkīrṇagajadantakaḥ ||
Saṅkīrṇa gajadanto'ayamulūkārthe niyujyate !

Meaning:

Gajadantau śliṣṭamukhau saṅkīrṇagajadantakaḥ = When two Gajadanta hastas are held face to face; Saṅkīrṇa gajadanto'ayamulūkārthe niyujyate = then it is saṅkīrṇagajadantaka hasta, it denotes the owl.

When two Gajadanta hastas are held face to face, then it is saṅkīrṇagajadantaka hasta, it denotes the owl.

5. गण्डभेरुण्ड

Gaṇḍabheruṇḍa (Huge size bird with two heads)

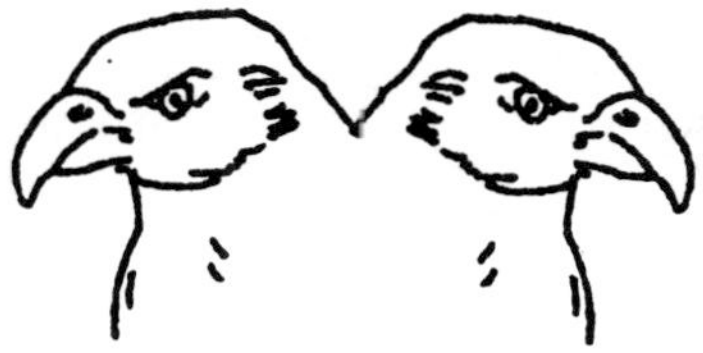

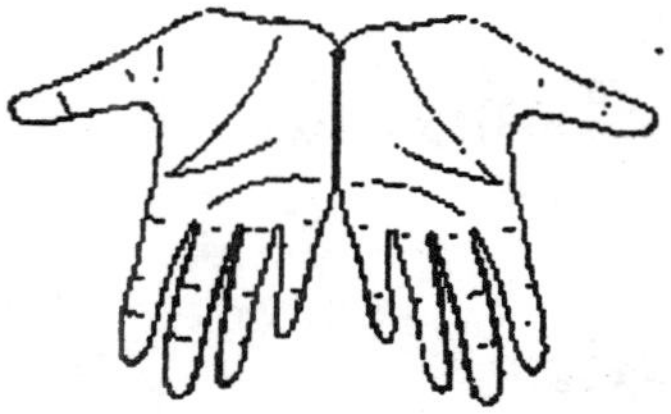

मणिबन्धे समाश्लिष्टा वर्धचन्द्रा वधोमुखौ ।।439।।
सर्वाङ्गुल्यस्तु विरला नाम्ना स्वतिकचंद्रकः ।
गण्डभेरुण्डकाख्यऽस्य विनियोगः प्रकीर्तितः ।।440।।

Transliteration:

Maṇibandhe samāśliṣṭā vardhacandrā vadhomukhau ||
Sarvāṅgulyastu viralā nāmnā svastikacandrakaḥ |
Gaṇḍabheruṇḍakākhy'asya viniyogaḥ prakīrtitaḥ ||

Meaning:

Maṇibandhe samāśliṣṭā vardhacandrā vadhomukhau = When two ardhcandra hastas join at wrists and point downwards; Sarvāṅgulyastu viralā nāmnā svastikacandrakaḥ = with all the fingers separated, it is called svastikacandrakaḥ; Gaṇḍabheruṇḍakākhy'asya viniyogaḥ prakīrtitaḥ = it denotes Gaṇḍabheruṇḍa.

When two ardhcandra hastas join at wrists and point downwards with all the fingers separated, it denotes Gaṇḍabheruṇḍa.

6. चातक

Cātaka (A kind of Cuckoo)

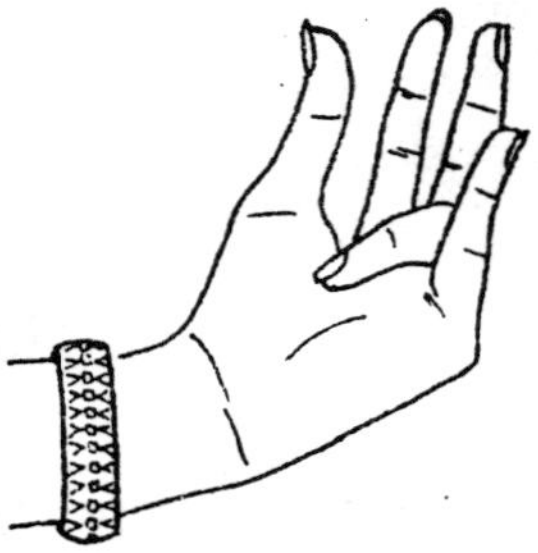

कांगुलश्चातके भूयात् पुंखितत्वम् उपाश्रितः ।

Transliteration:

Kāṅgulaścāṭake bhūyāt puṅkhitatvam upāśritaḥ |

Meaning:

Kāṅgulaścāṭake bhūyāt puṅkhitatvam upāśritaḥ = If Kāṅgula hasta performs puṅkhita hasta prāṇa. it denotes Cātaka.

If Kāṅgula hasta performs puṅkhita hasta prāṇa. it denotes Cātaka.

7. कुक्कुट

Kukkuṭa /Tāmracūḍa (ROO)

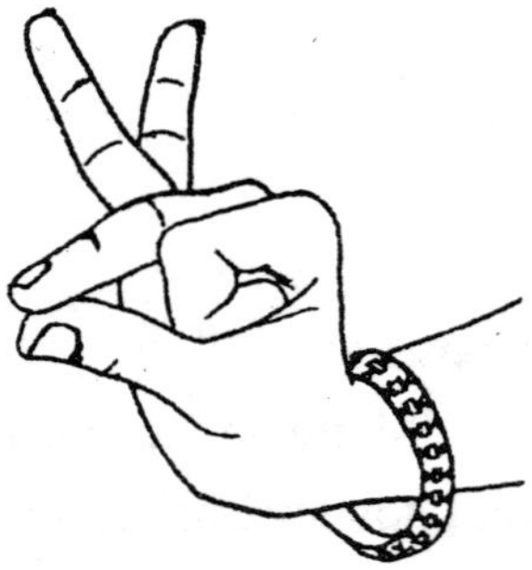

पूर्वोक्त भ्रमरौ भूयात् ताम्रचूड निरुपणे ।।441।।

Transliteration:

Pūrvokta bhramarau bhūyat tāmracūḍa nirūpaṇe ||

Meaning:

Pūrvokta bhramarau bhūyattāmracūḍa nirūpaṇe = Bhramara hasta described earlier, denotes ṭāmaracūḍa i.e. cock.

Bhramara hasta described earlier, denotes ṭāmracūḍa i.e. cock.

8. कोकिल

Kokila (Koel) (Indian)

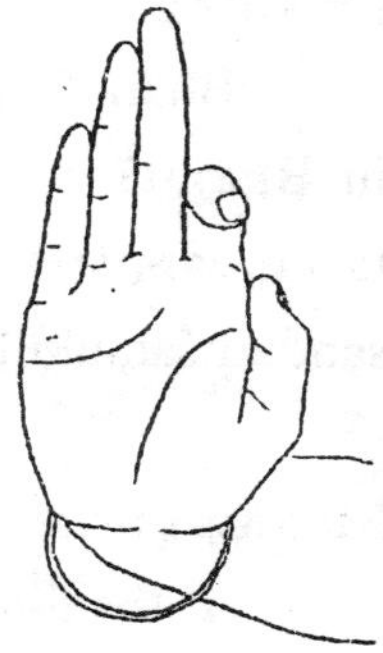

अरालः पुंखिताकारः कोकिलार्थे नियुज्यते ।

Transliteration:

Arālaḥ puṅkhitākāraḥ kokilārthe niyujyate |

Meaning:

Arālaḥ puṅkhitākāraḥ kokilārthe niyujyate = If Arāla hasta performs puṅkhita hasta prāṇa, it denotes cuckoo.

If Arāla hasta performs puṅkhita hasta prāṇa, it denotes cuckoo.

9. वायस

Vāyasa (Crow)

भरतार्णव संप्रोक्त भ्रमराङ्गुष्ठकः तथा ।।442।।
अग्रभागेन तर्जन्यमिश्रितो यदि पुंखितः ।
संदंश मुकुलो भूयात् वायसार्थे नियुज्यते ।।443।।

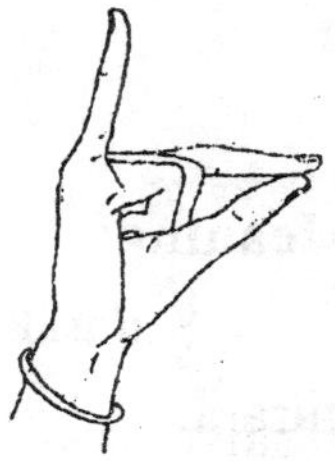

Transliteration:

Bharatārṇava samprokta bhramarāṅguṣṭhakaḥ tathāḥ ||
Agrabhāgena tarjanyamiśrito yadi puṅkhitaḥ |
Sandamśa mukulo bhūyāt vāyasārthe niyujyate ||

Meaning:

Bharatārṇava samprokta bhramarāṅguṣṭhakaḥ tathāḥ = If the thumb of Bhramara hasta as mentioned in Bharatārṇavam; joins the end of the forefinger and performs puṅkhita hasta prāṇa; Agrabhāgena tarjanyamiśrito yadi puṅkhitaḥ Sandamśa mukulo bhūyāt vāyasārthe niyujyate = it is considered as sandaṃśamukula hasta; it denotes the crow.

Meaning:

If the thumb of Bhramara hasta -joins the end of the forefinger and performs puṅkhita hasta prāṇa, it is considered as sandaṃśamukula hasta; it denotes the crow.

10. कुरर

Kurara (Osprey)

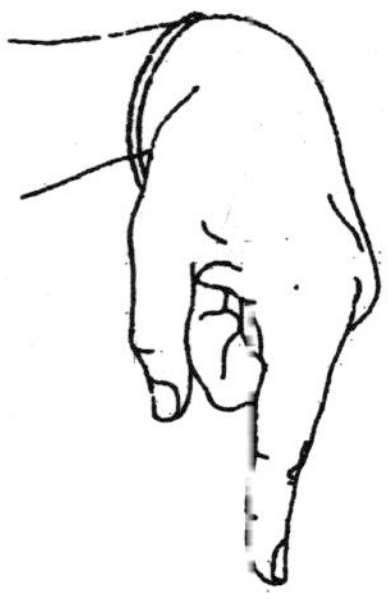

कुरराख्ये अपविद्धाख्यो सूचिरेव प्रयुज्यते ।

Transliteration:

Kurarākhye apaviddhākhyo sūcireva prayujyate |

Meaning:

Kurarākhye apaviddhākhyo sūcireva prayujyate = If Sūcihasta performs apaviddha hasta prāṇa, it denotes kurara.

If Sūcihasta performs apaviddha hasta prāṇa, it denotes kurara.

11. शुक

Śuka (Parrot)

शुकतुंडः प्रयोक्तव्यः शुकार्ते पुंखिताकृतिः ।।444।।

Transliteration:

śukatuṇḍaḥ prayoktavyaḥ śukārte puṅkhitākṛtiḥ ||

Meaning:

śukatuṇḍaḥ prayoktavyaḥ śukārte puṅkhitākṛtiḥ = If śukhatunda hasta performs puṅkhita hasta prāṇa, then it denotes the parrot.

If śukhatunda hasta performs puṅkhita hasta prāṇa, then it denotes the parrot.

12. सारस

Sārasa (Indian Crane)

नेतु कनिष्ठापि किंचित् वक्रितभावतः ।

ा प्रदेशमुकुलो योज्योऽअयं सारसार्थके ।।445।।

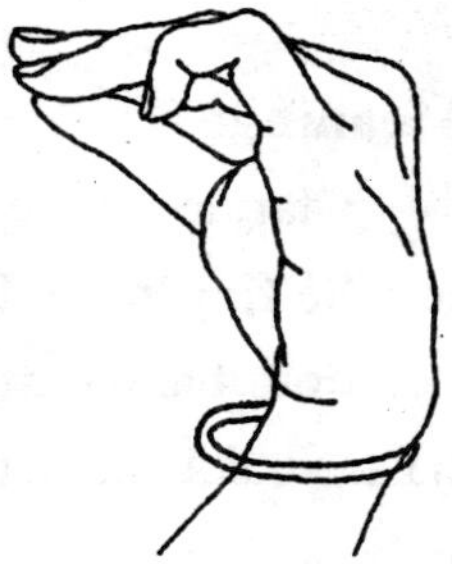

Transliteration:

Mukuletu kaniṣṭhāpi kiñcit vakritabhāvataḥ |

Nāmnā pradesmukulo yojyo'ayama sarasārthake ||

Meaning:

Mukuletu kaniṣṭhāpi kiñcit vakritabhāvataḥ = If the little finger of

Mukula hasta is bent slightly; Nāmnā pradesmukulo yojyo'ayama sarasārthake = it is considered as Pradesa mukula hasta; it is used to denote sārasa.

If the little finger of Mukula hasta is bent slightly, it is considered as Pradesa mukula hasta; it is used to denote sārasa.

13. बक

Baka (Heron)

तर्जन्याङ्गुष्ठ संयोगे मध्यमा अनामिकापि च ।
प्रसारिते कनिष्ठा चेत् वक्रिता तलमाश्रिता ।।446।।
नाम्ना संकीर्ण हंसोऽअयं शुक्राचार्य मतोदितः ।
बकार्थेमंत्रभेदेषु योज्यः संकीर्णहंसकः ।।447।।

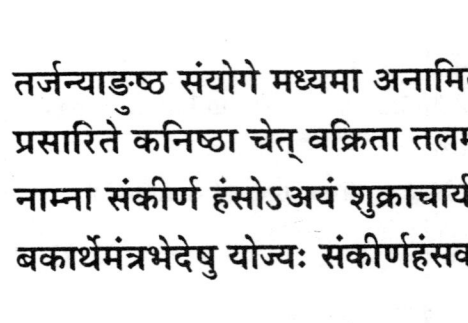

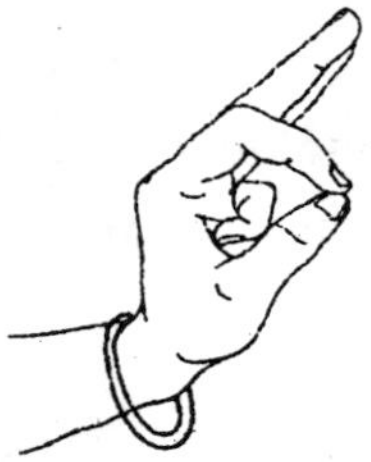

Transliteration:

Tarjanyāṅguṣṭha saṃyoge madhyamā anāmikāpi ca |
Prasārite kaniṣṭhā cet vakritā talamāśritā ||
Nāmnā saṅkīrṇa haṃso'ayaṃ śukrācārya matoditaḥ |
Bakārthemantrabhedeṣu yojyaḥ saṅkīrṇahaṃsakaḥ ||

Meaning:

tarjanyāṅguṣṭha saṃyoge madhyamā anāmikāpi kā = If the forefinger and the thumb are joined, the middle finger and the ring finger is extended, prasārite kaniṣṭhā cet vakritā talamāśritā = and the little finger is bent into the palm; nāmnā saṅkīrṇa haṃso-ayaṃ śukrācārya matoditaḥ = then it is known as saṅkīrṇa haṃsa hasta; bakārthemantrabhedeṣu yojyaḥ saṅkīrṇahaṃsakaḥ = this is the view of Sukrācārya; this denotes the baka as well as mantrabheda.

If the forefinger and the thumb are joined, the middle finger and the ring finger is extended, and the little finger is bent into the palm, then it is known as saṅkīrṇa haṃsa hasta; this is the view of Sukrācārya; this denotes the baka as well as mantrabheda.

14. क्रौंच

Krauñca (curlew)

पूर्वालपद्महस्ते कनिष्ठा तलकुंचिता ।
लीनालपद्म हस्तोऽअयं क्रौंचार्थे संप्रयुज्यते ।।448।।

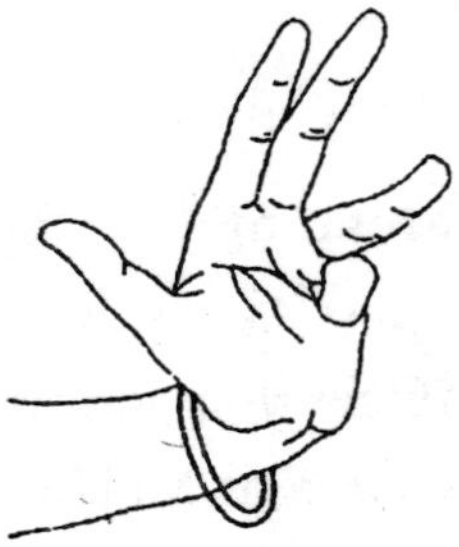

Transliteration:

Pūrvālapadmahaste kaniṣṭha talakuñcita |
līnālapadma hasto'ayaṃ krauñcārthe samprayujyate ||

Meaning:

Pūrvālapadmahaste kaniṣṭha talakuñcita = If the little finger of Alapadma hasta is bent into the palm; līnālapadma hasto-ayaṃ krauñcārthe samprayujyate = it is known as Līnālapadma hasta; it denotes krauñca bird.

If the little finger of Alapadma hasta is bent into the palm, it is known as Līnālapadma hasta; it denotes krauñca bird.

15. खद्योत

Khadyota (Firefly)

अंगुष्ठो मध्यमायाः स्याद् अग्रपर्वनि पीडितः ।
मुखा-हंसकरः सो अयं खद्योतार्थे-अपाविद्धकः ।।449।।

Transliteration:

Angusṭho madhyamāyāḥ syādagra parvanipīḍitaḥ |
Mukha-haṃsakaraḥ so-ayam khadyotārthe-apaviddhakaḥ ||

Meaning:

Angusṭho madhyamāyāḥ syādagra parvanipīḍitaḥ = If the thumb presses the topmost joint of the middle finger and performs apaviddha hastaprāṇa; Mukha-haṃsakaraḥ so-ayam khadyotārthe-apaviddhakaḥ = it is known as Mukhahaṃsa hasta. it denotes the fire fly.

If the thumb presses the topmost joint of the middle finger and performs apaviddha hastaprāṇa, it is known as Mukhahaṃsa hasta. it denotes the fire fly.

16. भ्रमर

Bhramara (Bumblebee)

प्रयोज्यो भ्रमरो हस्तः भृंगार्थे यदि पुंखितः ।

Transliteration:

Prayojyo bhramaro hastaḥ bhṛṅgārthe yadi puṅkhitaḥ |

Meaning:

If Bhramara hasta performs puṅkhitaḥ hasta prāṇa, it denotes the bee.

17. मयूर

Mayūra (peacock)

मयूरार्थे प्रयोज्यः स्यात् मयूरो पुंखितो यदि ।।450।।

Transliteration:

Mayūrārthe prayojyaḥ syāt mayūro puṅkhito yadi ||

Meaning:

Mayūrārthe prayojyaḥ syāt mayūro puṅkhito yadi = If ı puṅkhita hasta prāṇa, then it denotes the peacock.

If mayūra hasta performs puṅkhita hasta prāṇa, then it denotes the peacock.

18 हंस

Haṃsa (swan)

हंसास्योऽपि प्रयोज्यः स्यात् हंसार्थे नृत्तकोविदैः ।

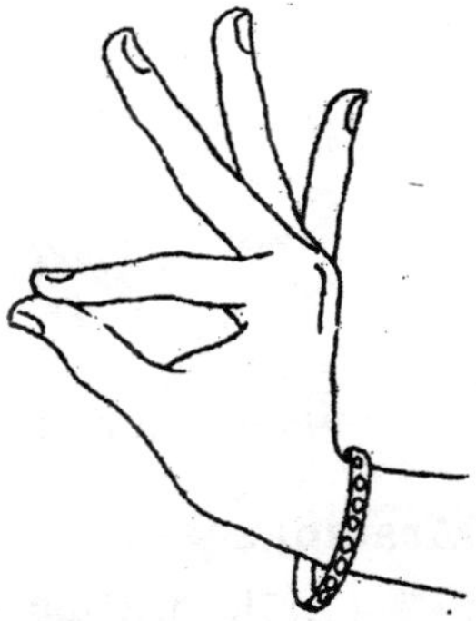

Transliteration:

haṃsāsyo'api prayojyaḥ syāt haṃsārthe nṛttākovidaiḥ |

Meaning:

Haṃsāsyo'api prayojyaḥ syāt haṃsārthe nṛttākovidaiḥ = Haṃsāsya hasta denotes the swan.

Haṃsāsya hasta denotes the swan.

19. चक्रवाक

Cakravāka (Ruddy goose)

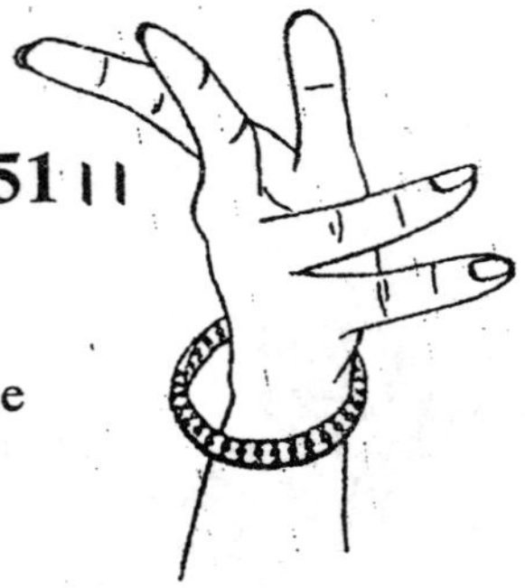

अलप ौ पुंखितौ चेत् चक्रवाके नियुज्यते ।।451।।

Transliteration:

Alapadmau puṅkhitau cet cakravāke niyujyate |

Meaning:

Alapadmau puṅkhitau seta cakravāke niyujyate = If Alapadma hasta performs puṅkhita hasta prāṇa, it denotes cakravāka.

If Alapadma hasta performs puṅkhita hasta prāṇa, it denotes cakravāka.

20. कोयष्टिक

Koyaṣṭika (Paddy bird)

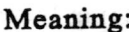

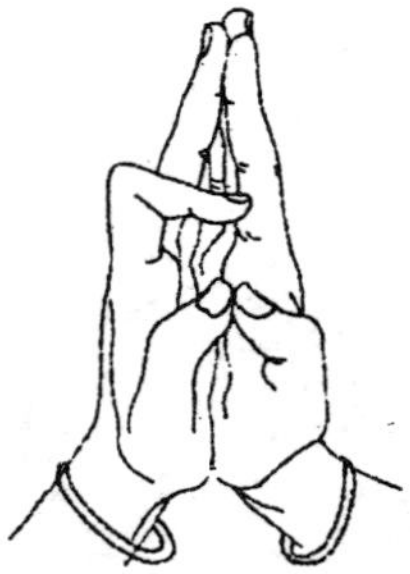

अरालो दक्षिणे वामे पताकेन विमिश्रितः ।
नाम्ना अरालपताकोऽयं कोयष्टिक निरूपने ।।452।।

Transliteration:

Arālo dakśine vāme patākena vimiśritaḥ |
Nāmnā arālapatāko'ayaṃ koyāṣṭika nirūpane ||

Meaning:

Arālo dakśine vāme patākena vimiśritaḥ = If the right hand in arāla hasta joins the left hand holding patāka hasta; Nāmnā-arāla-patāko-ayaṃ koyāṣṭika nirūpane = it is known as arālapatāka hasta. It denotes koyāṣṭika.

If the right hand in arāla hasta joins the left hand holding patāka hasta, it is known as arālapatāka hasta. It denotes koyāṣṭika.

Chapter 31

जलजंतु हस्ताः

Jalajantu hastāḥ

(Abhinayam for the acquatic animals)

1. भेक

Bheka (frog)

चक्रांगुष्ठौ च तर्जन्यौ हस्तयोः अंतरंगतौ ।
माध्यमे मिश्रिते दिर्घे कुंचिते च -अप्यनामिके ।।453।।
प्रसारिते कनिष्ठे च श्लिष्टचक्रो-अयमिष्यते ।
एतस्य विनियोगस्तु भेकार्थे संप्रयुज्यते ।।454।।

Transliteration:

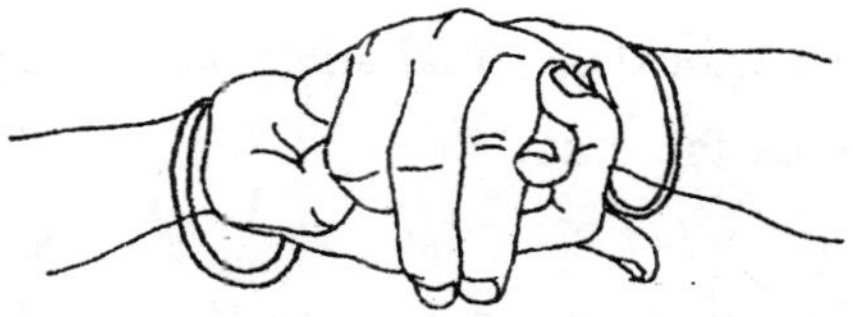

Cakrāṅguṣṭhau ca tarjanyau hastyoḥ aṃtaramgatau |
Mādhyame miśrite dirghe kuñcite ca-apyanāmike ||
Prasārite kaniṣṭhe ca śliṣṭacakro-ayamiṣyate |
Etasya viniyogastu bhekārthe samprayujyate ||

Meaning:

Cakrāṅguṣṭhau ca tarjanyau hastyoḥ aṃtaramgatau = If the thumbs and the forefingers of cakrahasta are bent into the palm; Mādhyame miśrite dirghe kuñcite ca-apyanāmike = the middle fingers and ring fingers are together and closed; Prasārite kaniṣṭhe ca śliṣṭacakro-ayamiṣyate = and when the little fingers are extended it is called as śliṣṭacakra hasta; Etasya viniyogastu bhekārthe samprayujyate = it denotes the frog.

If the thumbs and the forefingers of cakrahasta are bent into the palm, the middle fingers are bent and the little fingers are extended it is known as śliṣṭacakra hasta; it denotes the frog.

2. कुलीर
Kulīra (Crab)

दक्षिणः कर्कटो भूयात् अपवेष्टितरूपकः ।
वामहस्तोपरिस्थायी श्लिष्टा स्याङ्गुलिः क्रमात् ।।455।।
लीनकर्कटकः सो अयं कुलीरे संप्रयुज्यते ।

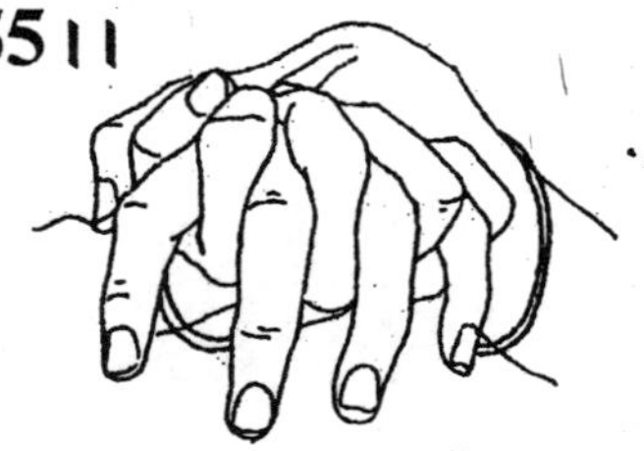

Transliteration:

Dakṣiṇaḥ karkaṭo bhūyāt apāveṣṭitarūpakaḥ |
Vāmahastoparisthāyī śliṣṭāścasyāṅguliḥ kramāt ||
Līnakarkāṭakaḥ so ayaṃ kulīre samprayujyate |

Meaning:

Dakṣiṇaḥ karkaṭo bhūyāt apāveṣṭitarūpakaḥ = If right hand holding Karkata hasta performs apaveṣṭita hasta prāṇa; Vāmahastoparisthāyī śliṣṭāścasyāṅguliḥ kramāt = and is placed on the left hand and the fingers are interlocked; Līnakarkāṭakaḥ so ayaṃ kulīre samprayujyate | = it is considered as Līnakarkaṭa hasta. It denotes the crab.

If right hand holding Karkata hasta performs apaveṣṭita hasta prāṇa and is placed on the left hand and the fingers are interlocked, it is considered as Līnakarkaṭa hasta. It denotes the crab.

3. रक्तपायि

Raktapāyi (Leech)

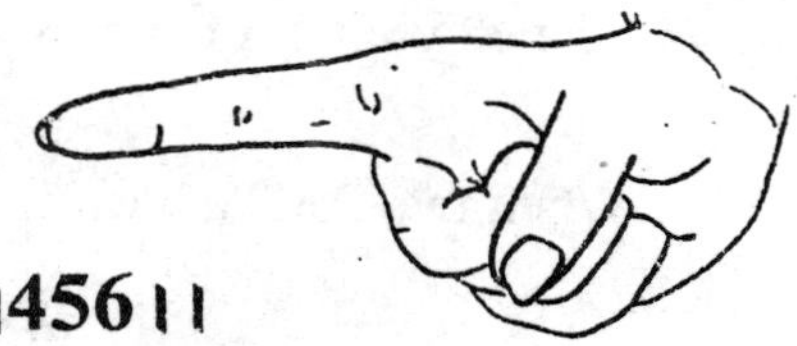

रक्तपायिनि सूचीस्यात् रेचिता तिर्यगेव च ।।456।।

Transliteration:

Raktapāyini sūcīsyāt recitā tiryageva ca ||

Meaning:

Raktapāyini sūcīsyāt recitā tiryageva ca = When sūci hasta performs recita hasta prāṇa and moved obliquely, it denotes the leech.

When sūci hasta performs recita hasta prāṇa and moved obliquely, it denotes the leech.

4. नक्र

Nakra (crocodile)

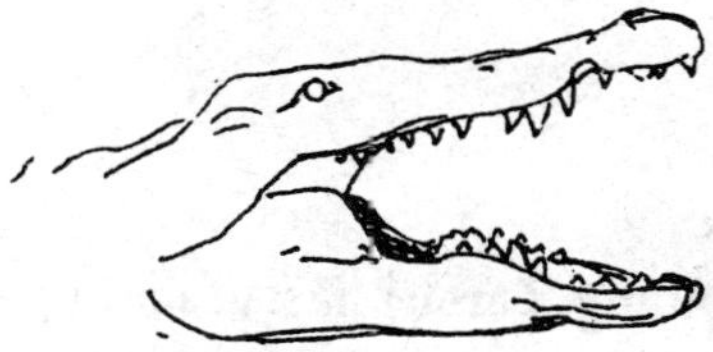

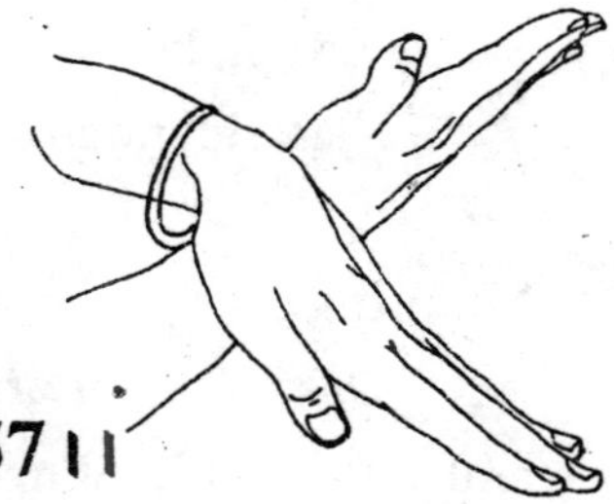

पताकस्वस्तिको हस्तो मिलितश्च विसर्जितः ।
नक्रार्थे पेटिकार्थे च योजितः पूर्वसूरिभिः ।।।457।।

Transliteration:

Patākasvastiko hasto militaśca visarjitaḥ |
Nakrārthe peṭikārthe ca yojitaḥ pūrvasūribhiḥ ||

Meaning:

Patākasvastiko hasto militaśca visarjitaḥ = When two Patāka hastas are crossed and held apart; Nakrārthe peṭikārthe ca yojitaḥ pūrvasūribhiḥ = is considered by the seers as a crocodile, as well as a box.

When two Patāka hastas are crossed and held apart, it is considered by the seers as a crocodile, as well as a box.

5. डुंडुभ

Ḍuṇḍubha (Boa constrictor)

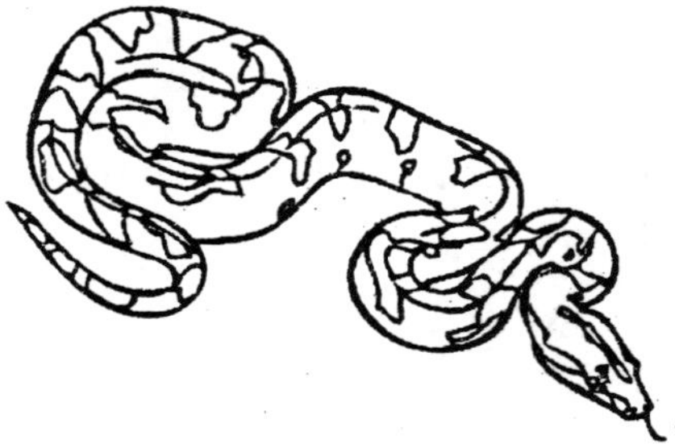

दक्षिणः कर्तरीभूतः कर-ऊर्ध्वमुखो यदि ।
अस्यप्रकोष्ठे वामः स्यात् कटकामुख रूपतः ॥458॥
कर्तरिदंडहस्तो-अयम् डुंडुभार्थे प्रयुज्यते ।

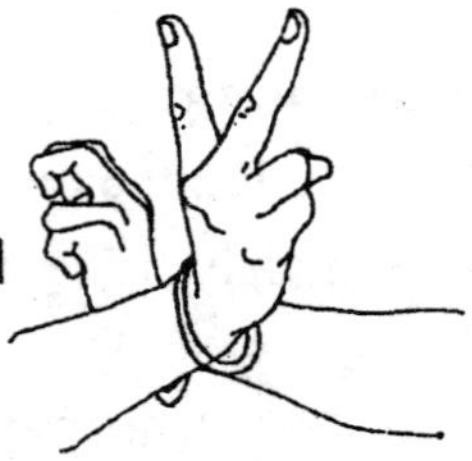

Transliteration:

Dakṣiṇaḥ kartaribhūtaḥ kara-ūrdhvamukho yadi |
Asyaprakosthe vāmaḥ syāt kaṭakamukha rūpataḥ ||
Kartaridaṇḍahasto-ayam ḍuṇḍubhārthe prayujyate |

Meaning:

Dakṣiṇaḥ kartaribhūtaḥ kara-ūrdhvamukho yadi = If the right hand holding Kartari hasta faces upwards and left hand holding Kaṭakamukha hasta is placed on the fore; Asyaprakosthe vāmaḥ syāt kaṭakamukha rūpataḥ = arm of the right hand, Kartaridaṇḍahasto-ayam ḍuṇḍubhārthe prayujyate = it is considered as Kartaridaṇḍa hasta; it denotes Dundubha.

If the right hand holding Kartari hasta faces upwards and left hand holding Kaṭakamukha hasta is placed on the fore-arm of the right hand, it is considered as Kartaridaṇḍa hasta; it denotes Dundubha.

6. व्याली

Vyālī (snake)

तर्जनी मध्यमे चाग्रे चापवद्वक्रिते युते ।।459।।
अनामिकां गुष्ठ-संधौ वक्रिता सुप्रतिष्ठिता ।
कनिष्ठ वक्रिता चायं व्याली व्याल्याम् नियुज्यते ।।460।।

Transliteration:

Tarjanī madhyame cāgre cāpavadvakrite yute ||
Anāmikāṅguṣṭha-sandhau vakritā supratiṣṭhitā |
Kaniṣṭha vakritā cāyaṃ vyālī vyālyām niyujyate ||

Meaning:

Tarjanī madhyame cāgre cāpavadvakrite yute = If the forefinger and the middle finger are bent like a bow, Anāmikāṅguṣṭha-sandhau vakritā supratiṣṭhitā = the ring finger is placed at the base of the thumb, Kaniṣṭha vakritā cāyaṃ vyālī vyālyām niyujyate = and the little finger is bent, it is known as Vyāli hasta; it denotes vyāli.

If the forefinger and the middle finger are bent like a bow, the ring finger is placed at the base of the thumb, and the little finger is bent, it is known as Vyāli hasta; it denotes vyāli.

A LEGACY OF CHANGE

The intent of this book is three pronged: firstly, to provide cohesive information to guide students into the tenets of practice, secondly, to establish by illustrations how movement vocabulary is an extension of nature and, the embodied art as essentially interdisciplinary and, thirdly, to encourage dancers/choreographers crafting their experience in movement to be informed of the historicity of the form in developing a frame of reference.

When the Abhinaya Darpana was written, the oral tradition of transmitting knowledge meant that the gestures and their usages were subjective to individual teacher's interpretation. By the time of its codification it was only natural that each text subsumed an interpretive version of the same gesture, defined by a different name. Hence the various manuscripts and publications of Abhinaya Darpanam contain various versions that differ from one another in the arrangement of topics and within the content of the same topic. In his 1934 edited version Manmohan Ghosh reconstructed of the contents of five manuscripts, available at the Madras Governmental Oriental Library, Visvabharati (Shantiniketan) and the Adyar Library, mentions the alternative versions of a gesture in this manner:

Kāṅgulaścalapadmakaḥ - Incomplete Palm leaf Manuscript from Adayar Library (No. XXII C.25), Lāṅgulasyolapadmakaḥ - Incomplete Palm leaf Manuscript from Adayar Library (No. XXII C.38), Lāṅgulaścālpadmakaḥ - Manuscript from India Office, Gāṅgalaścālpadmakaḥ, Paper Manuscript from Adayar Library (No. VIII J.9).

Besides these, there are many versions of verses and their suggested meanings. Conceptually these alternative textual versions and their subsequent interpretations within the various stylistic traditions posed a conundrum for all teachers to arrive at a consolidated methodology. At the level of performance however, these variations coupled with the socio-cultural context allowed diverse interpretations of the form. The last twenty years has particularly established a legacy of form with preoccupation in two aspects of the dance: one that is 'objective-formative' where the focus is on the dynamics of movement, its structure and rhythm, and the use of space, the other, the 'expressive-emotional' content that is best understood in a global context where the idea, process, purpose and function of dance occur (Sondra Horton Fraleigh, 1996). This articulation was again an extension of the legacy established by stalwarts like Rukmini Devi, Balasaraswati and Chandralekha whose dance reflected their preoccupation with the textual traditions and historicity of dance, the complexities of the revival and reform movement and the subsequent positioning of dance practice on the urban stage.

Since its compilation, the Abhinaya Darpanam continues to be the mandatory text of Bharatanatyam representing the timelessness of the art and the timeless flow of our tradition. I hope this illustrated version proves a useful guide to dancers and teachers in the tenets of its practice, to review past practices and their enduring presence in present day performances on the global stage.

I sincerely hope this book will heighten our sensibility to nature, expand our vision of the aesthetic constitution of Bharatanaatyam, allow an experience of the message in every movement and partake in the enduring legacy of change.

Anita Vallabh

REFERENCES

Appa Rao, P.S.R
Abhinaya Darpanam of Nandikeswara' (trans). Natyamala Publications,1997.

Bunce W. Frederick
'Mudras in Hindu and Buddhist Practices: An Iconic Consideration'.
'D.K.Printworld (P) Ltd. New Delhi, 2005.

Clippinger, Karen S.
'Dance Anatomy and Kinesiology - Principles and exercises for improving technique and avoiding common injuries.' Human Kinetics, U.S.A, 2007.

Desmond, Jane
'Embodying Difference: Issues in Dance and Cultural studies.' Cultural Critiques 26,Winter 1993-1994.

Fraleigh, Sondra Horton
'Dance and the Lived Body.' University of Pittsburg Press, 1987.

Franklin,Eric
'Conditioning for Dance- Training for Peak Performance in all Dance Forms.' Human Kinetics, U.S.A, 2004.

Ghosh, Manmohan
'Nandikesvara's Abhinaya Darpanam.' (ed & trans.) Manisha, 1975.

Ghosh, Manmohan
'Nandikesvara's Abhinaya Darpanam.' Metropolitan Printing & Publishing House Ltd, Calcutta, 1934.

Hanna,Judith Lynne
'To Dance is Human-A Theory of Non-verbal Communication.' The University of Chicago Press,1979,1987.

'Lakshana Mudra.'
Tiruvaduvadurai Adhinam. 1940.

'Mahābharata Chūdāmani.'
Kalakshetra, 1952.

McCutchen, Brenda Pugh
'Teaching Dance as Art in Education.' Human Kinetics, U.S.A,2006.

Nambeeshan, Narayanan
'Hasta Lakshana Dipika.' (ed) K.R.Brothers, Kozhikode, 1925.

O'Shea, Janet
'Bharata Natyam on the Global Stage.' Motilal Banarsidass, Delhi, 2009.

Ramachandra Sekhar P.
'Dance Gestures (Mirror of expressions).' Giri Trading Agency Pvt. Ltd. (2nd edition) 2008.

Unni, C.P
'Nātyaśāstra.' volume I, II, III, IV (ed. & trans) Nag publishers, 1998.